Las Newman has given us a welcom[e ...]
in nineteenth-century West Africa[n ...]
terprise. His book also highlights th[e ...]
no less than their white counterparts, had to grapple with the difficult issues of
how to make an informed Christian response to the indigenous religions and
cultures of Africa. These questions remain relevant today.

Brian Stanley, PhD
Professor of World Christianity,
University of Edinburgh, UK

Thoroughly researched and engagingly written, this book makes a significant contribution to African diaspora studies. Las Newman offers compelling evidence of the role of West Indian agents in the project of carrying Christianity to the Mother Continent, and he enriches our understanding of the West Indies from which the missionaries emerged. This book will be appreciated by the specialist and the general reader alike.

James W. St.G. Walker, PhD
Distinguished Professor Emeritus of History,
University of Waterloo, Canada

In this work, Las Newman weaves a comprehensive, fascinating story of the involvement of West Indians of African descent in the missionary enterprise in West Africa in the nineteenth century. These West Indian missionaries demonstrated great courage and persistence in the face of many and varied challenges including having to work under some difficult Western white missionary leaders and in the face of Western imperialist interests.

Newman's extensive use of archival sources enlivens his accounts and analyzes and lends solidity to his work. The reader is left with a better appreciation of the holistic nature of the *missio Dei* and what can be learnt from the experiences of these West Indian missionaries for the pursuit of mission in our own time and beyond.

This study fills a vacuum in both the academy and the church. I unreservedly recommend it to all students of mission history, the people of the West Indies and, of course, all those in Africa who continue to enjoy the fruits of the labours of the West Indians who offered to become missionaries to Africa in the nineteenth century.

Benhardt Y. Quarshie, PhD
Rector,
Akrofi-Christaller Institute of Theology, Mission and Culture, Ghana

To Die in Africa's Dust

West Indian Missionaries in Western Africa in the Nineteenth Century

Las G. Newman

Langham
ACADEMIC

© 2024 Las G. Newman

Published 2024 by Langham Academic
An imprint of Langham Publishing
www.langhampublishing.org

Langham Publishing and its imprints are a ministry of Langham Partnership

Langham Partnership
PO Box 296, Carlisle, Cumbria, CA3 9WZ, UK
www.langham.org

ISBNs:
978-1-83973-533-2 Print
978-1-78641-015-3 ePub
978-1-78641-016-0 PDF

Las G. Newman has asserted his right under the Copyright, Designs and Patents Act, 1988 to be identified as the Author of this work.

All rights reserved. No part of this publication may be reproduced, stored in a retrieval system or transmitted, in any form or by any means, electronic, mechanical, photocopying, recording or otherwise, without the prior written permission of the publisher or the Copyright Licensing Agency.

Requests to reuse content from Langham Publishing are processed through PLSclear. Please visit www.plsclear.com to complete your request.

Scripture quotations marked (NIV) are taken from the Holy Bible, New International Version®, NIV®. Copyright © 1973, 1978, 1984, 2011 by Biblica, Inc.™ Used by permission of Zondervan.

British Library Cataloguing-in-Publication Data
A catalogue record for this book is available from the British Library

ISBN: 978-1-83973-533-2

Cover & Book Design: projectluz.com

Langham Partnership actively supports theological dialogue and an author's right to publish but does not necessarily endorse the views and opinions set forth here or in works referenced within this publication, nor can we guarantee technical and grammatical correctness. Langham Partnership does not accept any responsibility or liability to persons or property as a consequence of the reading, use or interpretation of its published content.

The thesis of this book was a doctoral study originally submitted as "Mission from the Margin: A critical analysis of the participation of West Indians as agents of Christian mission in the western missionary enterprise in Africa in the nineteenth century, with special reference to their conception of Christian mission." The thesis was pursued at the Oxford Centre for Mission Studies (OCMS) in Oxford, UK, and completed in 2007 through the generous assistance of the Langham Partnership International. The author is a Caribbean Langham Scholar

Dedicated to the memory and legacy of the late
Professor Rev. Dr. Horace O. Russell, CD (1930–2021),
Jamaican Baptist scholar and pioneer in the
study of Caribbean church history
and
Professor Emeritus Terence O. Ranger, FBA (1929–2015),
Professor of African History, St. Antony's College, University of Oxford

Contents

Acknowledgements xi

Preface xiii

Abbreviations xv

Part 1: Formation – The West Indies and the Making of Christian Agents

Chapter 1 3
  Introduction
    The Problem 4
    The Objective 8
    The Structure 10
    The Methodology 14
    The Scope and Limitations 15
    Definition of Terms and Concepts 16
    Hypothesis 19
    Conclusion 26

Chapter 2 29
  The Making of the West Indian Church: Identity, Community, and Social Reconstruction
    The Moravian Community 34
    Forming Agents for Mission 40
    The Formation of Baptist Communities 45
    Development of the Baptist Mission in Jamaica 47
    Mission Formation 49
    The Church of England in the West Indies 61
    Conclusion 73

Chapter 3 77
  Emancipation and the Missionary Dream
    The Post-emancipation West Indies: A New Social Order? ... 78
    The Challenge of Africa 96
    The Western Missionary Establishment 99
    Summary and Conclusion 101

Part 2: Participation – The West Indian Missions to Western Africa

Chapter 4 107
The Basel Mission to the Gold Coast (1843–1850): Seeds of Failure, Fruits of Success
- Recruitment in the West Indies 111
- Participation in the Africa Mission 119
- Repatriation and Threat of Repatriation 133
- The Fruits of Success 137
- Conclusion 141

Chapter 5 145
The Baptist Mission to the Cameroon (1841–1888)
- Origin and Conception of the Baptist Mission to the Cameroon 146
  - The Reconnaissance Mission 148
  - Resourcing the Mission 151
  - Deploying the Mission 156
- The Challenge of Africa 164
- Moving to the Mainland 166
- Mission in Crisis 172
- The Final Phase 174

Chapter 6 179
The Anglican Mission to the Rio Pongas (1855–1897)
- Inventing a Mission 181
- Deploying the Mission 184
- Maintaining the Mission 190
- Reinforcements from Barbados 194
- Navigating under New Local Political Leadership 198
- The Third Phase 200
- A Major Breakthrough 203
- Black Leadership and the Challenge of Maintaining the Mission ... 207
- Impact on the Mission to Africa 212
- Eclipse of the Mission 215
- Conclusion 219

Part 3: Interpretation – Nostalgic Exiles or Missionary Enterprisers?

Chapter 7 225
Encountering Africa
- The Basel Mission to the Gold Coast 228
- The Baptist Mission to the Cameroon 231

The Anglican Mission to Rio Pongas 233
Challenges Faced in Encountering Africa..236
   A Plague of Locusts 236
   Contesting African Culture 239
   Witchcraft 242
Witchcraft Eradication..244
   Islam 245
African Slavery..248
   Fighting the Anti-slavery Cause in Africa....................................252
   Polygamy..259
Conclusion...263

Chapter 8 267
Conceptions of Christian Mission
Mission and Civilization..268
Church Planting..272
African Philology and Vernacular Scripture Translation 274
Education 277
Villages and Social Formation 280
Domestic Agriculture and Health Care 283
Marriage and Family, Death and Dying and the Struggle for
   Human Dignity..286
Temperance and Anti-slavery Societies..291
The Mission to the Rio Pongas...292
Summary..293

Chapter 9 297
Assessments and Implications
The Moravian Community in Jamaica...302
The Anglican Community..304
Reshaping Africa in European Imagination......................................305
Mobilizing for Missionary Participation 306
Fulfilment of the Emancipation Dream...309
Conceptions of Christian Mission..311
Mission as Justice and Freedom..314
Christian Mission as *Missio Dei*...315
Implications...318
West Indian Missionaries and The Modern Global Missionary
   Movement..321

Appendix I 325
  From the Archives of the Basel Evangelical Missionary Society, Basel, Switzerland

Appendix II 327
  From the Archives of the Baptist Missionary Society, Regents Park College, Oxford

Appendix III 329
  From the USPG Archives, Rhodes House, Oxford

Bibliography 331

Acknowledgements

This work has been long in the making. I owe a great deal to my supervisor, the late Terence O. Ranger, distinguished Cecil Rhodes emeritus Professor of African Studies at St. Antony's College, Oxford, whose extraordinary patience and encouragement was more than any student could reasonably expect. I also thank Professor Horace O. Russell, whose early direction and enthusiasm for this project inspired my feeble attempt. But even more I give thanks for their own significant contributions to the enterprise which inspired and guided my efforts.

My thanks also to the then faculty and staff of the Oxford Centre for Mission Studies (OCMS) when I was undertaking this work. Doctors Chris Sugden, Vinay Samuel, Paul Freston, Len Bartlotti, Ben Knighton, Bernard Farr, and David Singh all encouraged me along the way even when I appeared diffident and faltering. Hilary Guest, as Special Assistant at OCMS, was extraordinarily encouraging, as were my fellow OCMS research colleagues whose example of determination continued to inspire. Thanks to Professors James W. St. G. Walker, Michael Craton, and Ken Davis, who laid the early foundations in the history department at the University of Waterloo in Ontario, Canada, where I did my undergraduate studies. Thanks to Dr. Gloria V. Robinson, who read through the manuscript and offered sound advice. Of course, grateful as I am for the expert assistance of all these people, any errors of fact or judgement are mine, not theirs.

Every scholar knows the value of good librarians. This is especially so for those engaged in archival research. Special thanks to Paul Jenkins, long-time archivist (now retired) of the Basel Mission in Basel, Switzerland, Allan Lodge, assistant librarian (now retired) at Rhodes House, Oxford, Sue Mills and Jennifer Thorp, archivists/librarians of the Angus Library at Regent Park College, Oxford. They were remarkably generous in their time and attention.

I wish to thank Lindsay Brown, former general secretary of the International Fellowship of Evangelical Students (IFES), whose personal encouragement and generous leave of absence when I was on staff made this work possible, and also my colleagues in the IFES ministry. The Langham Trust provided the necessary financial resources and I express my deep gratitude to them. My thanks to Canon Paul Berg, whose gentle supervision was appreciated, and to the late Rev. Dr. John R. W. Stott, founder of Langham Partnership International, who was my principal source of inspiration.

Throughout this research the "family" in Oxford sustained my sojourns. My Oxford family consisted of Holy Trinity Church, Headington Quarry, Michael and Sue Neale, who combined extraordinarily warm hospitality and a shared passion for cricket, Robert (sadly now deceased) and Elizabeth Rivington, whose cultured hospitality, assistance in research, and generosity helped me along. Thanks also to Tom and Martha Kempton, Felicity "Fizzi" Gum, and John and Cecily Delderfield, who provided splendid accommodation and spiritual fellowship on innumerable occasions on my visits and sojourn in Oxford.

Above all, I am grateful to my wife, Margaret, my daughters, Minke and Anneke, and my son, Johnathan, who all endured a lot while this project was germinating and slowly bearing fruit. Without Margaret's incredible editorial assistance and forbearance, this publication would not have seen the light of day.

Of course, the publication of this book required a publisher that has great forbearance and insights into risk-taking. I am enormously grateful for first Vivian Doub, then Mark Arnold and the other staff at Langham Publishing for their incredible patience and encouragement. They have generously guided and shaped this material into something that is worthy of your time and engagement.

Deo gratias!

Preface

To help salvage the flagging Western missionary enterprise in Western Africa in the mid-nineteenth century, bold attempts were made to recruit and deploy African West Indians in the West Indies to the mission field. Between 1841 and 1897 African West Indians actively participated in five missionary expeditions from the West Indies, which were part of various European and American attempts in the nineteenth century to "remedy the problem of Africa." This study is a comparative analysis of three of these five expeditions. It is my intention and hope that such analysis would shed some light on the motivation, contribution, and success or failure of these transatlantic expeditions which took place in the margins of the British Empire, from one context of African enslavement in the New World to another.

The three expeditions examined originated from three different confessional ecclesiastical groups within post-Reformation Protestant Christianity. They are the Basel Mission (Moravian) to the Gold Coast, the British Baptist Mission to the Cameroon, and the Church of England in the West Indies (Anglican) Mission to the Rio Pongas (now The Gambia). These were initiatives organized by the newly formed West Indian church which emerged in the milieu of early and mid-nineteenth-century West Indian society. As a marginal group of missionary agents in what was widely considered a Western European-American project, the West Indian initiatives have raised historical questions about their suitability, motivation, and contribution (if any) to the enterprise. In addition to investigating the existential formation of these African West Indians in the context of the entrenched slave society in the West Indies, their participation in the nineteenth-century slave society of Western Africa may reveal ways in which encountering the motherland of Africa may have further shaped their conception of the missionary project which they had initially reluctantly embraced but to which they later passionately sought to contribute. The phenomenon of post-emancipation West Indian agents in Christian mission in Africa raises various historical, social, and intercultural issues, including the interplay between religion and factors such as identity formation, race, ethnicity, and the embrace of colonial empire, as well as the relationship between the margin and the metropole in the nineteenth-century missionary mind.

What was the real motivation of the West Indian agents who were recruited for the missionary enterprise in Africa? This study questions historical interpretations of the African West Indian participation in the Western missionary enterprise in Africa in the nineteenth century as being that of "nostalgic exiles" in a mythic pursuit of an imagined homeland or misguided adventurers in pursuit of personal career advancements and instead proposes that the African West Indians' engagement in Africa was a pursuit to further the emancipation dream for themselves and their fellow Africans in the motherland. Their participation reinforced and shaped a conception of Christian mission as an agency of justice and freedom, not unlike the conception of Christian mission exhibited by the apostolic group in the early first-century church, who sought to evangelize Gentiles and legitimize gentile Christianity as an act of providential design and divine justice. This conception of the missionary project appeared to have motivated a dynamic of engagement which enabled the missionary project in Western Africa in the nineteenth century to achieve its long-term goal of planting Christianity firmly in sub-Saharan African soil. In recent historiographies of Christianity in Africa, new focus has been brought to bear on the role of "native agents" and non-Western agents in the transmission of Christianity to Africa. In light of this new focus, the contribution of African West Indians in the nineteenth century warrants reinvestigation and re-evaluation.

Abbreviations

BHFA	Baptist Herald and Friend of Africa
BMS	Baptist Missionary Society
BEMS	Basel Evangelical Missionary Society
BLO	Bodleian Library, Oxford
BQ	Baptist Quarterly
CHJ	Cambridge Historical Journal
CQ	Caribbean Quarterly
EHR	Economic History Review
GPM	Gambia-Pongas Magazine
IBMR	International Bulletin of Missionary Research
ISER	Institute of Social and Economic Research
IMR	International Missionary Review
MF	Mission Field
MH	Missionary Herald
JHR	Jamaica Historical Review
JJ	Jamaica Journal
JAH	Journal of African History
JBS	Journal of British Studies
JCH	Journal of Caribbean History
JICH	Journal of Imperial and Commonwealth History
JRA	Journal of Religion in Africa
JNH	Journal of Negro History
S&A	Slave & Abolition: A Journal of Slave and Post slave Studies
SOAS	School of Oriental and African Studies, University of London

Part 1: Formation

The West Indies and the Making of Christian Agents

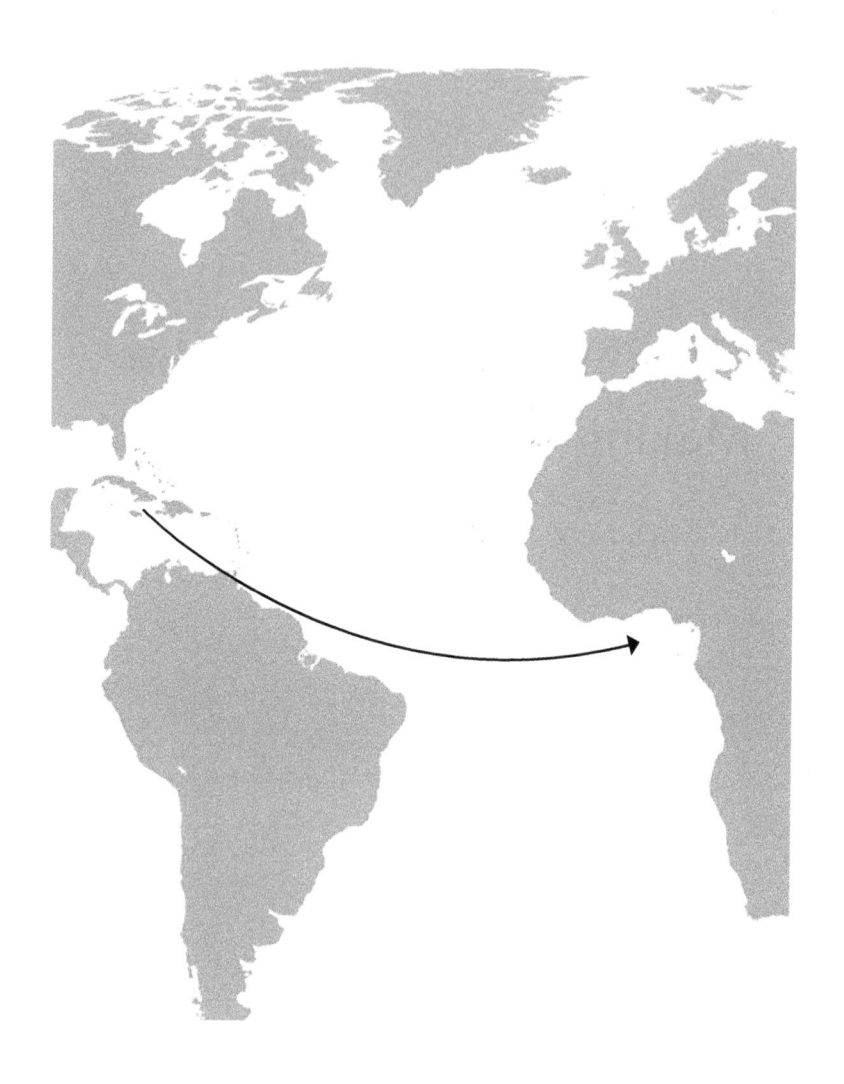

West Indian Missionary journeys to Africa

CHAPTER 1

Introduction

Between 1841 and 1897, five expeditions bearing over one hundred West Indians of African descent went to Western Africa to participate in the enterprise to plant Christianity in the soil of sub-Saharan Africa. These expeditions emerged from separate Christian communities in the British West Indies and represented a distinct mid-nineteenth-century West Indian desire to contribute to the advancement of Africa through the agency of Christian mission. The expeditions were: (1) the Basel Mission (with Moravians) from Jamaica to the Gold Coast in 1843, led by Andreas Riis, (2) the Baptist Mission from Jamaica to the Cameroon in 1844, led by John Clarke, (3) the Wesleyan Mission from Grenada to the Gold Coast in 1845, led by Henry Wharton, (4) the Presbyterian Mission from Jamaica to Calabar, Nigeria, in 1846, led by Hope Masterton Waddell, and (5) the Anglican Mission from Barbados to the Rio Pongas in 1855, led by Hamble James Leacock.

These enterprising mission initiatives from the West Indies in the mid-nineteenth century did not occur in a historical vacuum. At least three broad contexts provided the environment and conditions for their contemplation, formation, and deployment. The contexts were: (1) the immediate post-emancipation environment in the British West Indies following the political and moral achievement of freedom and liberation from the centuries-long enslaved bondage of Africans in British slavery, (2) the perceived and actual condition of sub-Saharan Africa in the mid-nineteenth century, and (3) the strategic geopolitical interests of the Western missionary establishment at the middle of the century. These three contexts intersected in the well-established, centuries-long linkages between Britain, Africa, and the West Indies through transatlantic trade. Given these factors, it is not difficult to understand how the interrelationship between these three contexts and their connections to the missionary enterprise would have helped shape new initiatives towards Africa in the aftermath of the official end of slavery in the British Empire in 1834. The transnational, and indeed transcontinental, nature and vision of the Western missionary enterprise of the nineteenth century provided sufficient geopolitical and moral grounds for the emergence of such initiatives. Utilizing the infrastructure of the triangular trade route between Europe, Africa, and the West Indies, the missionary establishment trumpeted and supported what was claimed to be the "overwhelming desire" of emancipated Africans in the West Indies to reverse the journey and bring badly needed light and salvation to Africa. The contribution by the West Indies towards the establishment of Christianity in Western Africa through these five missionary expeditions was, therefore, energized by a complex of motives which contributed as much to their failures as to their achievements on the field.

The Problem

Historians of West African Christianity such as Groves (1954), Neill (1964), Ajayi (1965), Ayandele (1966), Debrunner (1967), Kalu (1980), Sanneh (1983), Hastings (1994), Bauer (1994), Isichei (1995), and Sundkler and Steed (2000)[1] have generally acknowledged the presence and participation of West Indians in the Western missionary enterprise in sub-Saharan Africa in the nineteenth century.

The role and participation of West Indians, however, have been inadequately understood and insufficiently appreciated. Not only has their participation been interpreted in both colonialist and anti-colonialist terms but the meaning and motive of the contribution they sought to make to the African enterprise have been inadequately grasped. Ajayi, for example, in his work on Nigeria, focuses on the emigrationist aspect of what he called "these nostalgic exiles" and argued that whereas individual West Indian missionaries did play

---

1. Groves, *Planting of Christianity in Africa,* 1954; Neill, *History of Christian Missions,* 1964; Ajayi, *Christian Missions in Nigeria,* 1965; Ayandele, *Missionary Impact on Modern Nigeria,* 1966; Debrunner, *History of Christianity in Ghana,* 1976; Kalu, *History of Christianity in West Africa,* 1980; Sanneh, "Horizontal and the Vertical," 1983; Hastings, *Church in Africa,* 1994; Bauer, *2000 Years of Christianity in Africa,* 1994; Isichei, *History of Christianity in Africa,* 1995, and Sundkler and Steed, *History of the Church in Africa,* 2000.

a useful role in the Christian mission in Africa, the expectations of large-scale emigration efforts were not only false but also unrealistic.[2] Ajayi may well have been right on the question of emigration, but that was by no means the central concern of the mid-nineteenth-century West Indian initiatives in Christian mission to Africa. Following the emigrationist argument, David Jenkins, *Black Zion*, and Harvey Sindima, *Drums of Redemption*, interpret the West Indian missionary expeditions to Africa as part of a mythic "back to Africa" journey in which diasporic Africans were in quest of an imagined homeland, pursuing of a kind of Black Zionism by scattered exiles. Jenkins and Sindima argue that the motives of these diasporic Africans were the redemption and cultural sanctity of "Africa" through the means provided by the European civilizing missions.

In a more recent contribution to the understanding of the rise of West African Christianity, Sundkler and Steed dismiss the role of the West Indians without any explanation and with no attempt to understand their particular contribution; not even one West Indian is named in their work. Yet, at the same time, in writing about the Basel Mission in Akropong, Sundkler and Steed highlight the role played by Zimmermann (a white German Bible translator)– whom they describe as "the remarkable missionary" – without any understanding or appreciation of the contribution of the West Indians to Zimmermann's career in Akropong.[3] For the most part, the African West Indians who participated in the nineteenth-century mission enterprise in Africa have remained largely faceless and voiceless. Their thoughts, hopes, struggles, disappointments, triumphs, and contributions have not been adequately accounted for, if at all.

However, some historians of Christianity in Africa, recognizing the need for a reinvestigation of the nature of the transmission of Christianity to Africa, are giving increasing attention to the role and contribution of native agency in that process. The story of the participation and contribution of others – including the local Africans themselves and the West Indians who worked alongside and leveraged the efforts of Western missionaries in the

---

2. Ajayi, *Christian Missions in Nigeria*, 46.
3. Sundkler and Steed, *History of the Church in Africa*, 207–209.

nineteenth-century missionary enterprise in Africa – is yet to be properly told.[4] After C. P. Groves drew attention to the phenomenon in his multi-volume work, *The Planting of Christianity in Africa*, Lamin Sanneh, in *West African Christianity*, and Jaap van Slageren, in "Jamaican Missionaries in Cameroon," attempt to explore and give recognition to the contribution of West Indian agents as a matter of historical record and their significance to the missionary enterprise in Africa. Daniel Antwi – in considering "the African Factor" in the transmission of Christianity in sub-Saharan Africa – has also helped to reopen the subject. These recent approaches to the historiography of Christianity in Africa have been laying the foundation for further inquiry into the role of non-western missionaries in planting Christianity in sub-Saharan African soil.

It must also be noted that West Indian historians, for their part, are yet to give attention to this aspect of the post-emancipation history of the British West Indies. Little space has been found in the agenda of the emerging research discipline of Emancipation Studies in West Indian history to explore this phenomenon. In a century of West Indian church history, only three historians have paid attention to it. In 1898, Alfred Caldecott – who served as principal of Codrington College in Barbados in the late nineteenth century – included the mission to Africa in his narrative on *The Church in the West Indies*. But this work only mentions the Anglican Mission to the Rio Pongas. Arthur Dayfoot's *The Shaping of the West Indian Church (1999)*, written a century later, mentions the five missions from the West Indies and attempts to account for this development in the West Indian church.[5] So far, Horace Russell is the only West Indian historian to contribute a published full-length

---

4. In reflecting on the historical transmission of Christianity in Western Africa, Kalu and Sanneh not only highlight the need for the history of Christian mission to take seriously the important role of native agents in the missionary enterprise, but Kalu further suggests that the careers of some of these agents need to be examined more closely, and Sanneh argues for a more careful historiography which balances the role of Western missionary agency with that of native agents. Kalu and Sanneh believe that a new historiography is needed to demonstrate the complexities and ambiguities of the early Christianizing mission in Western Africa. Kalu, "Introduction," *History of Christianity in West Africa*; Sanneh, "Horizontal and the Vertical," 165–171 and *Translating the Message*.

5. Dayfoot did include a photograph of one of these missionaries to Africa, the Rev. and Mrs. W. A. Burris who served from 1896–1925 in the Anglican Mission to Western Africa, though not much was said of them, Dayfoot, *Shaping of the West Indian Church*, 219.

study of this episode in West Indian history.[6] Russell focuses specifically on one mission – the Baptist Mission to the Cameroon – and his bibliographic introduction to the problem shows the extent of colonial neglect of the subject as well as some post-colonial realities, both in the West Indies and in Africa, which have given rise to renewed interest in this subject. Russell argues that while the Baptist initiative was a failure in terms of its expectation and design, it had positive historical value for both the Baptist Union in Jamaica – "helping to define its final shape and structure"[7] – and the resultant Baptist churches of the Cameroon. In his judgement, this was "one of the finest stories of missionary endeavour."[8] Nevertheless, Russell raises significant questions about the motive, authenticity, and adaptation of the West Indians in Africa as participants in the western missionary enterprise.[9]

Given this problem then, this study attempts to critically assess the participation of West Indians in the enterprise of Christian mission in Western Africa in the mid-nineteenth century. While acknowledging that the historiography of the phenomenon is of critical importance, it is a more adequate understanding of the significance and contribution of West Indian participation in the nineteenth-century Western missionary enterprise in Africa that will inform a fairer and more accurate historiography. It is the latter, therefore, that is the focus of this research.[10] Of further historical interest would be the possibility of discovering what, if any, distinctive conceptions

---

6. Russell, *Missionary Outreach*. The Nigerian scholar Waibinte Wariboko has now courageously reopened the subject in the West Indies with a welcome contribution focusing on the West Indian missionaries to the Pongas Mission. Wariboko's work *Ruined by "Race"* follows on Vassady's concern regarding the issue of race and ethnicity and the extent to which these factors contributed to the success or failure of the West Indian missionaries in Africa. Although reference is made in Wariboko's work to the mid-nineteenth century agents, his concern largely focuses on mission work in Africa in the early twentieth century by missionary agents from the West Indies. As such, his work is largely outside the scope and limitations imposed on this research. This welcome contribution, however, has placed the subject squarely on the agenda of post-emancipation studies at the University of the West Indies, where he was recently engaged, and opens the prospects for research on other aspects and perspectives of this post-emancipation phenomenon in West Indian history. See Vassady's unpublished PhD dissertation, "Role of the Black West Indian Missionary."

7. Russell, *Missionary Outreach*, 262.

8. Russell, 250.

9. Neill, *History of Christian Missions*, and Bauer, *2000 Years of Christianity*, have also raised questions of adaptation.

10. Attention has been drawn to the complexities and importance of Mission Historiography. See Sharpe, *"Reflections on Missionary Historiography,"* 76–81.

of Christian mission may have characterized the participation of the West Indians in missions in Africa.

It must be borne in mind that the West Indians who participated as agents of Christian mission in Africa were products of an intensely charged immediate pre-and post-emancipation socio-political environment in the West Indies, in which the meaning and basis of human freedom were critical issues of daily practical negotiation and ontological quest. This quest for ontological and existential freedom was a major factor in shaping the mind and spirit of West Indians in the nineteenth century. The struggle for their own identity and meaning to some extent appeared to influence how the West Indian agents in mission in Africa in the nineteenth century viewed participation in the project that was aimed at transforming Africa. Therefore, Jenkins and Sindima might very well be right in their suggestion regarding the ideological or moral motivation for the West Indians' participation in the missionary enterprise. Viewed in this way, some reasonable explanation may be available to account for the failure of the emigrationist aspect of the project, as well as to shed some light on the reasons for success in other aspects of the enterprising West Indian missions.

The Objective

The primary objective of this study is the examination of the participation of West Indians in the missionary enterprise to Western Africa in the nineteenth century, with a view to critically assessing their participation and discerning any distinctive elements of their conceptions of Christian mission. In so doing, a secondary objective is to understand the significance or otherwise of the phenomenon of Christian missionary agency from marginal communities. From its origins, Christianity was a marginal religion in the Graeco-Roman Empire. In time, however, Christianity emerged as a dominant influence in the cultures of Europe and the Middle East. Missionary agency by people from marginal communities, especially within the margins of Empire, should not therefore be overlooked or disregarded. Historical precedents in the early church of the first three centuries AD suggest that such agency can be effective in the means and modalities of missionary intercultural transmission.

The case of the West Indian agents in the missionary enterprise in Western Africa, coming from the colonial margin of the British Empire in the West

Indies to the margin of the pre-colonial environment of sub-Saharan Africa in the mid-nineteenth century, gives rise to a variety of interesting questions. For example, given the history and sociology of slave society in the British West Indies, how was it that, in the mid-nineteenth century, West Indians came to be perceived and perceived themselves as prospective agents for Christian mission? Was the opportunity of a "back to Africa" mission an existential means of escape from the frustrations of the social and economic insecurity in the British West Indies, following the collapse of slave society and the dim prospects of the emancipation project? In Africa, how did the West Indians perceive their agency and engagement in the enterprise, including their ability to influence and shape mission policy and direct mission outcomes? How were they perceived by the Africans in whose environment they went to live and serve? Were they the only returnees from the West Indies or were there others representing other entities? What was the West Indians' conception of the missionary enterprise? In reality, whose mission was it, theirs or the masters? What legacy, if any, did the West Indians' involvement produce in Africa?

While exploring possible answers to these penetrating questions, a number of factors came to light. One, as already noted, is the relatively under-researched nature of the subject in West Indian history. The paucity of research of this phenomenon in West Indian history is matched by the absence of a body of knowledge (written or oral) in the West Indian church about this aspect of its history. In almost every case in the contemporary West Indian church, knowledge of the West Indian missions to Africa is sketchy and vague, and whatever memory exists is fast receding. In contrast, while precious little information can be found in the West Indies, a rich body of material about this subject exists in mission archives in Europe and America.[11] In the case of the three missions selected for this study – the Basel Mission to the Gold Coast, the Baptist Mission to the Cameroon, and the Anglican Mission to the Rio Pongas – a sufficient body of material exists in the archives of the

---

11. This body of material would have been further enriched if not for the loss of important documents by most of the West Indian agents in Africa through fires, floods, tribal raids, white ants, and other disasters on the field. For example, John Duport, the Anglican agent from Barbados who superintended the Pongas Mission, lost his entire collection of documents in several fires in his mission stations in the Pongas. Likewise, collections from the Jamaican Baptists Merrick, Fuller, and Pinnock were similarly lost in the Cameroon stations.

Basel Evangelical Missionary Society (BEMS – now called Mission-21.org) in Switzerland, the Baptist Missionary Society (BMS) in Regent's Park College, Oxford, and the United Societies for the Propagation of the Gospel (USPG) in the Bodleian Library, Oxford, for the contribution of the West Indians to the enterprise in Africa to be unearthed and the role they played more carefully researched and better understood. This is so particularly in the case of those who achieved significant careers and longevity in Africa, such as J. J. Fuller in the Cameroon, Catherine Mulgrave on the Gold Coast in Ghana, and John Duport and Phillip Doughlin in the Rio Pongas (The Gambia).

The Structure

This study is structured around three issues and divided into three parts. Part one deals with the issue of formation. It explores the dominant socio-historical factors upon which the idea that Christianized Africans in the West Indies in the mid-nineteenth century might be useful agents in the failing struggle to plant Christianity in sub-Saharan Africa was invented and promulgated. This issue of formation involves not only the formation of persons but, equally, the formation of institutions such as the West Indian church which, through its critical auxiliary missionary associations, played an important part in the organization of the mission initiatives in the Western missionary enterprise in Africa.

Part two deals with the issue of participation. It examines the recruitment, deployment, and engagement of the West Indians as agents of the Western missionary enterprise in Africa. Of the five mission initiatives from the West Indies to Western Africa in the mid-nineteenth century, three were selected for this study – the Moravian Mission to the Gold Coast, the Baptist Mission to the Cameroon, and the Anglican Mission to the Rio Pongas. These three were selected for several reasons. First, all three mission initiatives shared a broad sociological context of origins in the colonial margins of the British Empire in the West Indies and, even though they departed from the West Indies at different intervals, two of them – the Moravian and Baptist missions – were contemporaneously on the field in Africa, while the Anglican mission was embarked on a decade later. Second, while engaging in different aspects of the missionary enterprise in Western Africa, all three mission groups went through remarkably similar experiences. Discerning certain patterns of encounter and response in the enterprise in Africa may inform and improve our understanding of the participation of West Indians as agents of Christian mission. Third, from the point of view of external support, these three missions had to contend with very similar issues pertaining to resource scarcity, manpower and welfare needs, maintenance, supervision, and, ultimately, the issue of sustainability of the mission ventures. Yet, despite these similarities, there were significant differences in matters such as ecclesiastical tradition, philosophies and strategies of Christian missionary engagement, and approaches to mission in Africa. These similarities and differences may suggest and open up avenues for understanding the motivation of the West Indians ex-slaves in participating in the missionary enterprise in Africa and may even help to understand their subsequent response to encounters with African realities in Africa.

There are two reasons why the other two mid-nineteenth-century mission initiatives from the West Indies – the Presbyterian mission to Calabar in Nigeria and the Wesleyan mission to the Gold Coast from Grenada and St. Vincent – are not examined in this study. First, the Presbyterian mission overlapped with the Jamaican Baptists in the Cameroon in many respects and shared a number of things in common, including competing for the same general geographical space in Africa. Although smaller, the Presbyterian initiative of 1846 to Calabar was, in many respects, similar to the Baptist mission to the Cameroon. There were important points of contact between these two missions. Although the two missions were briefly rivals, contesting the same space in West Africa, they later collaborated with each other and supported one another's missionary engagement in the field. Hope Waddell and Bela Vassady have both shed some light on aspects of this project. However, Vassady's work has also highlighted the important contribution of the Jamaica Baptist Mission to the Cameroon pointing its significance and bringing to light some excellent material.[12] Horace Russell's substantial work on the Jamaican Baptist Mission to the Cameroon, has taken the matter much further.[13] In light of

---

12. Vassady, "Role of the Black West Indian Missionary."
13. Russell, "*The Missionary Outreach of the West Indian Church*". The Presbyterian initiative is worthy of further study as Groves, *Planting of Christianity*, and Walls, "*Mission Origins*," point out.

the questions they raise and the questions raised in this study, revisiting this mission seems necessary to attempt answers to new lines of inquiry.

Similarly, the Wesleyan mission from Grenada coincided with the Basel Mission from Jamaica to the Gold Coast. Although operating in the same section of Western Africa, the Basel Mission was the larger of the two and took on more significance given its fortunes in Africa prior to the arrival of the Jamaicans in 1844. Therefore, this study focuses on the Basel Mission rather than on the Wesleyan mission.

The Anglican Mission to the Rio Pongas, on the other hand, merits special attention for several reasons. First, of the three mid-nineteenth-century mission initiatives from the West Indies to Western Africa examined in this study, the Anglican Mission is the least researched and the least known; it is largely a neglected area of study. Focusing on this mission may shed some light on the ways in which a colonial church that had been established within the structures of West Indian slave society sought to reposition itself through missionary engagement in Africa, in the context of emancipation and the new freedoms and transition to a post-slavery West Indian society. A second reason is that despite the established position of the Church of England in the West Indies in the mid-nineteenth century, the Anglican Mission to Africa – which the Church of England promoted – suffered all the characteristics of marginality like the other two missions in this study, even as it attempted to represent a distinct and unique contribution to Africa by a West Indian church. As a mission from the then established Church of England in the West Indies, it not only offers fair comparison and contrast with the other nonconformist West Indian mission initiatives but also raises the interesting question of the extent to which its missiology was aligned to the missiology of Anglican agencies in the metropole such as the Society for the Propagation of the Gospel (SPG) and the Church Missionary Society (CMS) in the mid-nineteenth century. What characterized and shaped the missiology of the Anglican West Indian Mission to the Rio Pongas? Was it the missiology of the SPG or the CMS, or was it something else?

Third, despite its ultimate fortunes and the vicissitudes in Africa, the Anglican Mission to the Rio Pongas lasted more than eighty years and was thus the longest West Indian missionary initiative to survive in Africa. Although, as Wariboko and Gibba demonstrate, the Anglican Church in the West Indies was severely affected by the economic and political consequences of the marginalization of the West Indies in British imperial concerns in the late nineteenth century, the idea of a mission to Africa persisted within the church well into the twentieth century. In light of the problem of cultural identity in the British slave colony that surrounded the Church of England's presence in the West Indies throughout its history, vis-a-vis that of the African population in the colony, the question must be asked; what sustained the persistence, however dimly, of the idea of mission to Africa in this West Indian church, especially in the new socio-economic, multi-ethnic, and multiracial environment of post-emancipation West Indian society? Given its longevity and endurance, what legacy, if any, did this mission initiative from the West Indies leave in Africa?

Part three deals with issues of interpretation. The meaning and motivation of the West Indian agents participation deserve far more critical analyses than hitherto they have received. Since the goal of this study is a critical assessment of the participation of West Indians in the Western missionary enterprise in Western Africa in the mid-nineteenth century, the question of what their participation really meant to them must be ascertained and critically analysed. Given the secondary goal of trying to discern ways in which marginal groups contribute to the transmission of Christianity inter-culturally, the case of the West Indian agents in Africa in the mid-nineteenth century may be insightful, if not instructive. An informed understanding of their participation may be derived from an analysis of the ways in which they approached and encountered Africa as enterprisers of Christian mission and the ways they responded to these encounters. Their responses, in all probability, were influenced and shaped by a number of factors, including their conception of the project to which they were recruited and in which they exerted themselves. Therefore, this section will examine (1) aspects of the West Indians' encounter with Africa as agents of Christian mission and their responses to those encounters as West Indians from the margins of the British Empire, and (2) their indicative or implied conception of the Christian missionary project in which they were engaged. Attempts will also be made to interpret the phenomenon of the participation of this group from the margins of Empire.

The Methodology

This study is a historical investigation into one aspect of the modern history of Christian mission. It is appropriate, therefore, that the methodology employed be that of historical tools of investigation, employing extensive archival research of primary and secondary sources, complemented by other resources from other disciplines. For this study, significant time was spent in four archives: the archive of the Basel Evangelical Missionary Society (BEMS) (now called Mission-21.org) in Basel, Switzerland; the Angus Library of the Baptist Missionary Society (BMS) at Regent's Park College, Oxford; the United Society for the Propagation of the Gospel (USPG) archives at the Bodleian Library, Oxford; and the archives of the Church Missionary Society (CMS) at the University of Birmingham, England. These are the official archives of the mission societies that sponsored the West Indian missionary initiatives to Africa in the nineteenth century, extended logistical and other forms of support to them, and were the body to whom these missionaries reported. The four archives mentioned above are well preserved, and excellent materials relevant to this study were found in reports, Correspondence, minute books, memoirs, pamphlets, and, in some cases, photographic and other documentary evidence. Supporting materials were also found in the National Archives and the National Library of Jamaica. In addition to archival work, site visits were made to the "Moravian belt" in central and south-western Jamaica and the Baptist sites in north-western Jamaica. Several visits were made to Codrington College in Barbados, to Antigua and Trinidad and Tobago, in attempts to obtain historical site understanding as well as to investigate local archival sources and, where possible, collect oral testimonies and examine any legacy of oral tradition regarding the participation of West Indians in the missionary enterprise in Western Africa in the mid-nineteenth century. In Africa research visits were made to the Gold Coast and the Akropong-Akawapim mountains in Ghana, the location of the Basel Mission. No specific research visits were made to the Cameroon or The Gambia. However, several visits were made to other parts of Western, Eastern, and Southern Africa such as Cote d'Ivoire, Kenya, Ethiopia, Zimbabwe, and South Africa for other purposes which gave the researcher some contextual understanding of the varieties of African cultural and religious environments.

The Scope and Limitations

Recognizing that an inquiry into a subject of this nature inevitably encompasses an extensive arena of research, limitations were imposed on the scope of this study. Consequently, the African context of the study is confined to that part of Western Africa where the West Indian mission initiatives were deployed and which formed their field of engagement in the mid-nineteenth century. However, this was not the only part of Africa in which West Indians served in the missionary enterprise in Africa in the nineteenth century. There is, for example, the context of Central Africa, where James Hemans of Jamaica – who served the London Missionary Society's Africa Mission for eighteen years – did outstanding work.[14] But this study will not encompass West Indian missionary work in Central Africa.

The study also confines itself to the second half of the nineteenth century and focuses on the period from the first push of the West Indian church to engage itself in the Western missionary enterprise in Africa in the 1840s to the last recruitment effort for mission in Africa in 1895 and 1896. This last recruitment drive took place when two bishops of the CMS's mission in Africa – Bishop Ingham of Sierra Leone and Bishop Herbert Tugwell of Western Equatorial Africa, who was Samuel Crowther's successor once removed – visited the West Indies in successive years to recruit West Indians for mission in Africa.[15] The fact of their recruiting mission in the West Indies at the end of the century must be seen not only as an indication of the continued belief, held for over fifty years, that West Indians could make a useful

---

14. James Henry Emmanuel Hemans was a pioneer schoolmaster with the London Missionary Society (1888–1906) and served at Fwambo and Niamkolo near Lake Tanganyika. He returned to Jamaica in 1906 and died in 1908. *Register of Missionaries, Deputations*, entry no.23, LMS Archives.

15. From this renewed link between the emerging African church and the West Indian church, some West Indians went to Western Africa and rendered outstanding service to the African church. One such person was W. A. Thompson, who spent over thirty years in Nigeria, where he worked on the translation of the Bible and the Book of Common Prayer into the Nupe and Hausa languages. He was made Superintendent of the CMS mission at Ibori and Warri. Another such person was Lennon, who also spent over thirty years as a West Indian missionary in Nigeria, where he had a remarkable career. He was made Canon of Lagos Cathedral in 1929 and Archdeacon of Ondo in 1944. Lennon went to Nigeria to be a tutor at St. Peter's College, Oyo, and later built schools and churches in several parts of Nigeria. It is said that many of his former pupils rose to important positions as heads of colleges, ministers of state, and university lecturers. Lennon was awarded the MBE and CBE for his missionary work in Nigeria, where he also served for a time as a member of the Legislative Council in Lagos.

contribution to the missionary enterprise in Africa, but also as some indication of the impact some West Indians made in Africa during that period. This idea of the prospective usefulness of West Indian agency in Africa, nurtured in the exigencies of West Indian slavery and emancipation, did not seem to have ceased with the disruptive impact of European intervention in the "Scramble for Africa" – which led to the partitioning of Africa – following the Berlin Congress of 1884–1885. As dislocating and negating as those interventions were, the West Indian church continued to send missionary agents to Africa well into the twentieth century.[16] However, this study does not consider activities of West Indian agents in Africa in the twentieth century.

This study recognizes that the period selected (1841–1895) spans almost six decades, a fairly long timeframe, during which significant shifts in mission policy, strategic direction, missionary fortunes on the field, and personal and organizational interests might have taken place. Such shifts are taken into consideration in this study. While the length of time could be problematic, it does provide an opportunity to investigate and observe the persistence or otherwise of an idea over many decades.

A further limitation is imposed by the nature of the study. While a study of this nature may legitimately be pursued in a variety of academic fields, this research focuses on the emerging discipline of Mission Studies.[17] This represents, in part, the researcher's academic interest, but it is also the natural arena in which the questions concerning the subject of this research have arisen. Given its underlying theme and subtext, however, it may also be possible to place this study within the emerging field of Emancipation Studies.

Definition of Terms and Concepts

For the purposes of clarity of thought and argumentation, this section describes how key terms and concepts used in this study are defined and understood.

---

16. See Dayfoot, *Shaping of the West Indian Church*, 219; Wariboko, *Ruined by "Race."*

17. Mission Studies seeks to understand the processes, modalities, and meaning of Christian transmission as a way of understanding the Christian movement in history. The International Association for Mission Studies (IAMS) was established in 1972 and publishes a journal, *Mission Studies*, twice yearly. See www.missionstudies.org.

The term "West Indian" refers to individuals who, by virtue of birth or naturalization, had established an identity from the geographical and cultural environment of the West Indies. "The West Indies" is that geographical and cultural area in the mid-Atlantic region which is bordered to the north by the United States of America, to the west by the Gulf of Mexico and Central America, and to the south by the continent of South (or Latin) America. The term "West Indies" was used to designate the area where the first European explorer, Christopher Columbus, landed in 1492. In search of a passage to the East, towards India and China, Columbus made landfall on an island that he named San Salvador (now part of the Bahamas), where he encountered native Indians. Columbus thought then that he had arrived in the East Indies. In fact, he had travelled in a westerly direction, hence the designation of the first landing as the "West Indies" and its peoples as "West Indians." This same geographical and cultural area is today known as the Caribbean, after the native Caribs whom Columbus encountered in the area. History and geography have combined to make this area a specific cultural zone referred to as the "West Indies."

The term "missionary enterprise" refers to the organized efforts to mobilize and deploy Christian individuals as agents and "missionaries" of the Christian faith. The Christian movement believes that its founder, Jesus Christ, gave a mandate and commission to his early followers in the first century AD, following his crucifixion, death, burial, and resurrection appearances. This commission was to propagate the faith to every nation, to the "ends of the earth", until he returns.[18]

Therefore, Christianity emerged as a missionary religion in the first three centuries AD and travelled throughout the Roman Empire, mainly through the agency of marginal peoples from marginal communities throughout the Middle East. By the nineteenth century, the propagation of the faith became an enterprise in which courageous volunteers offered themselves or were selected to cross continents and oceans, to transmit the Christian message in other lands. This missionary enterprise was backed and supported by imperial powers of state or by voluntary organizations as auxiliaries of the church. By the nineteenth century, these organizations, sometimes driven by lay members of the church, mobilized public and private support to fulfil

---

18. See the Synoptic Gospels, Matthew 28:19; Mark 16:15; Luke 24:47; John 20:21.

this missionary mandate. In fact, the Christian missionary enterprise, as understood and practised by the nineteenth-century European and American church, was shaped by two different philosophies of Christian mission which impacted and shaped the strategies of missionary engagement of the missionary movement in the modern world.

In the first approach, Christian mission was practised as an enterprise supported by royal charter, in which church and state participated in close cooperation and collaboration with each other. Based on a Christian tradition that was largely Constantinian – in which church and state worked closely together – Christian missionary engagement was coextensive with state functions. Christian mission, as an agent of the state, was expected to perform and deliver the "civilizing task" of creating a new moral society in which religiously "redeemed" and appropriately acculturated human beings would function as effective moral agents for the good of society. The tools for achieving this goal were the mission work of the church in education, including the employment of Western understandings of science and technology in fields of endeavour such as agriculture, medicine, and other such practical, scientific, and professional pursuits.[19]

In the second approach, the understanding and practice of Christian mission was derived from the radical Anabaptist tradition in the sixteenth-century Reformation, in which church and state were understood and regarded as two very separate and distinct entities which existed for different reasons. State patronage and support of any kind were, as much as possible, to be eschewed in Christian mission. In this tradition, Christian mission was to be conducted entirely on the principle of voluntarism, independent of the political state.[20] In the Protestant-Evangelical tradition, influenced largely by the 16th century radical Reformation, the goal of Christian mission is personal conversion with the expectation that, through individual and personal religious transformation, communities and societies would be affected and ultimately transformed. The origin of the church in the British West Indies resulted from both these historical approaches to Christian mission. Therefore, the extent to which these historical missionary traditions influenced the origins, conception, and indeed the engagement of the agents

---

19. See Neill, *Colonialism and Christian Mission*, and Hastings, *The Church in Africa*.
20. Hinchliff, "Voluntary Absolutism," 363–369.

of the West Indian churches in their missionary initiatives in Africa in the mid-nineteenth century is something to consider.

The term "margin" is used in a spatial sense to refer to a position of some distance from the centre of primary activity or mainstream influence. In some discussions, the term "periphery" is used with a similar understanding. Periphery or margin not only implies some degree of distance but also a sense of relative importance or unimportance in relation to the centre of mainstream activity. In this study, the term "margins of empire" refers to the status of the British West Indies relative to its importance in the centre of the geopolitical interests of the British Empire by the mid-nineteenth century.[21] One indication of the increasing marginalization of the West Indies in the British imperial strategic outlook in the nineteenth century is the fact that even after three decades since the passage of the Emancipation Act in 1833, the 1865 peasant uprising in Jamaica was blamed on, among other things, "British neglect" of the West Indies.[22] Similarly, the 1876 popular rebellion in Barbados was blamed on, among other things, British imperial preoccupations that drew their focus and attention elsewhere, away from the West Indies, unlike in the two previous centuries.[23]

Hypothesis

Mission scholars such as Neill (1964), Ajayi (1965), Bauer (1994), Russell (2000), and Wariboko (2007) [24] have pointed to and raised historical ques-

---

21. The decline and marginalization of the British West Indies in relation to the expansion of the British Empire in the nineteenth century is part of the central argument of Eric Williams's thesis, *Capitalism and Slavery*. This sense of growing marginalization – to which attention was drawn by keen nineteenth-century observers of West Indian affairs such as John Trew (*Hints*) – may account, in part, for the rise of a sense of disempowerment and disillusionment experienced by black West Indians in the late nineteenth century. This cultural and political disillusionment parallels the rise of new struggles for cultural and political identity in the late nineteenth century, led by charismatic figures such as Alexander Bedward and, later, Marcus Garvey. Their movements not only carried distinct and strident anti-imperial overtones but also proactively embraced and promoted a Pan-Africanist political and cultural ideology, while turning away from the dominant British and Eurocentric colonial cultural influence. See Campbell, *Rasta and Resistance*.

22. Trew, *Hints*, 7, 8, 12–14, 19–24.

23. Beckles, *History of Barbados*.

24. Neill, *History of Christian Missions*; Ajayi, *Christian Missions in Nigeria*; Bauer, *2000 Years of Christianity*; Russell, *Missionary Outreach*; and Wariboko, *Ruined by "Race."*

tions concerning the suitability and adaptation of the West Indians agents who participated in the missionary enterprise in Africa in the mid-nineteenth century, particularly those who failed to sustain their participation. Other African scholars such as Kalu (1980), Sanneh (1983), and Antwi (1998)[25] have meanwhile called for a reinvestigation of the role of non-Western agents – in particular, native and diaspora Africans – in the process of the transmission of Christianity to African soil. Therefore, it seems appropriate that the case pertaining to participation of the African West Indians be reopened and re-examined in a study such as this. With regard to the issue of their adaptability to Africa, some historians claimed that, through their long sojourn in the West Indies, the African West Indians had lost knowledge of and affinity to Africa and that they and their successors had no intention of repatriating to Africa as their homeland.[26] The question is, were the issues of their participation in the missionary enterprise in Africa as clear-cut as that? Is this the way to adequately understand the West Indian presence in Africa in the mid-nineteenth century, as agents of Christian mission?

This study hypothesizes that, to fully understand the significance of the West Indian participation, the focus should not be on those who failed in the project but, rather, on those who succeeded. In particular, the focus should be on those West Indian who achieved long careers and produced significant results in Africa. It is their longevity and contribution that helped to secure the main goal of leveraging the planting of Christianity in sub-Saharan Africa which the Western (European) missionary establishment attempted to do in the first half of the nineteenth century. This was the primary reason for their recruitment and deployment. It is along this dimension that the significance of their participation can be truly and meaningfully measured. There are sufficient examples of West Indians who achieved such careers in Africa to make an adequate case for their significance.

The participation of West Indians in the missionary enterprise in Africa in the nineteenth century should, therefore, be placed in proper perspective. No attempt will be made in this study to overstate their case or their importance. To be sure, their participation in the project was marginal and

---

25. Kalu, "Introduction," *History of Christianity in West Africa*; Sanneh, "Horizontal and the Vertical"; and Antwi, "African Factor."

26. Wariboko, *Ruined by "Race"*, 189–212.

intended to be supplemental to the main task which, we assume, was led and controlled by white Europeans or Americans. But it is within the very perimeters of their marginality that investigations should be carried out to understand how these West Indians responded to encounters with Africa and to the vicissitudes and demands of their engagement in the mission to Africa that was led and directed by others with other interests. As black agents from across the Atlantic, from the margins of the British Empire, their presence and participation were bound to be fraught with difficulties and challenges. For them to succeed in the project in Africa would have required certain levels of motivation, desire, and character, as well as providential care.

Like missionaries from other climes and contexts, the West Indians struggled and often failed to overcome the varieties of obstacles in the way of missionary engagement in Africa, not least the torrid equatorial conditions to which they were thought to be immune. It came as a surprise to the promoters of the enterprise when some West Indians, like Europeans, succumbed to the equatorial climate and added to the catalogue of missionary mortality in Africa. The West Indians also struggled with obstacles to the missionary task in the form of various encounters with African primal religious traditions and the expanding and competing presence of Islam. Polygamous and other African constructions of family, the prevalence of the practice of bondage slavery and a domestic economy based on the practice of slave trading, fuelled by intertribal violence and warfare, and the normal hostility and resistance to exogenous change, all presented challenges for the West Indian missionaries agents in Africa. These issues were problematic for the West Indians in African lands in the late nineteenth century, as many were fomented and directed by local political elites against missionary intrusions. The prospects of the three West Indian missions in Africa were eclipsed as much by the political interventions of European imperialistic ambitions in the late nineteenth century, as by their own internal struggles and challenges in mounting and maintaining enterprising missions. There is sufficient evidence to show that despite these obstacles, and indeed in the face of them, the majority of West Indians agents in Africa responded proportionately to the challenges they encountered. Those who persevered and succeeded in the project demonstrated an incredible degree of passion and resolve to make the project succeed against the formidable odds faced in Africa.

The real issue, therefore, and perhaps the more important question then is this: what motivated the West Indians' passionate engagement in this enterprise? What enabled their survival and longevity, and what does that motivation tell us about their commitment to the project? As a necessary corollary, what was their contribution, and how important was this contribution, to the missionary enterprise? As people whose formation were by and large derived from the colonial margins of the British Empire and not from the metropolis of Europe or America, it is interesting to discern the factors, as far as they can be determined, which enabled their survival and longevity in Africa and which informed their engagement in the missionary outreach. The question must be asked: shaped by the grand narratives of Atlantic slavery and emancipation, to what extent did this psychosocial background influence a conception of the missionary enterprise in which they exerted themselves as agents of the West Indian church engaged in Christian Mission?

An interesting aspect of this phenomenon is the fact that in their missionary outreach the West Indian church appeared not only to have desired to engage Africa but also sought to compete with and challenge the Western missionary enterprise itself. This is evident in at least two critical areas. First, based on their acclaimed success in planting Christianity firmly in the West Indies by the mid-nineteenth century, the West Indian mission church leaders appeared determined to show that those in the margins of the Empire could participate in the missionary enterprise and make a real contribution, perhaps even more penetrating and effective than those from the metropole. At the very least they considered a lateral contribution from the margins as an act of divine providence and a prospect for which the West Indians were thought to be especially suited. The level of resolve and commitment displayed by the West Indian church leaders to achieve the goal of establishing Christianity in sub-Saharan Africa did not spring merely from what they described as their "elective affinity" with the ideals and values inherent in the evangelical enterprise. It also sprang from their own valorization of the instrumental role of education, moral training, and vernacular Christianity in producing short, medium, and long-term social change. They believed that they were in a credible and strong position to demonstrate the efficacy of Christian mission as a useful, if not a necessary agent of social change, such as was needed in Africa in the mid-nineteenth century. Their self-professed claims regarding their role in the collapse of slavery and in the attempts to bring about social transformation and a new social order in a post-slavery society engendered and bolstered such convictions and confident attitude towards the enterprise.

Based on their personal historical experience in the West Indies, most of the West Indian agents in Africa appeared to have been driven to tireless self-exertion, at great personal risk, to build the infrastructure, foundation, and physical framework upon which the missionary enterprise in Africa was established. They provided essential support to the project. Even if a key underlying motive was the supplanting of the African slave trade, their contribution to the social organization of mission work, church planting, building technology, housing stock, development of domestic agriculture, application of medicine, literary and educational work, and the introduction and employment of technologies appropriate for printing, bricklaying, manufacture of clothing, and the development of local food supply chains were all with a determined view to building a more stable and sustainable modern African society. These were the underlying civilizing goals of the Western missionary enterprise. These goals were also perceived as the instrumental means of "remedying Africa" and effecting new life chances for Africans. The West Indian agents accepted these goals and were determined to employ every means available to achieve them. Whether or not such determination was misguided, as some have argued, the fact is that this determination appeared to have been driven as much by the missionary experience in the West Indies as by a strong desire to engage in a bigger project – especially one involving social change of significant dimensions, such as emanated from and was led by metropolitan interests.

The West Indian church leaders who mooted and mobilized around the idea that the young West Indian church had an obligation to "do something for Africa", appeared ready to demonstrate that participation in the missionary enterprise in Africa by African West Indians was not only providential, it was driven and directed by a sense of divine justice. The notion of *"mission as justice"* [27], raised by the West Indian church as one justification for their engagement in the enterprise in Africa, brought to the table the question of reparations for Africa for what the leaders referred to as, *"wrongs hitherto*

---

27. Noted missiologist David Bosch, *Transforming Mission*, 400–408, traces the theological history of this notion of Mission as Justice. However, the notion was tested and proven in the laboratory of the historical environment of the mid-nineteenth century West Indies. That environment provided a concrete basis on which such a theology could be constructed.

inflicted upon her" by the trans-Atlantic slave trade.[28] Not only had African slaves in the West Indies believed and demonstrated by their long history of resistance and rebellion, that slavery was wrong and that Africa and Africans had been wronged, but now it was thought, providentially by the passage of the Emancipation Act, the British Government had understood and acknowledged that a fundamental injustice had been done to Africa. By the mid-nineteenth century reparations for Africa, conceived of in spiritual and material terms by the more evangelical sections of the Western missionary establishment, became the agreed moral response to the conditions of sub-Saharan Africa. As we will see, this idea was very passionately and persuasively articulated in London in 1833 and again in 1840 by British Baptist missionary to Jamaica, William Knibb. From his missionary engagements in Jamaica, Knibb deliberately and courageously took on the missionary establishment in the metropolitan environment, publicly raised the issue of reparations in Anti-Slavery conventions and demanded a response.[29] It is of note that today, over one and three-quarters of a century later, the question of reparations for Africa is still being debated.[30]

Despite this confidence, however, the West Indian initiatives in Africa proved difficult for the nascent West Indian church to sustain. In the end, these enterprises collapsed under the pressure of internal and external factors, yet not before helping to ignite the spark which kept the flame of the project flickering throughout the nineteenth century. Although such determination and vision were very evident among mission leaders in the West Indies, in

---

28. Trew, "*Africa Wasted . . . ,*" 2,5,9, 18, 35. Barrow, '*Fifty Years. . . .*' 13, Clarke, Dendy, Phillippo, *The Voice of Jubilee,* 25.

29. Thomas Fowell Buxton, successor to William Wilberforce in the leadership of the British Anti-slavery movement, picked up this theme and carried it even further in organizing a big institutional response in the Niger Expedition of 1841. (T. F. Buxton, *The African Slave Trade).*

30. See "The legal basis of the claim for Reparations", By Lord Anthony Gifford, British Queens Counsel and Jamaican Attorney-at-Law. A paper presented to the First Pan-African Congress on Reparations, Abuja, Federal Republic of Nigeria, April 27–29, 1993. The following websites show the current concerns and dialogue on the question of reparations within the Caribbean. www.msnbc.msn.com/id/13785355/;

http://news.bbc.co.uk/1/hi/world/africa/424984.stm; http://www.cbc.bb/content/view/12284/45/; http://www.emancipationtt.org/WCAR2001.htm http://www.jamaicagleaner.com/gleaner/20070214/lead/lead8.html

https://reparationscomm.org/reparations-news/david-comissiong-the-church-of-englands-giant-reparations-step/ accessed January 17, 2023.

https://www.leighday.co.uk/news/blog/2023-blogs/what-the-church-of-england-s-new-100m-slavery-fund-tells-us-about-addressing-historic-injustices/ accessed 1 February 2023.

the end, sending African agents from the West Indies to engage in Christian missions in Africa was not sustainable. For economic, administrative, and other logistical reasons alone, partnerships had to be developed with missionary societies in Europe and with other metropolitan interests globally. These partnerships, by virtue of their own constraints of vision and material resources, often inhibited the progress of the West Indian initiatives in Africa. Over time, the value of West Indian participation became apparent, and this realization prompted requests for more and more help from the West Indian church. Despite appeals and requests, however, the West Indian church was unable to deliver in effective terms, being increasingly incapacitated by the declining local, social and economic conditions in the West Indies. With such dramatic decline in the West Indies in the late nineteenth-century, the interplay between the margin of the Empire and the metropole, which was built into a competitive rivalry, resulted in the missionary dream among the West Indians declining and eventually being aborted. Nevertheless, some West Indian agents, especially those in the Pongas Mission, managed to find ways to sustain their initiatives in Africa for over eight decades and more, and left enduring legacies behind.

A part of the philosophy behind the recruitment of African West Indians as agents for mission in Africa was the belief that being of African descent they could serve as "native agents" to help implement the goals and agenda of the Christian Civilising missions. The idea that "native agents" could be employed and be useful in the project was articulated by Henry Venn, secretary of the Church Missionary Society (1841–1873) who was perhaps the most influential nineteenth-century theorizer of Christian mission.[31] Venn argued that whether or not a church was truly planted in any place depended on the critical involvement of the local native peoples. He proposed that a young church – planted by an external missionary agency – once grown, should exhibit a "three-self" set of defining marks and characteristic features. It should be *self-governing*, *self-supporting*, and *self-propagating*. When these three indicators were achieved, the planted church could be said to be a truly "native" or indigenous church. While it is arguable whether this philosophy of mission was ever fully accepted by the Western missionary establishment, it is a fact that the West Indian agents in Africa engaged in the missionary

---

31. Shenk (1998), *Henry Venn*, 698.

enterprise fully expecting the rise of a native African church with African leadership, not just as a matter of pragmatic necessity but also of divine justice. This, they believed, was the way the "wrongs" done to Africa would be "righted" and the true liberation of Africa achieved.

Conclusion

While the participation of African West Indians as agents of Christian mission in the missionary enterprise in Western Africa in the mid-nineteenth century is a phenomenon that has been acknowledged, it has not yet been adequately accounted for.[32] This phenomenon was motivated and organized by missionary leaders in the West Indies who wanted to contribute – even if competitively – to the missionary project in Africa from the margins of the British Empire. But these initiatives from the West Indies suffered from a complexity of mixed motives and what might be considered historical misfortunes. As a marginal group of people, the West Indians went into the enterprise in Africa apparently with a conception of Christian mission as an efficacious agency of social transformation, based on their existential experience in the West Indies. The theological underpinnings for these missionary initiatives was the doctrine of providential design which mission leaders in the West Indies and in England conceived of.[33] While this notion of providential design as an impulse for Christian mission might have been understood by the West Indian church in the concrete historical circumstances of African enslavement and emancipation in the context of the British Empire, it was a notion which bore similarities to and parallels the understanding of the impulse and motivation for Christian mission by the early Christians of the first three centuries AD, also in the context of Empire. Those early Christians felt impelled to spread the faith following the paradigm of Jesus and his convert, Saul of Tarsus, in the first century Roman Empire. Saul, also known as Paul, became the leading

---

32. Wariboko (2006a), "*A neglected Theme* . . ."

33. Sindima criticizes this doctrine of Providential Design as it relates to the missionary projects in Africa in the nineteenth century from the African diaspora. He claims that it is "erroneous" and an invention to give sanction to the failed emigrationist plans. While exercising justifiable suspicion of any doctrine that suggests that "God, in his inscrutable ways, had allowed Africans to be carried off into slavery so that they could be Christianised and civilized and return to uplift their kinsmen in Africa," how can you rule it out if God is, in fact, inscrutable? Sindima, *Drums of Redemption*, 69–73.

Christian missionary of the first century AD and spread Christianity beyond the margins of the Jewish world. He gave profound expression to this idea of providential design by the way he used the Greek word *kairos* in his letter to the Galatians:

> But then the chosen time [kairos] came. God sent his Son. A woman gave birth to him. He was born under the authority of the law. He came to set free those who were under the authority of the law. He wanted us to be adopted as children with all the rights children have. (Gal 4:4–5 NIRV).

As a marginalized group in the Roman Empire, the early Christians engaged the Empire with missionary fervour– in response to justice issues such as an oppressive level of state persecution and the need for social justice and freedom as citizens of the Empire.[34] This was an important historical paradigm of missionary impulse. As Orlando Patterson brilliantly demonstrates in *Freedom in the Making of Western Culture*, the struggle of these early Christians contributed to the birth of natal rights and freedoms, which left an indelible mark on Western civilization.[35]

This conception of mission as justice and freedom, based on the notion of Providential Design, not only reflects the early church's understanding of Christian mission, it also provides a basis for understanding Christian mission as *missio Dei*. The concept of Christian mission as *missio Dei*, emerged in Europe in the mid-twentieth century, in the aftermath of the Second World War.[36] It emphasizes that Christian mission is God's project and not merely a human agenda, that the missionary endeavour is God's programme and not the church's invention, and that God precedes the missionary and is in control of the enterprise. It is a theology of mission that calls attention to the fact that Christian mission is not a Western invention. Rather, it is a central characteristic in of the nature and being of the Sovereign Trinitarian God,

---

34. St. Paul, using his apostolic credentials, rose to the defence of gentile Christianity and argued passionately for the legitimacy of gentile Christian identity against the background of discrimination, resistance, and other forms of social injustice seeking to delegitimize gentile Christian claims (Galatians 5:1; Ephesians 2:11–19; 3:7–12 NIV). Thereby, Paul set the basis of a missionary engagement in the Roman Empire in which Christian mission was conceptualized in terms of mission as a pursuit of justice.

35. Patterson, xvi (*Preface*), 294–303, 326–331.

36. Bosch, *Transforming Mission*, 389–393.

who is a missionary God. Christian mission should, therefore, be central to the life of the church, not auxiliary to it. It is not be the exclusive domain of any one group or centres of power. The notion of Christian mission as *missio Dei* was particularly important for the church of the mid-twentieth century as it sought to grapple with its global mission in what the historian Eric Hobsbawm described as the "Age of Extremes." In that century, the contradictions and dialectics of the human condition were dramatically manifested in the dismantling of empires, the overthrow of imperialism, and the liberation of millions of subject peoples through two world wars and the unrelenting global struggle for freedom.

Therefore, a critical understanding of the role of marginal groups such as the West Indian agents in Western Africa in the mid-nineteenth century in missionary transmission may be of some historical significance and may require a different set of interpretive tools to fully comprehend it. Such tools should seek to discern, explicate, and understand the self-perception and self-understandings of these kinds of enterprisers of mission, especially those operating from the margins of imperial power and influence and as "native agents." The recruitment and missionary deployment of West Indians in Africa in the mid-nineteenth century must, therefore, be understood in the much larger context of their theological, psychosocial and geopolitical formation in colonial British West Indies and their deployment in the missionary field of Africa, in the sights of European imperial interests. That is what this study sets out to do.

CHAPTER 2

The Making of the West Indian Church: Identity, Community, and Social Reconstruction

One of the key concerns of this study is the question of why the West Indies in the mid-nineteenth century was seen as a possible source of missionary supply for the Western enterprising Christian missions to Africa. The answer to this concern lies in an understanding of the mission communities in the West Indies in which the initiatives for Africa were formulated and from which they were commissioned. The purpose of this chapter, then, is to examine the formation of those mission communities and consider how they developed into the West Indian church. Much of this development took place primarily in the nineteenth century in the context of West Indian slave society. The interest of this study is to determine, if possible, the extent to which the factors that contributed to the formation of Christian communities in a slave society might also have shaped the reconstruction of personal identities of those enslaved who became attached to these mission communities, as well as the extent to which such Christianized West Indian identities became missionary in outlook.[1]

---

1. This question of the role of institutions in identity formation has been examined by Jon Miller, *Social Control*, in his study of the Basel Evangelical Missionary Society. Drawing on Weber's theory of elective affinity, Miller argues that through the identification and sharing of mutual values and the voluntary subordination of personal identity to organizational control, missionary identity was formed in missionary training.

The relationship between Christianity and slavery has had a controversial, highly contested, and problematic history. One the one hand, Christianity has been seen as a justifier of the institution and practice of slavery and as a buttress for slave-based societies.[2] On the other hand, Christianity, and especially its evangelical message, has also been seen and interpreted as an agency of subversion,[3] a social threat and source of conflict, and an influence for civil disobedience. In a political economy based on plantation agriculture and a state-sanctioned regime of slave labour, attitudes towards Christianity have depended largely on which end of the social and theological spectrum was being represented. This study is set against the background of this problematic history, especially in light of the vigorously contested attempts to establish mission communities in the British West Indies after 1800, at the height of West Indian plantation slave society.

Although the Slavery Abolition Act was proclaimed in the British Parliament in 1833, the declaration of full emancipation of African slaves in the British West Indies took place on 1 August 1838. Since then, mission churches in the British West Indies have commemorated the historic achievement of emancipation with annual events that dramatize and memorialize the collapse of that most ignoble of institutions in the modern civilized world.[4] In 1842, on the fourth anniversary of emancipation, a London Missionary Society (LMS) missionary in Jamaica recorded a speech of an ex-slave at such a commemorative event at an LMS mission church in Chapelton, Clarendon:

> My dear brothers and sisters me heart quite full of joy to see you all so free and happy here today . . . at this hour in slave time, we all go to the field to dig cane holes, or pick coffee, and if we sick, Buckra flog we fi true, and no hear when we cry for mercy. But now no Overseer can come and drive we off to the field. Now we can work when we like and stay home when we sick. We can buy we own lands, build we own house, go to we own church. Me feel thankful to God and dem good people over dere

---

2. See Elkins, *Slavery*; Davis, *Problem of Slavery*; Genovese, *Roll Jordan Roll*; and Patterson, *Freedom in the Making*.

3. Turner, *Slaves and Missionaries*, 1–33.

4. Higman, "Slavery Remembered," 55–74.

in England for making we all free and for sending a minister to learn we a little manners of Massa Jesus.[5]

Several things are worth noting about this event and this ex-slave's speechmaking. First, the commemorative event was being celebrated within the environment of the mission church. With regard to the event, the missionary seemed very pleased that the event was hosted by the church, and that the community participated in this event with some degree of enjoyment and gratitude. In so doing, this mission church, like others, facilitated a process of ritualizing and institutionalizing the collective memory of this former slave community. The ex-slave speechmaker's evocative language on this occasion suggests not only an intentional correlation between the events of slavery and emancipation and the role of mission Christianity but also a degree of personal identification with that relationship. Whatever the speechmaker meant by "go to we own church,"[6] presumably the facilitating role played by the mission churches helped in strengthening the relationship between ex-slaves, the church, and the community – a relationship which had begun before the abolition of slavery. As the staging of the commemorative event implies, in post-slavery society, that relationship would have required sustained efforts to strengthen it.

A second point to note is the characterization of freedom in the speechmaker's discourse and the new feeling of personal identity displayed among the ex-slaves. In the speechmaker's mind, emancipation not only meant the mere absence of merciless physical punishment for any kind of abstention from enforced labour, even in sickness – "Buckra flog we fi true, and no hear when we cry for mercy" – but also the freedom to make life choices, to purchase and acquire land, to assemble or disassemble, to live in one's own house, and to go to one's own church – "we can buy we own lands, build we own house, go to we own church." Freedom involved the distinguishing right to possession of private property and the exercise of the self-dignifying and humanizing power of choice, as opposed to living in a state of perpetual bondage, coercion, and denial of basic natal rights. This characterization of

---
5. Holland to LMS Foreign Secretary, Correspondence West Indies, Jamaica - Box 11, LMS Archives, London.

6. Arguably, this expression could have multiple meanings, possibly including the freedom to openly attend African churches, where African religious rites were clandestinely practised during slavery.

freedom is significant in helping to understand the ex-slaves' existential quest in pursuit of the prospects and dream of emancipation.

A third significant observation is that the missionary, as an observer and eyewitness, found this speech noteworthy enough to record and despatch in his report to London. Without naming the speechmaker, the missionary noted the particular issues the speechmaker highlighted and conveyed these as if they represented the general feeling among the emancipated slaves; as perhaps they did.

It is clear that the ex-slave, in this speechmaking exercise, was spelling out the meaning of emancipation in personal terms. But by the repetitious and idiomatic use of the expression "we all" and "we," the speechmaker also appeared to be speaking collectively for fellow ex-slaves. In so doing, this ex-slave's speech revealed the general view – which was apparently shared among slaves in the British West Indies – that emancipation was achieved for them by "dem good people over dere in England." Where did such an idea come from? Was this idea derived from the association, which was often a complex relationship, between slaves and missionaries on the plantation and the missionaries' association with the British and American anti-slavery movement? Was this view an indication of a colonial mentality, derived from a set of critical subaltern relationships in the colonial state? Furthermore, to what extent was this feeling of self-confidence on the part of emancipated ex-slaves reliant on the actions of "good people over dere in England," rather than on what Beckles calls the "self-liberating ethos" of the slaves in slavery?[7] In the end, the larger question regarding the authentic meaning of emancipation is this: Did emancipation enable the recovery and reconstruction of personal identities for the African ex-slaves, giving them the opportunity for what Sheller describes as "lived freedom,"[8] or did it lead to a further denial of freedom? These important questions suggest that while looking at the formation of the West Indian church through the establishment of mission communities within the context of plantation slavery, it may well be worth looking again at the critical relationship between slaves and missionaries and the extent to which African slaves appropriated the message of the missionaries

---

7. Beckles, "Caribbean Anti-slavery", 869–878.
8. Sheller, *Democracy after Slavery*, 10, 103, 147–173.

and the mission church and could be perceived as having the possibility of becoming useful Christian agents.

This relationship between slaves and missionaries in West Indian slave society has received focused attention from scholars such as Turner, Lampe, and Hall.[9] In their examination of the cases of slave societies in the British and Dutch West Indies respectively, both Turner and Lampe contend that while the relationship between slaves and missionaries was critical in the colonial state during the regime of West Indian slavery, that relationship led to contrasting outcomes in these two colonial societies. Turner, for example, argues that in the British slave society of Jamaica, the problematic relationship between slaves and missionaries not only disturbed the status quo of plantation life, it eventually contributed to the undermining and disintegration of that society. Lampe, on the other hand, argues the very opposite for the Dutch West Indies and demonstrates that the relationship between slaves and missionaries served to enhance and prolong the practice of slavery in the Dutch West Indies. Hall, in her critical assessment of the relationship between the missionaries, in particular the English Baptist missionaries in Jamaica in the nineteenth century and the black African slaves in the British colony, focussed attention on how the radical dissenting tradition of the English Baptists in the metropole played out in the colony in the crucial formative period between 1830–1867, producing colonising subjects and racialised and gendered selves both in the Empire and at home.

If mission Christianity in the West Indies did in fact produce such contrasting and complex outcomes, it brings into question the real nature of the forms of Christianity delivered by the mission churches and the role played by the missionaries. Our interest here is to understand the extent to which mission Christianity in the British West Indies in the nineteenth century was instrumental in mediating real transformation in the persona and self-concept of the British West Indian slave, especially against the background of Orlando Patterson's characterization of West Indian slavery as "social death."[10] We shall now examine the importance of the formation of mission communities in the West Indies and reflect on the factors that helped to shape those

---

9. Turner, *Slaves and Missionaries*, 65–101, Lampe, *Mission or Submission?*, Hall, *Civilising Subjects*, 12–13.

10. Patterson, *Slavery and Social Death*, 10–14.

communities, paying particular attention to the three mission communities that played important roles in recruiting and sending West Indians to Africa as agents of Christian mission in the mid-nineteenth century.

The Moravian Community

The Moravian mission to the West Indies was one of the earliest Protestant groups to engage in Christian missionary activity outside of continental Europe since the Reformation. Almost sixty years before William Carey – the declared "Father of Modern Missions" – went to India, the Moravian Church, also known as the Church of the United Brethren, was already at work in the West Indies. The Moravian movement or the *Unitas Fratrum* (Latin for "Unity of Brethren") – which originated in the fifteenth-century Czech reform movement in Moravia and Bohemia, under the leadership of Count Nikolaus Ludwig von Zinzendorf (1700–1760) – found its organizational strength and unity in a community called Herrnhut (meaning, "the Lord's Watch") in Germany in the early eighteenth century. Reared in the strong pietistic tradition of the sixteenth-century German Reformation, these Brethren missionaries, as they were called, were sent to the West Indies as early as 1732 by Zinzendorf, who himself visited the West Indies in 1739.[11] The first Moravian missionaries to arrive in the West Indies were Leonard Dober and David Nitchmann, who went to the Danish West Indies in 1732 with a mission to Christianize the slave populations of St. Thomas, Santa Cruz, and St. Croix. By 1754, three other Brethren missionaries – Zacharias George Caries, Thomas Shallcross, and Gottlieb Haberecht – arrived in Jamaica on a mission to Christianize slaves on three plantations in the western end of the island.[12] Throughout the eighteenth century, Moravian missionaries spread across the West Indies, entering Suriname in 1735, Antigua in 1765, Barbados in 1766, St. Kitts in 1777, and Tobago in 1790.[13]

---

11. Lampe, *Mission or Submission?*, 36–40.

12. Caries, Shallcross, and Haberecht arrived in Jamaica on 7 December 1754 to commence Moravian work among nine hundred African slaves on the Barnham Plantations in St. Elizabeth and Westmoreland at the request of planters William Foster and Joseph Foster. William and Joseph were absentee planters who were converted to the Moravian movement in London and who wanted their slaves in Jamaica to be Christianized. See Hark and Westphal, *Breaking of the Dawn*, 8.

13. See Lewis, *Moravian Mission*, and Lampe, *Mission or Submission?*

Despite fifty years of dogged work, the efforts of the Moravians in Jamaica proved largely unsuccessful.[14] Encountering a variety of obstacles and challenges – including a high mortality rate, the political and social complexities of Jamaican plantation slave society, and the problem of language – the Moravian missionaries struggled to make any real progress in their mission work. By the beginning of the nineteenth century, the Moravian Mission in Jamaica had produced only meagre results. Perhaps the most difficult problem the Moravians faced during their early years of mission in the West Indies stemmed from its strategy of missionary engagement. This strategy was founded on the firm belief that Christian missionaries should eschew patronage and dependence of any kind and, as much as possible, be independent and self-supporting. The Zinzendorf-led community in Herrnhut held strongly to the German pietistic principles of brotherhood, community, simplicity of lifestyle, hard work, charity, and selfless service which included the principle of non-involvement and non-interference in civil politics, which was a principle that Zinzendorf preached in the West Indies[15] and which, Richard Price argues, was self-contradictory in practice when played out in the context of West Indian slave society.[16] These pietistic principles and the principle of non-interference in civil politics were, however, the guiding factors which informed the Moravian conception of the missionary vocation and missionary practice.

In Jamaica, the first Moravian missionaries – Caries, Shallcross, and Haberecht – found themselves dependent on the patronage of the British planters who had invited them and sponsored their mission. That sponsorship included the gift of a small plantation that required slave labour, a gift that the Moravian missionaries accepted in 1755. They named the plantation

---

14. Hutton, *History of the Moravian Church*, 11.

15. In his message, Zinzendorf appealed for faithfulness, diligence, and endurance of the state in which the slaves found themselves. He presented slavery as the will of God and suggested that what was most important was spiritual freedom, the freedom of the soul that liberates from all evil – "thoughts, deceit, laziness, faithlessness, and everything that makes your condition as slaves burdensome." The text of Zinzendorf's message to slaves in the West Indies is quoted in Lampe, *Mission or Submission?*, 38–39.

16. Price, *Alabi's World*, 418. As Lampe contends, it was a principle that was helpful to the Dutch colonial policy of first providing for the Christianization of the slaves in the Dutch West Indies before any granting of emancipation. This had the effect of delaying emancipation in the Dutch West Indies, despite the pressure exerted by British abolitionists and anti-slavery forces. Lampe, *Mission or Submission?*, 103–105.

"Old Carmel" and engaged in the practice of slaveholding while attempting to pursue their evangelistic mission. By accepting planter patronage, and engaging in the practice of slavery – which involved the selection and purchasing of slaves for their own use – and justifying it on social and theological grounds, they and other Moravian missionaries who did the same, effectively compromised their message and their status in the West Indies. In an environment seized with the problematic history of Christianity and slavery this was bound to be a negative factor in the pursuit of the Moravian mission in the West Indies. This practice of slave-holding by the Moravian missionaries, however theologically and pragmatically argued, made them appear too closely identified with the Plantocracy. In Jamaica, it contributed to the perception among the African slaves that the Christian message involved the tacit if not the overt acceptance of slavery. Jamaican slaves were therefore wary of embracing the Moravian mission[17].

It was not until the early nineteenth-century that real growth began to emerge in the Moravian mission in Jamaica. In a period of seven years, between 1831–1838, the number of persons under the care of the Moravians missionaries in Jamaica doubled from 4,800 in 1831 to 9,913 in 1837[18]. Within this period, six new Moravian mission stations were established. This sudden expansion in the Jamaican Moravian mission parallels a similar expansion in the Moravian mission in Suriname during the same period.[19] In Suriname the attraction of the African slaves to the Moravian mission was driven by very powerful social factors. By joining the mission and becoming "good brethren," the slaves could achieve some level of social respectability. As "good brethren," they obtained access to the prized commodity of education for themselves and their children, and thereby had a vehicle for improving their social status. It was a way out of the dehumanized and self-alienating status of the uneducated slave.

The growth in the Moravian mission community in Jamaica, on the other hand, may be attributed to several factors: one was the increase in missionary

---

17. Furley, *"Moravian Missionaries and Slaves in the West Indies"*.
18. Buchner, *The Moravians in Jamaica*, 27.
19. In the Suriname case, the Moravian strategy of missionary engagement focused on educating and Christianizing the slaves, even as slaveholders themselves. This strategy had the support of the Dutch colonial government and was used by colonial authorities to argue against Emancipation (Lampe, *Mission or Submission*, 49).

personnel during this period, including the arrival, in 1828, of Jackob Zorn, who would play an important role in the Moravian Mission at the time of emancipation; another was the role of the Negro Education Grant offered by the British Parliament in 1834, which allowed missionaries to do more towards the education of the slaves; as well as, the general state of anxiety and agitation for freedom on the part of the Jamaican slaves in the pre-emancipation period of the 1830s which gave greater organizational impetus to mission leaders.

In addition, two public events occurred which were pivotal in helping to catalyse the mission work of the Moravians in Jamaica in the early nineteenth century. The first was the public acknowledgement in 1823, by the leaders of the Moravian Mission in Jamaica that the practice of slaveholding was wrong and that the strategy of mission engagement they had been pursuing was, in fact, impeding the progress of the mission. By the 1820s, through comparisons with other mission communities on the island, these leaders had begun to realize that one of the key factors inhibiting Negro slaves from attending Moravian chapels was the slaves' perception of a close association and identification of these chapels with the plantation system and enslavement. Along with this public acknowledgment and repudiation of the practice of slaveholding in 1823, the Moravian elders also released the slaves they held at the Old Carmel estate and abandoned the mission station there. The changes that resulted in the fortunes of the Mission were noted by the mission inspector Peter La Trobe when he inspected the newly opened station at Irwin Hill during his visit to Jamaica in June 1828. As secretary of the Moravian Mission Board in London, La Trobe wrote from Irwin Hill to Brother Huffel, the mission leader, explaining the reasons for the growth in the Moravian Mission in Jamaica:

> The favourable disposition of many Proprietors of Estates and the increasing desire for the Gospel on the part of the slaves have afforded opportunities to the Brethren to extend their ministry . . . At Irwin near Montego Bay, eight Estates have been periodically visited for some years past, with considerable effect . . . but experience in that and in the other Islands, has proved that both the means of usefulness and the profitable results are much more effectually promoted where a chapel and mission House

can be erected in a central situation on land belonging to the mission. On such a spot of free ground Negroes from many miles round who are backward to visit Estates of other masters delight to assemble. In recent instances where this measure has been adopted, the congregations have greatly increased in a short time, so that the Chapels have occasionally been found far too small to contain the audience, and the state of the people has materially improved.[20]

La Trobe pointed out that the main reason for the new growth was the change in mission location to a spot of "free ground." His perceptive grasp of the resultant benefits to the Moravian Mission of the strategic move of separating chapel and mission house from the plantation reflected the new understanding among the leaders of the Jamaican Moravian Mission. They understood and recognized the need for a shift in their strategy of mission engagement. By taking such bold and public action, the Moravian Mission, for the first time, experienced rapid growth as the Jamaican slaves began to respond to the space and opportunity the mission provided for self-development, community association, and the formation of new identities.

The second event that helped to catalyse the Moravians' missionary work in Jamaica was the Pfeiffer case.[21] In the aftermath of the "Baptist War" – a major slave uprising in the western section of Jamaica during the Christmas break of 1831 – following the brutal putting down of the uprising by the local militia, several missionaries and their families were arrested, and charged with treason and sedition, based on allegations that they were preaching seditious doctrines of freedom to the slaves on several plantations and inciting them to rebel. Among those targeted for arrest and detention was Heinrich Gottlieb Pfeiffer, a German Moravian missionary, who was summarily arrested on 7 January 1832 at his New Eden mission station in Manchester. Amid heavy rains, Pfeiffer was dragged to the town of Mandeville to appear before a military court. Fortunately, the Moravian Mission leaders – led by John Ellis

---

20. Lampe cites documents from the Archiv der Bruder-Unität, Herrnhut, i. Letter of P. La Trobe to Br. Huffel, 19 June 1828. Lampe has brought to light and reproduced twenty-four important primary documents related to Moravian Mission work in the West Indies. Lampe, *Mission or Submission?*, 191.

21. Lampe, *Mission or Submission?*, 51–65. Lampe adds a few primary source documents relating to the Pfeiffer case in Appendix II, Documents 4, 5, 6, pages 196–201.

of the Fairfield station in Manchester – were apprised of the situation and they galvanized themselves into action. The circumstance of Pfeiffer's arrest, trial, and subsequent acquittal catalysed into action not only the Moravians but the entire mission community on the island. Quick intervention by the Moravian leaders delayed the trial until a fair process could be established.[22]

John Ellis knew or suspected that the trial would be very difficult for Pfeiffer because of his lack of command of English and his extremely humble disposition. Ellis observed, "Poor Br. Pfeiffer . . . his Germanisms made him more difficult to be understood and he did not command very great respect or manifest much acuteness."[23] Pfeiffer's trial before a military court in the town of Mandeville took place on 16 January 1832. Three witnesses were called. The evidence offered against Pfeiffer was so insufficient and contradictory that the court acquitted him of all charges. But Pfeiffer's release did not result in an immediate end to the targeting of missionaries. He and other missionaries continued to remain under suspicion and surveillance by colonial officials. They were subjected to public abuse from time to time, especially after the publication of a report commissioned by the Jamaican Assembly on the 1831 uprising. This report blamed the Protestant missionaries for the restiveness and rebellion of the plantation slaves in western Jamaica. The Moravian leaders were anxious to send Pfeiffer away from the island, for his own protection but were not able to do so for some time, and it was only in 1849 that Pfeiffer was sent to Bluefields in Nicaragua to work among the Miskito Indians.

The public acknowledgement by the leaders of the Moravian Mission and Pfeiffer's trial seemed to have had the effect of causing the Moravian Mission in Jamaica to reflect upon and re-examine their philosophy and strategy of missionary engagement, in particular the principle of non-interference in civil politics. Within two months of Pfeiffer's release from custody, the Moravian leaders felt it necessary to go public with a protest against the state's verdict on missionaries in Jamaica; and in April 1832, they published "A Remonstrance of the United Brethren in Jamaica, against the Report of the Committee of the House of Assembly on the late Rebellion."[24] In this report, they adopted

---

22. Letter of John Ellis on the trial of Pfeiffer, Fairfield, Feb 5, 1832, in Lampe, *Mission or Submission?*, Appendix II, Document 4, pages 196–197.

23. Lampe, *Mission or Submission?*, 196–197.

24. Lampe, 198–201. The Remonstrance denied the accusation of seditious teachings by the Moravian missionaries and defended the "meritorious behaviour" of slave helpers

a public stance against the political state, defending both missionary work in the island and Christian slaves who supported the mission churches. Since public protest was not the usual way Moravians addressed civil matters, the publication of this report was an indication of their recognition of the need to clarify, assert, and defend their work in the public domain. Although the Moravian leaders did not publicly change their policy and attitude towards civil matters, this close encounter with Jamaica's legal and political system over the Pfeiffer case in the early 1830s made them more keenly aware of and sensitive to the inadequacies of their position of avoidance of public issues and "civil matters"; and from that time on, they took notice of public issues of social justice, social equity, and due process in law within the state apparatus.[25]

Interestingly, in 1833, within two years of the 1831 slave insurrection in western Jamaica, the British Parliament passed into law the Slavery Abolition Act, which came into effect throughout the British Empire. In a sense, the abolition of slavery was anticipated by the African slaves themselves and by the mission communities in Jamaica. They had begun to reshape their strategy of mission engagement owing to a variety of circumstances, including the pre-abolition growth the mission churches were experiencing. By this time, the plantation slaves had begun to appropriate the message brought by the missionaries and were responding in large numbers. In the context of a long-established slave society, perhaps they saw in these mission churches the opportunity for salvation from the bondage of the demanding and discordant world of the plantation. To these people who had been treated as mere chattel, the Christian message became an instrument of hope and an opportunity for personal self-transformation.

Forming Agents for Mission

We have seen that, by the third decade of the nineteenth century, the sheer pressure of local circumstances forced mission communities in Jamaica, such as the Moravian community, to adjust their strategy of missionary

---

from their mission during the uprising. It also produced supporting testimonials attesting to their work.

25. In 1998, Livingston Thompson, a Moravian church leader, suggested that "the attitude of engaging in politics is emerging as the preferred approach among pastors" in Jamaica. Thompson, "Church and Politics," 12, 17.

engagement. Local circumstances had also caused shifts in other areas of mission work such as the area of the direct formation of persons in Christian beliefs through Christian rites and discipline. While the missionary strategy of focusing on slave education, moral formation, and family life training, and eschewing matters to do with civil politics was centred around plantation life, when this strategy proved problematic, a shift was made to work in "neutral space," which meant doing mission work away from plantation life. In this "neutral space," missionary work could be more directly applied and policies implemented to ensure the independent development of the mission community.

The close association that existed between the mission and the plantation was not the only factor that had accounted for the low level of response from the slaves before 1823. Another significant factor was the Moravian message of evangelical discipleship, which demanded public expression of one's faith commitment and submission to Moravian discipline. These demands were strictly enforced, and one practice in particular – the practice of "exclusion" – was employed as a policy of mission discipline, particularly for moral misconduct, to members of the mission or adherents hoping to become members. Whenever this policy was applied it meant that the Moravian slave adherent or member was excluded from the rites of Moravian worship. Exclusion was public shaming – a punishment without the use of physical whips. This public shaming was intended to induce the excluded member to repent and demonstrate contrition.

This Moravian policy came to light in the court case against Pfeiffer. One of the witnesses who testified against him was a Moravian woman named Ellen Dobbie. Dobbie had been "excluded" from the New Eden congregation for adultery before Pfeiffer was assigned to serve that congregation.[26] Regardless of whether or not Dobbie was motivated by anger or a desire for retaliation, her Dobbie's testimony during the trial described the policy and its effect:

Question: Do you know the prisoner?
Dobbie: Yes.

---

26. Lampe, *Mission or Submission?*, 196–197, Appendix 1, Document 4, John Ellis on the trial of Pfeiffer.

Question:	Did you ever hear the prisoner say anything about Negroes being free?
Dobbie:	Yes, he said that after Christmas we should all be free.
Question:	What do you mean by we all?
Dobbie:	The Negroes who are slaves.
Question:	When did you hear him say so?
Dobbie:	At Bogue church.
Question:	Was it in the open church before everybody?
Dobbie:	Yes.
Question:	Do you attend that church?
Dobbie:	Yes, but I do not now take speaking; it is long since I left the speaking room; I left it before the prisoner came there.
Question:	What do you mean by taking speaking?
Dobbie:	I do not go into the room with those he takes there.
Question:	How many go together into the room?
Dobbie:	Several go together.
Question:	What passes in this speaking?
Dobbie:	The person asks us what we have done for the Lord? If we have done good, he says we shall go to the Lord; if not we shall not go to him.
Question:	Are any left when the rest go into this room?
Dobbie:	Yes
Question:	What is the difference between those who go into the room, and those who do not?
Dobbie:	Those who do good go in, and the bad ones are kept out.[27]

This description and explanation of Moravian practice by an "excluded" member, given in court, was evidently intended to show how manipulative the Moravian Mission was towards the African slaves. In reality, it revealed the nature and effect of Moravian discipline in forming Moravian congregations. Those who were kept out or "excluded" had to either resolve to adhere to Moravian discipline or be shamed into being good members. In order to

---

27. Lampe, *Mission or Submission?*, 197.

enforce this practice and produce "good" members, a system of lay "helpers" was instituted to give catechetical instructions and provide some level of lay leadership. The lay leaders' duties included the important practice of "watching" over the brethren. While the movement was growing and new stations were being developed on "neutral" lands, the focus of Moravian engagement as a mission community remained the same: educational classes for religious and literary instruction, proactive encouragement of marriage and family life, development of moral character through acceptance of hard work, honesty, fidelity, community and pietistic devotion as Christian virtues and values. The enforcement of Moravian discipline then became the vehicle through which Moravian identity was to be formed.

The environment was patently decorated with a huge number of examples of the moral degradation of personhood by the brutal regime of slave society and the behaviour of the planter class. Chattel slavery provided the perfect conditions in which immorality thrived. Given the abusive and immoral environment of Jamaican slave society – a fact also highlighted in the diaries of Thomas Thistlewood, an eighteenth-century planter in Jamaica[28] – it is not difficult to understand why those who accepted the Moravian message and elected to identify with the mission community were required to submit to the demands of the discipline required for membership in the Moravian community.

As the Moravian community in Jamaica expanded and a cadre of "helpers" of proven ability emerged, the need for formal education and training of these native lay helpers became a key focus of activity for the mission in the immediate pre-emancipation period. By then, the mission was successfully engaged in enterprising mission work. In 1832, the "Female Refuge" – a shelter or hostel for orphaned or destitute girls – was founded at Fairfield in Manchester. In this mission-run facility, the girls received adolescent care and vocational education. The Earl of Mulgrave, the colonial governor, served as patron of the school and visited the institution in 1833. At the time of his visit there were twenty-four girls in its care. The Governor and his wife, Catherine Mulgrave, gave active charitable support to this venture. Catherine even took into custody a girl who had been rescued from a slave ship bound for Cuba, which had run aground on the coast of Jamaica. She baptized the girl and

---

28. Hall, *In Miserable Slavery, Thomas Thistlewood in Jamaica, 1750–86.*

gave her the name Catherine Mulgrave. The Moravian Mission in Jamaica also developed close links with the Mico Educational Trust in Kingston, whose Superintendent, J. Miller, was a member of the Moravian community. The young Catherine Mulgrave was educated as a teacher at Mico Training College in Kingston and later became one of the most outstanding missionaries in the Basel Mission in Akropong, on the Gold Coast of Africa.

Another factor which contributed to the growth of the Moravian Mission in Jamaica was the visionary leadership of Jackob Zorn, who served as its superintendent. Zorn was born in St. Thomas, in the Danish West Indies, of Moravian missionary parents, and his wife was also born in the Danish West Indies, in Santa Cruz. Jackob Zorn later travelled to North America to observe mission work there among the Indians. In 1828, Zorn and his wife arrived in Jamaica and were stationed at Fairfield in Manchester. His arrival and subsequent election to the position of superintendent coincided with a period of unprecedented growth in the Moravian Mission in Jamaica. While the policy of non-interference in civil matters remained the official position of the Moravians in Jamaica, particularly after the insurrection of 1831–32, there were leaders among them, like Zorn, who had international links with the British and American anti-slavery and abolitionist movements and who, like other nonconformist missionaries in Jamaica, began to anticipate the collapse of slavery in the British West Indies.

Zorn's international links gave him exposure to mission discourses and debates in Europe and America. In 1836, he attended the General Synod of the United Brethren in Herrnhut, Germany. He was in Correspondence with Thomas Buxton and the Africa Colonisation Society in Britain, as well as with the inspector of the Basel Evangelical Missionary Society in Switzerland. These international connections broadened his awareness of the transatlantic concerns about Africa and the role Christian mission could play in bringing about change and transformation in the continent of Africa. As Superintendent of the Moravian Mission in Jamaica, this stimulated his interest in envisioning how the local Moravian communities in Jamaica could become involved in and contribute to the Christian missionary enterprise in Africa.

By 1838, when full emancipation was declared in Jamaica, the Moravian communities in the island, despite their slow and difficult beginnings, were well established, with structured leadership and a sizeable following. This leadership now included "native helpers," who assisted in the mission churches and in various projects such as schools and other outreach development endeavours. They helped maintain Moravian discipline and gave real presence in the Moravian educational institutions. Zorn and his fellow elders took great pride in these accomplishments. They were proud of producing a growing number of Christianized African slaves in their mission communities and of being able to help them in their formation as they transitioned from slavery to emancipation. These Christianized Africans who embraced the Moravian ethic embraced an identity that had clear and distinct Christian beliefs, rites, and practices. The values and virtues of the Moravian social ethic, as modelled by the Moravian brethren in Herrnhut, were inculcated as key elements of the Christian message and witness.

Based on strong pietistic beliefs, the Moravian Mission in Jamaica forged a formation of personhood amid the challenges and moral conditions of the British West Indies slave society of the late eighteenth and early nineteenth centuries. As their mission churches grew numerically, their work in education and institutional development in Jamaica also grew. By the time of emancipation, with internationally aware leaders like Superintendent Jackob Zorn providing guidance and oversight, the Moravian mission community was among those mission communities in Jamaica which had begun to contemplate other fields of missionary endeavour once slavery was abolished. Dreams of contributing to the development of Christian mission in other lands – Africa, in particular – soon surfaced.

The Formation of Baptist Communities

The Baptist communities in the West Indies first emerged in Jamaica in the late eighteenth century.[29] Russell traces their formation not from Europe but from the liberated slaves of the American War of Independence which was fought for eight years from 1775 to 1783.[30] After the war, some freed African American slaves emigrated north to the British territory of Canada (Nova Scotia), while others headed south to the British West Indies. Between 1784

---

29. Stanley, *Bible and the Flag*, 68–105, and Russell, *Missionary Outreach*, have outlined in great detail the emergence and development of the Baptist community in Jamaica.

30. Russell, *Missionary Outreach*.

and 1802, three such black liberated slaves – George Leisle, George Gibbs, and Moses Baker – arrived in Jamaica with Baptist beliefs and practices and developed preaching missions in Jamaica's urban and rural centres in Kingston, St. Catherine, and St. James respectively. They proved quite effective in gaining interest among Jamaica's freed slaves, not only in the urban spaces but also among plantation slaves. Groups of slaves and freedmen gathered around these preachers, and this led to the formation of native churches which identified themselves as Baptists and adopted Baptist rules and principles. The preaching and organizing gifts of these black preachers proved quite successful and, within seven years, Leisle had baptized 400 people, enrolled 953 members, and set up schools for the instruction of children around Kingston. Baker, for his part, gathered 1,400 "justified believers" and 3,000 followers in western Jamaica by 1802.[31]

The spectacle of free black preachers preaching the gospel and teaching forms of Christianity that emphasized religious rites using potent eudemonic symbols such as baptism by immersion in large volumes of water, spirit mediums, and transcendental dreams resonated with the black slave population in Jamaica. At the same time, it raised suspicion among the planter class and among the more orthodox European missionaries of the established churches in Jamaica. The appeal of these black preachers added to the affinity of their message and rituals to African religious rites and aesthetics which were on the verge of a renaissance among the slave population in Jamaica at that time.[32] Therefore, the appearance of this phenomenon of black preachers espousing and modelling a black Christian identity was important at this stage of late eighteenth-century Jamaican society. As Russell points out, there is ample evidence to suggest that these Baptist leaders from America also had international connections and were very much aware of other black Baptist leaders and black churches in London, England; Nova Scotia, Canada; Sierra Leone, West Africa; and, of course, Savannah, Georgia (USA).[33] News of

---

31. Dayfoot, *Shaping of the West Indian Church*, 129–130.

32. After being a slave society for over a century, the British West Indian colony of Jamaica experienced a resurgence of African religious manifestations in the late eighteenth century. These manifestations, retained from Africa or reconstructed in the West Indies, were employed as instruments of resistance and revolt against the regime of slavery in the late eighteenth and early nineteenth centuries. Patterson, *Sociology of Slavery*; Brathwaite, *Development of Creole Society* and "Spirit of African Survival,"; and Lewis, *Main Currents*.

33. Russell, *Missionary Outreach*, 6.

Baptist exploits and developments on these three continents were published in John Rippon's *Baptist Annual Register* (1791–1802), and, inevitably, such news conveyed an important sense of a transnational identity and growth of a Baptist movement in the late eighteenth century. This movement was now being transmitted to Jamaican slave society by black agents, themselves victims of slavery in the New World.

However, in the delicate and highly charged sociopolitical environment of late eighteenth-century Jamaican slave society, the colonial authorities could hardly resist the temptation to take action against these black preachers, particularly when their preaching activities appeared to threaten the status quo of plantation life. Such was the case on the Adelphi Estate in the western parish of St. James, where Moses Baker drew large crowds to nightly meetings. In a clear attempt to curtail or shut down these Native Baptist churches, the authorities invoked a law which required a licence for public preaching and demanded that these black preachers obtain the requisite licence to preach in Jamaica. This licence had to be obtained from the Bishop of London, who, it was claimed, had jurisdictional and ecclesiastical authority over the British colony for such matters. Unable to obtain a licence from London, these black Baptist preachers in Jamaica were, for a time, effectively constrained in their evangelizing work. However, utilizing their transnational networks, Leisle and Baker contacted the British Baptists and invited them to undertake work for the Baptist Mission in Jamaica instead.[34] With the first arrival in 1814, the British Baptists not only came to Jamaica at the invitation of the black Baptist preachers but also came at a time when, for nearly thirty years, Baptist religious roots had already been laid among the slave population. These black preachers from America had set the pace for Baptist mission work in Jamaica.

Development of the Baptist Mission in Jamaica

As Brian Stanley notes, the beginning of Baptist work in the West Indies predates the formation of the Baptist Missionary Society (BMS), which was founded in Kettering, England, in 1792.[35] By 1813, the BMS was in a position to respond to the request for help from Jamaica, and John Rowe was sent out

---

34. Stanley, *History of the Baptist Missionary Society*, 69.
35. Stanley, *History of the Baptist Missionary Society*, 68.

to the colony, arriving in Jamaica in 1814. At first, Rowe and his successors tried to link with and assist the existing Baptist mission founded by the black American ex-slave preachers. But they soon ventured away to pioneer the formation of other Baptist communities. As is common with all evangelical mission societies of the period, there were strict policy guidelines under which BMS mission work was to be undertaken in Jamaica, including the policy of non-interference in the political order of the host society. Hence, the BMS missionaries were able to claim that their mission in Jamaica was not to "abolish slavery or to change the political institutions of the country." They insisted that their mission was "infinitely higher and holier" than political involvement. They had come, they claimed,

> out of compassion for the poor slave . . . [to] shed the light of faith upon his benighted soul, [to] bring the poor, forsaken wanderer into the fold of the Good Shepherd; that they might break off the shackles of his spiritual bondage, worse than that of his body, and brighten his desolate lot in the world with the hope of immortality in the world to come.[36]

However, for the enslaved black African, who had endured the long and entrenched institution of chattel slavery, the "shackles of his spiritual bondage" were manifested in the chains and whips of the regime of slavery. And what these people needed was the means of liberation from that bondage, not mere psychological escape from it. By the early 1820s, the BMS work in Jamaica was strengthened with the arrival of a new batch of missionaries. Among them were Joshua Tinson (1822–1850), Thomas Knibb (1823–1824), Thomas Burchell (1823–1846), James Phillippo (1823–1879), William Knibb (1825–1845), and John Clarke (1829–1875). William Knibb arrived in 1825 to take the place of his brother Thomas, who, within a year, had succumbed to the tropical conditions. This group of British Baptist missionaries from the Baptist Union of Great Britain vigorously pursued Baptist mission work in the four corners of Jamaica, establishing alternative Baptist congregations in population centres in St. Thomas in the east, Kingston, Port Royal, and Spanish Town in the south, Falmouth in the north, and Montego Bay in the

---

36. Clarke, Dendy, and Phillippo, *The Voice of Jubilee*, 7–11.

west. Their centres of operation became the foundation on which Baptist work in Jamaica was later to be organized and structured.

Mission Formation

The formation of Baptist mission communities and Baptist identity in Jamaica developed along three separate but interrelated lines. First, the principles of mission engagement, which included the organizing principle of autonomy of local congregations which Baptist polity required and the theological principle of conscientious dissent when moral conflict required it. Between 1823 and 1833, the Baptist mission in Jamaica grew rapidly, so much so that on a visit to London in 1840, William Knibb boasted that in 1834, there were twenty-four Baptist Missionary Society churches on the island of Jamaica with 10,838 members and by 1839, thirty-nine churches with 24,777 members, and 21,111 inquirers. In addition, there were 5,028 children in day school, 645 in evening school, and 9,159 in Sabbath schools.[37] These mission churches and educational institutions were organized around the mission stations with the BMS missionaries in full command.

Given this record of growth, BMS historian Brian Stanley points out that "in no other Baptist field was Church growth so spectacular, and nowhere else was progress towards the autonomy of the indigenous Church so rapid."[38] This rapid expansion of the Baptist Mission in Jamaica before 1838 encouraged and stimulated the missionaries to engage even harder after the abolition of slavery in building and maintaining more institutions (such as chapels and schools) and developing native leadership. They even attempted to create a national Baptist identity through uniting the regional centres of eastern, northern and western communities. Communication networks were established to foster and enhance Baptist identity through newspapers such as the *Baptist Herald and Friend of Africa*, which William Knibb began in 1839 in his centre in Falmouth, Trelawny.

---

37. Knibb, *Report of the Proceedings*, BMS Archives, Angus Library.

38. Stanley's observation of the spectacular growth of the Jamaican Baptist mission by the third decade of the nineteenth century is worth noting when compared with other Baptist missions and in the special circumstances of Jamaican slave society. Stanley, *Bible and the Flag*, 68.

On the matter of dissent, the British Baptist missionaries in Jamaica operated in constant fear of persecution. From time to time, because of their reputation as dissenters,[39] they were challenged to publicly defend Baptist principles and practices against two sets of protagonists in Jamaica – the colonial state and rival mission organizations. Not only did this challenge keep the Baptist missions in a constant state of defensiveness, it also strengthened their dissenting posture and self-identity. This was evident in each edition of the *Baptist Herald*, which communicated this sense of persecution, defiance, and resolve.

Since Baptist leaders faced constant challenges from the state, they felt compelled to defend themselves and their mission, and to publicly respond to charges of political interference which came from local authorities and managers of estates. As Baptist congregations grew in numerical strength, the relationship between Baptist missionaries and the black slave population in Jamaica strengthened and showed increasing signs of impact on both slave and missionary. This deepened suspicion about Baptist activities among state authorities and managers of estates.[40]

The turning point in the Baptist missionaries' relationship with the colonial state came in connection with their alleged role in the slave uprising of 1831–32. The circumstances of this "Baptist War" are themselves quite controversial. During Christmas 1831, slaves from several plantations in the western parishes of Jamaica – believing that freedom had been granted by the British government in England but was being denied by the local colonial authorities – covertly planned a strike, which was intended to be, at the very least, an act of non-cooperation with the slave regime. This strike was to take place when work on the plantations was expected to resume after the Christmas holidays. The proposed action was simply intended to be a non-violent withdrawal of labour as a form of protest against the continuation of the institution of slavery. However, before strike action could commence,

---

39. Watts, *The Dissenters*.

40. The relationship with the African slaves had produced such outstanding personalities as Richard and Joseph Merrick, who were mentored by John Clarke and who served the church as native pastors. But it also produced Samuel Sharpe, who, as a deacon in Thomas Burchell's congregation in Montego Bay, saw no dissonance between Christianity as taught by the church and the need for revolutionary action to bring about social change in the slave society of Jamaica. Sharpe, now a national hero in Jamaica, was implicated in the slave uprising of 1831–1832 and singled out as leader of the insurrection. He was executed by the state on 3 May 1832.

the plan was leaked to the planters. Acting out of fear, the planters took immediate preventive action by calling for militia reinforcement from as far away as Kingston. When the militia arrived in Montego Bay, their presence spread alarm in western sections of the island and triggered the setting of incendiary fires to seven estates by some the slaves. This act of insurrection involved over twenty thousand slaves on these estates in western Jamaica.[41]

The Jamaican establishment, including the local assembly and the planters, reacted with full force, resulting in some 200 slaves being killed, 540 executed, and martial law imposed. The strong reaction of the state was supported by some leaders of the established church in Jamaica, the Church of England in the West Indies, and especially from a new group of Anglican clergymen who formed the Colonial Church Union.[42]

One of the reasons this uprising was called the "Baptist War" was because many of the slaves were Baptist members – some connected with the Native Baptists – and many of the leaders were Baptist deacons.[43] Consequently, there were strong public allegations that the BMS missionaries were the chief influencers of this seditious anti-slavery activity that had turned into a violent insurrection. As a consequence of the dangerous nature of the uprising and the public allegation and suspicion of the role of mission churches in this slave society, there was an outbreak of attacks against evangelical mission leaders in Jamaica. The Baptist leaders were singled out for public attention, and several of their missionaries were arrested. They were not only charged with interfering with civil politics by selecting their leaders from among those chosen to be the "drivers" of the estate labour force but also, among other things, with being a "political party." It was believed that the insurrection was organized by the "drivers" of the estates, many of whom were leaders in the Baptist churches. The scale of destruction of property on the plantations was such that leading agitators were apprehended, tried, and sentenced to be hung for treason. Among these was the Baptist deacon Samuel Sharpe.

---

41. Patterson, *Sociology of Slavery*, 273; Turner, *Slaves and Missionaries*, 148–178.

42. As a reaction to this perceived Baptist-led insurrection, the Colonial Church Union was formed in the parish of St. Ann in 1832 by Rev. George Bridges, ostensibly to defend the colony against the seditious activities of nonconformist missionaries. This reactionary move among some members of the established church in Jamaica set off a bitter controversy and intense rivalry between the established church (Church of England) and the Methodists, Presbyterian, and Baptists churches.

43. Craton, *Empire, Enslavement, and Freedom*, 334.

The attack on the Baptist Mission saw thirteen Baptist chapels destroyed and five Baptist missionaries – Knibb, Burchell, Abbott, Whitehorn, and Gardner – arrested and detained. The arrest of Knibb and Burchell on charges of treason fired up the Baptists to cry out against unwarranted persecution by an immoral civil regime. The impact of the events of 1832 threatened to stigmatize Baptist work in Jamaica, but the mission leaders responded vigorously and defiantly and took their case all the way to Britain. In 1833, Knibb was in England, appealing to British public opinion by giving a first-hand report and explaining the missionaries' view of the situation in Jamaica. He appeared before the Baptist Missionary Society and spoke to large gatherings of the British public.[44]

The Baptist Mission in Jamaica faced constant charges and allegations from rival mission organizations in the island. There were allegations that the British Baptist missionaries were engaged unfairly and improperly in mission work. For example, the Presbyterians criticized and took them to task for allegedly issuing tickets to communicants and improperly admitting unqualified people to the sacred elements of Holy Communion, promoting unqualified persons too quickly to positions of leadership in the church, and – in their eagerness to claim large numbers as members – being weak in discipline and administration. The Presbyterians claimed that the actions of these missionaries had compromised the entire mission enterprise and went as far as to bring a formal report of these charges to the secretary of the Baptist Missionary Society in London as a "Remonstrance against the Baptists of Jamaica."[45] In response, the BMS missionaries in Jamaica were called upon to explain and give account to the BMS in London. Again, these

---

44. Sermon by William Knibb in London, 19 June 1833, and again in 1840. By 1830, the tide of considered opinion in Britain had turned towards reform even though Parliament had, as early as 1807, approved measures for "The Amelioration of Conditions of the Slaves." The rise of British and American anti-slavery movements between 1807 and 1830 had raised the tempo of the debate over slavery, and many evangelical missionaries who had direct evidence of slave conditions had joined the anti-slavery movement. This caused slaves in the British West Indies to regard evangelical missionaries working among them as allies in their quest for freedom and strengthened their belief that they had "good people over dere in England" who were championing their case for the ending of slavery.

45. The nine-point charges against the Baptist missionary practices in Jamaica were agreed by the Presbyterian missionaries at Goshen, St Elizabeth, on 14 July 1841 and signed in the name of the Presbytery by Peter Anderson, Moderator, and William Scott, Clerk. Included as Appendix 1 in Waddell, *Twenty-Nine Years, 1861/1970*, 663.

Baptist missionaries resolutely and defiantly defended themselves and refuted the charges. Having to defend Baptist work and principles of mission engagements both in Britain and Jamaica had the interesting effect of reinforcing and strengthening Baptist identity as nonconformist, independent, and resistant. This religious identity with quasi-political overtones certainly helped to embolden the formation of the nascent Baptist communities in Jamaica, but it also led to further antipathy towards the Baptists by the plantocracy and the colonial state.

As noted earlier, a second factor that helped in the formation and consolidation of Baptist communities and Baptist identity in Jamaica was the impact of the host society (the mission field) upon the missionaries themselves. In early nineteenth-century Jamaican society, this impact seemed to have had a transforming effect upon the British Baptist missionaries since their courage and conduct in missionary labours, against very trying odds, would otherwise be difficult to explain. The Jamaican mission field created conditions and behaviours that tested the operational policy guidelines of the BMS in metropolitan London. For example, with the strong influence of a dissenting tradition, particularly evident among Bristol Baptists in their background, the British Baptists in Jamaica soon found the BMS policy of non-interference in civil matters a difficult policy to strictly adhere to in practice in the strongly contested environment of Jamaica's nineteenth-century slave society. This was especially so when matters to do with actions of the colonial state conflicted with their religious conscience. As Turner has shown, the political behaviour of the Baptist missionaries in appearing to defend the interest and welfare of the African slaves led to what she termed the "disintegration of the Jamaican slave society" and the collapse of slavery.[46] After the 1831–32 debacle in Jamaica, it is evident that the BMS missionaries in Jamaica became much more open and strident in their growing opposition to slavery, a stand which inevitably conflicted with the BMS policy of non-interference in the civil politics of the host country.

The change in missionary behaviour was further evident when missionaries Knibb, Burchell, Phillippo, and Clarke attended the General Convocation of the British and Foreign Anti-Slavery Society in London in 1840. In public speeches around Britain, these missionaries once again took the opportunity

---

46. Turner, *Slaves and Missionaries: the Disintegration of Jamaican Slave Society*, 148–178

to publicly defend their work in Jamaica against charges of political interference by the new colonial governor, Sir Charles Metcalfe. For example, in a public forum at Exeter Hall, Knibb, who was in great rhetorical form, rousingly proclaimed to loud cheers: "If your missionaries are political, it is just, because the rulers make them so. The time is come when the Christian church will find that no Christian missionary can do his duty without being political."[47] Such bold and daring statements would previously have brought him in direct confrontation with the BMS since such sentiments ran counter to mission policy regarding instructions for engagement in foreign mission work. But, in the triumphalist mood of the 1840 anti-slavery convention in London, it was welcome news, even though theologically and operationally problematic for BMS policy. Knibb's theological justification for this bold new assertion was that when civil rulers overstepped their mark, as they were thought to have done in the aftermath of the 1831 uprising in Jamaica, "they have entered the sacred enclosure of conscience . . . and I for one will never rest until they are turned out of it."[48] In his speech, Knibb was reflecting the way in which Baptist missionaries in Jamaica had been transformed by the exigencies of the host society in which they laboured. Knibb's theological justification and interpretation of mission policy was very much in keeping with what Catherall calls "the logic of their beliefs."[49]

In Baptist theology, the supreme virtue of conscience as the final arbiter of human moral actions transcends any other consideration and must certainly be regarded as being above human political considerations. As the BMS missionaries stated in their Jubilee Statement, what they learned in Jamaica was that

> the gospel is the everlasting foe of every kind of bondage . . . Wheresoever it comes, it seeks to emancipate from every yoke. It has a natural and implacable antipathy to oppression, and cannot live in the same land with slavery. No sooner does the gospel enter, than the conflict begins. A struggle is inevitable. The doom of slavery is sealed, for the war will never cease till slavery receives its death-blow, and lies prostrate at the feet of its

---

47. Knibb, *Report of the Proceedings*, BMS Archives, Angus Library.
48. Knibb, *Report of the Proceedings*, BMS Archives.
49. Catherall, "Baptist War and Peace," 268.

glorious conqueror. So it was in Jamaica. Christian Missionaries did not come to abolish slavery; they came to preach the gospel, in its wonder-working power, having first of all provoked slavery to hostility and to arms, fought out the battle, until slavery was no more – until the fell monster, with its whips, and chains, and manacles, and bilboes, and every other instrument of torture was buried, never, never, never to rise again.[50]

Such an understanding of the "wonder-working power" of the gospel was certainly mediated through the exigencies of their mission engagement. How else did these missionaries arrive at such an understanding? They evidently came to appreciate the truly emancipatory power of the Christian gospel in the concrete historical environment of the slave society of the British West Indies. The evidence suggests that the Jamaican environment and experience reshaped and transformed their theological outlook.

Further evidence of this change in their theological outlook can be observed in the changed perspective, attitude, and understanding of the so-called "Negro character". In a benign and paternalistic kind of way, the British Baptist missionaries had arrived in the West Indies believing that they had a positive view towards the persona of the African slaves. They believed that the Africans, despite their physical condition in bondage, were redeemable and therefore worth evangelizing, which might have proved sufficient motivation for missionary endeavours among Africans despite the existence of slavery. To believe that the Africans had, at least, a redeemable soul was one thing. But the philosophical and cultural question of the "Negro character" had raised doubts about the ultimate value of such engagement. To believe that African slaves had the mental capacity for "higher living" and noble achievements required another level of appreciation.

This changed perspective on the African character was most evident in the theological work of David East, a BMS missionary in Jamaica at the East Queen Street Baptist Church in Kingston, and tutor at the Baptist Calabar Theological College. In the aftermath of emancipation, East and other BMS missionaries in Jamaica showed a new appreciation for Africa and the "sons of Ham." In 1844, he published a pamphlet on Africa, in which he gave an

---

50. Introductory Discourse by the BMS missionary to Jamaica, Rev D. J. East, in *The Voice of Jubilee*, 11.

interpretation of the then widely used text of Psalm 68:31.[51] In his pamphlet, East argued that not only was the text a fulfilment of prophecy, it also signalled the removal of a curse on the sons of Ham. This curse had been set in Genesis 9:22–27.[52] From East's point of view – and perhaps also the point of view of his BMS colleagues in Jamaica – now

> the believer in revelation sees in the condition of Africa the fulfilment of Divine prediction – the execution of a curse pronounced by the Almighty nearly four thousand years ago, and still standing on record in holy oracles (Gen 9:22–27, Ps 68:31), but the curse which for so many generations has rested upon the unhappy descendants of Ham, is not to be perpetual.... The same inspired authority which records the curse, predicts the blessing.[53]

This idea, just six years after the abolition of slavery, that Africa and black Africans were no longer under curse but under blessing was a new revelation, a new understanding and interpretation of the black person. It was also a new insight into biblical prophecy from the point of view of Baptist scholars. This new understanding led to what Russell calls the attempt to "reinstate the African into the human race."[54] Perhaps it was this new theological justification, among other things, that imbued the Baptist mission leaders in Jamaica with the passion and drive for the formation of Baptist

---

51. "Princes shall come out of Egypt; Ethiopia shall soon stretch out her hands unto God" (Ps 68:31 KJV).

52. "And Ham, the father of Canaan, saw the nakedness of his father, and told his two brethren without. And Shem and Japheth took a garment, and laid it upon both their shoulders, and went backward, and covered the nakedness of their father; and their faces were backward, and they saw not their father's nakedness. And Noah awoke from his wine, and knew what his younger son had done unto him. And he said, Cursed be Canaan; a servant of servants shall he be unto his brethren. And he said, Blessed be the Lord God of Shem; and Canaan shall be his servant. God shall enlarge Japheth, and he shall dwell in the tents of Shem; and Canaan shall be his servant" (Genesis 9:22–27 KJV).

53. East, *West Africa*, 2–3.

54. Russell, "*Emergence of the Christian Black*", 51–58. BMS missionary David East also made it very clear in his Introduction to the Jubilee record of the BMS work in Jamaica in 1864, *The Voice of Jubilee*, where he discusses the "Capability of the Black Man for Education". East said "the black man in Jamaica has been educated. He has been taken from some of the lowest positions in the social scale, and raised at least to positions of respectability and honour, in which no one can gainsay his ability to exercise those social rights which the British Constitution confers upon him as a British subject", 14–17.

communities in post-emancipation Jamaica. They were outstanding in their post-slavery reconstruction work in all centres of Baptist witness in Jamaica. East's theological interpretation of Psalm 68:31 – "Princes shall come out of Egypt; Ethiopia shall soon stretch out her hands to God" – was echoed by other BMS mission leaders in Jamaica. This text became the main biblical text that was used to shape the Jamaican Baptist vision for their missionary undertakings in Africa. For many, Psalm 68:31 became their chief missionary text for the call to Africa.

A third factor in the formation of Baptist community and Baptist identity in the West Indies – which followed directly from the previous two – was the ever-increasing need on the part of the Africans enslaved in the West Indies for the reconstruction of an Afrocentric identity in this New World environment.[55] With the arrival of the new team of British Baptist missionaries in 1823 and the spread of Baptist centres across Jamaica, encounters between the missionaries and the deep existential issues affecting the African slaves in bondage became inevitable. One of the effects of these issues on the slaves was to produce a pseudopersona – a disguised or masked self – characterized by the image of a docile, subservient "yes massa" personality, which Patterson, Brathwaite, Burton, and others have drawn attention to.[56] In this context, from the outlook of the BMS missionaries, it was clear to them that what was needed was a new Christian persona to combat the stereotype of the depressed, alienated persona of the Jamaican slave. According to Russell, they invented the "Christian Black" as their missionary project and as a major contribution to missionary enterprise in the West Indies.[57]

This became especially evident in the long and influential career of James Mursell Phillippo in Spanish Town. Of all the BMS missionaries, Phillippo had the longest career in Jamaica, spanning over fifty years (1823–1879). From his base in Spanish Town – the administrative centre and colonial capital of Jamaica under the British – Phillippo had intimate knowledge of the issues,

---

55. The inexorable drive for the establishment of African identity in the New World took many forms and began almost from the time European enslavement of Africans began. It certainly fed the debate on retention vs reconstruction of African cultural presence in the New World. Where this issue intersected with the engagement of Christian missionaries in Jamaica, began to emerge, as Russell contends, after 1823. "The Emergence of the Christian Black."

56. Patterson, *Sociology of Slavery*; Brathwaite, *Development of Creole Society*; and Burton, *Afro-Creole*.

57. Russell, "Emergence of the Christian Black," 51–58.

conditions, and yearnings of the slaves, and he was one of the pioneers of the reconstruction project undertaken by Baptist missionaries immediately following the proclamation of full emancipation in 1838. Phillippo also knew the power of Baptist preaching. The Baptist doctrines of regeneration and conscientious dissent were very attractive to slaves in bondage. Using the modality of the embodied rite of baptism by immersion – which the Baptists emphasized and which the African slaves were quick to appropriate in large numbers – the African slaves carved out a psychological and identity-shaping space for themselves in slave society. They adopted this Baptist rite as their own means of redemption and redefining of self,[58] and this was certainly one of the factors that explain the phenomenal growth of the Baptist mission communities prior to abolition of slavery.

The deep association and encounters of the British Baptist missionaries in Jamaica with the lives of the African slaves before emancipation were deepened even further after abolition. Inspired by their achievements and self-proclaimed contribution to the collapse of slavery, these missionaries formed new institutions for the development of the emancipated Africans. These included a native pastorate for the development of leaders for the emergent Jamaican Baptist church and a theological training institute in Calabar – which was officially opened on 6 October 1843 with ten students – to provide pastoral and theological training for the Jamaican church. They also launched the Jamaica Baptist Missionary Society in 1846, as a means to promote, recruit, and deploy Jamaican missionaries abroad. These programmes and measures certainly helped to establish a strong Baptist identity and a network of Christian communities across the island.

However, the need for recovery of an Afrocentric self on the part of the emancipated Africans in the New World environment like Jamaica, required much more than physical actions such as building institutions and training by the Europeans. It also required, among other things, a vigorous pursuit of the emancipation dream to realize the full benefits of emancipation – benefits such as those mentioned in the speech of the ex-slave during the celebration of the fourth anniversary of emancipation in Jamaica. It required the full redemption of persons from "natal alienation,"[59] the transformation of

---

58. Besson, "Religion as Resistance," 43–76.
59. Patterson, *Slavery and Social Death*, 7.

self-perception and self-concept, and the full recovery of the dignity of self, family, and community. Turner, Wilmot, Austin-Broos, Hall,[60] and others point out that the Baptist missionaries' tempered advice to the newly freed slaves following the proclamation of the Emancipation Act suggests that the missionaries were aware of these realities.

One such example is the advice given by William Knibb who, knowing of this need among the enslaved Africans, attempted to spell out to his congregation on the eve of emancipation, the meaning of freedom and define in very practical terms the nature of the responsibilities before them. In his charge, Knibb made it clear that "to be free you must be independent. Receive your money for your work; come to market with money; purchase from whom you please; and be accountable to no one but the Being above, whom I trust will watch over you and protect you."[61] Knibb highlighted three key elements that he believed African ex-slaves needed to grasp about the nature and use of freedom: that freedom for former slaves in bondage now meant independence, not dependence; that freedom meant the inherent right and power of choice, not obligation by coerced actions; and that freedom meant self-determination, not subservience. These three elements were intended to reinforce the character of the new "Christian Black."

While underscoring the value of work and its just reward, and the self-empowering and self-dignifying actions of free agents, Knibb also drew upon the dissenting tradition in Baptist theology and hinted at the moral right to freedom. His emphasis on ultimate accountability being to "no one but the Being above" implied the free exercise of conscience and the human and moral right to resist any authority which conflicts with the authority of the "Being above." To former slaves, this would have been good news and good advice. The just reward of money (cash) for expended labour was important and essential in the development of a market economy as an interdependent arena of community development. Therefore, the exercise of that free choice of spending earned money was not merely a self-empowering act of a free agent, it was also of great social value for the greater social good.

---

60. Turner, *Slaves and Missionaries (1982)*; Wilmot, "Emancipation in Action"(1986); Auston-Broos, "Redefining the Moral Order" (1992) and *Jamaica Genesis (1997)*, Hall, *Civilising Subjects (2002)*.

61. Hinton, *Memoir of William Knibb*, 283–285.

In his charge, Knibb also highlighted the values of enterprise, self-empowerment, and self-dignity that the Baptist missionaries sought to inculcate, especially during those last moments of slavery. But these values also formed part of the understanding of the freedom that the Africans pursued during slavery as well as after emancipation. In time, these values helped shape a new post-slavery West Indian character and cultural identity.

These three interrelated internal and external factors of Baptist organizational polity, with emphasis on the principle and tradition of nonconformism and dissent, undoubtedly helped to shape the formation of the Baptist communities in Jamaica. These communities in formation were forced to wrestle with their own internal organizational problems, while guarding against and responding to external threats directed at them. The Africans in slavery and freedom became skilled at appropriating what was most useful to them in the reconstruction of their post-emancipation identity.

The agitation and struggle for slave emancipation in Jamaica, in which the Baptist missionaries became embroiled, not only dislodged the BMS policy of non-interference in the politics of the host country, it also further fuelled the Baptist missionaries' desire to protect the black Christian populace they had helped to produce. These missionaries envisioned that once the evil system of slavery was abolished, this Christian population would become the vanguard of a new West Indian Christian society.[62] The creation of "civilized subjects" – to quote Catherine Hall[63] – was the missionary dream.[64]

---

62. The slave uprising in Western Jamaica in 1831–32 could have dealt a severe blow to this vision. But, as indicated earlier, the events of the so-called Baptist War were cleverly used by the Baptist missionaries such as William Knibb (1825–1845) as a great opportunity not only to agitate in Great Britain for the abolition of slavery but also to envision and challenge the British public regarding the usefulness of a black Christian population in the West Indies to the cause of bringing an end to the evils of African slavery.

63. Hall, *Civilising Subjects*, 84–139

64. The BMS missionaries were in no doubt about the means of achieving this dream. The instrumental means was the Christian missionary. In their jubilee statement affirming the role of the missionary they triumphantly stated, "How is the monster demon [of slavery] to be destroyed? By the policy of statesmen? By the power of the army? By the wisdom of philosophy? No – by the missionary. How is the mutual slaughter and merchandise in man to be put an end to? By the missionary. By whom is Africa to be covered by the blessings of civilisation? By the missionary. By whom are the sable millions of that wide continent to be lifted up to the fellowship of the free states of Europe? By the missionary. Let the gospel of Christ have free course, run, and be glorified throughout all its borders, then old things will pass away, and all things become new. In that hour her degraded sons will rise from the earth,

When the Emancipation Act of 1833 signalled the end of slavery in the British Empire, the BMS missionaries in Jamaica exulted in this triumph of "light over darkness" and, from the margin of the British Empire, felt ready for a new horizon of challenge. As Phillippo explains – in his Correspondence with Thomas Fowell Buxton in January 1839 – five months after the euphoric celebrations of "freedom" in the West Indies, that new horizon was Africa itself.[65]

The Church of England in the West Indies

The third West Indian church whose making and formation we will examine in this chapter is the Church of England in the West Indies, also referred to as the Anglican Church. In many respects, the formation of the Anglican Church in the West Indies was derived from the Church of England's pattern of ensuring pastoral ministration for the English people wherever they might be found throughout the British Empire. The presence of the Anglican Church in the West Indies goes back to the early seventeenth century, when, in the aftermath of Cromwell's Western Design, the English began to arrive and settle in the West Indies, taking with them religious chaplains who established chapels to serve the colonial settlers. These chaplains were licensed by the Bishop of London, who was expected to exercise episcopal supervision from his seat of authority in London. In reality, such supervision did not occur because it was difficult and impractical on two counts: first, the long distance of four thousand miles of ocean between London and the West Indies, and second, a general absence of direct and informed knowledge of the West Indies by presiding bishops of London. Preoccupied with matters of local domestic concern in the metropole, these bishops often neglected episcopal jurisdictional duties in the margins of the British Empire, such as the West Indies. In reality, as Alfred Caldecott points out, the expectation

---

feel that they are men, not brutes, and worship their creator." Clarke, Dendy, and Phillippo, *The Voice of Jubilee*, 269.

    65. Phillippo to Buxton, Buxton Papers, Correspondence, USPG Archives. By then, the Baptists and other evangelical missionaries in Jamaica were ready to embark on a new project, proposing a mission to Africa from the newly formed West Indian church. Although Phillippo's inquiry was primarily for information, it appeared open for other forms of assistance which those in the metropole might have been able to supply.

that the Bishop of London would exercise real episcopal supervision in the West Indies had no meaningful basis apart from the fact that it was the Bishop who issued licences for preaching in the colonies.[66]

As a consequence, for more than a century and a half, Church of England clergy serving in the West Indies had no effective episcopal supervision. Caldecott points out that during this period the Anglican Church in the West Indies was "an anomaly." It was "an Episcopal Church without Bishops; it was a professedly Diocesan system without dioceses."[67] As a result, from the seventeenth century onwards, Anglican clergy in the West Indies were, for the most part, unregulated, unsupervised, and virtually "a law unto themselves." Moreover, being paid by the state as agents of the Crown, and thereby under obligation to the social and political establishment, they were understandably more interested and involved in the welfare of the plantocracy than in that of the other constituent populations of colonial society. For this reason – in addition to other reasons such as its style of religious worship, with a structured prayer book liturgy fixed on English cultural attitudes – the Church of England in the West Indies developed a reputation for being pro-establishment, conservative, elitist, and favouring the status quo with its pro-slavery agenda. For the most part, and until the end of the eighteenth century, there was hardly any place in this church for plantation slaves who comprised a significant proportion of the population of the British West Indies. It did not help matters much when highly visible plantations associated with the church – such as the Codrington Estates in Barbados – practised plantation slavery in the name of Christianity.

By the beginning of the nineteenth century – after having been present in the West Indies for nearly two centuries – the Church of England in the West Indies found itself in the position of being compelled to adjust its orientation towards the larger population and needs of West Indian society. This became necessary for at least three reasons. First, the church was pushed by the imperial government to respond to the religious and humanitarian needs of the slave population. In 1823, in the aftermath of the 1807 Act for the Abolition of the Slave Trade, the British government passed so-called slave laws governing the regime of slavery in British colonies. Lord Bathurst, the Colonial

---

66. Caldecott, *The Church in the West Indies*, 49.
67. Caldecott, 49.

Secretary, outlined for all colonial interests what was described as "effectual and decisive measures for meliorating the conditions of the slave population in his majesty's colonies."[68] These measures gave evidence, perhaps for the first time, of the British government's interest in the humanitarian and moral aspects of a slave-based economic system. The measures also indicated the government's determination to use religious agency to improve slave conditions. By referring specifically to "the moral condition of the slaves," the expectation of the imperial government was that this would be the work of the church. As the established church, not only was its cooperation expected but this was presented as a real opportunity for engaging further in its religious work. As a branch of the Church of England, the Anglican Church in the West Indies was well placed to access funds from the imperial government for the education of the Negro slave population.

A second reason for the church's change in orientation was the fact that other British Protestant mission societies – which by then had commenced missionary work in several parts of the West Indies – had begun to make an impact on the majority slave population. These evangelical missions had altogether different cultural attitudes and assumptions about the Negro, about church and state relations, about Christian mission and religious conversion, and about the institution of slavery itself. Their vigorous pursuit of missionary work showed up the fact that the Anglican Church was not where the action was with regard to outreach to the African slave population. Not only was the work of the Church of England in the West Indies languishing, the Anglican Church in the West India was ill-prepared to respond to the new circumstances that resulted from the new laws of 1823.

The third and more immediate reason for change was the recognition of the need for a more structured organization, one in which there was more local and direct episcopal leadership and oversight, which could more effectively carry out the wishes and mandate of the Colonial Office. This was not the case which obtained by virtue of the largely unregulated state and absence of direct episcopal leadership in the West Indies. So, in 1823, the imperial government also made a grant available through the Society for the

---

68. Speech to the British Parliament by Secretary Canning on "Amelioration of the condition of the slave population in the West Indies". HC Deb 16 March 1824 vol 10 cc1091-198. https://api.parliament.uk/historic-hansard/commons/1824/mar/16/amelioration-of-the-condition-of-the

Propagation of the Gospel (SPG) for the establishment of two dioceses and colonial bishoprics for the West Indies. One bishop was to reside in Jamaica and the other in Barbados. The objectives of the grant were quite specific:

1. To effect those improvements in the moral and religious state of the Negroes which are contemplated in the new resolutions lately passed by the House of Commons.
2. To be under the jurisdiction of the Archbishop of Canterbury and to make annual report of the state of the Dioceses to His Grace.
3. To supply each Bishop with an Archdeacon, one of whom should reside in Jamaica and the other in Barbados or Antigua.
4. To provide the new Bishops with the powers of appointing in each principal island, one of the Revd. Clergymen to act as an Ecclesiastical Commissary whose duty it should be to make annual reports to the Bishop on all spiritual matters connected with the districts in which he resides.[69]

These objectives, as set out by the Colonial Office, were to ensure the better management and coordination of church affairs in the West Indies and offer more systematic supervision and coordination of the clergy. In this, the first attempt to regularize the Anglican Church in the West Indies and place it under direct episcopal supervision, it is of interest to note that the first and perhaps the overall mandate of Colonial Office was to attend to "the moral and religious state of the negroes." The establishment of episcopal order in the West Indies from 1824 – although long overdue – may, among other things, be seen as a recognition on the part of the British government of the need for change in slave conditions in the West Indies. Given the extent of agitation among the slave populations in the colonies, it could also have been as an admission of neglect of the ecclesiastical affairs of the West Indies for far too long. This new mandate prioritized and set an important new direction for the Anglican Church in the West Indies.

The two newly appointed bishops – Christopher Lipscomb (1824–1843) and William Hart Coleridge (1824–1842) – were consecrated at Lambeth Palace, London, on 24 July 1824 and despatched to the West Indies. Lipscomb

---

69. Reply of the Society, C/WIN/Bar 15, Correspondence, USPG Archives, Bodleian Library.

and Coleridge sailed together and arrived in the West Indies in January 1825. While their arrival in the West Indies eventually brought a new sense of order to the Church of England in the West Indies this was not without difficulty. There were several obstacles they had to overcome, including the less than friendly reception by the local clergy already in place. In carrying out their commission the two bishops increasingly moved the church in the West Indies beyond merely performing the role of chaplaincy to the English settlers and planter class. Both bishops – not unexpectedly – encountered resistance from sections of the local Anglican clergy. Some clergymen objected to the "interference" of a bishop in their parish. In private Correspondence with a friend, Lipscomb made reference to the opposition he faced in Jamaica and described such clergymen as "the old parsons," who, he said, were "prejudiced in opposition to all the late measures" and were generally attached to the planters in the old system.[70] He noted that the church in Jamaica had suffered due to inadequate attendance to duty by the clergy. Nevertheless, armed with the mandate from the imperial government, and through courageous determination and hard work, both bishops effected significant changes in the Church of England in the West Indies. They erected new churches, schools, and chapels of ease; within a decade (1825–1835), they increased the number of catechists, schoolmasters, curates, and clergy within their jurisdictions.

Bringing episcopal order to the Anglican Church in the West Indies occurred just in time, in the decade before the collapse of the British West Indian slave societies. As these societies entered the process of transition to a new social order, that new order demanded a new orientation and new ministrations from this church. In this new context of black freedom, the cultural attitude, religious style, and mission orientation of the church required change in ways more relevant to meeting the spiritual needs of a new, free, and multiracial society. This church needed to reposition itself in post-emancipation society.

An example of the new change in social context was expressed by a clergyman in Trinidad in a letter to Bishop Coleridge in Barbados, under whose episcopal supervision he operated. Pleading with the Bishop to support his request to the SPG for a grant of £150 to erect a chapel in his parish, he pointed out:

---

70. Lipscomb to Rev. A. M. Campbell, March 4, 1837, C/Win/Jam 2, Correspondence, USPG Archives, Bodleian Library.

> During the last 12 months about 600 from India, 100 Africans from Sierra Leone and St. Helena, and 100 Portuguese from Madera have been located in the parish. Large numbers are arriving and expecting to arrive from the same quarters of whom not one is, on his location here, a member of our church.... Surrounded as we are here by hundreds of Hindoos, and Mahomedans from India, and pagans from Africa, by a population speaking the English, French, Spanish, Tamil, Telugee, and three or four African languages, our work is essentially Missionary, and to whom shall we look for assistance but the Missionary institutions of our church at home.[71]

Similar requests also came from Guiana and Jamaica.[72] Given the realization that the work of the church in this new context was "essentially missionary," and to fulfil their episcopal mandates, the Bishop of Barbados and the Bishop of Jamaica responded in three ways. First, they took on the missionary challenge of education of the Negro slave population. This was challenging because – despite the orders of the imperial government in 1823, and again in 1825, proposing "effectual and decisive measures" – some colonial officials and planters in the West Indies resisted the implementation of the requirement of religious instructions for slaves. They argued that educating Negro slaves would only confer upon them new powers, which would make them even more ungovernable and, in any case, would be of little value to them in the afterlife.

In the face of strong opposition from some quarters, Lipscomb and Coleridge implemented the new measures, leaving their mark on the educational development of both Jamaica and Barbados. In 1836, Lipscomb formed a National Schools Association and appointed the Rev. George D. Hill as its superintendent. Hill served from 1836 to 1840. By 1841, the National Schools Association had 62 schools under their care and, in his final report to the Bishop before leaving office in 1840, Hill optimistically concluded that the National Schools have been "a powerful engine of religious instructions to which children of Jews, Roman Catholics, Baptists, and Methodists

---

71. Watson to Bishop of Barbados, C/Win/Bar 13, File # 13, Correspondence, USPG Archives, Bodleian Library.

72. C/Win/Jam 2, D 16, USPG Archives, Bodleian Library.

have submitted... that they might obtain the advantages of our branches of Education."[73] Hill praised the fact that the schools provided a good foundation for religious instructions but also noted that they were good schools for academic education. In Barbados, Coleridge expanded the number of schools to such an extent that within ten years there was an increase from 10 schools to 125, nearly all of which were supervised by the diocese.[74]

Despite the achievements of Lipscomb and Coleridge in education, however, the anticipated benefits of education to the Negroes of religious instruction and academic education so eagerly expected, produced mixed results. On the one hand, the church schools produced some excellent students. In his final report, Hill exulted in the fact that "in the best schools the class of boys have made themselves masters of the greater part of the Oxford Catechism with the proofs from memory and could answer occasional questions in the Gospels and Acts of the Apostles, with creditable acquaintance with the main points of Scripture, History, Chronology, and Geography."[75] On the other hand, this English church-based education had the effect of not only creating elite Negroes but, moreover, successfully alienating them from their cultural moorings. In addition, as the post-emancipation economy of the West Indies declined in the mid-nineteenth century, so did school attendance. The inability to pay even minimal fees was cited as the main reason for this decline. The noble goal of education as a means of social and economic improvement for the Negro, particularly in post-emancipation, valuable as it was, proved to be less achievable on a mass scale. As early as 1834, reports to the Bishop were beginning to point out that "the schools are not flourishing as we would have wished."

The second response of the church to this new dispensation was the formation of specific mission-oriented organizations to redirect and refocus the missionary activities of the church. This was evident in the variety of indigenous missionary societies which were formed to encourage, promote, and mobilize missionary activities within the dioceses. Local branches of the Society for the Propagation of the Gospel (SPG), Society for Promoting

---

73. Hill to Lipscombe, C/Win/Jam 2, File # 157, Correspondence, USPG Archives. Bodleian Library.

74. Caldecott, *The Church in West Indies*, 92.

75. Hill to Lipscombe, C/Win/Jam 2, File #157, Correspondence, USPG Archives. Bodleian Library.

Christian Knowledge (SPCK), and the British and Foreign Bible Society were formed in various parishes. Public appeals for subscriptions to these societies were launched from time to time, to meet local needs such as caring for new immigrants, relief for victims of plagues and other natural disasters, or to assist the poor and destitute on behalf of the church.[76] These auxiliary activities provided opportunities for practical parochial involvement for lay members of the church. As church-sponsored mutual aid societies, these societies provided opportunities for active church members of the Church of England to associate with each other in a social reality which would have made this difficult, and they were important not only in personal religious development but in community formation as well, especially as post-emancipation social and economic realities began to take hold.For the Anglican Church in the West Indies, there was now a new sense of the church's need to pursue a common, though varied, indigenous mission.

The third and most significant response was that the church, at least at the leadership level, began to embrace Africa as a region in need of practical and spiritual redemption. Before emancipation, some Church of England missionaries in the West Indies – such as Rev. John Trew – began to articulate a vision for the involvement of the Anglican Church in the West Indies in the missionary enterprise in Africa. After the failure of the highly publicized Niger Mission of 1841, that articulation became even more vocal. In a letter to the Lord Bishop of London in 1843, Trew put forward a case in which he argued that Britain owed a "national obligation to Africa" for all the "disgusting and dreadful accompaniments of slavery . . . brought into existence by Great Britain." Part of the discharge of that obligation, he contended, must be assistance to Africans themselves in supplying the "spiritual wants of Africa." Having embraced the idea that what was needed in Africa to make the project succeed was "African agency," Trew argued that the West Indian church must be involved so as to help create "a truly native African agency for introducing Christian civilization in Africa." Writing from Britain after his tour of the

---

76. One such appeal from the Trinidad Association of the SPG in May 1845 stated: "Appeal of the Trinidad Association For The Propagation of the Gospel, to the inhabitants of the island, for their benevolent co-operation in farther extending the means of religious instructions and improvements, especially to the immigrants from heathen lands who have arrived and are still arriving on its shores." The appeal requested funds to erect schools and churches and maintain clergymen and catechists. Trinidad Association, C/Win/Bar 13, file # 11, USPG Archives.

West Indies in 1842 as an agent of the Mico Charity Trust, Trew published a pamphlet in London in 1843, in which he pointed out that even in the West Indies this fact had been grasped and that "so fully persuaded of this truth . . . are the missionary societies now labouring in the West Indies, that there is scarcely one of them which has not already laid its plans for establishing an institution in connection with its own communion, expressly designed for supplying missionaries."[77] Trew was concerned that since every other missionary society in the West Indies was so engaged, the Church of England in the West Indies should also be part of the African enterprise; and essential to this was the embrace of Africa itself and of Africans in the West Indies. Trew's ideas were later picked up in Barbados by Richard Rawle, principal of Codrington College (1847–1864), and Thomas Parry (1842–1870), Bishop Coleridge's successor. They, too, desired to see the involvement of the West Indian church in making an Anglican contribution towards the establishment of Christianity in sub-Saharan Africa.[78] We will examine the implementation of this desire and the fortunes of this effort more fully later in this study.

These organizational responses helped the Anglican Church to move forward in the mid-nineteenth century towards the formation of a broader mission-focused church community. As a result of changes in West Indian society, including the arrival of new immigrant groups, the growing social welfare needs of the poor – caused by increased poverty and natural disasters such as hurricanes, smallpox, and cholera epidemics – and, generally, what Beckles calls the "crisis of the free order" from 1838 – 1897 – the Era of Emancipation,[79] demand for local mission work increased dramatically in the post-emancipation period. As this demand increased, the church expanded

---

77. Trew, *Africa Wasted by Britain*, 40–41.

78. It must be noted that the inclusion of concern for the material and spiritual state of Africa by this church was nothing short of a transformation in its mission orientation to include mission at home and abroad. Basing its new concern on the expedient arguments of the strong affinities of race and ethnicity between the majority population in the West Indies and Africa, the leadership of the Anglican Church in the West Indies in the mid-nineteenth century seemed to have been persuaded to incline its mission orientation towards Africa even though the church remained culturally ambivalent and infused with white racial attitudes towards Africa. This attempt at repositioning itself and its mission in the immediate post-emancipation period, it is noteworthy that it now looked, of all places, towards Africa. How successful the leadership was in spreading that vision throughout the whole church was certainly one of the key issues that belied the construction of its missionary plans for Africa.

79. Beckles, *History of Barbados*.

its organizational structures and established new dioceses with new bishoprics in Guiana and Antigua (1842), Bahamas (1861), Trinidad and Tobago (1872), the Windwards (1879), and British Honduras (1883). By the end of the nineteenth century, the Anglican Church in the West Indies had undergone significant structural changes and developed a more broad-based ministry to serve the changing West Indian society.[80] The major issue of disestablishment from the English Crown – which the church had to contend with during the period 1868–1870, especially in the diocese of Jamaica – brought its own crises and stresses. By 1870, the church in Jamaica was officially disestablished and separated from state patronage. In the end, disestablishment provided the West Indian church with the opportunity to chart its own course and develop its own institutional life in keeping with the cultural aspirations and demands of West Indian society.[81]

As mentioned already, one of the critical areas in which the Anglican Church in the West Indies was compelled to change was in its attitude to the issue of slavery and towards the Negro slave.[82] The history and practice of Anglican worship in the West Indies was neither pro-African nor Negro-friendly. Anglican chapels were not designed for Negro slaves, and those who ventured to attend them faced discrimination in receiving Anglican rites. In Barbados, Bishop Coleridge had abolished the practice of Negroes being compelled to wait to make their way up to the altar until the whites

---

80. These changes included disestablishment in 1869, formation of a distinct West Indian Province with the election of its very first archbishop in 1883, and the convening of its first Provincial Synod in 1889. These organizational developments were not without the influence and assistance of the international Anglican Communion. The four West Indian bishops attended the first Lambeth Conference in Canterbury in 1867 and were part of general discussions about the necessity, advantages, and disadvantages of disendowment in the colonial church. They also took the opportunity to call upon the assistance of the House of Bishops in Canada for advice and consultations following the Lambeth Conference Caldecott, *Church in the West Indies*, 150.

81. By the end of the century, sixty-five years of episcopal order brought a new organizational sense of belonging and a repositioning of the Church of England in the West Indies into a mission-minded church. Although haltingly achieved, the seeds were sown for the creation of a truly West Indian Anglican Church. The realization of this, however, was only to be fully appreciated towards the end of the twentieth century with the election of native bishops and the introduction of more indigenous liturgies.

82. It was well known that during slavery some Anglican priests argued that the Negro slaves' lack of knowledge of the English language would make church attendance of little benefit to them and that, therefore, there was no missionary necessity to reach out to them. Where Negro slaves did make the effort to attend Anglican mission churches, the small size and structure of some chapels precluded any sense of welcome and belonging.

had participated in taking the consecrated elements of the Eucharist. He had also encouraged the use of music in the liturgy, even though this was not the norm in the colonial Anglican Church of that period.[83]

Perhaps nowhere was an attitude adjustment towards slavery and the Negro slaves needed more than in the churches' attitude towards emancipation and its prospects. Given its historic alignment with the colonial establishment, the Church of England in the West Indies could hardly have been expected to welcome emancipation and be enthusiastic about the prospects of the new post-slavery society. It is not surprising, therefore, that the church's attitude towards emancipation was lukewarm and apprehensive. At the time of emancipation, other Protestant missionary groups throughout the West Indies experienced a general feeling of triumph in their moral fight over the evil and "sin" of slavery. As far as the Anglicans were concerned, however, as Caldecott says, "we were nearly being excluded altogether."[84] Missionaries and mission societies that were more closely engaged with the Negro slaves and their cause, such as the Baptists and Methodists, were able to reap great benefits in the form of large numbers of liberated slaves who flocked to these mission churches for celebration and thanksgiving on the eve of emancipation.

As already noted, one of things that was an embarrassment and a source of contradiction for the Anglican Church was the existence of the Codrington Estates in Barbados as a Christian slave plantation.[85] This was problematic for a church which needed to reposition itself in post-emancipation, away from its pro-slavery allegiances. The story of the Codrington Estates centres on Christopher Codrington, a son of the Barbados planter class, born in 1668 in Barbados and educated at Christ Church, Oxford. Christopher Codrington became a fellow of All Souls College, Oxford, before returning to the West Indies as an officer in the military service of the imperial government. He served as one-time governor of the Leeward Islands before finally returning to settle on the Codrington Estates. Christopher Codrington saw no incompatibility between his espousal of Christianity and the practice of slaveholding. He held large numbers of slaves on the estates and believed

---

83. Caldecott, *Church in the West Indies*, 95.
84. Caldecott, 99.
85. Papers for the Codrington Estates are deposited in this collection, C/Win/Bar-12, USPG Archives, Bodleian Library.

that he had a mission to Christianize them and make them into Christian slaves. When he died, in 1710, the Codrington Estates were bequeathed to the Church of England's Society for the Propagation of the Gospel (SPG) for the purpose of establishing a college for the study and practice of "Physick, Chirurgery, and Divinity." Codrington's idea was to link the study of medicine and mission in order to supply medical missionaries for Christian mission. In the early eighteenth century, such a concept was perhaps the first of its kind and certainly among the earliest proposals for medical missions in the Western world.

It took some time for the SPG to take possession of the properties and put Codrington's will into effect. Richard Rawle, when he became principal of Codrington College in 1847, astutely tried to link Codrington's expressed will with John Trew's idea of the Church of England in the West Indies becoming a missionary church and contributing to the missionary project in Africa. Rawle converted the principal's lodge at Codrington College into a training centre for West Indian Anglicans (both black and white) to prepare them for missionary service in Africa. Codringtonians who went to Africa to engage in the work of Christian mission faced the problem of trying to reconcile Codrington College's pro-slavery legacy with an ostensibly pro-African, anti-slavery missionary project in Africa. It was a legacy that would continue to haunt the missionary efforts of the Barbados church in Africa.

Given the critical adjustments it had to make in post-emancipation West Indian society, the Anglican Church, like other mission communities, took several steps towards readjusting and redirecting its mission. For Anglicans in the West Indies, the challenge – particularly with the process of helping to recover and reshape identities – was even greater. It included working towards the psychosocial, economic, and material advancement of the newly freed Negro slaves. Through its schools, chapels, structured worship, catechisms, ritual practices, and community organizations, the means were there for the formation of an Anglican identity, especially in those who were associated with the church as members or adherents. This identity emerged with three characteristic features: (1) the cultivation of a sense of religious duty, which meant regular attendance at church and participation in the ritual practices of the church; (2) ethical living, which meant monogamy, honourable family life, and trustworthiness; and (3) a dignified persona, which meant propriety in dress, good manners, and proven character. Although these were generally the marks of Christian identity that mission Christianity sought to inculcate in the West Indian churches, for the Anglicans, it was much more clearly defined and more socially pronounced. Church members who breached these requirements faced some form of church discipline, in small or large measure. Such discipline could include temporary exclusion from participation in the Anglican rite of Holy Communion or being debarred from appointment to the church leadership.

An example of this was demonstrated when the black West Indians who professed to embody this Anglican identity publicly embraced or displayed other identities such as the radical revolutionary identity of the frustrated emancipated peasants who participated in the 1865 uprising in Jamaica or the 1876 Confederation Rebellion in Barbados. Anglican leaders not only expressed their surprise and disappointment but applied "discipline" to their former members.[86] For the black West Indian in post-emancipation society, such discipline at times represented a conflict of loyalties and identities. In such instances, they had to choose between the identity inculcated by mission Christianity and the identity derived from ethnic ancestry and social status. In a free post-slavery society, the choice was often made in favour of the latter.

Conclusion

The question of why the West Indies in the mid-nineteenth century was seen as a possible source of missionary supply for Africa is an important one. The outline presented in this chapter makes it clear that, by the middle of the century, the objective of establishing mission communities in the British colonies in the West Indies was accomplished beyond reasonable expectations. Mission administrators in Europe and agents in the West Indies were pleased with their success. For almost every Protestant group which engaged the West Indies as a mission field at the beginning of the century, success in terms of church planting, church growth, and the establishment of viable

---

86. In citing as an example of church discipline, the measures he employed when his clergy, "to their dismay, found that not only the major portion of their flocks had been concerned in this wholesale plundering, but that several of their communicants were gravely compromised" in the 1876 Confederation Rebellion, the Lord Bishop of Barbados, The Rt. Rev. J. Mitchinson, suspended them from communion, required them to make restitution where possible, and give a public confession. After their act of contrition, he gave them formal absolution. Mitchinson, "Church Discipline," *MF* (1 February 1888): 41–44, USPG Archives, Bodleian Library.

mission communities was achieved beyond reasonable expectations. In the process, the African slaves in the West Indies (later ex-slaves) to whom the missionary message was largely directed, appropriated those elements which appealed to them in their existential condition and utilized them in the restoration of their ontological well-being.

Since the making of the West Indian church involved missionary engagement in the peculiar context of an entrenched slave society, this had to be a highly negotiated task. In the end, the formation of these mission communities was the product of an experience which was (1) intensely contested, being challenged, on the one hand, by the existence of a repressive colonial state and a dominant planter class interest and, on the other, by rival mission organizations, (2) significantly successful, in both quantitative and qualitative terms, as far as conversions, imperial slavery amelioration, and institution-building measures were concerned, and (3) identity-forming, as it offered a new sense of being and new communities of belonging. The interplay of all these factors, which began at least three decades before the end of slavery, became even more important post-slavery.

It was this missionary engagement in the slave societies of the British West Indies that became the basis on which necessary and vital social reconstruction work took place post-emancipation. Perhaps the coded thanksgiving message of the ex-slave speechmaker at the celebration of the fourth anniversary of emancipation in the mission church in Chapelton, Jamaica, implied as much when he spoke of his thankfulness for missionaries from England who came "to learn we a little manners of Massa Jesus." Learning "a little manners" might have been pointing to the adoption and embrace by the African slaves of an identity inculcated by mission Christianity. But, as later reactions to the failure of the promise of emancipation showed, ethnic and ancestral identities were never far from the surface.

With their vast tested experience of missionary engagement in the West Indies and the success achieved in working successfully in a complex and dynamic cross-cultural context, mission leaders in the West Indies found the challenge of participation in missionary endeavours further afield irresistible. In the making of the West Indian church, the formation of the Moravian, Baptist, and Anglican churches illustrates the successful planting of these churches with the help of "native" leadership – elders, deacons, pastors, catechetical helpers, teachers, poor relief and social welfare workers, community builders, and so on – and the supportive infrastructure of training institutions. The mission leaders were convinced that, based on this experience, the ground was set for the newly planted West Indian church to engage in the pursuit of the missionary dream elsewhere, as part of its contribution but, equally, as part of its own development and self-understanding. Therefore, the conditions were set for the West Indian church to dream of engaging fully in the Western missionary enterprise in the mid-nineteenth century.

CHAPTER 3

Emancipation and the Missionary Dream

If the Western missionary establishment succeeded in establishing a truly West Indian church in the mid-nineteenth century, as it believed it did, the question then arises: to what extent were the products of the newly planted mission churches ready and able to respond to the challenges of missionary engagement further afield? And why did they set their missionary sights on Africa? What was it that ignited the West Indian church's missionary vision for the African continent?

To answer this question satisfactorily it is important to explore further, to understand the sociopolitical dynamics of at least three broad geopolitical contexts in the mid-nineteenth century that provided the environment, opportunity, and motivation for a transcontinental and transnational missionary vision to emerge from the West Indian churches. The combined effect of these contexts gave rise to the enterprising mission initiatives to Western Africa. What were these contexts? They were (1) the social and economic dynamics of a transitional, post-emancipation British West Indian society, (2) the condition of sub-Saharan Africa in the mid-nineteenth century in its actual and perceived state, and (3) the geopolitical interests of the Western missionary establishment by mid-century, with its attendant successes, failures, and strategic goals. The driving force that motivated and propelled the participation of West Indians in the missionary enterprise in Africa arose from the dynamic interplay of these three contexts. This interplay generated feelings of optimism on both sides of the Atlantic that the West Indian churches were ready and able to respond to the challenge of missionary engagement beyond their shores.

The Post-emancipation West Indies: A New Social Order?

When the British Parliament passed the Slavery Abolition Act of August 1833 which was for the total abolition of Colonial Slavery it changed the legal status of chattel slaves in the British Empire and offered the opportunity for transformation in the circumstances and fortunes of vast numbers of enslaved Africans. It also laid open the possibility and prospect for a new social order in colonial places like the West Indies. That prospect, however, as bright and promising as it appeared, was jeopardized by the failure of British legislators to consider seriously the post-slavery future of the West Indies as a free society. The Act resulted in a new social order, but, arguably, no clear vision or direction was given by the British government about what that new social order should entail. The legislators in the British Parliament were focused more on the economic consequences of abolition than on measures for social reconstruction for a new social order that would necessarily result from the historic legislation. British parliamentarians expressed greater concern about investors in the slave-based economy and the maintenance of "law and order" than about the victims of the regime that they had just abolished. Possibly fearing political backlash from the powerful pro-slavery West Indian lobby in Britain, Parliament made provision in the Act for £20 million to be paid as compensation to the owners of slave estates in the West Indies. No provision was made in the same legislative act for the newly emancipated slaves. The Negro Education Grant of 1834 was a mere gesture, that in no way compensated for the damage done by slavery; nor was it intended to be compensatory.

The expectations by the planters, such as they were, presumed that the newly freed African slaves would earn their living on West Indian plantations through a period of apprenticeship.[1] This apprenticeship programme was intended not only as a means for the ex-slaves to earn wages on the estates

---

1. The proposal for a period of apprenticeship was not accepted by all British colonies in the West Indies. While Jamaica, Barbados, and Guyana implemented it, Antigua and Trinidad did not and thus set their slaves free in 1833. In Jamaica the proposed apprenticeship period of six years was reduced to four, thus ending slavery in that island in 1838.

but, perhaps more importantly, for them to learn the habits and social meaning of freedom before full emancipation could be enjoyed.[2] This "earn" and "learn" expectation was not a sufficient response either to the enfranchisement needs of the ex-slaves or to the negative psychological and material legacies of "miserable" slavery which the British slave-investors had caused.

The lack of provision for a new social order notwithstanding, the pursuit of freedom was a long-established dream of slaves on the British West Indies sugar plantations. To a large extent, by the time the British Parliament passed this Act, these slaves were already prepared for it. As shown in different ways by Patterson, Jakobsson, Genovese, Craton, Turner, Beckles, and Sheller,[3] not only was freedom the primary object of slaves throughout the existence of British Atlantic slavery – and certainly during the nearly fifty years leading up to the passage of the Abolition Bill – but that freedom had an existential and ontological character to it that could not be denied forever.[4]

Patterson, for example, in his early sociological study of the structure of West Indian slave society, drew attention to the typologies and causes of slave resistance and revolts, highlighting some characteristics of the slaves' relentless struggle for freedom.[5] He later pursued this interest in the nature of slave struggles for freedom in a provocative thesis, first in "Slavery: The Underside of Freedom," and later in *Freedom in the Making of Western Culture*. Patterson argues that it was the nature of modern slavery in the Atlantic world that gave rise to the valorization of freedom and democracy in the Western world. He argues that freedom "began its career as a social

---

2. Despite the passage of the British emancipation bill, it was not universally agreed that freedom from British slavery was a good thing for the Africans on plantations in the West Indies. There were those, even in the Colonial Office – like Earl Grey – who believed that the bill was "a leap in the dark" and that regulations should have been imposed to require "managed freedom." Bell and Morrell, *Select Documents*, 383–389; Morrell, *British Colonial Policy*, 269.

3. Patterson, *Sociology of Slavery (1967)*, *Slavery and Social Death (1982)*, "Slavery: The Underside of Freedom," (1984) and *Freedom in the Making of Western Culture (1991)*; Jakobsson, *Am I Not a Man and Brother? (1972)*; Genovese, *Roll Jordan Roll (1972)*; Craton, *Testing the Chains* and "Continuity Not Change" (1982); Turner, *Slaves and Missionaries (1982)*; Beckles, *History of Barbados (1990)*; and Sheller, *Democracy after Slavery (2000)*.

4. Craton, in particular, focuses on patterns of slave revolts pre- and post-emancipation, focusing on continuities and discontinuities in these revolts. Since 1816, resistance and rebellion against the system of slavery in the British West Indies escalated and effectively sensitized local opinion as well as the British public to the inhuman and violent nature of the slave system. These resistance movements also highlighted the quest for freedom on the part of the enslaved.

5. Patterson, *Freedom in the Making*, 402–406

value in the desperate yearnings of the slave to negate what for him, and for non-slaves, was a peculiar inhuman condition." Without slavery, therefore, he posits that "freedom would not today stand unchallenged as the supreme value of the Western world."[6]

For her part, Sheller contends that the black radical and revolutionary tradition in West Indian historical consciousness not only emerged from this value placed on freedom in slave society but was the basis on which a truly democratic tradition emerged in the West Indies. She argues that this democratic tradition in the West Indies emerged dialectically against the background of the strong anti-democratic tendencies that were so much part of the behaviour of the white oligarchic planter class, which for centuries dominated local assemblies in the colonies.[7]

If this quest for freedom, both in its existential and ontological dimensions, was significant in the collapse of West Indian slavery – as argued in the work edited by Beckles and Shepherd[8] – emancipation itself, as "lived freedom,"[9] remained a key challenge. By "lived freedom," Sheller means the need on the part of the ex-slaves to reconstruct life in families and communities, and negotiate with former slave owners and managers of estates the terms and conditions of labour employment, housing, land access, and so on. For ex-slaves living in the post-emancipation period, "lived freedom" meant doing whatever was required to meet basic subsistence needs. Sheller also includes, in this very apt phrase, the need for "sustained mobilisation of protest and political claim-making" against both local and metropolitan governments in order to protect the achievement of freedom and prevent any regression or denial of it. This "lived freedom" was, for her, the real challenge of the emancipation dream.

In broad terms, this challenge was manifested in at least three areas. (1) The need for the establishment of an economic basis for sustaining the freedom achieved at emancipation. In a free, post-slavery society, labour now commanded wages. Liveable wages required bargaining, negotiation, and productivity. (2) Goods and services in the new society needed reorganization

---

6. Patterson, *Freedom in the Making*, Preface, 1–5.
7. Sheller, *Democracy after Slavery*, 174–225.
8. Beckles and Shepherd, *Caribbean Freedom*, ix–xi
9. Sheller, *Democracy after Slavery*, 4, 18–40.

and redistribution for a new market economy. (3) Most importantly, laws governing slave conduct and the master-servant relationship in a free society needed to be enacted in order to provide requisite protections for free citizens. Where was the political will to create this new social order following the enactment of emancipation in law?

The first challenge to establish and develop an economic basis of freedom for the ex-plantation and ex-household slaves was access to viable land, affordable housing, and education.[10] As the dream of full emancipation unfolded, these critical needs were, in the main, unmet, and this often proved an impediment to developing the economic freedom needed by the ex-slaves. Measures to ensure these fundamental requirements were slow in coming from the colonial state or the plantocracy, and their tardiness tended to undermine and delay the delivery of the benefits of freedom that were generated and promised by the Slavery Abolition Act in 1833. Therefore, the economic basis of freedom for the ex-slaves was, at best, insecure; at worst, non-existent. Nevertheless, the emancipated Africans in the West Indies never slackened their vigilance and struggle for full freedom. As Michael Craton and Gad Heuman show, significant acts of resistance to the requirement of a period of apprenticeship, for example, took place in places like St. Kitts, Dominica, Guyana, Barbados, and Trinidad.[11] Strikes, street protests, and other overt and covert acts of resistance, particularly involving women, pushed the final button for full freedom.[12] The dream of realizing full freedom had remained. The long slave tradition of resistance and revolt throughout the history of

---

10. Although, since the early 1800s, the development of a slave economy and society in the Negro villages on the estates provided a semi-autonomous social existence in which the slave hut, provision grounds, and Sunday markets provided key sources of income and economic activities, landholding and housing after slavery were critical determinants of real freedom. See Higman, *"Slavery Remembered"*; Mintz, *"The Historical Sociology"*; and Burton, *Afro-Creole*, 38–41.

11. Craton and Heuman point out the persistence of a pattern of resistance among slaves in the British West Indies in their relentless struggle for freedom in slavery and after abolition. Craton, "Continuity Not Change," 192–206; Heuman, "Riots and Resistance," 135–149.

12. Craton also points out that in Jamaica there were "dozens of riots hitherto unpublicised between 1838 and 1865." Noting the causes for these riots, which included problems of adjustment, official opposition to any return to traditional ways – especially in religion – tensions occasioned by questions of rent, wages, and the availability of land, and conflict with new immigrants, government surveyors, and the police, he argues that "these incidents multiplied and spread in times of economic slump such as the late 1840s, early 1860s and mid-1870s, or in times of natural disaster, such as drought, flood or cholera epidemic." Craton, "Continuity Not Change," 324–347.

West Indian slavery was never abandoned, as evidenced in Heuman and Trotman's edited work.[13]

The second challenge to the full achievement of the emancipation dream was the social organization of freedom itself. The labour-intensive agricultural economy of the British West Indies required new sources of labour to augment a decline in locally available labour and for the optimal upkeep of productivity levels on the plantations. The cultivation of sugar was, after all, the mainstay of the economy of the British West Indian societies. In the 1840s, new pools of labour from the Indian subcontinent and Africa were contracted to supply the labour needs of the West Indian plantations. The influx of new immigrants added a new social dynamic to the new order of post-emancipation West Indian societies.

Accommodations and adjustments of various kinds were required for this new, multiracial social order. Ex-slaves from the plantation now had to compete with these new sources of labour for jobs, housing, and other benefits.[14] As the price of labour became more competitive and the sugar economy of the West Indies began to decline – especially in the face of new global competition for sugar on the world market – negotiating their freedoms became a real challenge for the ex-slaves. Therefore, in this situation, how freedom was conceived and utilized was of utmost importance. If it was intended that a free peasant class were to emerge in an ordered state following the collapse of slavery, this required the active intervention of the colonial state. The British Parliament and the local assemblies were responsible to put such measures in place. Failure to do so meant that non-state agencies such as the mission churches – especially as they had developed into community organizations – would have had to step in to fill the breach in the public organization of freedom for the ex-slave population. The failure of the British Parliament to make social provisions in the Abolition Bill left this vacuum to be filled by others.

In this respect, the activist and energetic role pursued by Christian missionaries in the British West Indies in the early nineteenth century, particularly those who were closely associated with the British and American

---

13. Heuman and Trotman (eds) *Contesting Freedom: Control and Resistance in the Post-Emancipation Caribbean*, xv-xxx.
14. Holt, *The Problem of Freedom*.115–178

anti-slavery movements, was a welcome intervention in the immediate circumstances of post-emancipation. Their role in the society prior to abolition had prepared them to respond to this challenge in the aftermath of the end of slavery. The mission leaders responded in several ways to this challenge of organizing freedom in a post-slavery society: via Free Villages, native leadership, and community associations.

In Jamaica, for example, one of the first projects to be undertaken by the mission churches, following the proclamation of full and final emancipation in August 1838, was the land settlement of the newly freed slaves. The missionaries, knowing the mood and controversy surrounding the imperial government's decision to end slavery and the local assembly's disposition towards slave emancipation, and knowing the disempowered state of the former slaves in terms of their inability to function as an organized "autonomous peasantry,"[15] took it upon themselves – without the necessary external support – to create villages in which the ex-slaves would have access to the means of resettlement. This project involved venturing into land settlement schemes, housing construction, and community building projects. The missionaries rallied to raise funds from family and friends abroad in Europe and America and also pooled their own resources to purchase lands to resettle the ex-slaves. Lands so acquired were then resold at discounted rates to the former slaves, especially those who had been part of the mission churches.

These land settlement schemes were the basis on which "free villages" were established throughout Jamaica post-1838.[16] They were called "free villages" because they were intended to be gardens of freedom and cradles of a free, Christianized post-slavery society, and they were named after important anti-slavery champions of freedom such as William Wilberforce, T. F. Buxton, and Joseph Sturge.[17] These "free villages" were expected to be model

---

15. Burton, *Afro-Creole*, 92.

16. As Burton, citing Mintz, noted, "By 1845, 19,000 families – perhaps 100,000 people in all, or a third of the ex-slave population of Jamaica – had settled in such villages." Burton, *Afro-Creole*, 92; see Mintz, "The Historical Sociology of the Jamaican Church-Founded Free Village System," 46–70 (downloaded from Brill.com 02/14/2024).

17. The very first post-emancipation free village for ex-slaves in Jamaica was created in 1840 near the colonial capital, Spanish Town, and named after Lord Sligo, the colonial governor, who proclaimed the Imperial Act of Emancipation in the island. Sligoville, which was spearheaded by the Baptist missionary J. M. Phillippo, is an important historical village in Jamaica today. At the inception of the village, Phillippo was unanimously chosen president of the Sligo-Town Agricultural and Horticultural Society for the Improvement of Husbandry

communities, designed to show how the "Christian Black," liberated by the Christian gospel, could be a good example of Christian social virtues such as industry, domesticity, and good family life, thereby demonstrating the true African character that Baptist missionary D. J. East had identified in his 1844 pamphlet. At the centre of village life was the chapel or place of worship. The chapel was surrounded by dwelling houses and other institutions like Sabbath schools and a local market.[18] To develop economic empowerment and a proper work ethic, a variety of projects were encouraged in the free villages. These included housing construction, domestic agriculture, animal husbandry, primary health care, horticultural guilds, and school education. What could not be achieved within the confines of the plantation could now be realized in the freedom available outside of it.

These villages played a vital role in the social structure of post-emancipation West Indian society. They provided the basis for the rise of an independent peasantry and the development of communities of small farmers and indigenous entrepreneurs, and they formed the bedrock of the modern Caribbean states.[19]

The development of native leadership was another project that was strategically important in the organizing of a free society. This project was begun prior to the abolition of slavery and was considered important in the development of the nascent Christian communities. All the mission churches of the various Christian denominations instituted programmes to develop and nurture a pool of native leaders to help with the missions. The Baptist mission churches in particular produced some outstanding leaders such as deacons Samuel "Daddy" Sharpe – who led the slave protest of 1831 in western Jamaica – Edward Barrett, Henry Beckford, and Richard and Joseph Merrick. In 1840, Barrett and Beckford were taken to London by William Knibb to attend the British-American Anti-Slavery Convention. They travelled around

---

and Gardening in the District. *BHFA* (15 July 1840), BMS Archives, Angus Library. Phillippo gave a good description of the village layout and noted that, since emancipation, about one thousand acres of land had been purchased and some 150–200 free villages set up in Jamaica. See. Phillippo, *Jamaica: Its Past and Present State*, 228.

18. According to Phillippo, the ex-slaves in the free villages named their dwelling houses in the most descriptive terms such as Happy Home, Comfort Castle, Content My Own, Thank God To See It, and Save Rent. Phillippo, *Jamaica: Its Past and Present State*, 229.

19. Paget, "*Free Village System*", 7–19 (*available online*); Mintz, "*From Plantations to Peasantries*", 127–153.

Britain with Knibb and spoke at public meetings about the situation in Jamaica. In 1842, Richard Merrick and Alexander Fuller were part of the Baptist scouting mission to Western Africa led by John Clarke.

This project of developing native leadership even in slave society was accelerated and given new impetus following emancipation. With the support of funds from the Negro Education Grant, mission churches rapidly expanded their building programme and constructed a large number of schools and chapels. As the mission churches grew numerically, additional personnel were required to share in leadership tasks, and so ex-slaves were recruited and trained as apprentices.

Educational projects undertaken to produce a black native leadership pool were supplemented by in-service systems such as the deacon-leader system in the Baptist churches, the system of "helpers" in the Moravian churches, the eldership system in the Presbyterian churches, and the class system in the Methodist churches. The preaching, teaching, and leadership development programmes became important in the organizational development of parochial and eventual national churches and communities, and they also helped to reinforce the emerging feeling that the West Indian church was a "church in mission" whose goal was to grow up and serve the community, making it stronger and self-reliant. The development of trained native leadership was seen as a fundamental requirement for the realization of this vision.

It must be noted, however, that while this benevolent and paternal missionary activity of creating and developing native agency was being institutionalized in the mission churches, the slaves in slave society had already initiated their own leadership development. Genovese, Burton, and Shepherd and Beckles show the many ways in which enterprising slaves, in an act of self-leadership, created and exploited opportunities to develop a world of their own within the permitted spaces within the regime of West Indian and American slave societies.[20] They created internal market systems to provide ground provisions and supplemental sources of food supply, established their own dwelling huts, received and exchanged goods, sang and danced together in self-created pantomimes, and prayed and held faith together in weekly

---

20. Genovese, *Roll Jordan Roll*; Burton, *Afro-Creole*; and Shepherd and Beckles, Section XI, Subaltern Autonomy: Social and Economic Culture, 713– 783, *Caribbean Slavery in the Atlantic World*.

Negro hut prayer meetings. The slave culture created from this Creole existence produced lay preachers who operated particularly among the Native Baptist churches. These preachers, some of whom began preaching in the mission churches, accepted the salvation and hope-filled message of mission Christianity and communicated it in the aesthetic and idiomatic understandings of their fellow slaves. Although their leadership was not always to the liking of mission church leaders, it was well recognized by their kith and kin, and this led to the growth of native organizations such as the Native Baptist Church.

A third project in the organizing of freedom in post-emancipation West Indian society was the formation of indigenous mutual aid societies and community associations. Organizations such as temperance societies, burial societies, anti-slavery societies, and literary societies such as local branches of the Society for the Propagation of Christian Knowledge (SPCK), and home and foreign mission societies were set up in local communities. These societies were meant to encourage the advancement of social causes, improve and promote the welfare and well-being of the local communities, and strengthen the missionary enterprise of the church. These societies and associations not only provided mutual aid but were critical to the provision of social capital in which social trust, interdependence, community well-being, and democratic decision-making could be developed.

For the missionaries in the British West Indies, capitalizing on their successes – first in the Christianization of the population of African slaves in the difficult political environment of West Indian slave society, and then in the eventual dismantling of the system of slavery itself and the relatively peaceful transition into emancipation – the task of social reconstruction seemed a natural next step to take among the newly freed population in the post-emancipation period. For these missionaries, the collapse of slavery represented the triumph of mission Christianity over the monstrous evil of slavery. They saw it as a sign of divine justice, a triumph of "right over wrong," light over darkness, good over evil. In his characteristic flamboyant style, Baptist missionary William Knibb saw it as a triumph for the "Moral Governor of the Universe."[21]

---

21. Knibb, "Spiritual Prospects," BMS Collection, BMS Archives. In his sermon in London in 1834, Knibb asserted, "Whatever may have been the designs of man, whatever he

It was in this immediate post-emancipation West Indian mood of Christian triumph that new horizons and new prospects for Christian mission were envisioned. The challenge of wider missionary involvement, particularly to Africa, was considered a "duty" and a "natural obligation," given their experience with Africans in the West Indies and the ancestral linkages to Africa. To this end, a mission to Africa became a big dream for the West Indian churches to operationalize.

The third and most important of the formidable challenges of emancipation was that of engineering the reconstruction of a new moral order for West Indian societies based on repeal of the slave laws and creation of new laws to govern a free society. The nature of the challenge was how to move a moribund colonial state from what Austin-Broos describes as "a morally disordered world" to a world governed by new sensibilities of innate human rights and human dignity.[22] That world – comprising free, self-determining human beings – was the new reality of the British West Indies that abolition opened up. As Austin-Broos explains, the "morally disordered world" was the mental and psychological world in which both slave and slave master lived. In this world, the human condition of both the slave masters and the enslaved was significantly disordered and alienated by the physical and spiritual damage caused by the long history of African enslavement. From time to time, visitors and observers who travelled in the West Indies during the regime of slavery have described this disorder. For example, a European visitor to Jamaica in 1778 – at the height of the regime of the British slave society – recorded his observations, noting that

> the souls of the slaves have been injured by a system which overthrows all morality ... where marriage is illegal, where overseers and book-keepers, and drivers know no bounds, no obstacles to their evil lusts ... when he finds himself the victim of evil passion, and beholds the most unblushing immorality in those

---

may have contemplated in enslaving Africa, we know the Moral Governor of the Universe had other designs, superior to them all."

22. Austin-Broos, *Jamaica Genesis (6–13, 133–233)*, has shown one way in which Jamaican ex-slaves set right the "disordered world" of slave society by the construction of a new moral order over against the old, using the European rite of mission Christianity and the African rite of healing disorders.

who profess to be his superiors, and when he sees his equals treated as beasts of the field.[23]

This observer was particularly drawn to note and highlight the comparison between the moral state of the slaves and that of the white European officials who administered the slave system. The contradictions he observed on the plantations in Jamaica led this visitor to conclude that slavery was "a morally contradictory system."[24] Indeed, to this visitor, slavery appeared as a system that "overthrows all morality." The moral situation in the British West Indies did not change much for a century and a half, and, arguably, it grew worse as time went on. As Altink shows, between 1780 and 1834, the violent abuse of slaves – the women in particular – grew increasingly outrageous.[25] By the early nineteenth century, observers of the moral state of the British West Indian societies – such as the evangelical missionaries – finally came to refer to the moral system of the slave societies as "immoral" and "evil."[26]

The evil of the system of slavery lay not merely in its capacity to morally corrupt and dehumanize, but according to Patterson, it was expressed most profoundly in the alienation it produced in the most natal form.[27] "Natal alienation" or "social death," as Patterson terms it, is the most brutal form of dishonouring the human being. From birth to death, it was the social disfigurement and self-estrangement which was inflicted upon the African slaves on West Indian plantations. They were given the status of chattels and regarded as properties of the slave owners. Overcoming this disfigurement and self-estrangement in a post-slavery world required significant personal and social reconstruction. If slavery was indeed "social death," then "resurrection to life" required not only economic opportunity and social engineering but also some form of exorcism and healing of the memory and conditioning of slavery. This was the promise and prospect of emancipation. But where

---

23. Hark and Westphal, *Breaking of the Dawn*, point out the observations of M. Mack during his visit to the Moravian communities in Jamaica.

24. Hall, *In Miserable Slavery*, 172–240, demonstrates the arbitrary brutality, benevolence, and reckless sexual exploits of a plantation owner like Thomas Thistlewood on his estates in Jamaica highlighting the moral contradictions of the slave society.

25. Altink, "Outrage on All Decency."

26. For an analysis of this change of attitude towards slavery in Protestantism, see Davis, *Problem of Slavery*.

27. Patterson, *Slavery and Social Death*, 7, 10–14, 99–101.

was healing and redemption for the ex-slaves to be found? If it was not to be found within the state apparatus, it had to be found outside it. And it was into this space that the missionaries jumped in the aftermath of the abolition of British West Indian slavery, especially the repealing of the slave laws.

Whatever optimism there had been about the prospects of a new social order in the British West Indies following the proclamation of emancipation, it soon faded away. During the 1840s, sugar prices fell sharply on the world market. Wages on the estates were low. The anticipated productivity of indentured workers from India, Africa, and China barely managed the keep the economy of the sugar industry viable. And in this agriculture-based economy, other commodity crops such as bananas had not yet risen in economic value. As a result of this downturn in the economy, poverty swept the Caribbean. In 1844, one mission leader reported:

> During the last twelve months a gradual reduction has taken place in the wages of the peasantry; so that at the present time few Estates are paying more than 1s per day. . . . It is now broadly asserted that such is the poverty of the planter, that 9d. per day, is the highest price they can give for labour.[28]

In addition to economic hardships, outbreaks of cholera and smallpox throughout the West Indies in the 1850s further drained the resources of the population.[29] Thousands of deaths occurred, and mission churches were once again called upon to mobilize assistance in response to a social crisis. Reports from Jamaica, Barbados, Antigua, and Guyana during the period 1851–1854 describe the struggles the mission churches experienced in responding to these domestic crises.

Meanwhile, as poverty grew among the peasantry, it was accompanied by an increasing sense of alienation from the colonial state. The inertia in repealing or amending slave laws governing master-servant relationships, landholding, private property, and so on to correspond with the new social status and relationships of ex-slaves added to the increasing levels of social frustration. Many ex-slaves were frequently taken to court over debt, vagrancy, and petty theft. Payment of court fines and attorney's fees threatened to

---

28. *BHFA* (20 August 1844), BMS Archives, Angus Library.
29. Phillippo, *Cholera in Jamaica*.

further impoverish the labouring classes whose wage earnings were increasingly jeopardized by bankrupt estates, high prices of imported goods, and crop failures caused by excessive rains one year and severe drought the next.

In Jamaica, Barbados, Trinidad, and Guyana, as in other islands and territories of the British West Indies, a growing sense of betrayal and injustice increased the levels of frustration among the peasantry and landless proletariat. They had looked forward to enjoying their freedom and the benefits of emancipation. But, after two decades of the emancipation dream, there was a growing feeling throughout the British West Indies that this freedom had been betrayed. The liberation from bondage slavery that had been physically achieved was indeed unfinished business.

Throughout the 1850s, the impact of the deterioration in the social and economic condition of the West Indian peasantry was manifested in significant decline in community involvement, including church attendance. Reports of great poverty and distress increased. James Phillippo, the British Baptist missionary in Spanish Town and Sligoville, reportedly lost half of his sizeable congregation within six years of emancipation. In his report in 1844 he noted:

> There is very great poverty, and that to a very considerable extent. Cases of real distress are very numerous. Their circumstances are far inferior to what they were three or four years ago; their clothing is not good, either in quality or condition, as formerly. . . . Nearly one-half of my congregation absent themselves from public worship from this cause alone.[30]

In the northern parish of St. Ann, from Brown's Town, John Clarke reported:

> There is much poverty and distress, more than I have known since emancipation. Until lately the peasantry in this district were among the most prosperous in the Island. They cultivated bread-kind, coffee, pimento, and sugar. They were accustomed to dress well. Their houses generally were good and substantial, and many of them well furnished. The greater part of them attended places of public worship; their children were sent to day

---

30. Phillippo's report, *BHFA* (20 August 1844), BMS Archive, Angus Library.

and Sabbath schools. The amount of crime was comparatively small; but during the last two years they have suffered severely from scarcity of food, want of clothing, and other privations of poverty.[31]

One of the consequences of this deteriorating state of affairs was that mission leaders in the West Indies were reluctantly compelled to make urgent, and perhaps embarrassing, appeals for relief assistance to their mission headquarters in Britain. Missionary societies in Britain did not always respond well. For the Anglican missions, both the Society for the Propagation of the Gospel (SPG) and the Church Missionary Society (CMS) of the Church of England rejected the Bishop of Kingston's appeals for help.[32] For the Jamaican Baptists, who had declared with great ceremony their independence from the Baptist Missionary Society in London, this turn of affairs put them in the unexpected and embarrassing position of admitting that they needed external aid and were dependent on the BMS in Britain. In 1859–1860, the BMS responded by sending its secretary, E. B. Underhill, to investigate and assess the state of the Baptist churches in Jamaica. Underhill, in his report, described the poverty he had witnessed in Jamaica, drawing attention to some root causes and strongly asserting that the colonial government showed little interest in the colony and neglected the black peasantry in the West Indies.[33] As social frustrations mounted, a black political leadership of the peasantry began to emerge. This leadership continued the tradition of black radical resistance to an oppressive social order, especially as there were strong perceptions that justice was being denied and impoverishment and social neglect were on the increase. One such leader, who emerged in Jamaica's eastern parish of St. Thomas, was Paul Bogle, a black Native Baptist deacon and landowner. Bogle was said to have owned some five hundred acres of land in the parish and, therefore, as a landowner, had the right to vote. On 7 October 1865, almost

---

31. John Clarke, Pamphlets on Jamaica, II and III, containing missionary reports 1863–1865, BMS Archives, Angus Library.

32. Kingston to Bullock, Bullock to the Bishop of Kingston, Venn to Bishop of Jamaica, West Indies 1860–1867, D28A, 179, Correspondence, USPG Archives, Bodleian Library. This rejection surprised the Anglican Church in Jamaica and it was then left to struggle to find resources in a depressed economy. The Baptist Missionary Society of London was also hard pressed to get involved again in the Jamaica Mission.

33. Underhill and Brown, *Emancipation* (1861).

three decades after abolition, a black man from Bogle's village of Stony Gut in St. Thomas was arrested, charged, and faced trial in the Petty Session of the court in the parish capital, Morant Bay. The charge was for trespassing (squatting) on an abandoned plantation. The man was pronounced guilty as charged by the court. On hearing the verdict, and believing the trial to be unfair, Bogle and a small group of supporters intervened and tried to prevent the man from being jailed. They demanded the man's release and further demanded action by the colonial government and the local assembly to alleviate the plight of the impoverished peasantry of St. Thomas. The disturbance they caused led to arrest warrants being issued for Bogle, his brother William, and about twenty-five other men from Stony Gut. On 10 October, local policemen were despatched to Stony Gut to issue the warrants, where they were met by a crowd of over two hundred angry peasants. The policemen were blockaded, beaten, and sent back to Morant Bay; and some were forced to take oaths in support of black brotherhood and solidarity with the African peasantry. That night, the peasants of Stony Gut made preparations for a general protest the following day.

On 11 October, Bogle led a march to Morant Bay to demand better justice for blacks. When the white officials in the parish vestry saw the mob, they reacted out of fear and gave orders for the local volunteer militia to open fire. Seven black peasants were killed, and a riot broke out in the town. The Court House was set on fire. In the melee that followed, twenty-one whites were killed, including the German Custos, Baron von Ketelhodt. Edward John Eyre – who had served as Lieutenant Governor of New Zealand (1846–1853), Governor of St. Vincent (1854–1860), and then became Colonial Governor of Jamaica in 1864 – believing that this action was part of an islandwide conspiracy to murder all whites in the colony, responded with brutal measures. On 12 October, he declared martial law in the county of Surrey, which covered the eastern third of the island. Troops were despatched to quell the rebellion and, under the cover of martial law and with a force of soldiers, sailors, and co-opted Maroons, white vengeance was exacted on the black population in the name of state justice. After three days of rioting, 580 persons were killed, 600 publicly flogged, and more than 1,000 houses destroyed.

On 17 October, George William Gordon – a prominent mulatto politician, who was associated with Bogle in the Native Baptist church in St. Thomas and was a member of the Jamaican Assembly – was arrested in Kingston on charges of high treason against Her Majesty's Government. He was accused of a being a co-instigator of the Morant Bay uprising. Gordon was taken to Morant Bay, tried under court-martial on 21 and 22 October, pronounced guilty on 23 October and hanged. On the same day, Paul Bogle was caught by Maroons, arrested, and taken to Morant Bay by the police. He was similarly tried, pronounced guilty, and hanged on 24 October.[34]

Those twelve days of October 1865 marked a turning point in the emancipation journey of freed slaves in Jamaica.[35] These events received widespread publicity in Britain and divided British public opinion over the question of British colonial rule and attitudes towards the Negro race.[36] Prominent individuals in England – such as Ruskin, Dickens, Carlyle, and Tennyson – publicly defended Governor Eyre's actions. On the other hand, people like J. S. Mill, Darwin, Huxley, and Spencer supported the Commission's report and attacked British colonial policy and attitudes in the West Indies. Sir Henry Storks led the Commission of Inquiry that was set up by the British government to examine the causes and conduct of the Jamaica rebellion and its suppression. The Commission blamed the Governor for excessive use of force in putting down an unarmed rebellion, and their report resulted in the recall of Governor Eyre in 1866 and his dismissal from the Imperial Service. The results of their inquiry led to the dissolution of the assembly by

---

34. Both Bogle and Gordon were declared national heroes in 1965, in a ceremony at the Morant Bay Courthouse. They, along with Sam Sharpe, are now two of Jamaica's seven national heroes.

35. Underhill, *Tragedy of Morant Bay*; Black, *History of Jamaica*; Bakan, *Ideology and Class Conflict*; Heuman, *Killing Time*.

36. The *London Times* commented that the "insurrection in Jamaica comes very home to the national soul. Though a fleabite compared to the Indian mutiny, it touches our pride more and is more in the nature of a disappointment. . . . Jamaica is our pet institution, and its inhabitants are our spoilt children. We had it always in our eye when we talked to America and all the slaveholding Powers. It seemed to be proved in Jamaica that the Negro could become fit for self-government. . . . Alas for grand triumphs of humanity, and the improvement of the races, and the removal of primeval curses, and the expenditure of twenty millions sterling, Jamaica herself gainsays the fact and *belies herself, as we see today. It is that which vexes us more than even the Sepoy revolt.*" Bolt, *Victorian Attitudes*, 77. A London publication sensationalized the uprising with a racy and wildly exaggerated account published as "Special and Authentic Details of the Inhuman Butcheries & Ruthless Atrocities recently perpetuated in JAMAICA, being a Thrilling and Horrible Narrative of the Revival of the Days of Revolutionary Terror in 1865. FIVE THOUSAND MEN, WOMEN AND CHILDREN MURDERED IN COLD BLOOD!! EIGHT MILES of ROAD STREWN with DEAD BODIES! Concluding with the TRUE STORY OF GEORGE WILLIAM GORDON". This was sold for one penny. (See copy in Appendix II).

the imperial government in 1866 and the imposition of direct rule through a Crown Colony administrative system.

The October 1865 events in Morant Bay had repercussions throughout the West Indies as well as in the southern United States, where slavery was still in force. White-dominated local assemblies became fearful of such events. In Barbados, where precautionary measures were taken against any such uprising, the local assembly formed a Barbados Defence Association, whose services were called upon in the local insurrection of 1876, which was known as the Confederation Revolt.[37] The Barbados Revolt took place when the British Parliament proposed a confederation of small states in the Windward Islands with the governing body located on Barbados and linked this to a kind of Crown Colony system of government. In 1875, a constitutional debate erupted between the new governor, John Pope Hennessey, and the local House of Assembly. Filled with accumulated grievances over disenfranchisement and the hegemony of the planter class-controlled economy, some of the disenfranchised blacks seized the opportunity and staged a rebellion in April 1876. The rebellion lasted five days and led to 8 blacks being killed, 36 being wounded, and 450 being taken prisoner. Many whites fled to safety. However, as Christine Bolt points out, "by the mid-nineteenth century the West Indies had ceased to be of real importance – or even interest – for Britain, but the race prejudice aroused in 1865 was to be of incalculable importance not just for the former, but for the whole world."[38]

The 1865 peasant uprising in Jamaica not only brought to light the slow pace of transition from slavery to real freedom in the West Indies, it also marked a turning point in the relationship between mission Christianity and the substream of African religious practices in the West Indies. As part of the tradition of African resistance in slavery and emancipation, manifestations of African religious traditions began to emerge as separate forms of Christianity, over against that of the mission churches. Those Afro-West Indian religious forms which had previously been suppressed or condemned outright by mission Christianity found free expression after 1865.

This became noticeable by the beginning of the 1860s, as African West Indians increasingly began to turn away from mission churches and turn,

---

37. Belle, "Abortive Revolution," 181–191.
38. Bolt, *Victorian Attitudes*, 82–83.

instead, to newer forms of religious experience that were more in keeping with their existential needs, anxieties, and religious styles.[39] Among these were Zion Revivalist religions which were aided by the new influence of American Revivalism, the precursor of American Pentecostalism. These newer religious forms offered greater physical and psychological space for personal empowerment, healing, and transformation of body and soul. In their religious imagination these newer religious forms, being "washed in the blood of the lamb" and "sanctified by the Holy Ghost" through the Christian embodied rites of baptism and saint-making by the Spirit, offered new sources of personal identity and power. The practical benefits to the users of Afro-West Indian religious rites differed in marked ways from those who practised the religion of westernized mission Christianity. Although mission Christianity emphasized what Austin-Broos calls "eudemonic rites," it was, she notes, "a religion of ethical rationalism" shaped by the European Enlightenment, which stood in contrast to African primal religious traditions.[40]

All these factors indicate that the British West Indies was experiencing significant social and political post-emancipation crises between 1840 and 1860. Although compounded by many internal and external factors, these were, in essence, crises of freedom. The peasant uprisings of 1865 and 1876 brought matters to the fore in both Jamaica and Barbados. But they also reflected and highlighted the general problem throughout the British West Indies of the unfulfilled promises of emancipation. As British imperial interest in the West Indies waned even further towards the end of the nineteenth century, with severe consequences on the West Indian economy, the church in the West Indies realized that it had to stand on its own feet and find its own ways of carrying out its mission. This mission included the challenge of responding to the needs of the local population and helping to create a new social order in post-emancipation West Indian society.

---

39. Some scholars – like Dale Bisnauth, *History of Religions* – see this development as the period of the "Africanization of Christianity" in the West Indies.

40. Austin-Broos, *Jamaica Genesis*, 36–42.

The Challenge of Africa

The second context that must be factored in is the context of continental Africa itself. In the nineteenth century, Africa represented a formidable challenge to Europeans, and particularly to Christian missionary endeavours. As Philip Curtin points out, prior to the nineteenth century, Africa had a strong, positive image as a land of reputable kingdoms and highly developed civilizations.[41] However, by the nineteenth century, that image changed, principally through Africa becoming the centre of focus of the transatlantic slave trade. To the European mind, Africa became "the dark continent." The image of Africa was of a land that was slave-infested, economically backward, and out of step with the modern civilized world.

This nineteenth-century European perception of Africa was cultivated and used extensively by the Western missionary establishment in propagandizing and mobilizing resources for civilizing missions to rescue Africa, the "dark continent." As Bediako notes, the description of Africa by the Irishman Hope Waddell, who served as a Presbyterian missionary in Jamaica for seventeen years before leading the Presbyterian mission from Jamaica to Calabar in 1846, was used in this way.[42] In Waddell's view, Africa and Africans represented the lowest levels of civilization known to humanity:

> At this day the Negro race stands before the world in a condition disgraceful to itself and to humanity. Divided into innumerable tribes and languages, – without literature, laws or government, arts or sciences, – with slavery for its normal social condition, and the basest and bloodiest superstition in the world for religion, – a religion without reference to God or their souls, to sin or holiness, to heaven or hell, and even without the outward insignia of temple, priest or altar, – has sunk so low as to be regardless alike of conscience and of shame, to reckon a man's life at his market value as a beast of burden, and to practice cannibalism, not from want, but revenge, and a horrid lust for human flesh.[43]

---

41. Curtin, *Image of Africa*, 9–10.
42. Bediako, *Theology and Identity*, 255–256.
43. Waddell, *Twenty-Nine Years*, 227.

Waddell's views both reflect and echo the perception then in Europe that Africa in the mid-nineteenth century was a problem that needed to be remedied. Recalling the high attainments in arts and arms of ancient Egypt and Carthage, he asks ruefully, "How should it [Africa] have fallen so far behind the nations of Europe and Asia?" Not only was Africa perceived by Europeans as "the dark continent," it was also seen as "the closed continent," as the German missiologist Gustav Warneck stated at the beginning of the twentieth century. After describing the early nineteenth-century European perception of Africa as a closed continent, with its waterways barely providing access to more than its coastal margins, Warneck describes missionary response in terms of an opportunity and challenge as "the rest of the Continent formed an inaccessible Colossus, and it is not a missionary duty to open up the doors of the world, but to go where they have already been opened."[44]

As far as sub-Saharan Africa was concerned, Christianity was largely unknown beyond the coast. It was not until the 1850s that Christian penetration into the regions beyond the Niger Delta and the estuary of the Rio Pongas took place. Perhaps more than any other single factor, it was David Livingstone's arrival in southern Africa in 1841 and his travels and research in the interior of Africa that opened up and galvanized European knowledge of and attention to the "heart of Africa."[45]

At the same time, the spectacular failure of the high profile, British-sponsored Niger Mission of the Church of England's Church Missionary Society (CMS) in 1841 drew British public attention to the well-publicized dangers and pitfalls of European efforts to introduce Christianity to Africa.[46] Africa was indeed "the White Man's Grave."[47] However, by the time of Livingstone's death on the banks of the Zambezi in 1873, thirty years after his arrival on the African continent, Christianity had taken root in Central and Western Africa with far-flung mission stations manned by European, American, African, and West Indian agents. During those three decades, the church in the North Atlantic, including the church in the West Indies,

---

44. Warneck, *History of Protestant Missions*, 214.

45. Livingstone, *Missionary Travels*; Walls, "Legacy of David Livingstone."

46. In the West Indies, the collapse of the Niger Expedition was lampooned in the press as a piece of "knight-errantry" driven by "ignorance and cupidity." *Jamaica Standard and Royal Gazette.* Wednesday, 2 February 1842. Kingston, National Library of Jamaica.

47. Curtin, "White Man's Grave," 94–110.

was awakened and responded to the missionary opportunity and challenge that Africa represented.

The number one challenge, however, was the fact that Africa was at the centre of a modern global market in human slavery. The "mystery" of the "heart of Africa" lay in the fact that both the internal and external marketing of African slaves emanated from the vast interiors of Africa that remained largely unknown to Europeans. By the mid-nineteenth century, publicly, the tide had turned against the slave trade and the transatlantic anti-slavery movement was particularly concerned with the challenge of discovering the source of this trade in Africa. Despite British efforts to eradicate it, slavery continued unabated. In 1839, Thomas Fowell Buxton – the publicly acknowledged successor of Wilberforce in the British anti-slavery movement – put forward a proposal for a "remedy" for Africa. This proposal involved a scheme to eradicate the trade in African slaves by supplanting it with legitimate commerce and the introduction of Christian civilization. This scheme was to be aided by the "civilizing" work of Christian missionary agency and the use of "native agents."[48] Buxton's proposal was well publicized in the West Indies. However, prior to emancipation, West Indian mission leaders had developed their own ideas of "native agency."[49] And although Buxton's plan was already known in the West Indies, in 1840, when his book *The African Slave Trade and its Remedy* was published, it was widely received with great interest and read throughout the West Indies.[50]

---

48. Buxton, *African Slave Trade*; see also Newbury, *British Policy*, 147–148, 292; and Walls, "Legacy of Thomas Fowell Buxton."

49. Buxton, as a parliamentarian and leading humanitarian in Britain, was at the receiving end of correspondence from missionaries in almost every British West Indian colony and was, therefore, very well informed about slavery and mission practices. He invited John Trew, the experienced CMS missionary to Jamaica, to become the secretary of his organization, the Africa Colonisation Society (ACS). The ACS, patronized by the British establishment, made it publicly clear in its programme that only Christian mission could "bring Africa into the concourse of modern Civilisation" through practical programmes of Christianity and commerce, the Bible and the plough. As long as the African slave trade continued, despite British attempts to outlaw the trade, so long would Western missionaries have a moral cause in Africa to eradicate this evil, as had been done in the West Indies.

50. Blyth, the Scottish Presbyterian missionary in Jamaica, in his autobiography, *Reminiscences of a Missionary Life*, 174, recounted the impact of Buxton's published plans on missionaries in Jamaica. "The appearance of Buxton's *Slave Trade and Remedy* also encouraged them (the Baptists) to persevere, as it led them to hope that missionaries might enjoy protection, and be safe both as to life and property, in some of the spots where the slave traffic had given place to legitimate trade. The Presbyterian missionaries accordingly took up the subject

Although the idea of social transformation through Christian evangelization involving the employment of native agency was already present in the West Indian church in 1840, what was lacking was a mechanism and the resources to implement it. In the West Indies, the missionary strategy of using the civilizing tools of education, agriculture, trade, and household domesticity to achieve social change had been tried and proven. Therefore, there was good reason to believe that valuable expertise could be found there to mount a mission to Africa in the mid-nineteenth century.

The Buxton plan called for the establishment of Christian colonies or villages in Africa. In this model of evangelization, the vision of social transformation, however, was to be in European cultural terms of self-dignity, Victorian ethical conduct, and Christian civilization. Christian enlightenment through the English Bible, the moral teachings of the church, and Christian moral practice in family life and educational attainments were to be the hallmarks of Christian witness. Additionally, in this plan, African markets would be open for "legitimate commerce" through African productivity and European market relationships. Such was the conceived vision of a "remedy" for the "problem" of Africa in the mid-nineteenth-century metropolitan mind.

The challenge of Africa, therefore, became the missionary dream and the driving agenda of Western missions in the mid-nineteenth century. This vision was embraced by highly placed members of the Western missionary establishment and accepted in principle by the West Indian church as part of their own experience in missionary work and ambition for future missionary exploits.

The Western Missionary Establishment

The third context that must be factored into this study is that of the status and vision of the Western missionary establishment and its strategic global interests in the nineteenth century. The Western missionary establishment was the network of missionary societies that had sprung up throughout Europe and North America from the late eighteenth century. The mission initiatives

---

in earnest and all of them solemnly, and with earnest prayer, dedicated themselves to the evangelisation of Africa, declaring their readiness to go to that country, should God in His Providence appear to countenance it."

from the West Indies to Africa occurred with knowledge of and insights into the state of the global missionary enterprise at the time. The leaders and initiators of the West Indian missions to Africa were members of that enterprise and part of the global chain involved in the project. However, the question arises as to whether the Western missionary establishment had any real interest in Africa in the mid-nineteenth century.[51] The evidence seems to suggest that it did not. The fact is that, by mid-century, European mission societies were almost ready to give up on Africa as a viable mission field. Most of these societies had no clear policy or plan for Africa.[52] The British Baptist Missionary Society (BMS) – founded in 1792 in Kettering, England, with such promise of missionary endeavours from the margins of the Empire – had given up on Africa after the failure of its early efforts in Sierra Leone.[53] During the forty years that followed, the BMS sent no missionary to Africa. By the mid-nineteenth century – after two decades of failure, due mainly to the high mortality rate of its agents – the Basel Evangelical Missionary Society in Europe was also about to foreclose on its efforts on the Gold Coast of Africa.[54] And when the greatly publicized Niger Missionary Expedition of the Church Missionary Society (CMS) collapsed in 1841, Europeans were convinced that not only was Africa the "white man's grave" but, if it was to be evangelized, it was increasingly unlikely to be by European agency. In the wake of the tragedy of the Niger Mission, one member of Buxton's large family, sharing the public disappointment, wrote:

> I confess I do not see what are we to do next for Africa. I hope in due time the right way may open. Certainly the climate seems

---

51. Most of the missionary societies were connected to large church denominations such as the Church of England, and the Church of Scotland, or the Baptist, Methodist, or Moravian churches. Others were interdenominational and operated from European urban centres such as London, Edinburgh, Paris, Basel, and so on.

52. Groves, *Planting of Christianity*, 212. The Church Missionary Society (CMS), for example, founded in 1799, had a few agents in Sierra Leone at the beginning of the nineteenth century. After their failures, no clear strategic plan for Africa was laid out between 1804 and 1824; the CMS suffered the loss of fifty-three of their seventy-nine missionaries. Hewitt, *Problems of Success*, 12.

53. Stanley, *History of the Baptist Missionary Society*.

54. Miller, *Social Control*, 16–22.

like a wall of fire around the land and it is a hindrance which no time nor perseverance can overcome.[55]

Thereafter, organizers and supporters of the Niger Mission began to believe that "by black agency alone that realm of thick darkness can be touched" and began to circulate this idea in popular mission discourse.[56] Buxton himself confessed, "A cloud seems for the present to rest on all our endeavours, but I have the strongest confidence in the agency of black men."[57] It was a confession which reflected disappointment in the failure of the efforts of the Western missionary establishment to "remedy" Africa through its own agencies. But it was also a confession which, perhaps, presaged the beginning of an acknowledgement of the possible usefulness of Africans to evangelize Africa.

By the mid-nineteenth century, following the openings created by imperial commercial interests, the strategic interest of the Western missionary establishment had shifted its sights to new fields in Asia (India, China, and the Far East) and British North America (USA and Canada).[58] Nevertheless, the challenge of Africa remained. It was this sense of European failure in Africa, coupled with a sense of confidence and triumph in their own missionary experience in the West Indies, which prompted West Indian mission leaders to contemplate mounting missionary expeditions to Africa in the mid-nineteenth century.[59] That Africa became the focus of the missionary dream of the West Indian church followed the logic and triumphalist mood of the missionary engagements of its leaders in the West Indies.

Summary and Conclusion

The final emancipation of African slaves in the British West Indies by 1838 presented a real opportunity for the British government to demonstrate its

---

55. Edward North Buxton to Priscilla Johnston, Buxton Papers, Reel #9, Correspondence, USPG Archives.

56. Mrs. Johnston to Dr. Philip, Buxton Papers, Reel #9, Correspondence, USPG Archives.

57. Buxton to Ramsey, Buxton Papers, Reel #9, Correspondence, USPG Archives.

58. Porter, *Imperial Horizons*.

59. Russell questions the basis of this claim that the West Indies was an established mission field by the mid-nineteenth century. He points out that it was this acclaimed mission success in the West Indies that led the Jamaican Baptists to prematurely sever a formal relationship with the parent society in Britain and that this, in turn, led to further problems in sustaining the work in this newly pioneered field. Russell, "Question of Indigenous Mission," 86–93.

true humanitarian interests in advancing the welfare of the Negroes, as it ostensibly professed. It could have done so had it been so minded. However, as the post-emancipation experience for the ex-slaves demonstrated, the promise of full freedom was not backed up by any plan for rehabilitation or social reconstruction to benefit their well-being. The slave societies of the British West Indies, which had been built over nearly two centuries needed to be deconstructed and a new social order established upon new legal foundations of free citizens. That social order remained a challenge both for the colonial state and for the newly freed ex-slaves.

It was left to non-state actors like Christian missionary agents on the field to step into the social vacuum and help put organizational structures in place that would add personal meaning to the opportunities which the emancipation dream afforded. Given their experience working with the African population in the West Indies prior to abolition, the missionaries believed they were well equipped to help with the post-emancipation reconstruction efforts. By the second decade of the post-emancipation period, however, the West Indies began to feel the effects of the social crises caused by the imperial government's neglect. By the middle of the century, the influx of new immigrants, droughts, crop failures, bankrupt estates, and widespread epidemics such as cholera and smallpox called attention to the social and economic state of the colonies in the British West Indies. As commodity prices for primary agricultural products such as sugar fell on the world market, landowners, labourers, and peasants in the West Indies began to show signs of increasing impoverishment. In the mission churches, church attendance that rose dramatically in the 1830s began to slowly decline by the end of the 1840s.

As new fields and opportunities opened up in Asia (India and China), North America, and the South Pacific, no longer was the West Indies seen as an attractive economic zone – unlike in the late eighteenth century. Feeling marginalized in an Empire which was now looking elsewhere, West Indian leaders were ready to explore new opportunities. Just as some estate owners and members of the planter class abandoned their estates and retired in Britain, missionary leaders looked for new opportunities for missionary work abroad.

Emancipation as "lived freedom" proved a tough challenge for the ex-slaves, and the emergence of black political leadership on their behalf was vital. While bearing the identity of "Christian Black," this black Christian leadership – which had already been nurtured by the church to meet its own need of auxiliary leadership in response to the growth in church attendance in the 1830s – had no difficulty pursuing black resistance and advocacy for social justice against the white oligarchic ruling class.[60] What drove people like Sam Sharpe and Paul Bogle – as deacons of the church and, at the same time, leaders of the underclass of slaves and peasants – was this dream to see freedom fully realized for the black population.

As the Western missionary enterprise began to turn its attention away from Africa – due to its history of failure to successfully establish Christianity on the Continent – West Indian church leaders saw the opportunity to make their contribution to the challenge of social transformation in Africa. Based on their track record, these mission leaders believed that the West Indian church was not only ready but also "best suited" to make this contribution, and so they set their sights directly towards Africa.

---

60. Russell, "The Emergence of the Christian Black," 55–58; Austin-Broos, *Jamaica Genesis*, 39.

Part 2: Participation

The West Indian Missions to Western Africa

CHAPTER 4

The Basel Mission to the Gold Coast (1843–1850): Seeds of Failure, Fruits of Success

The mission initiative led by the Basel Evangelical Missionary Society (BEMS) from the West Indies to the Gold Coast of Africa in the mid-nineteenth century was the first organized missionary project to leave the West Indies and land on African soil. The twenty-five African West Indians, who landed in Christiansborg (now Accra) in April 1843, were recruited from the Moravian Mission in the West Indies, mainly from Jamaica. Since the Moravian Mission was present throughout the West Indies from the mid-eighteenth century, some questions arise: Why were the Jamaican Moravians chosen for the Africa mission? What, if anything, did the Jamaicans contribute to this enterprise? Did the Jamaican Moravians make any distinctive contribution by their participation in the Africa project?

These questions raise three specific issues that require further examination: first, the nature of the relationship between the BEMS in Basel, Switzerland and the Moravian movement in Germany, and their connection to the Moravian Mission in the West Indies; second, the kind of response the recruiting agents from the BEMS received in the West Indies; and third, the experience of the Jamaican Moravians on the field as they encountered and engaged in the BEMS project in Africa.

The BEMS had come into being in 1815 as a Swiss-German missionary society in Basel, Switzerland. A product of the Swiss Reformation of the sixteenth and seventeenth centuries, its roots lay in South German Pietism. As a religious movement, Pietism has been described as "an emotionally intense set of beliefs and practices that placed especially strong emphasis on spiritual rebirth, close individual reading of scripture, personal asceticism, discipline, and social conservatism."[1] It emerged strongest in the Wurttemberg region of South Germany in the late eighteenth or early nineteenth century, where the "Wurttemberg Pietists," as they were called, formed themselves into a Bible study movement in Basel in 1780 and called it the German Society for Christianity. By the first decade of the nineteenth century, this movement had developed a passion for missionary evangelism and set up the BEMS in 1815 to train young men for missionary service.[2] By 1821, the BEMS decided to move from being only a training institution to become a sending agency and sent its first agents to the Far East. Missionary interest in Africa initially began in 1828. The BEMS sent five agents to Liberia but, as a result of illness and death, the missionary endeavour failed. Within twelve months, three of the pioneer missionaries from Basel died on the field, and the others were forced to withdraw. In 1831, finding that Africa was not favourable to European missionaries, the BEMS decided to abort its mission in Liberia.[3]

In 1828, the BEMS had also responded to an invitation of the Danish Crown and the Danish Lutheran Church to provide agents for a mission in the Gold Coast, in the Danish-controlled Christiansborg. The four agents who were sent to the Gold Coast attempted to generate real missionary engagement with Western Africa.[4] However, between 1828 and 1838, the BMS suffered heavy losses of personnel in the Gold Coast Mission, losing eight missionaries in twelve years. In addition, their mission did not even produce a single baptized African convert. In November 1838, when news came of the death of yet another missionary in the Gold Coast Mission – a man called J. Murdter – the Basel Committee lamented the fact that even after a decade in

---

1. Miller, *Social Control*, 12.

2. Initially, the BEMS was a training institution, not a sending agency. In the early years, having produced missionaries trained for service, the Society channelled its agent through organizations such as the Church Missionary Society. When the BEMS decided to send out its own agents, its focus was towards the Far East in Russia.

3. The pioneers of the Basel Mission to Liberia were J. C. S. Handt, C. G. Hegele, J. F. Sessing, G. A. Kissling, and H. H. Wulff. Groves, *Planting of Christianity*, 295.

4. The four pioneers to the Gold Coast – K. F. Salbach, J. G. Schmidt, G. Holzwarth, and J. P. Henke – landed in Christiansborg (Danish Accra) in December 1828. Within eight months, three of them had died. Groves, *Planting of Christianity*, 300.

Africa they had "no visible results, no fruits of the work."[5] The haemorrhaging of its personnel mirrored the haemorrhaging of morale and confidence in any prospect of success in Africa.

This repeated failure in Africa had given rise to doubts within the Basel Committee about the real prospects of success in the African environment, and they were faced with the question of whether they should withdraw from the Gold Coast as they had done in Liberia. After Murdter's death in November 1838, the Danish missionary Andreas Riis – the sole surviving Basel missionary in the Gold Coast – was recalled to Basel for consultation as the Basel Committee contemplated the future of the Gold Coast Mission. Pioneer and visionary that he was, Riis managed to persuade the Committee to make one more attempt, this time with the aid of a new source. This new source was the Christianized Africans in the West Indies, who had been trained by the Moravian Brethren. Fortunately for Riis, the new inspector in Basel, Wilhelm Hoffmann (1839–1850), was personally determined to see the Gold Coast Mission survive and was willing to make one last attempt.[6]

As described in chapter 2, the formation of a Moravian community in Jamaica was based on a strategy of missionary engagement that focused on strong conservative religious virtues and social values. These included the virtues of honesty, fidelity, and religious devotion and the values of labour and community. The Moravians took great care in the formation of their community and placed emphasis on personal discipline, moral conduct, hard work, and avoidance of civil political matters. In this community, the social advantages of moral character, exemplified in personal conduct, marriage, and family life, constituted the basis of Christian witness in what was considered a "heathen" environment. In this respect, Moravian identity shared strong affinities with the religious and social values of the Basel Evangelical Missionary Society. It is of interest to note that after having existed continuously for 186 years the BEMS in 2001 consolidated and transferred its global missionary work into a new organization called *Mission-21.org*, also based in Basel, Switzerland.

---

5. The news affected feelings in Basel towards their missionary attempts in Africa. They noted, "We are bowed down at the hearing of all the sad news. We are dismayed at the utter failure of our plans. We do not understand the thoughts of the Lord with this deeply affected work." Reindorf, *History of the Gold Coast*, 226.

6. Groves, *Planting of Christianity*, 24.

In addition to shared affinities in origins, doctrines, and practices, there were other factors that led to a natural partnership being forged between the BEMS and the Moravians in the West Indies. The transatlantic anti-slavery movement of the 1830s had opened lines of communication between European missionaries serving in the West Indies and the British and American anti-slavery movement. Through these channels, European missionaries in the West Indies – such as the Moravian superintendent Jakob Zorn, Baptist missionary William Knibb, and Anglican CMS missionary John Trew in Jamaica – were in direct contact with Basel and London regarding missionary work in the slave societies of the West Indies. Indeed, John Trew, who spent many years as a CMS missionary to Jamaica, returned to Britain in 1835 to become secretary of Buxton's Africa Civilisation Society and, later, the Mico Educational Charity Trust.[7] Meanwhile, J. F. Sessing, a Basel missionary to Liberia, was transferred to Jamaica in 1842 to serve on behalf of the CMS.[8] These links not only opened lines of communication through which information passed back and forth, they also provided the opportunity to build transatlantic relationships among the missionary communities, which proved useful in designing the post-emancipation missionary projects in Africa.

In Europe, the proclamation of slave emancipation throughout the British Empire attracted attention, especially to the West Indies, and also raised awareness of the continuing practice of slavery by other European colonial powers. In addition, in the euphoria of emancipation in the British West Indies, those enterprising missionaries who were part of the anti-slavery movement, and whose dissenting and risk-taking activities had earned them recognition among the African slaves, drew attention to the claims of the role of missionary work in bringing about the collapse of slavery in the British West Indies during the period 1834–1838.

As the largest British colony in the West Indies, Jamaica was at the centre of powerful anti-slavery focus and activities in the early 1830s. Agitation among the slave population in various parts of the island and the testing of the chains of slavery on various plantations were strong undercurrents during that period. While the question of why the Jamaican Moravians were

---

7. Buxton to Trew, Trew to Buxton, Buxton Papers, 14, 15, Reel #5, Correspondence, USPG Archives.

8. Groves, *Planting of Christianity*, 295.

chosen for the Africa mission can be answered through an understanding of these relationships, it should be understood more directly in the context of the affinities between the South German Pietists in the Basel movement and the Zinzendorf-led Moravians in Germany. And if, as Andreas Riis believed, the Basel agents were to recruit in the West Indies with a view to finding strong support for the Gold Coast Mission in Africa, there were reasonable grounds on which to expect favourable responses from Zorn and the Moravian Mission in Jamaica.

Recruitment in the West Indies

Having secured the approval and blessing of Inspector Hoffmann and the Committee in Basel to commence recruitment of West Indians for the Gold Coast Mission in Africa, Andreas Riis proceeded to make the necessary arrangements. With his commission to make a final attempt to secure the West Africa mission on the Gold Coast, he immediately set about obtaining logistical support for this mission and was encouraged by the response he received from several sources, including Buxton's Africa Colonisation Society.[9] In May 1842, a delegation of four sailed from London to the West Indies to recruit agents for the Gold Coast Mission. The delegation included Riis, his wife, Margarethe Anna Wolters, a German Basler named George Widmann, and a black African called George Peter Thompson. The inclusion of Thompson in this recruiting party was of great significance to the Basel Mission because Thompson was a black Liberian, who had been trained in both Basel and Germany and spoke fluent German. Orphaned at an early age, Thompson was privileged to have been raised in the home of Governor J. Ashmun of Liberia and later sent to Europe for his education. Trained at the mission headquarters in Basel, he had met Thomas Fowell Buxton's sister – Lady Gurney of Norfolk – and one of Fowell's sons who had visited the Basel Mission in Switzerland.[10] Thompson was also acquainted with the Basel missionary Jakob Sessing, who had previously served in Liberia and

---

9. Buxton made a grant of £500 to Riis's mission recruitment effort in the West Indies.

10. While he was in Jamaica with Riis, recruiting agents for Africa, Thompson outlined the story of his life in a letter of gratitude to Buxton. Thompson to Buxton, Buxton Papers, Reel #9, Correspondence, USPG Archives.

was now Island Curate in Jamaica. As a black African, Thompson's presence in the recruiting party added great hope and esteem to the project.[11] As an African who was German-speaking, had trained in the Basel school, and received a European education, the hope was that he would be a role model of the benefits of European education and civilization to the West Indians and other Africans on the Gold Coast.

Although the planned destination for Riis and his delegation was the British West Indies, this was not where they first landed and attempted to recruit for the mission in Africa.[12] When the delegation arrived in the West Indies, they first landed at St. Croix in the Danish West Indies. Although cordially received by the colonial governor and Moravian church leaders, they failed to secure any Africans for the mission in Africa.[13] From St. Croix, the delegation moved on and arrived at Antigua on 20 July 1842. Again, they were disappointed because the Moravian leaders had failed to prepare for their visit. The mission leaders in Antigua appeared not to have been informed of the recruitment drive and, therefore, no advance preparations had been done. Riis did, however, manage to recruit one Antiguan teenager – Jonas Hosford, age 16 – to accompany the mission. From Antigua, their next stop was Jamaica, where they arrived in December 1842.

The Basel delegation was much better received in Jamaica because Jakob Zorn, the Moravian superintendent, was prepared for their visit and had prepared the Moravian community for the recruitment effort. Riis and the Basel delegation spent over six weeks in Jamaica and claimed to have travelled over five hundred miles as they communicated their vision for Africa in pursuit of their recruitment drive.[14] Having spent Christmas in Jamaica,

---

11. Debrunner, *History of Christianity*, 107.

12. Perhaps they had hoped to select agents from several parts of the West Indies. But although the Moravian Mission was spread throughout the West Indies by the mid-nineteenth century, realistically, in 1842, the only place where there was an available pool of potential recruits was in the British West Indies. At that time, despite the strong pressures exerted upon them by the British anti-slavery movement, slavery had not yet been abolished in the French, Dutch, and Danish West Indies. African slaves in these West Indian slave societies, however Christianized, would not have been available for such a venture.

13. The colonial governor appeared to have thought that the prospect of taking Africans from the West Indies back to Africa for Christian missionary work was unlikely to succeed. Given the low estimate of the African character held by colonialists in the slave societies of the West Indies, this would not have been surprising. Hall, *Slave Society*, 41–50.

14. A full account of the delegation's activities in Jamaica was published in the Basel *Mission Magazine* (1843): 231–242, Afrika III 1842–1848, BEMS Archives, Basel, Switzerland.

Zorn wrote to La Trobe in London on the day following Christmas Day with the announcement that "a whole party is making preparation to proceed to Kingston to sail early in the New Year."[15]

In Kingston, Widmann and Thompson took the opportunity to visit the Mico Charity Trust and other educational institutions to observe the work being done with a view to transplanting the Mico model of education practised in Jamaica to the Gold Coast Mission in Africa.[16] On 5 January 1843, Zorn again wrote to La Trobe, noting that "Riis had found in our congregations the requisite number of Christian families willing to devote themselves to the service of our saviour among the Blacks in the Aquapim mountains on the West Coast of Africa. The party consists of 6 families, numbering 23 souls, exclusive of Catherine Mulgrave, now the wife of Br. Geo Thompson."[17] Zorn named the six families, which included John and Mary Hall, and their son, Andrew, from the Irwin Hill congregation; John and Mary Rochester, and their children, John Paul and Ann, from the Fairfield congregation; Joseph and Mary Miller, and their children, Rose Ann, Robert, and Catherine, also from the Fairfield congregation; James and Margarethe Mullings, and their daughter, Catherine, from the New Bethlehem congregation; Edward and Sarah Walker, and their son, John, also from the New Bethlehem congregation; and James and Catherine Green, and their son, Robert, from the Nazareth congregation.[18] There were also two young bachelors – Alexander Worthy Clerk from the Fairfield congregation[19] and David Robinson from the

---

15. Zorn to La Trobe, 26 December 1842, Africka - III (1842–1848): vol. D-1, 2. Correspondence, BEMS Archives.

16. While at Mico, Widmann catalogued the list of recruits and classified them according to date and place of birth, congregation, date of church membership. Widmann to Inspector Hoffmann, Mico Institution, Africka - II (1842–1848): vol. D-1, 2, Correspondence, BEMS Archives, Basel, Switzerland.

17. Zorn to La Trobe, 26 December 1842, Africka - III (1842–1848): vol. D-1, 2, Correspondence, BEMS Archives. The news of George Thompson's marriage to Catherine Mulgrave added more appeal to the project since Catherine's background was remarkably similar to that of Thompson's. Both were trained black teachers, of whom it was expected that they might be able to implement the Mico model of education in the Gold Coast Mission in Africa. Thompson's letter to Buxton from Mico suggested as much.

18. These congregations were located amid the agricultural plantations in the south-western and central part of Jamaica, where Moravian work originated and took root. It is part of the section of Jamaica in which a strong independent proto-peasantry emerged following the collapse of British slave society in 1838.

19. Debrunner, *History of Christianity*, 108.

Fulnec congregation[20] – and Catherine Mulgrave, whom George Thompson married before the end of December 1842, and the Antiguan teenager, Jonas Hosford, completed the list of recruits. In preparation for their departure for West Africa, the selected group assembled at the Moravian church in Lititz, St. Elizabeth, on 4 January for a valedictory service before departing from Alligator Pond to Kingston, from where they would make their transatlantic journey.[21]

As enthusiastic as the mission leaders in Jamaica might have appeared at the prospect of making this contribution to Africa, there were at least two fundamental issues underlying the project which needed to be addressed. One was the question of expectations and the extent to which they were mutually understood, shared, and agreed by all parties – exactly what was expected of the West Indian recruits while in Africa, and what could they expect from their participation in the missionary enterprise. The second issue was the matter of confidence on the part of the mission leaders in the West Indians' ability to contribute meaningfully to the Africa project. To address the first issue, a contractual relationship was established which obligated the BEMS to secure necessary provisions for the recruits and their families. Reciprocally, the West Indians were bound by the contract to offer their services for a stated period of time. Beyond that, the contact was imprecise with regard to what options were legitimately available if there were breaches or mutual failures to meet the agreed obligations. The contract – negotiated by Andrea Riis, and agreed between the BEMS and the United Brethren in Jamaica (Moravians) – stated the following:

1. The Forms of Services for the congregations and regulations for Church Discipline of the Moravians to be maintained.
2. The recruited West Indians were to serve willingly the Mission, who will care for all their needs in the first two years.
3. The Mission Society takes the obligation to provide houses for the West Indians and gardens and to give one day a week free.

---

20. Widmann to Hoffmannm 30 January 1843, Africka - II (1842–1848): vol. D-1, 2, Correspondence, BEMS Archives, Basel, Switzerland.

21. Zorn to La Trobe, 26 December 1842, Africka - III (1842–1848): vol. D-1, 2, Correspondence, BEMS Archives.

4. After two years they may either work for themselves or for the Mission Society for a reasonably low wage.
5. If anybody wants to return after two years the Mission Society will pay the passage, provided that they have not been guilty of moral (sexual) aberration.[22]

While a contract was the basis of dealing with the question of expectations, the issue of confidence was dealt with more subjectively. Like other Christian mission communities in Jamaica at the time, the Moravian community were deeply suspicious of any relationship between the Moravian faith and the religious culture of Africans in the Jamaican slave society. The strong principles of German Pietism which shaped the missionary engagement of the Moravian missionaries in Jamaica did not always dispose them to understand and interface well with what Austin-Broos describes as the "politics of moral orders" in Jamaican colonial society.[23] As already explained, these "moral orders" were the political, social, and cultural structures in which the Creole society of Jamaica was formed vis-a-vis the contrasting structures of mission Christianity which the European missionaries had brought with them. These often conflicted within the West Indian cultural context as the missionaries negotiated entry into Jamaican slave society.[24] The mission Christianity practised by the European missionaries in the West Indies was, to a large extent, influenced by the assumption that outside of European understandings of Christianity, all religious and cosmological claims were suspect, if not altogether false. Mission Christianity tended to focus on rational and ethical Christian practices while downplaying supernatural religious experience.[25]

---

22. Zorn to La Trobe, 4 January 1843, Africka - III (1842–1848): vol. D-1, 2, Correspondence, BEMS Archives. Zorn and Riis communicated these elements of the contract to London and Basel. See also Correspondence from Riis, Widmann, and Thompson, January 1843, to Inspector Hoffmann, Letter-books Correspondence, missionaries' personal files, vols. D-1, 1 to D-1, 4, and abstracts from Correspondence.

23. Austin-Broos, *Jamaica Genesis*, 233–239.

24. In the slaves' quest for meaning, transcendence, and survival, these structures – shaped by the world views of post-Enlightenment Eurocentric mission Christianity, on the one hand, and an Afrocentric world view that informed the world the slaves made for themselves in the context of New World slavery, on the other – often conflicted in their struggle for effective liberation.

25. Austin-Broos, in her study of the origins of Jamaican Pentecostal rites and practices, argues that in the nineteenth-century mission Christianity practised in Jamaica, "animated ideas of good and evil embodied in a natural-social environment made little sense to the Christian concerned with the internalised evil of sin." Those ideas came from a religion and culture that,

As they engaged in the West Indian colonial environment, the European missionaries tended to repudiate as "heathenish superstition" religious claims and expressions, particularly those of African origin, which were beyond the orthodoxy they understood and prescribed. The Moravians were particularly resistant to any suggestion of exposure to or syncretism with African-Jamaican religious practices. Practices such as obeah or myalism were roundly repudiated.[26] Obeah was a practice that appeared similar to witchcraft and might have been derived from the Twi culture on the Gold Coast. The practice was brought to the West Indies by the slaves and reconstructed as part of slave religion in the Creole West Indian society. The object of the practice was to obtain protection against evil forces and to succeed in personal plans. This was achieved by "putting on of spirits" by a leader – an "obeah man" or an "obeah woman." Myalism was also a practice of slave religion. It was the "taking off of spirits" as a defensive strategy to conquer evil. Myal practice incorporated many elements of Christianity – including the use of hymnody, the Psalter, and ablution – and was intensely focused on the Trinity.

It was not surprising, therefore, that before their departure from Alligator Pond in the parish of Manchester to Kingston – in preparation for the transatlantic journey to the Gold Coast of Africa – Superintendent Zorn and other elders of the Moravian community charged the Jamaicans, warning them to "keep entirely clear from African superstition and not countenance them even by an approving smile." Zorn cited the Biblical text "Little children keep yourselves from idols" (1 John 5:21) and urged them to have unity among themselves, and to "perfect candour in their intercourse with their future ministers, to industry, temperance and to everything that is lovely and of

---

she claimed, "remained opaque to them." Even less threatening matters such as the significance of a ceremonial dress code were not always grasped. Austin-Broos, *Jamaica Genesis*, 40. Buchner cites a case in point: "The wearing of gold trinkets and artificial flowers is not tolerated among us, or at least is reproved as vanity. At the marriage ceremony the bride appears in much state, richly clad, sometimes as well as any lady, with silk stockings, an embroidered robe, and costly veil. It would be impossible to recognise the same person a few days after in her common dress. We take pains to discourage all extravagance on such occasions, as this proves a stumbling block and a snare to many. Not having the means to make a rich wedding, they often fall into the sin of concubinage." Buchner, *Moravians in Jamaica*, 140.

26. Buchner, *Moravians in Jamaica*, 140–141; Brathwaite, *Development of Creole Society*; Austin-Broos, *Jamaica Genesis*, 43. See Erna Brodber's novel *Myal* for the significance and persistence of this form of Afro-Jamaican religious experience in Jamaican society.

good report."[27] He admonished them to uphold five of the key values of the Moravian ethic which was inculcated in the Moravian community from which they were being sent out as ambassadors. These five key values were the socioreligious values of brotherhood (unity among the brethren), openness (not secretiveness), physical labour (hard work), self-restraint (temperance), and exemplary moral conduct. Since these values reflected the social and religious characteristics considered essential to Moravian witness, Zorn urged them to take these values with them to the missionary project in Africa as part of their contribution and model products of the Jamaica Moravian Mission. Perhaps the coincidence of the timing of the recruitment drive in Jamaica at the time of the outbreak of the open practice of obeah and myalism in the western part of Jamaica in 1842 – despite prohibitions and laws banning such practices – was at the back of Zorn's mind as he bade farewell to the Jamaican missionaries.

For their part, the Jamaican recruits seemed to have been contemplating with some anticipation contact with Africa and the prospects of being in their ancestral homeland. Edward Walker from the New Bethlehem congregation, as he thought about his departure for Africa and the reality of leaving behind his congregation of Moravians, addressed the assembled gathering in Lititz, St. Elizabeth, with these words, which Zorn recorded in his letter to La Trobe:

> If I leave you, I go not to a foreign country. Africa is our country. Our fathers and grandmothers have been brought here by force and we have brethren and sisters to pray for Africa and for us . . . when we go there . . . pray that the Lord may help us and bless us. [28]

Although Walker's voice in this instance is being heard through Zorn, his remarks raise two important questions. First, what was the significance of Walker's apparent embrace of Africa as "our country"? How authentic was it? And was that a clue to his motivation for participation in Christian mission work in Africa? Second, did Walker's embrace of Africa imply a rejection of Jamaica as "home"? Several things may be inferred from Walker's

---

27. Zorn to La Trobe, 4 January 1843, Africka - III (1842–1848): vol. D-1, 2, Correspondence, BEMS Archives.

28. Zorn to La Trobe, 4 January 1843, Africka - III (1842–1848): vol. D-1, 2, Correspondence, BEMS Archives.

remarks: (1) There was an apparent open and publicly displayed willingness to identify with Africa; whatever Walker might have imagined Africa to be, it was not "a foreign country"; (2) There was some expectation that participating in the mission in Africa could make a difference; going there with "the help and blessing of the Lord" was qualitatively quite different from the way their "fathers and grandmothers" came; and (3) There was no intimation of abandoning or cutting ties with Jamaica; instead, Walker was depending on continuing links with Jamaica for emotional and prayer support – "we have brethren and sisters to pray for Africa and for us . . . pray that the Lord may help us and bless us." In Walker's emotional remarks, the reference to ancestral affinity with Africa seem to have been a motivational factor in his offer to go with the Basel team to spread Christianity in Africa,[29] and no doubt this was also a motivating factor for the other recruits.

The question of confidence, however, depended on the personal acquaintance with and knowledge of the individuals selected by the Moravian leaders. There seemed to have been a reasonable expectation on the part of these leaders that those they had chosen possessed the ability and capacity to make a worthwhile contribution to the project in Africa. Zorn, in his letter to La Trobe on the eve of their departure from Alligator Pond, expressed full confidence in the Jamaicans recruited and noted, "I feel confident that they go from proper motives and Christian principles, their whole conduct and their parting address convince us of it."[30]

Before bidding farewell from the shores of Jamaica, the Basel delegation and the Jamaican recruits attended a public meeting in Kingston at the Coke Methodist Church. At this meeting Riis, Widmann, and Thompson delivered addresses in which they informed the public of the object of their mission and solicited support for the mission. One Jamaican newspaper took note of Thompson's role in the delegation and highlighted his speech while describing the departure of the mission from Jamaica on 8 February 1843.[31] The journey to West Africa, symbolizing the reversal of the transatlantic slave trade, took over nine weeks, in sometimes rough and unsettling conditions. When the missionary party landed in Christiansborg at Easter on 17 April 1843, the

---

29. Zorn to La Trobe, 4 January 1843, Correspondence, BEMS Archives, Basel, Switzerland.
30. Zorn to La Trobe, 4 January 1843, Correspondence, BEMS Archives.
31. *The Falmouth Post*, 15 February 1843, National Library of Jamaica, Kingston.

arrival of the West Indians marked a new phase in the Basel Mission's work in Africa. This was a final attempt to establish the mission based in Akropong and, as Noel Smith notes, this "second attempt" (1843–1850) proved critical to the future of Christian mission on the Gold Coast.[32]

Participation in the Africa Mission

As noted in chapter 2, one of the issues which arises in this study is the lack of voice and visibility of the West Indians who were engaged in the nineteenth-century missionary enterprise in Africa. Even though, in aggregate terms, they were not numerically significant, some questions must be asked: Why have they been so voiceless and faceless in the historiography of Western missions in Africa?[33] Did they not, in fact, leave any record of their presence and participation in the enterprise? Did they make any contribution to the enterprise and, if so, was it important or not? The archives of the BEMS clearly contain sufficient valuable documentation relating to the experience of the Jamaicans to make it possible to hear their voice, know their concerns, and understand their experience in the missions in Africa, yet they have remained mute and invisible.[34] It is upon this material I now wish to draw in my examination of the case of the Jamaicans who participated in the Basel Mission on the Gold Coast.[35]

The Jamaicans' participation in the Basel Mission in the Gold Coast took several forms. From the records, it is clear that the intention and plan of the

---

32. Smith, *Presbyterian Church in Ghana*, 39.

33. It has already been noted that Groves, in his groundbreaking work *Planting of Christianity in Africa*, acknowledges and highlights the role and contribution of the West Indians in the rise of West African Christianity. Nevertheless, they again remained nameless and voiceless. Smith, *Presbyterian Church in Ghana*, and Debrunner, *History of Christianity in Ghana*, on the other hand, name the recruited West Indians who were the earliest members of the Basel Mission church in Akropong-Akwapim. In 1939, this mission church became the Presbyterian Church of Ghana. Smith and De Brunner try to represent their experience in that pioneering mission but fail to let the West Indians speak for themselves.

34. Recent attempts have been made to correct a colonialist history of the work of the Basel Mission. See Antwi "African Factor," 55–66. Following Sanneh, "Horizontal and the Vertical," Antwi offers a new perspective to the understanding of the missionary enterprise in Africa in the nineteenth century.

35. I am very grateful to Paul Jenkins, retired archivist of the Basel Mission (now called Mission-21.org), for his enthusiasm for this project and his encouragement to examine the Basel archival records.

Basel missionaries was to model their mission work on the basis of establishing a Christian village in Africa, in which the West Indians would live and work as black Christian colonists. The missionaries' vision was that, through this model village, exemplary witness to the values and virtues of Christianity would be communicated to the surrounding African communities.[36]

On arriving in Africa, therefore, the first task of the West Indians was to settle down and organize themselves to begin the process of establishing this Christian village. There was, however, one big problem. No physical accommodation was available or prepared for them and their families. Andreas Riis, the mission leader, had been away from the Gold Coast for three years (1840–1843), and there had been no one to oversee the preparation of accommodations for the new mission party he had brought back with him. Further, it had never been Riis's intention to settle on the coast if he did return to Africa. Before leaving Africa in 1840, for consultations in Basel, Riis's plan for the future of the Gold Coast Mission had been to establish the Mission in Akropong among the Akwapim people. Akropong is an area away from the coast, in the hills above Christiansborg, and Riis's intention had been to settle down there and establish a permanent base for outreach to other areas in the hinterland. So before his departure for Europe, he had secured a house in Akropong for this purpose. The house had been given to him before his recall to Basel by the king of the Akwapim. However, controversy surrounded the acquisition of the house and this had been one of the reasons for Riis's recall. Considerable energy, time, and physical resources had been expended on this house, and some in Akropong, and even in Basel, questioned why a mission house on such a grand scale was needed in Africa.[37] In Akropong itself, the houses available at the time were woefully inadequate for the group of new missionaries. In any case, no provisions had been made

---

36. Although not spelled out in very clear terms, the basis of the contract made in Jamaica both required and implied cooperation and commitment to this vision on the part of the recruited Jamaicans.

37. Jenkins, "Scandal of Continuing Intercultural Blindness," 67–76. In his summons to appear before the Committee in Basel in 1839, Riis was asked to answer questions regarding the controversy. It should also be noted that as a place name in the nineteenth century, the spelling of Akropong-Akwapim varied, and so different spellings would be seen throughout this study. The spelling varied from Akuapim, Acuapim to Aquapim, and Acropong.

for their overall needs.[38] The only option was to construct new houses to accommodate the Jamaicans and their families. For this, resources of timber and labour had to be found, and the Jamaicans were put to work immediately. For over three months, while the housing problem was being sorted out, the Jamaicans remained on the coast in temporary, makeshift accommodations.

Therefore, the Jamaicans' first act of participation in the Africa mission was in housing construction. Some of the Jamaican men – like Miller, Rochester, and Walker – were active in the logging and sawing of timber. During this early exercise, one of the issues which arose was the interface between the robust physical experience of the West Indians against the technology of the Europeans. To cut timber for housing, the Jamaicans had been given a European saw, which had been designed precisely for the purpose of logging and brought to Akropong by the young German missionary Hermann Halleur, who had joined the mission. The Jamaicans soon found the European instrument clumsy and impractical, and they abandoned it in favour of their own manual technique. George Widmann, who was German, observed this and realized that the Jamaicans might indeed have a very useful contribution to make in the Africa mission. In a report to Inspector Hoffmann, Widmann commended the Jamaicans for their practicality and efficiency, noting that "the sawing machine is not being used. It is a heavy machine, needing 6–8 people to be moved and used and has to be transported from tree-to-tree. The West Indians are much better at sawing by hand."[39] By July 1843, after three months at the coast in Christiansborg, the Jamaican missionary group moved to Akropong to occupy the newly built houses which they themselves had built.

The Jamaican missionaries also became involved in establishing a source of food supply for the Mission. As part of their intended contribution to Africa, they had collected and brought with them samples of food crops grown in Jamaica, which included yams, bananas, plantains, mangoes, oranges, breadfruit, coffee, and cocoyams. This food investment was later to prove important, not only for the agricultural and domestic food needs of the Mission but also

---

38. Conditions in Akropong at the time were very unsettling as a tribal dispute between King Ado and King Dankwa turned into violent tribal war in the 1840s.

39. Widmann to Hoffmann, 16 January 1846, Letter-books Correspondence, missionary personal files, vols. D-1, 1 to D-1, 4, Correspondence, BEMS Archives, Basel, Switzerland.

for the local economy of Akropong.[40] Some of the Jamaican women, like Mary Rochester, were also involved in the agricultural work. Mrs. Rochester was particularly good at producing oil from nuts, and she was the first to make groundnut oil in Akropong. George Widmann even contemplated the possibility of an export trade for her groundnut oil but seemed to have been dissuaded by the lack of infrastructure in the Mission to make such a venture efficient and cost-effective.[41] Dieterle, another Basel missionary, observed in his report to the Committee: "The West Indians, esp. Rochester, plant much yams, plantains and bananas. Mrs. R. makes ground-nut oil. They had 2–300 plantains, 5–600 little coffee trees, and 1000 yams."[42] Sadly, Mary Rochester died in childbirth in 1849, six years after her arrival in Africa.

One of the key tasks of the Mission in its early establishment on the Gold Coast was the setting up of a mission school. George and Catherine Thompson were deployed to Christiansborg to start the school. As both were trained teachers, and had such varied and cultured backgrounds, they were expected to be able to adjust to the cosmopolitan culture and urbanized life of mid-nineteenth-century Christiansborg (Danish Accra). They managed to open a school in Christiansborg with five pupils and began their educational work. These early engagements suggest that, despite organizational shortcomings, the Jamaicans were willing to participate in and contribute to the development of the Mission. They were deployed and engaged in the work of the Mission according to their skills, training, and aptitude for particular types of work, which was the basis on which each one had been selected in the West Indies.

Soon, however, tensions began to develop in Akropong between the Jamaicans and the Basel missionaries. Disappointed in the lack of provisions and, more particularly, the attitude of the Basel missionaries, especially the mission leader Andreas Riis, the Jamaicans began to show their disappointment and displeasure by making a series of demands upon the Basel

---

40. Dickson, *Historical Geography*, 120–126; Odamtten, *Missionary Factor*.

41. Widmann to Hoffmann, November 11, 1847, Letter-books Correspondence, missionary personal files, vols. D-1, 1 to D-1, 4, Correspondence, BEMS Archives.

42. Dieterle to Hoffmann, 19 February 1848, Letter-books Correspondence, missionary personal files, vols. D-1, 1 to D-1, 4, Correspondence, BEMS Archives, Basel, Switzerland. This indicates that five years on since their arrival in Africa the food supply which the Jamaicans helped to create was an important source of sustaining the Mission in Akropong.

missionaries. They demanded more clothing, more food, more allowances, and better conditions. The more they complained, the more Riis and his Basel colleagues became irritated and embarrassed at their inability to satisfy the needs of the Jamaicans. The complaints and requests of the Jamaicans were a source of much aggravation in the Mission and had a negative impact on the progress of the work. Given the racial dynamics of the mission environment in Akropong, it might have been quite easy to determine the real source of the West Indians' displeasure. The fact is that, as emancipated African West Indians from a very robust environment, where struggle for self-determination in colonial Jamaica was normative behaviour for ex-slaves, they would not have been content and compliant with what they perceived as arbitrary and less-than-affirming white European leadership. They were not afraid to voice their complaints about their welfare and make requests for better treatment. As they complained continuously about the terms and conditions of their work, their complaints became the basis on which some of the Basel missionaries, like Widmann and Sebald, assumed that the West Indians had problems adjusting to life in Africa.

As the tensions became more problematic for the Basel leadership, and assuming that adjusting to life in Africa was the source of the problem, Widmann wrote to the Committee in Basel stating what he thought were the difficulties being experienced by the Jamaicans. He noted that "they seem not to take true root, they behave like all emigrants."[43] In his view, they were simply restless like all new emigrants in a new environment. These were, after all, New World Africans transported back to Old World Africa. He dismissed the problem stating that "it does not matter, as long as they form some sort of a nucleus for a Christian congregation and make a contribution to civilization." In other words, as long as they persevered with the task of the Mission, they would somehow adjust to the situation and settle down. But then, in the same report, he added cryptically, "liberation does not predispose them to obedience and order." What the European missionaries seemed to have expected of the Jamaicans was subordination, cooperation, and compliance, not challenge or critique of their leadership.

---

43. Widmann to Hoffmann, Letter-books Correspondence, missionary personal files, vols. D-1, 1 to D-1, 4, 5–6, Correspondence, BEMS Archives, Basel, Switzerland.

George Widmann did notice a difference, however, between the West Indian men and the West Indian women, and he observed that "the men are willing to work, if they can do it their own way, but the uninstructed women are lazy – they have the pride of English ladies, but not their intelligence."[44] What Widmann and the Basel leadership in Akropong did not understand was the nature of the problem against which the Jamaicans were constantly agitating. It was a problem with which, as post-emancipation African Jamaicans, the West Indians were quite familiar and against which they instinctively and relentlessly rebelled. Two situations brought the real problem to light, both of which involved the role of Andreas Riis as leader of the Mission.

The first had to do with steps taken by the Jamaicans to get their complaints addressed. As the tensions between the Basel missionaries and the West Indians increased, and as their sense of collective security was threatened, they took the initiative to write directly to the Committee in Basel. On 13 January 1845, they took the bold step of writing a letter to the Committee in which they complained about the conditions in which they lived for two years. In their letter, they specifically complained about the leadership of Riis, stating that "living with Riis is too bad."[45] They complained that he "always quarrel with us" and that this was not "for the Gospel sake but only worldly affairs." They mentioned his constant murmurings about them and indicated not only their own insecurity about Riis's actions and disposition towards them but also his behaviour towards his European colleagues. They specifically mentioned Riis's treatment of the young German missionary, Hermann Halleur, stating that "how he treats Mr. Halleur it is too bad." Exposing their fears and insecurity, they added, "how he goes on with his own colour . . . we don't know how will do to us," suggesting that if he could behave towards his own fellow white Europeans in such bad and arbitrary ways, they were uncertain as to how he would behave towards them as black West Indian people.

In their letter, the West Indians did not ask for action to be taken against Riis. Instead, they appeared to indicate that his conduct was something they were not prepared to live with. It was in that context that they raised the

---

44. Widmann to Hoffmann, Letter-books Correspondence, missionary personal files, vols. D-1, 1 to D-1, 4, 5–6, Correspondence, BEMS Archives.

45. Letter from West Indians, Letter-books Correspondence, Afrika III (1842–48): vol. D-1, 2, Correspondence, BEMS Archives, Basel, Switzerland.

matter of repatriation, stating that "we wish to return back to Jamaica . . . all the brethren agree together how Mr. Riis goes on with us in Africa." Their expression of a desire to return to Jamaica before the end of the agreed contractual period was certainly, on the basis of their own testimony, a result of the treatment meted out to them by Andreas Riis. It was an expression of disappointment in the Mission, especially the ill-treatment and lack of protection and recourse available to them. While it is arguable that the West Indians found adjusting to life in Africa difficult, the fact that they arrived with families and young children into a situation that was unclear and without basic provisions did not help them to adjust. At that time, the Basel leadership in Akropong was under severe strain as they attempted to acquire resources for the Mission. Riis's mission house in Akropong, which had been so carefully, if controversially, built, had been abandoned during his long absence. The effort required to renovate and rehabilitate it took considerable physical as well as emotional resources; given the need to provide accommodations for the West Indians and their families, as well as food and clothing, this took its toll.[46]

However, the real underlying source of the West Indians' insecurity appeared to have been based on the inadequate and unclear expectations of the contractual arrangement made between the Moravian leadership in Jamaica and the Basel Mission. On the face of it, the terms of the contract appeared both generous and reciprocal. The contract identified conditions for service which would contribute to the advancement of the Mission and achievement of its goals. It provided some space, on both sides, for adjustments and termination of the contract. However, what the contract did not specify was the consequences and recourse, if any, if the Basel missionaries failed to deliver on their agreed obligations. The Jamaicans knew, and appeared to have accepted, that they were being recruited as auxiliaries and that the Mission would be led by the Basel missionaries. What they did not know, and what they did not expect, was the manner in which this leadership was executed. Given the affinities and goodwill which surrounded the inception of the

---

46. Under these circumstances, patience as well as physical resources were in short supply and, in his leadership of the Mission, Andreas Riis became increasingly temperamental, abusive, erratic, and confusing.

partnership, they were taken aback at the way they were treated by the Basel missionaries and their position in the mission. What recourse did they have?

In its response to the letter from the West Indians in Akropong, the Basel Committee believed that conditions in the mission were the result of the leaders being overstretched and that the problem would be alleviated by the addition of more manpower from Europe to assist Riis, Widmann, and Halleur.[47] Early in 1845, three new missionaries – Hans Nicolai Riis, (nephew of Andreas), Ernst Sebald, and Friedrich Schiedt – were commissioned in Basel and sent out to strengthen the Mission in Akropong-Akwapim. Their presence did not, however, bring about the expected abatement in the tensions in the Mission. In addition to the continued failure to receive promised provisions, the West Indians were further surprised and disappointed by the strained relations and constant disagreements among the Basel missionaries themselves.[48] Nonetheless, they continued to agitate for the Basel Missionaries to live up to their side of the contract to provide for the welfare of the West Indians. This attitude on the part of the West Indians only added to Riis's irritation and arbitrary behaviour as Mission leader. The West Indians became, like others in the Mission, the object of Riis's increasingly abusive behaviour. His intemperate and erratic behaviour caused further division among the Basel missionaries, some of whom, like Widmann, concluded that Riis was now out of control.

The second situation was the brutal violence, abuse, and humiliation meted out to one of the West Indian missionaries at Akropong, which highlighted the problem of Andreas Riis's character and leadership of the Mission and led to his ultimate undoing. Sometime before May 1845, Riis had given orders that Jonas Hosford, the young West Indian teenager from Antigua, be publicly flogged by his household African slave, Aschong, because of allegations of theft and of accusations that he had left the Mission compound

---

47. Letter-books Correspondence, 14 May 1845, Afrika III (1842–1848): vol. D-1, 2, Correspondence, BEMS Archives. In May the Committee acknowledged receipt of the letter but did not take any decision to specifically address the West Indians' concerns. See also Miller, *Social Control*, 208, note 23.

48. Miller draws attention to the practice of peer surveillance or "mutual watchfulness" among the Basel missionaries that became integral to their social relationships and created interpersonal estrangements. He argues that "in the field the bitterness this caused sometimes made it impossible for the missionaries to work together productively and caused recurrent injury to the organisation." Miller, *Social Control*, 142.

without permission. The severity and public humiliation of the flogging was only made worse by Riis's participation in it with his boots and fists after the stick broke over Hosford's back.[49] The Basel missionaries, Widmann and Sebald, protested and tried to protect Hosford. On 16 May 1845, Sebald wrote to Basel and complained about Riis's treatment of the West Indians.[50] He described the flogging incident and confirmed that, among other things, the West Indians were being treated unjustly and denied adequate blankets, clothing, furnishings, and tools. On 26 May 1845, Widmann also wrote to Basel, appealing for "real justice to be done to the West Indians" and intimating that he might resign from the Mission if something was not done about Riis.[51] According to Sebald, the incident plunged the Mission into a period of "prolonged depression."[52]

Consequent to this terrible event, young Hosford never seemed to recover his emotional balance and position in the mission. He experienced great difficulty fitting in and later ran away from Akropong, deserting the Mission. Hosford's disappearance was apparently not only a response to the way he was physically treated by the Basel missionaries but also a reaction to the restrictions placed upon the West Indians with regard to contacts with African cultural life. According to Dieterle, Hosford was upset and offended by the restrictions and prohibitions that kept him from watching funerals and pagan performances.[53] Sometime later, Hosford returned and was assigned to work with Friedrich Schiedt in the school at the new mission at Ussu. In 1847, however, he left Africa – after four years – and returned to the West Indies.

The growing sense of insecurity, humiliation, and disappointment on the part of the West Indians heightened the question of repatriation on their part.

---

49. Miller, *Social Control*, 124.

50. Sebald to Hoffmann, Afrika III (1842-1848): vol. D-1, 2, Correspondence, BEMS Archives, Basel, Switzerland.

51. Widmann to Hoffmann, Akropong, May 26, 1845. BEMS archives. Months later, on 7 January 1846, after Riis was recalled to Basel, Widmann again gave his opinion that "the treatment of the West Indians by A. Riis was wrong and harsh. He had an unhappy way to use ironical and sarcastic words and to defame the other missionaries before the West Indians." Widmann to the Basel Committee, Akropong, January 7, 1846, Missionary personal files, Afrika III (1842-1848): vol. D-1, 2, Correspondence, BEMS Archives.

52. Sebald to Hoffmann, Afrika III (1842-1848): vol. D-1, 2, no.13, Correspondence, BEMS Archives.

53. Dieterle to Hoffmann, 17 February 1848, Afrika III (1842-1848): vol. D-1, 2, Correspondence, BEMS Archives.

Their prospects in Africa did not, from the immediate circumstances, look very bright or promising. Once again, they made a written appeal, directly to the Committee in Basel, mentioning the option of repatriation. As expected, the request for repatriation was refused on the grounds that it would violate the terms of the contract, which called for conditional repatriation only after honourable service to the Society for a period of five years.

Meanwhile, Basel received more complaints about Riis and his leadership of the Mission in Akropong, including serious concerns and complaints about his extra-Mission commercial interests.[54] In 1845, in response to increasing pressure from the field, the Basel Committee recalled Riis to Basel for consultations. Riis travelled with his wife, Margarethe, but sadly, she died at sea en route from Western Africa to Basel. In Basel, Riis was asked to respond to charges of contravening mission policy with regard to private ownership of lands and private trading activities by missionary agents of the Society. Riis failed to give satisfactory account to the Committee and was quietly released from the mission in Western Africa and sent back to his homeland in Denmark. He never returned to Western Africa and died in Norway in 1854.[55]

With Andreas Riis gone, George Widmann was appointed leader of the Mission in Akropong. As the new superintendent, Widmann, clearly embarrassed by the Mission's inability to supply the promised material needs of the West Indians under Riis's leadership, also became intemperate in his conduct and often complained to Basel about not having the means to provide for and remunerate the West Indians.[56] However, as new supplies of missionaries arrived from time to time from Basel, every arrival provided new opportunity for fresh leadership and progress in the mission. In February 1847, four new missionaries arrived, all from south Germany: J. C. Dieterle, F. Meischel, J. Stanger, and J. Mohr. Accompanying them was twenty-one-year-old Rosina Binder, who had been selected and sent by the Committee to marry George Widmann, who had earlier submitted a request for a wife to Basel. Rosina's

---

54. It was reported to Basel that Riis had purchased a farm and was involved in private trading in muskets and gunpowder, in contravention of Mission policy.

55. Jenkins, "Andreas Riis," 571.

56. Widmann to Hoffmann, Akropong, 8 January 1846, personal file, Afrika III (1842–1848): vol. D-1, 2, Correspondence, BEMS Archives. "In our loneliness here, the West Indians are our consolation and encouragement. We lack badly cloth linen and shoes for them – not available on the coast."

story highlights the critical yet ambivalent role of women in the early years of the Basel Missionary Society. As the eldest of ten children in a pietistic family of German peasant farmers, she was considered a "well brought-up farmer's daughter and a truly simple-hearted Christian." She had no advanced education but had been trained in an Institute for Girls and seemed quite suitable. Arriving in Akropong on the evening of 20 January 20 1847, she was married the next day. She described the occasion in her diary:

> This was one of the most important days in my life, because it was my wedding day. Admittedly, it was a very quiet wedding. In the morning my dear fiancé was very much occupied. All the people who had carried the loads from Osu had to be paid in goods. All our baggage has been carried from the coast as head-loads. So there were a great many porters. At three o'clock the marriage ceremony took place. Brother Meischel carried it out and took as his text Genesis 14. Our little community and lots of natives were present. A lot of people were standing by the windows. But we felt the Lord was close to us, so it was easier to bear the fact that my loved ones from home were not there.... The gathering, almost entirely of black people made various impressions on me.[57]

Rosina went on to have a remarkable career of nearly thirty years in Africa and had eleven children. In 1876, when George Widmann died in Akropong, she returned to Germany. She died in 1908, at the age of eighty-two.

The addition of new personnel created a new dispensation in the Mission. The West Indians worked alongside the new missionaries, and this proved to be the turning point in the psychological acceptance for some and the beginning of the end for others. One of the casualties of this new phase of the Gold Coast Mission was the celebrated marriage of the African Basler George Peter Thompson and Catherine Elizabeth Mulgrave, a Jamaican. While the Thompsons were in charge of the mission school in Christiansborg, they began a family and had two children in three years. However, George Thompson's emotional and moral balance appeared to have slowly disintegrated as he struggled with a devastating personal identity crisis in the

---

57. Haas, "Nineteenth-Century Basel Mission," 34.

Mission.[58] On the one hand, having been trained in Basel and chosen to be part of the recruitment team to the West Indies, he might have considered himself an insider, a "Basler." However, while engaged in missionary work in Africa, he was excluded from leadership decisions and effectively marginalized by the white "Baslers,"[59] perhaps because he was a black African and also not an ordained minister. Unable to find a meaningful and secure identity in the creolized, cosmopolitan environment of Christiansborg, his personal life fell apart.

Plunged into this identity crisis, Thompson began to violate Mission policy regarding the personal use of alcohol and "fraternization with the natives." When George Thompson's moral lapses, in particular his infidelity, were "discovered" by his fellow missionaries, it was reported to Basel. He was placed under discipline and relieved of all his duties. For her part, Catherine found in Rosina, George Widmann's young wife, a listening ear, and she also received support from the other missionary wives. As her journal reveals, Rosina Widmann also needed a confidant like Catherine to cope with her own personal crisis in the Mission.[60] The missionary wives offered each other important mutual support in the complex world of the mission environment in Western Africa.

After several failed attempts to reconcile the couple, in 1847, when the matter appeared unresolvable, the Basel missionaries in Akropong agreed to permit a divorce. The Thompsons had been married five years at the time. After suffering the embarrassment of marital failure and divorce, George Thompson struggled on in Christiansborg for several years without employment. No Basler wanted to hire him. In a report to Basel (October–December 1851), a missionary named Locher stated that he had employed Thompson, commenting that Thompson had "fallen so low that for a time nobody wanted to give him a job, he was near suicide."[61] Later, while in Christiansborg, Thompson remarried, this time marrying a local African Creole woman.

---

58. Haas, 40.

59. In Miller's study of the Basel Evangelical Missionary Society (now called *Mission-21.org*), he noted that to be a "Basler" was such an important aspiration for the South German missionaries but that very few measured up to it.

60. Haas, "Nineteenth-Century Basel Mission," 30–44.

61. Locher appeared to have taken a keen interest in Thompson's welfare and noted that Thompson was the reason why he had entered the mission. "I tried to contact him and to see him employed personally. He is engaged to an African girl – I will help pay for her."

Catherine also remarried, and the story of her remarriage, her new family, and her role in the Mission (a story to which we shall return later) became one of the more celebrated aspects of the new phase of the Mission in Akropong.

Other West Indian families also felt the effects of the stresses and strains of the conditions in the Mission and tried to come to terms with their situation. The Rochesters and the Mullings became spokespersons for the West Indians and gained the sympathy and respect of some of the newly arrived Baslers like Dieterle. They continued to agitate for adequate remuneration and better conditions or repatriation. Widmann, however, identified them as the "ring leaders" who tested the loyalty of the rest. He wrote to Basel at one point noting that "only the Hall family has yet decided to remain here."[62]

This ongoing agitation in the Mission, which lasted for the better part of three years, was now not only an "irritation" but required external intervention or some effective action by the Basel Committee. Certainly, it required effective leadership from the Baslers in Akropong. By June 1847, the missionaries on the field in Akropong met in Accra and developed a response to the situation. The response came in the form of a new set of conditions for the continued participation of the West Indians in the Mission. The new conditions stipulated the following:

1. The West Indians must give notice of their staying or returning before the 1st of July, [1847]. The decision of each one will be accepted by the missionaries.
2. No passage of a West Indian brother staying in the country after April 16th, 1848 will be paid.
3. Nobody leaving before this date without the consent of the agents of the Mission will have his passage paid.
4. It will not be possible to send all returning families in the same vessel.
5. Those returning will have their house kept in repair and their salaries paid till the day of departure.
6. The mission engages to build new stone houses containing three rooms each for those remaining. If Brethren are employed by the Mission they will receive 15 strings of cowries a day, but

---

62. Widmann to Hoffmann, 12 July 1847, Afrika III (1842–1848): vol. D-1, 2, Correspondence, BEMS Archives.

the Mission is not obliged to employ them and to find work for all. The mission is ready to buy land for those remaining and to present it to them as property.
7. Aged people and invalids will be supported by the Mission. The mission will take care of fatherless or motherless children. The children of those remaining in the country will be allowed to learn any trade suitable on the expenses of the society, so that they can earn their keep afterwards.[63]

As Widmann reported, these new conditions, although ameliorative, did not satisfy the West Indians.[64] Their continuing discontent precipitated a conference of all the Basel missionaries in Akropong to decide on the fate of the West Indians. This conference, proposed by Schiedt – whose opinion of the West Indians was that "many of them are not yet ready to consider this country as their permanent home"[65] – was convened in Akropong in March 1848. The main agenda item was the future of the West Indians. The conference revised the terms of the June proposal and further proposed that "after three months everyone must have made up his mind whether to return or to stay. Those remaining shall get stone houses according to the earlier proposal. They shall be encouraged to plant – not only the usual yams, etc. but also cocoyams, coffee, groundnut, ciyam, pepper, and cotton."[66] The conference also marked a turning point in the attitude of the Basel missionaries to the Jamaicans. Widmann and other Basel missionaries admitted and confessed that they were wrong in their treatment of the West Indians. Widmann recorded his regret and reported to Basel that "in certain cases I did wrong."[67]

The action taken by the Basel missionaries in convening this special meeting and setting down new terms proved effective in bringing about the needed change. Two reasons accounted for this. The first was that the West Indians

---

63. "Stipulations," Danish, Accra, Afrika III (1842–1848): vol. D-1, 2, No. 6, BEMS Archives.
64. Widmann to Hoffmann, 12 July 1847, Afrika III (1842–1848): vol. D-1, 2, Correspondence, BEMS Archives.
65. Schiedt to Hoffmann, Accra, 27 May 1847, Afrika III (1842–1848): vol. D-1, 2, Correspondence, BEMS Archives.
66. Report on Missionaries' Conference, Afrika III (1842–1848): vol. D-1, 2, No. 7, BEMS Archives.
67. Widmann to Hoffmann, 7 March 1848, Afrika III (1842–1848): vol. D-1, 2, Correspondence, BEMS Archives.

were given an ultimatum to which they had to respond. The second reason was the admissions of injustice meted out and wrongs done to the West Indians. The influence of new Basel missionaries who had joined the group in Akropong also injected genuine attempts to make good the situation and respond positively to the call to accommodate the welfare needs of the West Indian agents.

Repatriation and Threat of Repatriation

Although the 1848 conference in Akropong proved effective in bringing about some resolution to the ongoing conflict and agitation on the part of the West Indians, there were those among them who still remained dissatisfied and disaffected. One such person was Edward Walker, who had been singled out as a ringleader by Widmann. Walker was the speechmaker from the New Bethlehem congregation who had given that emotional address – in which he referred to Africa as "our country" – at the farewell gathering in Lititz, St. Elizabeth. Meischel, a Basel missionary in Akropong, believed that Walker thought that the letter following the 1847 meeting in Accra – which had stipulated new terms and conditions of their participation in the mission – was a "bad letter" because it gave them such a short deadline (only one month) in which to decide to remain or repatriate.[68]

In November 1848, Walker, acting on his own, sent a personal letter to Meischel, to whom he had been assigned, asking him to find a replacement for him because he was intending to leave the Mission by January.[69] Walker did not say in his letter that he was leaving the Mission in order to repatriate to Jamaica but merely stated that his reason for leaving was because he wanted "to provide for himself." This was perhaps an indication that he had concluded that his welfare in Africa had been betrayed and that his enforced deprivation was driving him to consider preparing or planning for some form of self-support for himself and his family in Africa. What he was intending to do is not certain, but repatriation to Jamaica was not an expressed desire as

---

68. Meischel to Hoffmann, 20 May 1848. Afrika III (1842–1848): vol. D-1, 2, Correspondence, BEMS Archives. See item no. 1 in the list of terms. Footnote #53.

69. Walker to Meischel, 10 November 1848, Afrika III (1842–1848): vol. D-1, 2, Correspondence, BEMS Archives.

it had been in 1845 under Riis's leadership of the Mission. Walker was taking the initiative to ensure adequate welfare for his family through means of self-help. He was granted the release he requested and left the Mission sometime before the end of the year.

In January, however, Walker wrote to Meischel again, this time begging and pleading to be taken back into the Mission because, as he put it, "hunger is on me and my wife, noting to eat."[70] It was, it appears, harder for him to survive outside the Mission than inside. In his letter, Walker asked pardon for his "sins," but blamed Meischel for driving him away and asked, "Why should you delt with us in this way?" He wrote, "Forgive us our sins we beg you, dear sir and let us come and hear the words of God or God's word, and also that we may return to our place and work." He compared himself to the prodigal son and pleaded: "I will never do the like any more dear sir. . . . I beg you and all the others. Let me get something to eat and not die." Reflecting a state of extreme vulnerability and powerlessness, Walker surrendered himself and wrote, "Till you know what to do with me, whether you will send me home or no, I left all in your hands, but I beg you to remember me to life and not to despair." In evident desperation, he pleaded again, "Since you drove me away, I came to you, but you would not take nor pardon me, but in the name of Jesus I beg you again. If you will never take my word any more I cannot help. I would come to you without write, but I fear you will run me away. I cannot say much to you, dear sir, for my heart and hands weak." He ended his letter, "I am the transgressor."[71]

Perhaps on account of Walker's evident fear of Meischel's response and because Walker had taken the initiative to write, Meischel reconsidered. Walker was made to appear before all the Basel missionaries at Akropong, make public his confession, and sign an agreement. Walker did so, not only making a public confession but also admitting that he had "cost the missionaries many troubles about my going home." Walker also put his confession in writing and signed the agreement. The new agreement he signed required, among other things, that he would "not engage in any other business or

---

70. Walker to Meischel, 21 January 1849, Afrika III (1842–1848): vol. D-1, 2, Correspondence, BEMS Archives.

71. Walker to Meischel, 21 January 1849, Afrika III (1842–1848): vol. D-1, 2, Correspondence, BEMS Archives.

trade or agriculture work for my own purposes which might drain off my attention from the property of the mission, and that I will in every respect strictly follow the directions of Mr. Mohr, [the new Missionary to whom he was assigned] and never leave the Mission premises without his special permission."

The case of Edward Walker is perhaps illustrative of one of the major problems the West Indians faced with regard to their participation in the Basel Mission to the Akwapims. His case was not just an isolated personal problem or a small episode in the struggle of the West Indians in the Mission but reflects the ambiguities and confused state of the West Indians in Africa as missionary agents in a European-originated and European-controlled project. Walker's case demonstrates the nature of the relationship between the West Indians and the Basel missionaries in Akropong. The West Indians were effectively marginalized in the mission, and Walker's humiliating pleas reveal the position of powerlessness and extreme dependence to which they were relegated by the Baslers. When they agreed to participate in the enterprise in Africa, the West Indians would not have expected the negative relational environment in the Mission, nor the kind of treatment meted out to them by the white missionaries whom they trusted. Deepening insecurity, continuing privations and, perhaps above all, effective marginalization would have been enough to cause their discouragement, disappointment, and discontent, and to warrant considering repatriation. Under those circumstances, they could not have been expected to have the freedom of spirit and enterprise necessary to make a meaningful contribution to the project in Africa.

The reality, however, was that the Basel missionaries themselves were also often disappointed and frustrated, embarrassed by their inability to provide the promised housing and clothing for the West Indians. Widmann wrote to Basel, explaining, "we lack badly cloth linen and shoes (for the West Indians) – not available on the coast." On 10 November 1847, he reported how embarrassed he was because "no cloth came from Basel to pay the labourers with."[72] Widmann, Dieterle, and Stanger, in particular, wanted to find ways to encourage the West Indians to stay. They contemplated and put forward a variety of proposals from time to time to improve their situation.

---

72. Widmann to Hoffmann, 6 January 1846, missionary personal files, Afrika III (1842–1848): vol. D-1, 2, Correspondence, BEMS Archives.

As time went on, however, the main concern of the Basel missionaries was that internal squabbles within the Mission were impeding their progress among the Akwapims.

This study has found no evidence to suggest that repatriation by the West Indians was a factor in the slow progress of the Basel Mission in the Gold Coast between 1843 and 1850. In fact, the evidence shows that – despite their discontent and their constant challenge to the Basel missionaries to live up to the contractual agreement to provide for their well-being in Africa – of the twenty-five West Indians (which included sixteen adults and nine children) who arrived in Christiansborg on 17 April 1843, none returned to the West Indies before the contractual period expired; and only James and Catherine Green, Edward and Mary Walker (of Jamaica), and Jonas Hosford (Antigua) returned to the West Indies before 1850. As early as 1844, Catherine Green had written to the Basel Committee seeking permission to go to another country to find medical help for a protracted problem of a sore breast. Although Andreas Riis had provided some medication, it did not result in the healing of her breast. In her letter to Basel, Catherine explained:

> Since coming to this country, I am troubled by a very bad sore breast, and we tried all means we know, but instead of it getting better, it rather getting worse and worse. And besides, this plaster which Mr. Riis gave me, it does not agree with me at all. Therefore, I send to ask you whether it would not be better for me to change to the country to see whether I could get rid of this sore breast. For I do not feel hearty on account of it.[73]

Two of the original party from the West Indies – David Robinson and Mary Rochester – died in Akropong. The majority had stayed on in Akropong. They struggled with the Mission work, raised their families, and, in the end, helped to produce the first generation of Christians in the Gold Coast Mission. The West Indians and their families formed the nucleus of the first mission church in Akropong-Akwapim. By the end of 1850, the congregation at Akropong numbered thirty-one, of which twenty-five were West Indians and six were young native Africans. After 1850, having tasted the first fruits of success, the

---

73. Green to Inspector Hoffmann, 12 December 1844, Afrika III, vol. D- 1, 2, Correspondence, BEMS Archives.

Basel Mission in Akropong began to look towards expansion of the Mission to the neighbouring Twi and Ga peoples.

The Fruits of Success

Between 1850 and 1870, with things a bit more settled, there began a new phase in the Basel Mission's work in Akropong. This new phase in Akropong coincided with a new phase in the leadership of the BEMS, with Joseph Josenhans (1812–1884) being appointed as successor to Inspector Hoffmann. During the time Josenhans led the Society (1850 to 1879),[74] and during this phase – which Noel Smith (1966) refers to as a period of consolidation – the Mission was able to settle down and attend to the primary task for which it had been deployed in Africa. This included beginning in earnest the work of language translation, which was an important aspect of the missionary enterprise and foundational for the transmission of Christianity to Africa. The work of translation had been tentatively begun by Andreas Riis, who had prepared a Twi-English dictionary consisting of 1,200 Twi words. Riis had taken this dictionary with him on his journey to the West Indies, and the West Indians had used it as a textbook for studying the Twi language on their way across the Atlantic to the Gold Coast. Upon his arrival in Akropong, Johannes Zimmermann took on this task and significantly expanded translation work in the Mission.[75] Soon the fruits of success began to emerge. New stations were opened at Kibi, Odumase-Krobo, Anum, and Aida. Eight stations – including Akropong, Christiansborg, Abokoi, and Aburi – were opened during this period. From 1846, attempts had been made to initiate new stations such as the one at Ussu, but disagreements among the missionaries about resources, strategy, and appropriateness of each proposed new site, as well as disaffection by the West Indians, had been major obstacles to any real advance.[76]

From these stations, important mission work was carried out to generate the rise of a truly African church in the hinterlands above the Akwapim

---

74. Jenkins, "Scandal of Continuing Intercultural Blindness," 344.

75. Antwi, "African Factor," 61.

76. Mader to Josenhans, 29 September 1851, Missionary personal files, Afrika III, vol. D-1, 2, Correspondence, BEMS Archives, Basel, Switzerland. (The Basel Evangelical Mission Society is now called *Mission-21.org*.)

mountains. At each of these stations, schools were established to enable the Mission to concentrate on education and the development of literacy, which was an important vehicle to plant Christianity in African soil. Native workers were trained in industrial crafts and skills for trade and commerce. Domestic agricultural food networks were developed, where experiments with cash crops – notably cotton, coffee, and cocoa – proved quite successful. And to produce native leadership for the emerging African church, a school for theological training was established in Akropong. The West Indians were actively engaged in each of these mission activities and made important contributions in these areas. Alexander Worthy Clerk, for instance, was only seventeen years old when he left Jamaica in 1843 with the missionary group. In 1857, he married a local African girl in Akropong and, together, they made an outstanding contribution to the Mission. Clerk was significantly engaged in extending the work of the Mission outside of Akropong. One of his sons, Nicholas Clerk, became the first clerk of the first synod of the church in Akropong.

One of the significant events that took place in the Mission after 1850 was the marriage of Basel missionary Johannes Zimmermann to Catherine Mulgrave – a woman whose contribution to the Basel Mission in Akropong was outstanding. Catherine Mulgrave had a remarkable background. She was born in a coastal town in Western Africa, probably Sao Paolo de Loanda in Angola. As a child, she had apparently been kidnapped by Portuguese or Spanish slave traders and was bound for Cuba in a slave ship when the ship ran aground off the coast of Jamaica (ca. 1833?). The crew and the slave cargo made it safely to the shore of Jamaica and were taken to Kingston. Since this incident took place after the passage of the Emancipation Act, Jamaica was considered British soil and, so, the slaves were set free. Catherine was entrusted to the custody of Lady Mulgrave, wife of the Earl of Mulgrave, Jamaica's governor (1832–1834). She was baptized and given the name Catherine Mulgrave. In 1834, when the Mulgraves were due to return to England, Catherine had to remain in Jamaica because medical doctors deemed her condition "too delicate to withstand the English climate." She was placed in the care of the Moravians, who had established a boarding school for girls in Fairfield, in the parish of Manchester. After completing boarding school, Catherine was sent to the Mico Training College in Kingston to be trained as a teacher. As mentioned earlier, George Thompson, a Liberian, met Catherine when he accompanied Andreas Riis to Jamaica in 1842, as part of the recruiting delegation from the Basel Missionary Society, and married her in that year. So elated was Thompson about his marriage to Catherine that he wrote to Thomas Buxton in England to thank him for what he was doing for the people "of my race" and to introduce his wife Catherine, giving a brief biographical description of her background.[77]

Johannes Zimmermann (1825–1876) joined the Basel Society in 1851 and was sent to the Gold Coast to work in Akropong. As a South German "Basler," his presence and contribution became one of the success stories of the Mission. Zimmermann was a specialist in linguistic translations. As soon as he arrived in Africa he began, in earnest, the pioneering work of translation that led to the development of an African vernacular Christianity in the Gold Coast Mission.[78] On 2 June 1851, Zimmermann shocked the Basel Society with a letter informing the Committee that he had taken in marriage Catherine Mulgrave. He had not requested permission to be married, as the Basel rule governing marriage required. These rules had been introduced in 1837 by Inspector Blumhardt with the approval of the Committee, and every Basel missionary was expected to know and adhere to them, which state, among other things:

> Without firm permission from the Committee, which is to be obtained beforehand, no marriage may take place.... Permission can only be given in cases where the Committee has reliable knowledge of the Christian character and the suitability of the person suggested as a woman missionary.... If a Brother refuses to accept the ruling of the Committee, he is free to resign. However, anyone who marries without permission will be regarded as having been dismissed.[79]

Johannes Zimmermann had merely announced what he had done and presented his action as a *fait accompli*. To justify his bold action, Zimmermann stated that he had married Catherine "to prevent her from becoming a Methodist" since a Methodist missionary was showing too keen an interest in her. However, Zimmermann knew he had the support of his Basler

---

77. Thompson to Buxton, Buxton Papers, Reel #9, Correspondence, USPG Archives, Bodleian Library.

78. "Johannes Zimmermann," in Anderson, *Biographical Dictionary*, 762.

79. Haas, "The Nineteenth-Century Basel Mission and Its Women Missionaries," 17.

colleagues in Akropong. In his report to the Basel Committee, the missionary Stanger commented on Zimmermann's marriage to Catherine and noted that "she is a good woman." He also expressed the feeling that it "is good that Zimmermann is tied a little and will roam less."[80]

With the precedent of Andreas Riis's disregard for the Society's rules before them, Zimmermann's action in matters that required the missionary's best judgement on the field, placed the Committee in a very awkward position. They contemplated all possible options and replied to Zimmermann stating that he was thereby to consider himself permanently stationed in Africa, to which Zimmermann replied that he would be happy to stay all his life in Africa[81] and that he would also encourage other European Christian males to marry African women and, by so doing, ensure that Christianity would take root in African soil.[82]

Catherine and Johannes Zimmermann raised a family of five children. As a trained educator, Catherine became very involved in Johannes's pioneering and groundbreaking work of translation. Despite the Society's unfavourable disposition towards this interracial marriage and their earlier direction to him, Johannes requested home leave in 1872. He took his family with him to Europe in an attempt to rehabilitate his failing health. They travelled to his hometown in Gerlingen, Germany, and spent two years away from the Mission in Africa. Although they returned to Akropong in 1874, within two years, they had to return to Germany again as Johannes's health deteriorated rapidly. On 13 December 1876, shortly after returning to Europe, Johannes died. Catherine remained in Germany for some time but later left the elder children in the Zimmermann home and returned to Africa in 1877. She

---

80. Stanger, Missionary personal files, Afrika III, vol. D-1, 2, BEMS Archives.

81. Zimmermann to the Basel Committee, 2 June 1851, Personal file, Afrika III, vol. D-1, 2, Correspondence, BEMS Archives.

82. The case of Johannes Zimmermann's conduct and career in the Basel Mission in Akropong has been of interest in organizational sociology and culture studies. Miller, *Social Control*, highlights the relationship between religious zeal and organizational control in his study of the Basel Mission and points to the careers of Riis and Zimmermann as examples of the inherent contradictions and complexities involved in organizations such as the BEMS. Young, *Colonial Desire*, on the other hand, discusses theories of racial and cultural hybridity that draw upon European attitudes to Africa such as Zimmermann's in relation to his view of African women and European men.

continued her work as a teacher and died in the Mission at Akropong in 1891, in what Basel said was "an honoured position in the Mission."[83]

Conclusion

The Basel Mission on the Gold Coast of Africa was initiated at the beginning of the nineteenth century. However, by the end of the third decade of the century, its survival was in doubt. By mid-century, hopes for survival were revived by the novel idea of employing Christianized Africans in the West Indies. That novel idea became part of the story of the struggle for the survival of the Western missionary enterprise in Africa in the nineteenth century and also the contribution of transplanted Africans of the African diaspora and native Africans in Africa to enable its survival.

This re-examination of the case of the participation of the West Indies in the Gold Coast Mission in the mid-nineteenth century highlights several things. First, it shows the extent to which there was transatlantic support for the idea of employing West Indians as agents of the missionary enterprise in Africa in the mid-nineteenth century. While the idea had its roots and origins in the West Indies and predated the collapse of British West Indies slave society, it also found expression and support in Europe at a time when European missionary interests were on the verge of giving up on Africa owing to the high mortality rate of their agents. At that time, the emerging West Indian church, anticipating the collapse of West Indian slave society, began investigating opportunities to contribute to the spread of "Christianity and civilization" in Africa through their African converts in the West Indies. This transatlantic support, nurtured against the background of the British and American anti-slavery movement, helped to mobilize sponsorship resources for the project, as well as ensuring the required response in terms of finding West Indian recruits. If there were initial misgivings, hesitations, and even doubt – either in Europe or in the West Indies – as to the real likelihood of such a scheme succeeding, the general goodwill and optimism on the part of the Western missionary establishment towards this novel idea provided a

---

83. A photograph of her tombstone is included in Schweizer's *Survivors on the Gold Coast* collection of records of the Basel Mission work in Akropong-Aquapim.

sufficient basis of support and moral encouragement to enable it to proceed with a venture to the African mainland.

Second, re-examination of this case shows the weaknesses and inadequacies of the European leadership of the Gold Coast Mission in Akropong-Akwapim. The first four years of the West Indians' presence in the Mission were largely unproductive. No African convert was made. Not much was achieved. This lack of missionary success occurred not because of any unsuitability on the part of the West Indians for this type of enterprise. As the evidence indicates, the problem of poor leadership and superintendence by the Basel missionaries contributed greatly to the unproductive environment of the Mission in its first few years. Their inability to mobilize resources and provide the promised basic material security and provisions – such as adequate housing, clothing, stipend, and food – for the West Indian recruits was not only an irritant but a stumbling block that caused the mission to falter and almost fail. In addition, the limitations imposed upon the West Indians, who were mainly enterprising Jamaican ex-slaves, confined them to the Mission community and restricted their contact with native Africans outside the community. This further marginalized them from meaningful participation in the enterprise and placed them in a disempowered position in the Mission. It effectively circumscribed and sanitized their encounter with Africa and rendered impractical the idea of establishing a Christian colony with African West Indians.[84] As the West Indians began acting in their own self-interest, for their own well-being, their agitations served to test and broaden the Basel missionaries' capacity to lead. During the leadership of Andreas Riis (1832–1845) and George Widmann, it became evident that the problem against which the West Indians struggled in the initial phase of this second attempt of the Basel Mission on the Gold Coast was that the Basel Mission leaders did not understand the essential struggle of the West Indians for dignity, respect, and the meaning and expectations they attached to their participation in the project.[85] Their struggle with the Baslers resulted

---

84. This may very well have been part of the reason the black male agents in the Mission such as George Thompson, Jonas Hosford, and Edward Walker suffered apparent crises of identity and personal disorientation.

85. Widmann, for example, showed this in his comment about "liberation." In a Correspondence to Basel, Widmann wrote that "liberation does not predispose them to obedience and order." What he did not understand was that for the West Indians, "liberation"

in policy decisions on the field that benefitted the Mission and increased the leadership capacity of the Basel agents.

Third, a re-examination of the case of West Indian participation highlights the character of the West Indians (mainly Jamaicans) who participated in the Gold Coast Mission in the Akropong mountains. Though some Basel missionaries thought these West Indians unsuited to and maladjusted in Africa, the agitations and threats of repatriation on the part of the West Indians must be carefully assessed. Were these mere expressions of personal pique and maladjustment in Africa or were they indicators of a struggle for dignity, respect, and meaningful participation? Were these agitations manifestations of the self-perceptions of the West Indians with regard to their status, treatment, and position in the Mission or were they symptoms of reactions to racial attitudes and decision-making on the part of the white European missionaries? There is no doubt that it was the intention of the Basel missionaries to set up a Christian colony in Africa and the black West Indians were to be the nucleus of this colony. Their role was to be subalterns, and they were treated as such by the white Basel missionaries. The Baslers, whose social origins were mainly from the small agrarian rural environment of South Germany, had their own similar struggle for power and social status. For them, as for the West Indians, the missionary enterprise – piety notwithstanding – was an opportunity for self-empowerment and social advancement. In the mid-nineteenth century, being a missionary and going overseas to fight the good cause on behalf of European civilization gave a certain nobility, respect, and social status to young, enterprising Europeans. From their testimonies, the newly emancipated West Indians imagined and desired no less for themselves.

And yet, although emotionally disempowered, the Jamaicans in the Akropong Mission were unrelenting in their struggle for dignity and respect. Coming from the environment of the newly emancipated, post-slavery British West Indies, in which sensitivity to power and powerlessness was a very strong and emotive social force, the Jamaican West Indians apparently expected more from their participation in the Christian enterprise in Africa

---

was not a gift. It was the result of a long, painful, and persistent struggle for freedom and the restoration and rebuilding of self-identity and dignity. This was essential to the persona of post-emancipation West Indians. At the very least, participation in the enterprise in Africa to bring "the light of Christianity" was perceived by them as an enhancement of that inner personal drive, not a further denial of it.

than the mere role of subalterns, and they were not inclined to accept acts of indignity towards their personhood. They had come to Africa to make their contribution to a great cause. And, in the late 1840s, the growing sense of being on the margin of Empire – especially after the impact of the Sugar Duties Act of 1846 on the West Indian economy – nurtured an even stronger desire for self-actualization, self-determination, and the realization of patrimony.[86]

Fourth, the contribution of the Jamaican West Indians to the mission shows that, by and large, despite the problems and setbacks they experienced in Akropong, they remained with the Mission and eventually participated in all aspects of its development. The broad range of their participation extended beyond building the infrastructure of the Mission to involvement in its agriculture, education, evangelization, and church-planting ventures. At the critical stage of the Mission's establishment, their contribution – from 1844 onwards – set the framework and foundation for the rise of an African church among the Akwapim and Ga peoples in Western Africa.

The original vision and dream for which Andreas Riis struggled hard in Africa, and subsequently travelled to the West Indies to secure help for, was achieved despite his own personal failings as leader of the Mission. Therefore, the role and contribution of the West Indies from 1843 onwards must be interpreted in the light of what it was – an attempt to find a source of missionary supply for the enterprise in Africa to help establish Christianity beyond the Gold Coast into the hinterlands of sub-Saharan Africa. To the extent that this venture succeeded – in the face of four decades of repeated failure – credit must be given, in part, to this new source – the West Indians – as much as to the new conditions which occurred in the Mission after 1850.

---

86. Curtin, "British Sugar Duties."

CHAPTER 5

The Baptist Mission to the Cameroon (1841–1888)

I could fly to Africa, without being permitted to see England anymore and to live and labour there, and die there when my work below is brought to a close.[1] John Clarke, 3 June 1842.

Of the five missionary initiatives from the West Indies to Western Africa in the mid-nineteenth century, the Baptist Mission to the Cameroon is perhaps the best known. In addition to Groves and Stanley,[2] Gwei, Vassady, Koua, and Briggs[3] have published on various aspects of this mission, while local Cameroonian interest in the subject has been shown by Emmanuel Aloangamo Aka in two articles in the *Cameroon Tribune*.[4] However, the only major study from the perspective of the Jamaican church is by Russell.[5] While

---

1. John Clarke, *African Journal*, vol. 2 (3 June 1842): 744, Box 1: *Journals of West Africa*, BMS Archives, Angus Library. These words of British Baptist missionary John Clarke, recorded in his journal while in Jamaica in 1842, preparing to return to Africa, reflect a passion for mission in Africa similar to that of the white Barbadian Anglican missionary Hamble James Leacock.
2. Groves, *Planting of Christianity*, 23–44, treats the subject significantly, and Stanley, *History of the Baptist Missionary Society*, 106–117, has also given sufficient prominence to it.
3. Gwei, "History of the British Baptist Mission"; Vassady, "Role of the Black West Indian Missionary"; Koua, "Planting of Christianity in Cameroon Town"; and Briggs, *Church in the Cameroons*.
4. Aka, "Joseph Merrick" and "How the Basel Mission was Established."
5. Russell, *Missionary Outreach*. As a Jamaican Baptist churchman and scholar, Russell pioneered significant interest in this subject and this major work was the publication of his 1972 doctoral dissertation at Oxford University.

145

it may be important to outline the contours of the main events and draw upon their significance, this chapter will focus on the nature of the participation of Jamaicans Baptists in this mission in the Cameroon and attempt to examine the meaning and impact, if any, of their participation in what was regarded, at that time, as a Western and European enterprise. How did the Jamaican Baptists come to participate in this enterprise?

Origin and Conception of the Baptist Mission to the Cameroon

The Jamaican Baptist Mission to Western Africa in the mid-nineteenth century originated in the context of two things. First was the attempt by British Baptist missionaries in Jamaica to create a stereotypical black Christian identity for African slaves in Jamaica during the period immediately before the collapse of British West Indian slavery in 1838. As noted in chapter 3, Russell, as well as Catherine Hall, have drawn considerable attention to this aspect of British Baptist missionary work in Jamaica.[6] Second was the Baptist missionaries' response to opportunities to engage in a new enterprise during the post-emancipation period following the dramatic end to African enslavement in the British West Indies. Their eagerness to capitalize on the opportunity for a big venture such as this was made known in England by the Baptist missionaries who worked in Jamaica through the channels of the British Baptist Missionary Society (BMS). On 1 August 1838, a mere five months after euphoric celebrations of "freedom" in the West Indies, the Baptist missionaries in Jamaica expressed their readiness to embark on a mission to Africa, and they did so even without a clear strategy – for there was no clear plan for the reconstruction of the post-slavery society. On 21 January 1839, James Phillippo – on behalf of the Jamaican Baptist missionaries – wrote to Thomas Fowell Buxton, organizer of the Africa Civilisation Society, to inquire how the Jamaican missionaries could assist and participate in the missionary enterprise to Africa. In his letter, Phillippo noted:

> Sensible of its difficulties, after imploring direction from on high and giving to our serious attention, feel ourselves placed under

---

6. Russell, "Emergence of the Christian Black," 16, 51–58, and Hall, *Civilising Subjects*, 84–264.

the most serious obligations to use all our efforts to commence a Mission to the Negro tribes in the interior of Africa, with as little delay as possible. There being no direct communication between this island and Africa and few sources of information respecting that country being opened to us, we are at a loss to fix upon any plan to carry our desires into effect and are therefore anxious that the Committee should give it all the considerations it demands and as early as possible communicate these sentiments to us.[7]

Although the idea of a mission to Africa from the West Indies was apparently conceived in Jamaica in the early 1830s, it was only after abolition that several proposals to lead such a mission emerged. One such proposal came from a Thomas Ward, who wrote to Buxton in 1839 offering to lead such a venture.[8] Ward indicated that he had worked for several years in Calcutta, the Mauritius, and Bourbon and had spent more than twelve years in Jamaica as a missionary, and he claimed to have published several papers on the subject of a Christian mission from Jamaica to Central Africa. He stated that he was confident that, in less than three months, he could recruit twenty to twenty-four families in Jamaica to accompany him on such a mission, adding that finding others with more education and training could come later. Buxton received the Correspondence while in Rome, where he was recuperating from illness. He replied to Ward expressing joy at the interest shown in the West Indies but declined to give practical assistance in respect of funding.[9] Buxton did, however, offer Ward a copy of his soon-to-be published treatise *Remedy for Africa*. Ward was probably acting on his own and did not seem to have had the support of other Baptist missionaries in Jamaica. In the end, it was John Clarke (1828–1879) who was chosen by the Baptist missionaries

---

7. Phillippo to Buxton, Buxton Papers, Correspondence, USPG Archives, Bodleian Library.

8. Ward to Buxton, Buxton Papers, Correspondence, USPG Archives. Missionaries in Jamaica and other parts of the West Indies, such as Antigua and Trinidad, also wrote to T. F. Buxton in March, May, and July 1839, communicating the "deep interest" and the readiness among African West Indians in the "evangelisation of their fatherland of Africa." Some even identified by name those who could be recommended for this enterprise. See Thwaites to Buxton, Anderson to Buxton, and Kennedy to Buxton, Correspondence, USPG Archives, Bodleian Library.

9. Buxton to Ward, Buxton Papers, Correspondence, USPG Archives, Bodleian Library.

in Jamaica for the task of leading the Baptist Mission to Africa, perhaps because of his background as a scholar and linguist, as well as his passion for Africa and its evangelization. Clarke's twelve years of outstanding missionary experience in Jamaica, beginning in Port Royal in 1828, would also have weighed heavily in his favour.

Clarke devised a plan involving three elements for the Baptist Mission to Africa. The first element was a reconnaissance mission to Western Africa, both to assess the possibilities for a mission from the West Indies and to scout for a suitable site on which to locate such a mission. For this, he sought and was given the blessings and support of the Baptist Missionary Society in London. Based on these findings, the second element of the plan – procuring resources and logistics such as transportation, finance, and key personnel to launch the mission from the West Indies to Western Africa – could be put in place. The third element of the plan was the careful recruitment and selection of agents in the West Indies and their effective deployment and management in Africa.

The Reconnaissance Mission

The mandate for the reconnaissance mission was worked out by the Jamaican Baptist missionaries in Jamaica and the BMS in London in 1840. They agreed that a deputation comprising John Clarke and George Prince – a medical doctor, who also worked as a BMS agent in Jamaica – should proceed to the regions of Western Africa with a view to establishing a Baptist mission in that area. Their brief, as Clarke noted, was "to examine the island of Fernando Po, the adjoining continent and banks of the Niger, if practicable, as high as to Egga, Babba, and Boussa."[10] It was clear, from this mandate, that although they were to "examine the island of Fernando Po," Fernando Po was not their intended destination and that they were to move into the Niger Delta as high upstream as possible.

It is worth noting that the BMS in London was initially reluctant to support the Jamaican proposal. Although they admired the missionaries' success in Jamaica and their enthusiasm for Africa, the BMS was apprehensive,

---

10. Clarke, *Journal of West Africa*, vol. 1, 12 October 1840, Box 1: *Journals of West Africa*, BMS Archives. There are two versions of this document. In the original manuscript, the date is 12 October 12 1840, and in a transcript version the date is stated as 13 October 1840. Both versions are in the same file collection.

both because of the Society's previous failures in Africa and because of the significant financial obligations of such a venture – which would make demands on the Society's limited resources and have implications on its existing commitments.[11] Clarke and some senior leaders of the Baptist Mission in Jamaica – including William Knibb, James Phillippo, and John Hinton – attended the 1840 World Anti-slavery Convention in London and seized the opportunity to advocate and secure support for the idea of an early mission to Africa from the West Indian church. They promoted the idea as being "the overwhelming desire" of the Christianized African Baptists in Jamaica,[12] and Knibb's rhetoric ignited British interest. At Buxton's request, Knibb met with him to clarify the West Indian plan and consider to what extent it agreed with or varied from Buxton's own grand plan for the Niger Expedition to be launched in 1841.[13] The Baptist missionaries' successful track record among the African slaves in Jamaica – which had been well publicized in Britain – and the enthusiastic rhetoric of the missionaries in Britain proved persuasive enough to spur the BMS into active partnership in the proposed venture.[14]

The first phase of the reconnaissance mission commenced with a farewell service at Park Street Chapel in London, attended by Knibb and Hinton from Jamaica and Angus and Cox from the BMS. Following the blessing received, Clarke and Prince departed from London and set out for Africa. They travelled in the *Golden Spring*, a coal-carrying vessel belonging to the West African Company. During their ten-week journey, Clarke used the time to read Jamieson's *The Niger Expedition*, work on his linguistic studies in

---

11. Underhill (1895), the BMS Secretary, noted the level of reluctance the Jamaican missionaries had to overcome. See also Groves, *Planting of Christianity*, 28–29, and Stanley, *History of the Baptist Missionary Society*, 106–107.

12. Knibb, for example, gave rousing speeches to Baptist audiences in several parts of Britain; during one of these speeches, he pledged £1,000 from his church in Kettering, Jamaica, for the project.

13. Buxton to Knibb, Buxton's Papers, Correspondence, USPG Archives. Interestingly, the meeting between Buxton and Knibb took place at the Brewery.

14. Part of the rhetoric used to promote the mission to Africa was the use of the biblical text "Princes shall come out of Egypt; Ethiopia shall soon stretch out her hands unto God" (Ps 68:31 KJV). This verse was interpreted in eschatological terms to mean that the historic moment had come when Africa's condition was beckoning for Christian mission to bring the gospel to that land. This text was widely used, not only by Jamaican Baptist leaders like William Knibb and John Clarke but also by Jacob Zorn, the Moravian superintendent, Bishop Thomas Parry, the Anglican bishop of Barbados, and Richard Rawle, principal of Codrington College in Barbados, in promoting their mission to Africa.

Hausa and Arabic, and write specimen African numerals from books and notes which he had recorded from Africans he met in Jamaica.[15] Arriving in Western Africa on 1 January 1841, at Clarence Bay on the island of Fernando Po, opposite the Cameroon, the two BMS scouts spent fourteen months exploring the Cameroon mainland and Calabar in Nigeria. Given the mandate they had received, it is surprising that Clarke and Prince established their base at Fernando Po. However, perhaps their decision was based on the reception they received at Fernando Po and the opportunity to build the mission on the Cameroon estuary from Clarence Bay. Clarke and Prince established their base at Clarence Bay in Fernando Po and established a church there with about 200–300 members.[16]

During this reconnaissance mission, Clarke and Prince sent back reports to Jamaica, and Knibb published these reports periodically in his publication *The Baptist Herald*, which referred to itself as the "Friend of Africa." These reports gave updates about the progress of the mission and generated further interest in the real prospect of a Jamaican mission to the western coast of Africa. In March 1841, Clarke reported:

> It appears to us to be no longer a doubtful question whether Africa be open to the preaching of the gospel. We think we have already had enough to convince us that the set time to favour her has come, and that the Baptist Missionary Society may, without fear, send forth its agents in large numbers as its resources will admit.[17]

With their initial mission accomplished, Clarke and Prince set sail for England on 3 February 1842 in a barque named *Mary*. Although their plan was to report first to the BMS in London, their ship was blown off course by a storm at sea and they landed, instead, in the West Indies, in Demerara (British Guyana), on 11 April 1842. From there, Clarke wrote letters to his missionary colleagues in Jamaica – William Knibb and his pastoral successor

---

15. Clarke, *Journal of a Mission to Africa*, vol. 1 (2 November 1840): 32, Box 1: *Journals of West Africa*, BMS Archives, Angus Library.

16. Groves, *Planting of Christianity*, 29–30.

17. "Letter from the Rev. John Clarke, 3 March 1841," *BHFA*, Wednesday, 3 November 1841, BMS Archives.

in Jericho, Richard Merrick.[18] On 27 May, they landed in Jamaica and, as a matter of historical irony, were able to report first to the Jamaican church rather than to the BMS in London.[19]

Resourcing the Mission

The second aspect of the Clarke-led plan was to find resources and logistical support for a Jamaican Baptist mission to the western coast of Africa. During their fortuitous stop in Jamaica in 1842, Clarke and Prince had begun the business of identifying and procuring resources for the proposed mission to Africa. Acting on the assumption that there was a feeling of unity and shared enthusiasm among the Jamaican Baptists about proceeding with the proposed plan, they travelled across the island to various Baptist communities, giving first-hand reports of the reconnaissance mission and attempting to galvanize support for what seemed to be a real prospect of a Baptist mission in Africa, led from the West Indies. On 8 June, for example, at a meeting of the Western Union at Knibb's station at Kettering in Trelawny, they received pledges of a boat, a sloop, a printing press, and a chapel for the proposed mission.[20] Moving west to Montego Bay, on 12 June, Clarke preached to 3,000 people at Thomas Burchell's station, using as his text Psalm 67:1–2: "God be merciful unto us and bless us; and cause his face to shine upon us; That thy way may be known upon earth, thy saving health among all nations" (KJV). On 1 July, a crowd of 2,000 gathered in St. Ann's Bay, and by 12 July, Clarke was in Kingston at the East Queen Street Church. There, £100 was raised by Baptist women through a bazaar and £10 raised by children of the mission school.[21] In these exciting circumstances, local chapters of the Jamaica Baptist Missionary Societies (JMBS) were formed in major town centres. No doubt, these events emboldened the belief that ample supplies of equipment,

---

18. Extract of a letter from the Rev. John Clarke to the Rev. Richard Merrick, George Town, Demerara, 12 April 1842, *BHFA* (1842): 154; Letter from the Rev. John Clarke to the Rev. William Knibb, Demerara, 13 April 1842, *BHFA* (1842): 142; BMS Archives. Angus Library.

19. Clarke, *African Journal*, vol. 2 (27 May 1842): 740, Box 1: *Journals of West Africa*, BMS Archives. Their arrival in Jamaica was also reported in the *BHFA* (Wednesday, 1 June 1842): 168, BMS Archives, Angus Library.

20. Clarke, *African Journal*, vol. 2 (8 June 1842): 745, Box 1: *Journals of West Africa*, BMS Archives.

21. Clarke, *African Journal*, vol. 2 (8 June 1842): 761, Box 1: *Journals of West Africa*, BMS Archives.

manpower, and money could be found in Jamaica to support a mission from the Jamaican church to Africa.

In their promotional campaign, in addition to mobilizing practical and logistical resources to enable the implementation of the mission to Africa, Clarke and Prince also tried to recruit some Jamaican Baptist agents for the next phase of the mission plan. They recruited two Jamaicans – Joseph Merrick and Alexander Fuller – to accompany them as vanguards of the Jamaica Baptist Mission to Africa. Joseph Merrick, a twenty-seven-year-old Creole mulatto, was the son of Richard Merrick, who had been among the first native Jamaicans to be placed in a position of pastoral charge of a Baptist congregation. Merrick and his family were members of the Baptist church at Port Royal and Kingston and had later moved to Spanish Town, the administrative capital and centre of governance of the British colony of Jamaica. Having shown great promise in the field of journalism, Merrick had been employed by the local paper, *The Watchman*, before Clarke took him under his scholastic wing and taught him Greek and Latin. After being baptized in 1837 by Clarke's cousin – John Clarke of Brown's Town – he had been introduced to church work and assigned responsibility for emerging churches in the Jericho-Mt. Herman circuit of Baptist churches in the parish of St. Catherine.[22] Young Merrick became a protégé of John Clarke – the leader of the mission to Africa – and, from his close association with Clarke as a fellow missionary, he also developed a keen interest in languages.

Fuller, an African Jamaican, was also an inhabitant of Spanish Town. He and his family were members of James Phillippo's congregation in Spanish Town. He was a skilled labourer, with considerable talents in building construction, carpentry, and mechanics, and specialized in cabinetmaking and joinery. Fuller also demonstrated strong character and piety. Both men were to play important roles in laying the foundation for the Baptist church in the Cameroon. By September 1842, Clarke and Prince were on their way once again to England to report to the BMS, and they took with them three Jamaicans – Joseph Merrick and his wife, and Alexander Fuller.

After reporting to the BMS in England and making logistical arrangements for the transportation of a missionary group from Jamaica to Western

---

22. John Clarke, *Memoirs of Richard Merrick and Joseph Merrick*. London: 1850, BMS Archives. Angus Library.

Africa, Clarke split the advance mission party into two. He himself travelled back to Jamaica on a chartered vessel, the *Chillimark*, to collect a contingent of Jamaicans and transport them to Africa, accompanied by Alfred Saker (1844-1876), a newly appointed BMS agent in London. Saker and his wife, Helen, and their daughter became a very important part of this Jamaica-BMS initiative to the Cameroon. Although Saker proved quite contentious and controversial, he was later regarded by the British as the hero of the mission.[23] Meanwhile, Prince and Merrick, their wives, and Alexander Fuller were sent on ahead to proceed to Africa to the place that had been earmarked for the Mission at Clarence Bay in Fernando Po.

Clarke, accompanied by a temperamental and quite recalcitrant Alfred Saker, arrived in Jamaica in September 1843. They spent six to eight weeks interviewing and processing prospective agents from among the Baptist churches throughout the island. At the end of this recruitment drive, thirty-eight Jamaicans were selected, although Clarke had – perhaps unrealistically – hoped for more.[24] In reality, the much publicized idea of a missionary contribution from the Jamaican church to Africa – involving Christianized Africans from Jamaica – had not been as enthusiastically embraced by everyone as the Baptist missionaries in Jamaica had hoped. Many of the newly freed African slaves, although strongly Christianized – were reluctant to return to Africa because of a strongly held fear of possible recapture and enslavement. On the other hand, some who volunteered to go were rejected. For example, during the recruitment process, Clarke noted, "On this day, I examined an applicant and although he appears now as one of the best of men, he after his baptism was guilty of flagrant sin and though he immediately confessed his sins and had truly repented, yet such a person could not be accepted for the Africa Mission without giving a precedent for a practice which would injure if not ruin the Africa Mission."[25] In addition, the black population in Jamaica were greatly disturbed by rumours circulating across the island, suggesting that the ship Clarke had hired for the journey was too small and, therefore,

---

23. Underhill, *Alfred Saker*.

24. Clark, *African Journal*, vol. 1-2, 12 October 1840-June 1842, Box 1, *Journals of West Africa*, BMS Archives.

25. Clarke, *African Journal*, vol. 1 (11 June 1842): 746-747, Box 1: *Journals of West Africa*, BMS Archives.

both inadequate and unsafe for a transatlantic journey from Jamaica to Africa with such a large number of people.

Three categories of Jamaican agents were recruited, selected on the basis of both practical skills and Christian character. The first category were teachers, who were expected to play an important part in the establishment of mission schools. In keeping with the strategic vision of the Western missionary enterprise at the time, the preferred strategy for mission engagement was through schooling native children. Clarke had assessed the requests and reported receiving requests for establishment of schools as a missionary contribution to Africa by European missionaries. Clarke, in one report from King Bell's Town in 1841, said, "The people here rejoice to hear the word; and they say they want Teachers among them." He was convinced that "they ought to have Teachers from Jamaica immediately."[26] The second category of recruits were skilled tradesmen, bricklayers, carpenters, and agricultural workers who would be required to help build the physical infrastructure of the mission. Clarke and Prince had decided that, as a cost-saving measure, in-house personnel were preferred. They knew that local manpower was available, but this was at a price that the Mission, with its slender resources, could ill afford. A third category was Christian families, who were needed to help form the nucleus of a black Christian settler community in which young black families would be raised as role models of the virtues of Christian family life. This was expected to be one of the key components of the Baptist strategy for Christian witness in Africa.

In addition to these employable skills, which formed the basis on which the Jamaicans were selected, the recruits were also expected to possess another set of qualifications. As publicized in an editorial of the *Baptist Herald and Friend of Africa*, the additional qualifications included first, "ardent piety of a decided and elevated character," second, "sound religious knowledge and aptitude to teach," and third, "humility, patience, and zeal and willingness to endure privation and suffering for Christ's sake."[27] While emphasizing that "the great duty of the missionary" is to "preach the Gospel," the editorial also pointed out that candidates for the Africa mission should understand what

---

26. Letter from the Rev. J. Clarke to the Rev. J. Merrick, King Bell's Town, Feb 6, 1841, *BHFA* Wednesday June 23, 1841, 184, BMS Archives, Angus Library.

27. Editorial, *BHFA*, September 6, 1842, 271–272, BMS Archives, Angus Library.

was expected of them as agents of the Christian missionary enterprise. Among these expectations was readiness to "encounter hardship, reproach, and suffering both mental and bodily, and should he be placed in circumstances to require it, to provide the necessities of life by the labour of his own hands."[28]

In Clarke's recruitment strategy there was an indication of the mission structure he intended to establish in Africa and the way in which the Jamaicans were to be deployed. In this recruitment process, Clarke not only outlined the types of qualifications of those to be recruited, he also sought the assistance of his missionary colleague at the various stations located throughout Jamaica to ensure that the right individuals were identified and recommended. For example, in a letter to William Knibb, Clarke requested that the Baptist missionaries engage the Africans in their congregation with a view to learning in "what part of Africa they or their forebears originated, the tongues they speak, the customs with reference to war, worship of idols, Islam, cultivation, and such like questions." He requested that they take the trouble to procure "as full a vocabulary as possible, nouns, adjectives, pronouns, verbs, etc." and forward this information to him.[29] His vision and strategy for the missionary recruitment process was to ensure, as far as possible, that those with appropriate local language and culture interests were selected and that their interests and aptitudes were used as vehicles for conversion and transmission of the missionary message in Africa.

At the end of the recruitment drive, thirty-eight Jamaicans were selected. Together with the four who had travelled to Jamaica on board the *Chilimark*, this made a party of forty-two. On 30 November 1843, this group was given an emotional farewell at the Falmouth harbour in the north-western section of Jamaica and sent on their historic journey to Africa.[30] Thus commenced the project to launch the Jamaican Baptist Mission in Africa.

---

28. Editorial, *BHFA*, September 6, 1842, 271–272.

29. Letter of the Rev. John Clarke to the Rev. William Knibb, New Providence, August 12, 1842, *BHFA* Wednesday, September 14, 1842, BMS Archives, Angus Library.

30. The *BHFA* (Wednesday, 6 December 1843): 4, BMS Archives, noted that "they go amidst the rejoicing of angels, the deepest sympathies of their brethren, the united prayers of the church."

Deploying the Mission

The third component of Clarke's plan was the deployment and management of the Jamaican Baptists in the enterprise in Africa. This missionary initiative lasted over four decades – from their arrival in Africa on 16 February 1844 until the departure of the last agent in 1888 – and may be divided into four phases. The first phase (1844–1846) was the establishment of the Mission foothold in Clarence, on the island of Fernando Po. The second phase (1846–1858) involved the relocation of the Mission from the island to the mainland and the struggle to establish it there. The third phase (1858–1876) involved the development of the Mission as a mission to the Isubus and the Dualas and the attempts at expansion into the upper reaches of the Cameroon. The fourth phase (1876–1888) was the final struggle for maintenance and survival, which concluded with the eventual demise of the Mission.

The task of deployment and management proved to be the most difficult aspect of the Baptist Mission to the Cameroon. For one thing, the island of Fernando Po, which was used as its first base of landing, was a small naval base on the west coast of Africa, lying twenty-five miles off the coast of the Cameroon, not far from the Niger Delta. This island was approximately forty-two miles long and nineteen miles wide. It had been intermittently occupied by Portugal and Spain from the sixteenth century onwards and abandoned by Spain in 1782 on account of its inhospitable climatic conditions, and its tendency for severe cases of malarial infestation.[31] In the early nineteenth century, when the British government tried to impose its anti-slave trade campaign in the Atlantic, they leased the island from Spain (1827–1834) and used it as a naval base to block and interdict those still engaged in the slave trade. During that period, the island was administered by Lieutenant Colonel Nicholls, who served as colonial governor.[32] The island possessed many natural resources, including an abundance of palm oil and timber that was suitable for shipbuilding. As a result, Fernando Po became a well-known stopping point for vessels travelling to the Niger Delta. In the 1840s, the island became a centre for the rehabilitation of recaptured slaves. Although T. F. Buxton had offered to buy the island on behalf of the Africa Civilisation

---

31. Groves, *Planting of Christianity*, 31, footnote 2; Le Vine, *Cameroon Federal Republic*, 2–4.

32. Groves, 29.

Society, Spain refused to sell it. Fernando Po had developed a polyglot population of Africans, Europeans, Americans, and Asians,[33] but its environment and climatic conditions were notoriously unhealthy.[34]

It was in this environment that Clarke decided to set up the first Baptist mission base. From there, he had hoped to eventually launch the enterprise to the African mainland. But Clarke's predetermined plans for the deployment and management of the Jamaicans had to be changed when, on arrival at Fernando Po, a set of internal and external problems combined to force him and his agents into a defensive and reactive mode. In a way, the conditions and experiences of the eleven-week transatlantic voyage from Jamaica to Western Africa both contributed to and symbolized the trials and ordeals the missionary group would encounter in their missionary venture in Africa. This reverse transatlantic journey "back to Africa" might have evoked forebodings of the infamous "Middle Passage" of the slave trade from Africa to the West Indies, even though the motives and purpose of this return voyage were quite different from the first and the conditions slightly more ameliorative. For example, space on the *Chilimark* was extremely cramped. Food and water were rationed and when available, poor. Several of the Jamaicans became ill, especially the women and children. Clarke noted that "the smallness of the vessel, 179 tons, causes her to have a great rolling motion, and with two boats upon the deck, there has been very little room for so many to move about and the Captain does not allow many of the people to come up on the roof." He added, "storms and calms and rain were generally severe trials as crossness and swearing and insulting conduct, often accompanied these natural visitations." As far as the food on board was concerned, Clarke noted that "the brown biscuits given to the people are such that the hogs will scarcely eat. They are very old – water has got to some of them. They are yellow and blue with mould on some parts and worms are in nearly all of them. There

---

33. Buxton to Ward, Rome, December 27, 1839, Buxton Papers, Correspondence, USPG Archives.

34. Stanley, *History of the Baptist Missionary Society*, 108, cited the *Times* description of Fernando Po in 1848 as "the most pestiferous land which the universe is known to contain." See also Curtin, *Image of Africa*, 343–344.

are plenty of white biscuits on board. The water is sometimes red with rust from the tanks and sometimes clear and good."[35]

When they landed in Africa, Clarke overflowed with thanksgiving to God for "not commissioning death to cut any of us down" on the way. The cramped and hostile conditions of the vessel he had hired to transport the Jamaicans across the Atlantic had severely tested the commitment and fortitude of this missionary group. On 19 January, shortly after leaving Jamaica, fire broke out in the vessel. A Jamaican named Gallimore saw the fire and shouted for water. Phillips, Duckett, and Fuller ran to the spot and extinguished the blaze with water, cloth, and their bare hands. Clarke believed that "had the fire prevailed the Captain and seamen would have taken the long boats and in both boats and on some sort of raft we might in a few days perhaps have reached Antonia from which we were more than 150 miles. More probably most of would have died miserably in the fire or in the water."[36] For the young J. J. Fuller – the eldest son of Alexander Fuller, who was already in Africa with Merrick – the traumatic experience probably aided his conversion to the Christian faith.[37] According to Fuller, to their precarious and unnerving journey was added the sour note of having "a wicked Captain and crew," who made their sufferings "very great." He noted that the Captain and crew "swore at us on every side" and badly managed the food supply with the result that most of it rotted.[38] By the time they landed in Africa the missionary group was not just relieved but dispirited, and some of them might even have lost the desire to take on the daunting enterprise before them.

Joseph Merrick and a group of local residents were on hand to welcome the group when they landed in Clarence Bay on Friday, 16 February 1844. Joseph Wilson, one of the local residents, reportedly expressed joy at the arrival of the Jamaicans with these words: "Mr. Clarke used to tell us how the people in Jamaica felt for us; how they subscribed money to send us the Gospel; but now we see with our own eyes that the Jamaicans friends love us . . . look at the houses which they brought with them. I am so glad they do

---

35. Clarke, *African Journal*, vol. 3 (August 1843–1844): 123, Box 2: *Journals of West Africa*, BMS Archives.

36. Clarke, *African Journal*, vol. 1 (August 1843–November 1844): 123, Box 2: *Journals of West Africa*, BMS Archives.

37. Fuller, MS *Autobiography*, 17–18, BMS Archives, Angus Library.

38. Fuller, 18, BMS Archives, Angus Library.

this, for we shall soon be able to put up one here and another there, among the poor Bubies."[39] Despite the welcome they received, the Jamaicans were immediately confronted with three shocking realities that shattered their expectations. First, there was the shock of discovering that there was no prepared accommodation for them and their families. John Clarke himself was concerned and noted:

> All was going on quietly, though fears were entertained respecting the intentions of Capt. Becroft towards us. Two large houses I had counted on had been taken down, one to be rebuilt for Br. Merrick, the other had been sold to Mr. Lynslager, by the Agent of the West African Company. This cast a damper on my mind for some time until I could tell where my friends were to be sheltered when they reached the shore.[40]

The second shock was a chilling reminder of the continued dangers and ongoing struggle over the issue of slavery and the trade in African slaves. Within two days of their arrival, a slave ship was captured in the Cameroon Bay and brought to Clarence Bay. In a letter to William Knibb in Jamaica, Joseph Merrick reported that an inquirer at the Clarence church, who had assisted in the capture of the ship, was killed and brought to Clarence for burial. The BMS missionary Thomas Sturgeon performed the funeral service.[41] Although, through the agency of Christian mission, their efforts were expected to help eradicate this scourge of slavery and the slave trade, this was certainly a very close encounter with the realities of African slavery.

The third shock was the impact of the climatic conditions in Fernando Po. Despite knowing the ill effects of the Western African climate on Europeans generally, it was presumed that the Jamaicans at least would prove more resistant. In the same letter to Knibb, Merrick also reported that illness was beginning to affect the Jamaicans, as well as their mission leader John Clarke and his wife:

---

39. *BHFA*, 30 July 1844, BMS Archives Angus Library.

40. Clarke, *African Journal*, vol. 3 (Friday, 16 February 1844): 154, Box 2: *Journals of West Africa*, BMS Archives.

41. Merrick to Knibb, Clarence, Fernando Po, 8 March 1844, *BHFA* Tuesday, 30 July 1844, BMS Archives.

You will be concerned to hear, that our friends Mr. and Mrs. Clarke have been very poorly of fever since their arrival. Mr. C. took ill on the 29th but has through mercy been free of fever for the last two days, and will I hope soon be strong again. Brother Clarke became ill on Monday last and has suffered much from vomiting, but is, I trust, in a fair way of recovery. Miss Cooper is also laid down with fever, and is at present very weak. Fuller's sons have been very ill of fever, and the younger one is still poorly: White and his wife are likewise ill, the former of fever, the latter of asthma. Mr. Bundy is poorly of ague and fever; and one of Mr. Norman's daughters has fever. I am however, thankful to be able to say, that the only dangerous case is that of Mr. Fuller's younger boy, and he has, I apprehend, passed the worst stages of his fever, which Dr. Prince thinks is similar to the fever of which so many of the Niger Expedition party died. A few weeks ago I was laid with pain in the bowels, and vomiting, but again, I am now recovered and am through mercy quite well recovered.[42]

While contending with his own illness as well as that of the Jamaicans, Clarke tried to organize the Mission, assigning tasks to the Jamaicans according to their skills and the tasks for which they had been recruited. Despite the poor conditions under which the Mission had been started, and the ill health suffered by most of its staff, their initial activities gave some direction to the work of the Mission. This work included establishing a church in Clarence, two types of schools, an industrial school for boys, and a normal school for boys and girls. In the Clarence church, organizations such as an anti-slavery society and a temperance society were formed to further a community-based social campaign on these two issues.

However, the station soon ran into major internal administrative difficulties. Upon their arrival, due to the lack of available housing in Clarence, most of the Jamaicans had been accommodated in the same house. In describing the housing situation in Clarence at that time, Clarke noted:

---

42. Merrick to Knibb, Clarence, Fernando Po, 8 March 1844, *BHFA* Tuesday, 30 July 1844, 242, BMS Archives.

We (the Clarkes) still occupy a garret-room. Mrs. Merrick has another – Miss Stewart sleeps still in another we use as a dining-room – the fourth is our pantry – below is our school and chapel, the printing office, and my library – below, on the ground floor, are stores and four rooms, two for Mrs. Duckett, and two for Mr. & Mrs. Phillip. I have bought three houses in the town, one for Mr. Fuller, one for Mr. Ennis, and the other for Mr. Duffis. One has been built of the Jamaican-framed wood for Mr. Norman who teaches the school there. Another for Mr. Trusty at Bassualla. A house has been put up at Bassipu, which Mr. Gallimore occupies, and three framed houses are putting up at Bimbia. Mr. Sturgeon has put up a shed for a school and temporary chapel. Mr. Merrick has rebuilt a house here. Dr. Prince is in a small house, and Mr. Saker occupies the Doctor's until it can be repaired. Mr. Sturgeon is still in his former one, and Mr. Ennis has built a small house at Bassikatta.[43]

These temporary, makeshift accommodations were arranged to house the mission group until something more satisfactory could be worked out. Although Alexander Fuller and the Jamaican men erected the six houses brought from Jamaica, the housing situation was still inadequate and unsatisfactory.

Within the first month, internal problems arose among the missionary group that not only distracted them from pursing the real purpose of the Mission but also threatened to derail it. These included deteriorating interpersonal relations among the British missionaries – particularly between Prince and Sturgeon – between the British missionaries and the Fernandians, and also among the Jamaican recruits. These interpersonal relationship problems threatened to undermine any possible progress in the work during this initial phase.[44] Not only was the frequency of illness among the Jamaicans a constant source of worry and anxiety, the necessity of housing the entire party in the same compound caused great difficulties among such a large group. Some of the Jamaicans, particularly those with children, became dissatisfied with their makeshift and inadequate accommodations, and there was a general

---

43. "Letter from John Clarke, 16 September, 1844," *BHFA* (11 March 1845): 78, BMS Archives, Angus Library.

44. Stanley, *History of the Baptist Missionary Society*, 109.

sense of insecurity and uncertainty over the lack of provisions. The apparent lack of effective management of the Mission only added to their disaffection.

As dissatisfaction mounted, there was increasing pressure on John Clarke, as leader. After just two months, following another round of contentions, Clarke noted, "Mrs. Showers (a Fernandian) was very insulting and impudent . . . she treated me with bold contempt and seemed full of rage against Mr. and Mrs. Norman, supposing they had told me of her cruel action. I must get them from under this roof as quickly as I can."[45] A few days later, Clarke had to respond to yet another problem that had to do with housing and interpersonal relationships. As he recorded:

> Mr. & Mrs. Wilson (Fernandians and members of the church at Clarence) have placed before me the painful situation they are in with Brother Saker. Often he will not speak to them and often interferes with servants. For the sake of peace, I must get another house for Br. Saker as soon as possible. Certainly he is a valuable man, but his temper is peculiar and his judgment not always wise.[46]

Clarke noted that he was also building a house for Mr. Norman "to get him a place for his large family."[47]

The problem for John Clarke was not just how to manage the housing issue and the interpersonal squabbles but also how to find other resources such as food and cash to pay the teachers and move the work of the Mission forward. In a letter to the BMS Committee in London, Saker made his own report of the problems of food shortages and the destitution of the missionaries. He reported that there was "no biscuit, no flour, no sugar, no butter, no meat of any kind, except sometimes a fowl, a squirrel, or a piece of good mutton. Yam, our chief dependence, is now getting scarce."[48] In this situation, the Jamaicans began to talk about going back to Jamaica. The first to indicate his desire to return was Bundy, whose state of mind, according to Clarke, was

---

45. Clarke, *African Journal*, vol. 3 (11 April 1844): 212–213, Box 2: *Journals of West Africa*, BMS Archives.

46. Clarke, *African Journal*, vol. 3 (20 April 1844): 218, Box 2: *Journals of West Africa*, BMS Archives, Angus Library.

47. Clarke, *African Journal*, vol. 3 (6 May 1844): 228, Box 2: *Journals of West Africa*, BMS Archives, Angus Library.

48. Underhill, *Alfred Saker*, 24.

"very bad" and who seemed determined to leave "by any opportunity." Bundy managed to drag on for two years but did very little work in the Mission and was a constant source of irritation for Clarke.[49]

To add to these internal problems, there were also external pressures. On 10 June, Captain Becroft, the Spanish agent in Fernando Po, visited Clarke and read to him instructions from Spain that stated that they were not allowed a place to settle on the island. Becroft, however, indicated that he would not enforce those instructions nor forcibly remove the newly arrived group. Clarke, nonetheless, was quite troubled as this had been, perhaps, his greatest fear. Three days later, he described his "painful feelings," noting that he was "low in spirit" and that the anxieties connected with the Mission "threaten to overwhelm me."[50]

Despite these significant internal and external pressures, however, some attempts were made to commence the work of the Mission and make as much progress as possible. By October 1845, things began to settle somewhat. One of the Jamaicans, Gallimore, moved to Bassipu on the mainland to open a station which he had initially visited with Merrick. There they gathered a group of about fifty-six people. Others such as Bundy, Duckett, and Ennis also travelled with Merrick to the mainland to commence their itinerant evangelistic work. Meanwhile, Clarke and Prince consulted with each other on the issues facing the Mission, including what to do with the Jamaican teachers who were, among other things, protesting that the £50 per annum stipend which they were being paid was not enough to take care of themselves and their families. Apart from taking note of the lack of zeal and devotion and the "spirit of jealousy, envy, and pride" among some of the Jamaican teachers, nothing was resolved. Prince seemed anxious to send to America for resources, including material to build more houses, but Clarke was hesitant about the quality and cost of the American material being proposed.

To ease the pressure in the Fernando Po station, Merrick, who had scouted the mainland, decided to move his family to Bimbia at the start of the New Year in 1845. Saker followed in June 1845, to begin his work among the

---

49. After Bundy left the Mission without Clarke's knowledge, on 24 March 1846, Clarke admitted that he should never have been recruited.

50. Clarke, *African Journal*, vol. 3, 13 June 1844, Box 2: *Journals of West Africa*, BMS Archives, Angus Library.

Dualas. Others, such as the Trusty family, settled in Clarence, and their children began to acquire the local dialects to the extent that they "seemed happy in their work."[51] Joseph and Samuel Fuller, the sons of Alexander Fuller, were stationed in the printing house in Bimbia as "compositors" apprenticed to Merrick, helping to produce texts in the Isubu language.

The Challenge of Africa

While attempts were being made to advance the work of the Mission, the problem of illness continued to plague the missionary group. To Clarke, who had stated his wish to "fly to Africa . . . to live and labour there, and die there," Africa now seemed to be "a land of perpetual sickness and death." The Sakers had lost their infant daughter just five months after their arrival in Africa. Almost all the Jamaicans had been ill. The first death among the Jamaicans was old Francis Duffis, who died in Fernando Po on 2 June 1845 at the age of sixty-one.[52] He had been in Africa only a year and four months.

The first ten months in Africa had been most traumatic, not only for the Jamaicans but also for the British missionaries. By the end of 1845, the Baptist Mission in Cameroon had to face more bad news. A consul general from Spain arrived in Clarence to inform them that they could no longer preach, teach, or remain on the island of Fernando Po, except in a private capacity. Clarke, Prince, Sturgeon, and Merrick met with him on 29 December on behalf of the BMS. Although they rejected the Consul General's notice, they were fearful of its consequences. One issue at stake was the question of what would become of the Fernandians who had accepted the Baptist faith and joined the church in Clarence should the Mission be forced to abort its work in Fernando Po. The Baptist missionaries wavered between remaining and defending the civil right of the Fernandians to worship as they wished or removing everything to the mainland, taking with them those Fernandians who wished to accompany them. In the end, it was agreed with the Spanish representative that one missionary would remain, particularly in the interest

---

51. Clarke, *African Journal*, vol. 4, 25 February 1845, Box 2: *Journals of West Africa*, BMS Archives, Angus Library.

52. The Jamaicans who died in Africa were Francis Duffis (1845); Alexander Fuller (1847); Joseph Merrick's son, Richard Merrick (1846); and George Williams (1851), who had married a local Fernandian woman. Joseph Merrick died at sea in 1849.

of continuing the school. When the Mission relocated, Thomas Sturgeon, as pastor of the Clarence church, remained on the island. The year ended, as Clarke noted, with "sore trials for the Mission."[53]

Dissatisfied with conditions, the Jamaicans continued to complain about their welfare and passively resisted following Clarke's instructions. Those who had been recruited as settlers, in particular, appeared to have had expectations of playing a greater and more important role than that assigned to them and, certainly, better conditions and remuneration than were offered by Clarke. Not only was the frequency of illness among the Jamaicans a constant source of worry for Clarke, the strategy of keeping the entire party in the same compound, rather than spreading out into smallholdings, caused him to rethink the deployment plan he had devised. Among other things, keeping the group together under one roof undermined the possibilities of advancing the work.[54]

Clarke concealed his disappointment with the Jamaicans and tried his best to appease them. He made adjustments where he could and tried to reassign individuals like Gallimore to make better use of their talents and abilities. But he, too, began to wonder if perhaps the selection of the Jamaicans had not been "a good one."[55] Gallimore, for example, was singled out as a ringleader among the disgruntled Jamaicans who were constantly agitating for improvement and change, and Clarke appeared to have regretted his selection.

Clarke's leadership was severely tested by the difficulties encountered by the Mission in this initial phase, the most serious being the internal dispute over his leadership and the question of superintendence of the Mission.[56] Apart from the dissatisfied and disgruntled Jamaicans, Clarke also had to contend with the BMS missionaries, in particular, the temperamental Alfred Saker, who tested and challenged Clarke's leadership of the Mission almost on a daily basis. After John Clarke left the Cameroon and returned to Jamaica, he wrote to the BMS about Saker in extremely unflattering terms:

---

53. Clarke, *African Journal*, vol.5, 31 December 1845, Box 2: *Journals of West Africa*, BMS Archives, Angus Library.

54. Stanley, *History of the Baptist Missionary Society*, 109.

55. Clarke, *African Journal*, vol. 3, 19 October 1843, Box 2: *Journals of West Africa*, BMS Archives.

56. J. J. Fuller later described this period as the period of "mismanagement" of the Mission. Fuller, MS *Autobiography*, BMS Archives, Angus Library.

My mind revolts from the work of recalling all the times and occasions in which ill-temper was manifested . . . my judgement of Mr. Saker's want of suitability for the work in which he is engaged remains the same. My fear is that the use of strong drink causes some of those unaccountable manifestations of temper, nasty at one time and sullen at another, to which he is prone.[57]

Anxious to get to the mainland to pursue his missionary career, Saker left the Clarence community after a year on the island. In a sudden and typically irascible manner, he relocated to the mainland in 1845 to create his own station at Ambas Bay in the Cameroon. While this may have helped to relieve some of the tensions in the Mission at Clarence, it created a negative atmosphere in Fernando Po, on account of both the manner in which his departure occurred and the fact that this highlighted the tension between himself and Clarke. In the end, however, Saker's move proved to be a good and strategic one, for himself, as well as for the Mission, as we shall see later.

In 1846, the internal problems of the Mission were compounded when a Spanish squadron led by Don Carlos arrived and reasserted Spanish claim to the island on behalf of the Government of Spain. This new development resulted in the imposition of a set of restrictions on Protestant missionary activities and the curtailment of the freedom British subjects had enjoyed thus far. With missionary activities now officially proscribed, the Mission could no longer operate with the degree of liberty it had anticipated and enjoyed thus far. Accordingly, a final decision had to be taken about the future of the Fernando Po Mission.[58]

Moving to the Mainland

Phase two of the Baptist Mission began with the relocation to the mainland on 3 February 1846. The original vision and goal of the Baptist initiative

---

57. Clarke to Sir Morton Peto, Br. Trestrail, and E. B. Underhill, Savanna la Mar, Jamaica, 13 March 1862, BMS Archives.

58. Sturgeon, who was allowed to continue in Fernando Po to look after what remained of the church and BMS activities there, had a tough time trying to ensure the Mission's survival. However, with the repossession of Fernando Po by Spain, which included the renaming of Clarence Bay as Santa Isabel and the arrival of a Roman Catholic bishop and Spanish priests to enforce Catholicism, by the end of 1845, the future of the BMS Mission in Fernando Po seemed at an end.

had been to engage in mission work on the mainland. The year 1846 had begun with continued pressure on the Mission leadership, with nearly all the Jamaican teachers asking to be sent home. The houses on Fernando Po were being dismantled for transportation to the mainland, and these teachers refused to relocate. When the first load of passengers (thirty-eight in all) and materials left Clarence for Bimbia on 3 February 1846, "to seek refuge from Spanish intolerance" as they claimed, Clarke noted the coincidence and irony of the date – for four years previously, on that very date, he and Prince had left Clarence and set sail for England but, fortuitously, landed instead in the West Indies. He lamented that "Clarence exists no longer and the Spaniards now call the town, Santa Isabel." Several trips had to be made and, according to Joseph Fuller – who, along with the other young men in the Mission – had now begun to throw his weight around, it seemed that "the whole year was spent in removing from Clarence."[59]

Those who relocated to the mainland tried to establish a new base of operations at Bimbia to help advance the work of the Mission; but, once again, major problems arose and the missionaries faced significant personal challenges. Joseph Merrick suffered a severe blow when his son died at Bimbia during that same month of February. Clarke gave a chilling account of the death of Merrick's son at night, describing how Merrick slept until daybreak with the cold, lifeless body.[60] In March, Bundy left the Mission.[61] The rest of the Jamaicans continued to agitate for better conditions and significant changes in their welfare in the Mission. By mid-1846, it was decided that those who wished to return to Jamaica would be allowed to do so. In November 1846, Clarke arranged for Mr. and Mrs. Ennis, Mr. and Mrs. Norman, and the bereaved widow, Mrs. Docket, to return to Jamaica by means of the Scottish Presbyterian vessel, the *Warree*. As 1846 drew to a close, Clarke also contemplated returning to Jamaica for reasons of health as well as to report to the Jamaican churches and, by the end of the year, had decided to return to Jamaica. John Clarke eventually left Africa on 15 May 1847 and arrived in

---

59. Clarke, *African Journal*, vol. 5, 3 February 1846, Box 2: *Journals of West Africa*, BMS Archives, and Fuller, MS *Autobiography*, BMS Archives, Angus Library.

60. Clarke, *Memoirs of Richard Merrick and Joseph Merrick*, BMS Archives; and Clarke, "J. Merrick, Missionary from Jamaica to Cameroon 1843–1849," 13.e.11.

61. Mr. Bundy was the first Jamaican to leave the Mission. He appeared not to have been suited for the work in Africa and perhaps should not have been recruited for it.

Jamaica on 5 July that year. He was never to return to Africa. At that point, and to that extent, it appeared that the project had collapsed and the Mission had failed.

However, the Jamicans who remained in Africa persisted with their mission work. By the mid-1840s, the areas surrounding Mt. Cameroon were populated by Bantu-speaking peoples from the hinterland who had formed themselves into autonomous villages. Bantu migrations to the coastal areas had been occurring from as early as the sixteenth century.[62] The Bantus were divided into two main subgroups, the Dualas and the Isubu, with the Dualas occupying a large area east of Mt. Cameroon. By the nineteenth century, the Dualas had been organized into a centralized state, which was controlled by rival kings, King Bell and King Awka. Duala politics of the nineteenth century revolved around these two kings.[63] The other subgroup, the Isubu, occupied the area west of Mt. Cameroon, which was controlled by King William, a wealthy ruler, who exercised political control over the merchant town of Bimbia. King William, whose mother was of the Bimbia ruling family and whose father was a Duala, exerted enormous influence over the area until his death in 1879. In 1833, William had persuaded the British to recognize him as king over the entire coastal region from Bimbia to Rio del Rey. The security and tenure of the BMS Mission on the mainland now depended upon King William.

King William generously met the Mission's need for land for the establishment of schools, mission houses, and chapels. In negotiating for these resources, the Jamaicans, like Merrick and Fuller, played active roles.[64] The new mission strategy on the mainland involved establishing two separate operating bases. Saker's stations at Ambas Bay, among the Duala, and Merrick's station at Bimbia, among the Isubu, were strategic positions from which the BMS work reached out to the Bantus of the Cameroon. Even though this strategy of separation had been driven by different personal visions, it had

---

62. Alagoa and Elango, "Niger Delta," 725–791.

63. Alagoa and Elango, 725–791.

64. Vassady suggests that King William favoured Merrick and assisted him in his endeavours, for while Merrick was a Jamaican of African descent, "the people of Bimbia did not distinguish him from a white man, probably because he was a very light skinned quadroon and because he came to them as an ordinary missionary like the European missionaries." Vassady, "Role of the Black West Indian Missionary," 84–85.

the advantage of approaching the Mission's task from the two most important directions. Neither base proved easy from an operational standpoint, but both produced important results, which we will examine later.

At Bimbia, Merrick set up a printing press, with J. J. Fuller as his apprentice, and it was as a Bible translator that he made his most valuable contribution to the Mission before his untimely death in 1849. Merrick pursued his work in Scripture translation, translating the Gospel of Matthew into the Isubu dialect in 1846, Genesis in 1847, and selections from John's Gospel in 1848. He also translated extracts from other parts of the Old Testament. He prepared a grammar and comparative dictionary of the Isubu, Baquiri, Monggo, Balung, Duala, and Balimba dialects, as well as schoolbooks, lessons, and a hymnbook in Isubu. He also founded the first Christian church in the Cameroon at Bimbia – with thirty-three members – on land that he had purchased from King William. He named his mission station "Jubilee" and, together with the others who had come over from Clarence, organized the church that he and John Clarke co-pastored. After Clarke's departure, Merrick continued to exercise full pastoral leadership of the church.

However, as in Fernando Po, so also in Bimbia, the climatic conditions were inhospitable and hard on the health, and sickness and death continued to plague the missionary group. Merrick's response was to establish a sanatorium in the mountains so that the missionaries could go there for a "change of air," to recover their health. Merrick encouraged those who needed a change to make use of this facility. When Merrick later died at sea in 1849, on his way to England for medical treatment, young Fuller thought that if only Merrick had made use of this facility himself, perhaps his life would have been spared longer.[65]

Meanwhile, in 1848, Clarke attended the annual meeting of the Baptist Missionary Society (BMS) in Exeter Hall in England and continued to vigorously defend the mission to Africa, even against concerns raised that, thus far, the expenses of the Mission were more than the results justified.[66] In his address before the BMS, Clarke outlined the progress, the difficulties, and

---

65. Fuller, MS *Autobiography*, BMS Archives, Angus Library. Unfinished draft MS.

66. See Clarke's response to the letter from the Committee outlining those concerns. "I can only mourn over this circular," he said. *MH* (May 1847): 76, BMS Archives, Angus Library.

the setbacks of the Mission and pointed out that "only five deaths of adults have taken place in Africa." He argued that

> out of all the numbers who had gone there, there have been but thirteen deaths, including children; and three deaths have occurred among those who returned to Jamaica, and in sickly state reached that land, making only sixteen, out of about eighty missionary teachers, settlers, their wives and children, who have been engaged in some way in this work for Africa.[67]

Three times in his address, Clarke insisted, "We have no cause to be discouraged." He placed before the gathering, the passion that drove him and others to continue supporting the enterprise, declaring, "we have suffered, and are willing to suffer in the service for such a Master, and in such a work of mercy, as that in which we are engaged."

Clarke's views regarding the mission in Africa and the nature of the missionary enterprise itself mirrored the views of Joseph Merrick, who shared his thoughts on the subject in his Correspondence with a British supporter in England. Going even further than Clarke, Merrick compared the sufferings and slow results of the mission in Africa with mission in Biblical times and mission in the history of the church. Reflecting on the subject historically, he wrote:

> Must we be surprised at the lapse of years which often takes place, even under the faithful preaching of the truth, ere the Holy Spirit is poured forth.... Four thousand years elapsed before the first promise was fulfilled; many hundreds before the promise made to Abraham, that his posterity should inherit Canaan; and many thousands will perhaps yet roll on before the promises made to the Messiah will be fully accomplished....
> It is God's usual mode to try long the patience of his people.[68]

Unfortunately, despite such a passionate and optimistic argument, however, the mission in Africa was soon being brought to its lowest ebb. On 22 October 1849, at the age of thirty-one, Joseph Merrick died at sea, en route

---

67. Clarke, *MH* (June 1850): 85–88, BMS Archives, Angus Library.
68. Clarke, *Memoirs of Richard Merrick and Joseph Merrick*, 92; Merrick to H. H. Dobney, 3 August 1848, BMS Archives.

to England for medical treatment. Realizing the potential loss the Mission would suffer by his death, Saker had written an impassioned letter to the BMS Committee in London a few weeks before, describing Merrick's condition as he prepared to leave for England. He pleaded for more manpower to help reinforce the Mission should Merrick not survive:

> The return of our brother Merrick is a deep affliction to us. But I am quite apprehensive that you will not see his face again. His stay of four weeks here, waiting a passage, has been a severe trial to his constitution. He has gradually declined every day, and I almost fear he will be prevented from embarking. His lungs are thought to be diseased; his sleep is broken by a painful cough, his energy is gone; his debility is so great he cannot walk but for a few seconds; he cannot ride. We fear he cannot live many days, but our hope is in God. . . . If he goes hence, who is left? Who will work? Who will pray? . . . Our choice is to send him to you where there is hope, or lay him in the grave, where he will rest from all toil. In such a dilemma we cannot hesitate and yet we grieve.[69]

Merrick's death was a real blow to the struggling Mission. This was noted by the BMS in its public meeting on 25 April 1850; and a Rev. T. F. Newman even stood up and complained that Merrick's loss required more than two or three lines in the annual report. "It should," he argued, "constitute elements of the future history of the Society."[70] But none felt the loss more keenly than J. J. Fuller and John Clarke. Fuller said that Merrick's death "cast a dark shadow over the mission," and Clarke immediately published a two-volume memoir of Merrick and his father, with whom he had worked closely in Jamaica.[71]

---

69. Saker's letter to the BMS Committee in London, *MH* (February 1850): 24, BMS Archives.

70. *MH* (May 1850): 73, BMS Archives.

71. Published in 1850, the book was sold to raise funds for both the Merricks' widows and granddaughter, Rosanne.

Mission in Crisis

In March 1850, Saker and his wife left for England, and Dr. Newbegin became the new leader of the Mission. Newbegin died within a month, leaving the Mission leaderless. In May, following Newbegin's death, Hope Waddell – leader of the Jamaican Presbyterian mission in neighbouring Calabar – went to Clarence Bay and called a meeting of the teachers and assistant missionaries to discuss the future of the Baptist Mission in the Cameroon. Waddell then wrote to the BMS in London expressing his earnest desire for speedy repair to the "desolation which has been made in your mission," for "it cannot long subsist in its present state."[72]

Alfred Saker later returned to Africa and took charge of the Mission and the church in Clarence. He received additional missionary help from England and trained native teachers. But the final blow came on 22 May 1858, when Don Carlos Chacon, Commander of the Spanish Squadron and Governor-General of all the Spanish islands, arrived in Fernando Po. Accompanied by six Jesuit priests, he proclaimed the religion of the island to be Roman Catholic and also proclaimed, upon the orders of the Spanish Crown, that no other religion would be tolerated. The reading of this edict was accompanied by the firing of cannons. On 2 June 1858, Saker relocated the remaining BMS interest in the Clarence church to the mainland, ending this venture that had begun in 1841. The BMS agitated with the Spanish government for compensation claiming damages, loss of property in schools, houses, and chapels and, eventually, received £1,500 as compensation.[73]

The period 1858–1876 represents the third phase of the BMS Mission to Cameroon. While this phase was characterized by struggles to survive in Africa, there were also renewed attempts to establish the Mission and consolidate the mission enterprise. In 1858, Alfred Saker, now Superintendent of the Mission, established the town of Victoria on the mainland. If Bimbia, founded by Merrick, proved to be particularly bad for the health of the missionaries, Saker's move to the south among the Dualas proved much healthier. It was from this base, supported by his native Cameroonian pastor, Horton Johnson, that Saker did his main work in the Cameroon. Johnson was key to the

---

72. Details of the meeting, as well as Waddell's letter to the Society, were published in the *MH* (August 1850): 115, BMS Archives.

73. *MH* (December 1879): 359, BMS Archives.

survival of Bethel Church, the church that Saker had founded in Cameroon Town. Saker and J. J. Fuller worked very closely together, especially when, for one reason or another, European missionaries were absent from the field. Saker's priorities were, as he put it, "first to provide a home for all where freedom to worship God must be the first requirement, then employment, and, if possible, prosperity." He sought to consolidate the Mission on the mainland by closing down the Bimbia station and concentrating his work among the Dualas in Victoria, which he had named after the English queen. As the senior missionary, he directed the Mission from Victoria under very difficult and controversial circumstances, until his final departure from Africa in 1876.[74]

In establishing the town of Victoria, Saker's vision was the creation of a naval port for British trade, with the hope that it would become a leading centre for trade between Britain and the Cameroon.[75] His dream, as Stanley suggests, was inspired by Buxton's vision for the introduction of commerce and Christianity in Western Africa, as well by Livingstone's similar vision in relation to the Zambezi.[76] Although Saker's dream did not materialize in the way that he had hoped, yet the scope of his missionary engagement encompassed a broad vision of social, economic, and political activities to the extent that his work dominated the legacy of the BMS in the Cameroon.[77] Victoria did see a great deal of commercial activity between African traders and Europeans, with the John Holt Trading Company becoming a leading British trading store in Victoria.[78]

---

74. Alexander Innes, a BMS missionary, aborted his career in the Cameroon and returned to England in 1859 to publish a blistering attack on Saker's treatment of the Africans. In 1863, following Innes's public charges against him, the BMS launched a Commission of Inquiry into Saker's running of the Mission, which led to Saker's dismissal.

75. When Saker relocated to the mainland, he proclaimed, "Cameroon is ours, a fine station and an open door to the interior of the land. . . . Bimbia is ours with room enough for a town and large trade. But a port is wanted where there can be British protection, British capital, and laws, a depot for coals for the navy, a safe harbour for our merchant vessels, a free port for the commerce of these rivers, and a refuge for the oppressed slaves." Underhill, *Alfred Saker*, 88.

76. Stanley, *History of the Baptist Missionary Society*, 110.

77. Eugene Stock, in his history of the Church Missionary Society's role in Western Africa in the nineteenth century, concluded that "the old Baptist Mission in the Cameroon was an interesting one, and had one name much honoured, that of Alfred Saker." Stock, *History of the Church Missionary Society*, 53.

78. DeLancey and Mokeba, *Historical Dictionary*, 107. John Holt (1842–1904) succeeded James Lynslager as the British commercial agent in the Cameroon, and his company lasted until the mid-1960s.

During this third phase, other Jamaican agents such as Francis Pinnock and his wife joined the mission in Victoria and served from 1857 to 1879.[79] Another Jamaican family, the Richardsons, also came to Africa and worked in the Mission at Victoria. Highlighting the Richardsons' work, van Slageren notes that they opened an inland mission station in Bakundo and served there from 1879 to 1886.[80] John Diboll and Alexander Innes, BMS missionaries from Britain, also came to work in the Mission at Victoria. The problem of strife among the European missionaries on the field was highlighted by the disastrous relationship between Saker and Innes, which resulted in the dismissal of Innes and a BMS inquiry into Saker's work in Victoria.[81] Despite his temperamental and often belligerent conduct, Saker survived thirty-five years in Cameroon and completed the translation of the entire Bible into the Duala language in 1872. In November 1876, he left Africa a worn-out man and died in London in 1880.

The Final Phase

The fourth and final phase of the BMS Mission to the Cameroon (1876–1888) began with the recall of Alfred Saker to Britain in 1876. Being the subject of two Commissions of Inquiry by the BMS (1863 and 1869) signalled the end of Saker's controversial but outstanding missionary career in Africa. His departure left the Mission facing a long period of struggle for survival before it finally came to an end. Although other BMS missionaries – such as George Grenfell, Thomas Comber, and Thomas Lewis – came to the Cameroon after Saker's departure, the Mission was virtually in the care of the long-serving

---

79. BMS Secretary, Underhill, who went to inquire into the work of Saker in Victoria in 1869, wrote, "Mr. Pinnock's house became our home during our brief stay. We found the colony to consist of some 200 persons, all of who were under the efficient instruction of Mr. Pinnock; either in the day school, which he personally taught, or his Bible class and Sunday school or in the sanctuary." Pinnock, Africa file A/1 BMS Archives. Unfortunately, King Abo confiscated all Pinnock's records and papers at his station in the interior. Not much of his work survived.

80. van Slageren, "Jamaican Missionaries in Cameroon," 152, draws attention to the fact that Paul Steiner noted, in 1926, that the Richardsons were servants of Christ whose humble presence and patience in that "dark place of Africa was a sign of the Kingdom to come and a test and a testimony of the birth of Christ in the darkness of Bethlehem."

81. Stanley, *History of the Baptist Missionary Society*, 110–112.

Jamaican, Joseph Jackson Fuller.[82] Fuller, who had grown up with the Mission from its inception, was ordained to the ministry in 1859 and became a full missionary agent of the BMS.[83] In many ways, he is the forgotten hero of the Jamaican participation in the missionary enterprise in Western Africa in the nineteenth century.[84] This may have been due partly to Fuller's own reticence and deference in the work of the mission. George Grenfell's comment that "no other man could have fought the battles as he has done" and Brian Stanley's observation that "the character who emerges with greatest credit from the difficulties in the Mission is J. J. Fuller" speak not only to the strength of character that Fuller displayed as a career missionary but also to the importance of his contribution to the enterprise.[85] Fuller has sometimes been criticized for being "a victim of excessive respect for white men"[86] and considered naive for assuming that his symbolic burning of collected artefacts of witchcraft in the middle of town could end the African cultural practice of witchcraft. Perhaps Fuller's response to issues such as this reflected the extent to which he supported the values and practices of the Western missionary enterprise. He saw himself as very much a part of this enterprise, even though, on many occasions, he could have acted otherwise, as we have already seen. But if Fuller was naive about this, so too were his colleague missionaries from the metropolitan environment for thinking that they could in fact eradicate the practice of witchcraft with rational Enlightenment Christianity.

In a remarkable career spanning over four decades (officially, 1850–1888), Fuller participated in every aspect of the Mission's work. He founded over five stations and made important contributions to the work of translation into vernacular languages. He suffered as much as anyone in the field. In 1888, when the Mission was compelled to close down, he was the last BMS agent

---

82. In 1878, George Grenfell and Thomas Comber were commissioned by the BMS to explore the Congo as a prospective new mission field. The BMS was on the verge of abandoning the Cameroon for the vast interior of Africa that the Congo River afforded.

83. His public ordination took place at the Victoria church and was conducted by Saker, Diboll, Pinnock, and Innes.

84. For example, although the work of Merrick, Saker, and Clarke are mentioned in DeLancey and Mokeba's *Historical Dictionary of the Republic of Cameroon* and Anderson's *Biographical Dictionary of Christian Missions*, Fuller's work is completely ignored. He receives no mention in either of these works.

85. Stanley, *History of the Baptist Missionary Society*, 114.

86. Ardener, "Kingdom on Mount Cameroon," 272–273.

left in the field and had the painful and difficult task of handing over his and his colleagues' life's work to the German agents of the Basel Evangelical Missionary Society on the instructions of the Baptist Missionary Society in London. Fuller remained on hand to witness the ruthless destruction of what they had laboured to produce over a period of forty years.[87] As Stanley comments, "The society could have wished for no more faithful servant to guide the Cameroon church through the new challenges which confronted it in the 1880s, than J. J. Fuller."[88]

The last decade before the Mission closed was the final round of a difficult struggle for survival. Mission work in the Cameroon had been slow, hard, and incremental. It had exacted a high price in terms of missionary mortality. Several times, the BMS had threatened to close it down, but Fuller had always argued against such a move and pleaded with the Society for the continuation of the Mission. Promised support from the West Indies ebbed and flowed according to prevailing economic conditions in the West Indies. In 1878, George Grenfell and Thomas Comber were commissioned by the BMS to explore the Congo as a new prospective mission field, because the BMS was on the verge of abandoning the Cameroon for the vast interior of Africa that the Congo River afforded. The death of David Livingstone in 1873 in northern Zambia had attracted widespread interest in missionary work in the African interior.[89] In 1884, the rising German leader Bismarck, through his emissary Gustav Nachtigal, had expanded Germany's imperial interest in Africa by annexing the Cameroon. The British government, seeing this as an opportunity to contain the Germans in the Cameroon – by keeping them out of the Niger protectorate – had ignored desperate pleas for British protection by local chiefs and the colony at Victoria and quickly agreed to the German annexation. Accordingly, the British Foreign Office had withdrawn its protection from the colony at Victoria, leaving British subjects, including the missionaries, unprotected and vulnerable.[90]

---

87. Newman, "West Indian Contribution," 220–231.

88. Stanley, *History of the Baptist Missionary Society*, 114.

89. H. M. Stanley's travel up the Congo River in 1877 led to great interest in the Congo region. The "highway into the African interior" had been found.

90. Edward Hewitt, the British consul, arrived one week after the annexation and was faced with a *fait acompli*. Le Vine, *Cameroon Federal Republic*, 4.

The Baptist Mission to the Cameroon (1841–1888)

By 15 December 1885, the BMS had committed itself to withdraw from the Cameroon and were looking for ways to get out without making the Cameroonian church feel that they were being abandoned.[91] As the only missionary left in the field, Fuller tried to provide leadership at yet another perplexing moment for the Cameroonian churches that the mission had planted at various stations. By 1886, however, Alfred Baynes, secretary of the BMS, wrote to Fuller, advising him that the Committee was unlikely to continue the Cameroon Mission "unless there was good prospect of opening up the interior to Christianity." Baynes pointed out that "for nearly forty years we have occupied the Cameroon and yet we have never once reached to any distance in the interior. Our mission today is exactly what it was during the first year of its existence – viz; a purely coast mission."[92]

Meanwhile, the BMS had begun negotiations with the Basel Evangelical Missionary Society for the Cameroon mission stations to be taken over. Eventually, an agreement was reached to sell the Cameroon stations to the BEMS for the sum of £2,000.[93] Fuller was appointed by the BMS to be its agent in handling the delicate matter of preparing the inventory and effecting the transfer of all BMS property in the Cameroon to the BEMS. This he did, with great patience, fortitude, and skill, despite having expressed to the BMS his own disappointment. At the end of his career, Fuller found himself in the very difficult situation of having to defend the BMS against charges of abandonment by the Cameroon church. There were accusations by the Cameroonian churches that the BMS had abandoned them to suffer at the hands of Germans – who had arrogantly imposed unwelcome and unfamiliar confessions upon them – and Fuller bore the brunt of the backlash against the BMS.[94] He was commended by the BMS for acting "wisely and well" in regard to the transfer of the mission and given the option of going to the Congo or

---

91. Stanley, *History of the Baptist Missionary Society*, 116.
92. Baynes to Fuller, Fuller, "MS notes on Cameroon and Fernando Po," BMS Archives.
93. Stanley, *History of the Baptist Missionary Society*, 116.
94. Between January and March 1888, Correspondence between Fuller and Baynes accelerated, with Fuller pleading for information, guidance, and instruction from the BMS. On 19 March 1888, for instance, Fuller wrote to Baynes indicating the sad position he was in and offering to go to Calabar to await further instruction. He made it clear how abusive the Germans were and said, "I cannot write to you all I have suffered nor the shameful way in which I have been treated but when d.v. I see you I can tell you better." Fuller to Baynes, "MS notes on Cameroon and Fernando Po," BMS Archives.

retiring in England with his family. Fuller opted for retirement. He left the Cameroon in 1888 and retired in London, where he died in Stoke Newington on 11 December 1908, at the age of eighty-three.[95] After forty years, the Baptist Mission in the Cameroon had collapsed, and the missionary dream of the Jamaican Baptist Mission to Africa had come to an end. But what of the legacy of this initiative from the West Indies towards the larger goal of planting Christianity in sub-Saharan African soil? The flame of Christian Mission in the Cameroon lit by the Jamaican Baptists from 1842-1880 had given rise to a Cameroonian church.

---

95. *MH* (1909): 55–56, BMS Archives.

CHAPTER 6

The Anglican Mission to the Rio Pongas (1855–1897)

"I will thankfully go to bed in Afric's dust . . ."[1] H. J. Leacock

The participation of the Church of England in the West Indies (the West Indian Anglican Church) in the missionary enterprise in Western Africa in the nineteenth century began after other Protestant denominations in the West Indies had already been engaged in missionary work in Africa for a decade or more. The Anglican Church's mission project represented yet another attempt to mobilize an indigenous mission from the West Indies, this time from a church which had the longest and perhaps the most controversial relationship with the West Indies. Though late from the point of view of West Indian interest in missionary endeavours in Africa, and beset with great difficulties throughout, the project somehow managed to sustain itself for more than eighty years and occupied some attention in the affairs of this West Indian church during the nineteenth century.[2]

---

1. These were the words of Hamble James Leacock, the pioneer West Indian Anglican missionary to Africa, from his speech before the Barbados Mission Society on 16 May 1855. Leacock communicated similar sentiments on the eve of his departure for Africa in a farewell correspondence to the then Archdeacon of the Bahamas, John Trew. Unfortunately, Leacock's passion and determination for mission work in Africa were not widely shared by other Barbadian churchmen, and he was the only candidate to volunteer for the Pongas Mission. Caswall, *The Martyr of the Pongas*, 68.

2. Caldecott, *Church in the West Indies*, 220–224; Barrow, *Fifty Years*; Ellis, *Diocese of Jamaica*, 147–150; Evans, *History of the Diocese of Jamaica*, 109.

That participation of the Anglican Church developed in two ways. First, there was the adventurous mission to the Rio Pongas area on the west coast of Africa, an area some 130–150 miles north of Sierra Leone. This mission emanated from the diocese of Barbados. Despite hopes that this would become a project of the entire Anglican Church in the West Indies, it remained a project of just this diocese. The Rio Pongas Mission, as an initiative from the West Indies, continued until 1935, when it became part of a new African diocese – the diocese of The Gambia and the Rio Pongas. In 1935, John C. S. Daley was appointed and consecrated as the first bishop of this newly created diocese in Western Africa, and his appointment and commissioning represented the culmination of eighty years of mission work pioneered by the West Indian Anglican diocese of Barbados. The new diocese was created to bring episcopal supervision to the scattered Anglican mission posts in The Gambia, French Senegal, and French and Portuguese Guinea. It was Bishop Daley's episcopal tour of the West Indies in 1937 – to thank the West Indian church for its contribution to mission in Africa and to encourage further support for the initiative – that led to the historic creation of this new diocese of The Gambia and the Rio Pongas.[3]

A second phase of the Anglican mission from the West Indies emerged in the late nineteenth century, in the aftermath of the imperial interventions of various European powers in the "Scramble for Africa". France, for example, occupied the Pongas area from the 1860s and forced British interests, including the West Indian mission, to move elsewhere. This second phase – which involved attempts to assist the often stalled but developing efforts of planting Christianity in the upper regions of the Niger Delta – was taken up largely by the diocese of Jamaica.[4]

This mission to the Rio Pongas from the Anglican Church in Barbados raises several fundamental questions, some of which have, in part, been addressed in chapter three. For instance: How was it that this church, which was so closely connected with the colonial structure of West Indian slave society, came to be involved in the enterprise of Christian mission in Africa in the

---

3. *G-PM*, A New Bishopric, (October 1938), USPG Archives.

4. Ellis, *Diocese of Jamaica*, 150; Evans, *History of the Diocese of Jamaica*, 109; Dayfoot, *Shaping of the West Indian Church*, 219.

mid-nineteenth century? What explains their participation in that project and what, if anything, did their participation achieve?

Inventing a Mission

Noel Titus has drawn attention to the circumstances in which the Anglican Mission to the Rio Pongas originated in Barbados in the early 1850s.[5] Outlining the difficulties surrounding the proposition and implementation of the idea, Titus points to the conflicts in the local sponsoring board and the controversies surrounding the competing yet contrasting visions of a rival group, the Barbados Africa Colonization Society, and questions the sincerity of the principal promoters of the mission, Richard Rawle and Thomas Parry.[6] His analysis raises questions about the authenticity of the mission and the motives that underlay the design and implementation of the project. But, notwithstanding the sincerity or otherwise of the promoters of the mission, perhaps the more relevant question is this: What was envisaged by the West Indian Anglican Church leaders, and what conception of the enterprise did they demonstrate in their proposal for the participation of the Anglican Church in the West Indies?

As already noted in chapter 2, the idea of a mission to Africa from the Church of England in the West Indies had been publicly advocated in England as early as 1843 by Rev. John Trew. But it was the combination of circumstances towards the end of the 1840s which provided the opportunity for this idea to come to fruition.[7] Those circumstances included a compelling need to reposition the Anglican Church in the West Indies in a post-emancipation society and to make good use of Codrington College, which, as part of the Codrington Estates, had been bequeathed to the United Societies for the

---

5. Titus, "West Indian Mission to Africa," 93–111.

6. The problems that Titus, "West Indian Mission to Africa," identifies are not unlike those that Russell, *Missionary Outreach*, identifies in the Jamaican Baptists' mission to the Cameroon a decade earlier. The similarities are instructive, forming a pattern that demonstrates the difficulties that the idea of a mission to Africa encountered in the West Indies.

7. On the whole, the Barbadian society in the 1840s was quite aware of various initiatives for Africa, including Buxton's Africa Colonisation Society that advocated the need to bring a real end to the slave trade and "bring Africa into the concourse of 'civilized nations'"; however, there was no practical scheme in place for the ordinary Barbadian churchmen of the 1840s to become involved, as part of their contribution to the solution of the problem.

Propagation of the Gospel (USPG), which was the missionary society of the Church of England. There was also the social and economic issue of providing opportunities for the new Christianized peasant class, especially in view of their difficulties in gaining access to land and their lack of employment opportunities in the immediate post-emancipation Barbadian society. These were stimuli for the birth of a vision for the creative employment of free black Christianized Barbadians. These circumstances conveniently converged in a vision shared by three key members of Barbadian society – Richard Rawle, Thomas Perry, and Colonel Sir William Colebrooke.

Richard Rawle, who had arrived in Barbados in 1847 to assume duties as principal of Codrington College, stirred the vision for the mission to Africa from the Barbados church and was initially its main driving force. An Englishman from Trinity College, Cambridge, Rawle was persistent and energetic, and fully aware of the parliamentary debates and discussions in London concerning Africa. He was anxious to engage in the enterprise for Africa, seeing it as a noble cause with which Codrington College could be associated, ostensibly in keeping with the missionary intentions of its benefactor, Christopher Codrington. After Rawle's death at Codrington in 1889, his executors, Mather and Blagg, co-wrote his biography in 1890.[8]

Rawle was happy to form an alliance with Thomas Parry, who had succeeded William Coleridge to become the second bishop of Barbados in 1842. The third person in this alliance was the newly arrived colonial governor of Barbados, Colonel Sir William Colebrooke, who took office in 1848. Colebrooke supported Rawle's idea and served as patron of the project. All three men were well aware of the transatlantic debate concerning Africa and the need to remedy its conditions using the agency of Christian mission.[9] Rawle quickly set about linking Trew's ideas with his own vision for Codrington College to be used as a training school for the preparation of West Indian agents to serve in Africa. On 15 November 1855, the proposal for an African mission from the Barbadian church was put before a meeting of the Barbados Church Society in Bridgetown. This was unanimously accepted.[10]

---

8. "The Life of Bishop Rawle," *MF* (1 December 1890): 458–463, USPG Archives.

9. Caswall, *The Martyr of the Pongas*, 62.

10. "Proposed Mission," *Barbados Church Society,* (1850), 1900, USPG Archives. See also Barrow, *Fifty Years in Western Africa* , 11–15.

However, it took five years to find a suitable representative to send to Africa on behalf of the Barbados church. The lack of volunteers and the difficulty of recruiting willing agents surprised and almost discouraged the mission proposers. In 1851, in a somewhat deflated mood, Rawle commented, "In blowing the trumpet of the mission, I am *vox et praeterea nihil*. It is heavy business agitating here, much like pulling the ears of a very fat dog, with a strong backward tendency. In the case of a pig, one would have the hopeful alternative of pulling the tail; but the Barbadian character has not even the energy of obstinacy and contradiction."[11] Rawle attributed the difficulties he encountered to the "Barbadian character" that, he thought, made it difficult to generate enthusiasm for popular causes. In addition to the manner in which the mission to Africa was proposed, constant outbreaks of cholera and other threats to public health kept the population preoccupied with pressing domestic concerns that threatened their daily survival. Nevertheless, Rawle and the Barbados Church Society persisted with their vision of a mission to Africa from the Anglican Church in the West Indies.

An examination of the proposal reveals three interesting features about the way in which it was framed. The first is the link made by Rawle between the African origins of the populations of the West Indies and the church. As Rawle put it, "A Mission to Western Africa would be a work peculiarly suited to the church in the West Indies where the population consists of persons so largely deriving their origin from that country."[12] This was an audacious connection to make, given the racial attitudes that prevailed between white and black Barbadians in the Barbadian church. Rawle's suggestive linking of the Barbadian population and the Barbadian Anglican church in a joint foreign missionary project was either religiously prophetic and optimistic, or otherwise openly racialist and insincere.

The second feature, addressed by Parry, was that "gratitude, justice and fitness for the work was uniting in the call upon the West Indian church for help to Africa."[13] This suggests that the proposal appeared to have been premised not solely upon notions of racial and ethnic affinities between the West

---

11. Mather and Blagg, *Bishop Rawle*.

12. Rawle to Hawkins; Parry to Rawle; Rawle to Hawkins; Rawle to Parry; Parry to Hawkins; Correspondence, USPG Archives.

13. Mather and Blagg.

Indies and Africa. Implied in it were also considerations of justice for Africa in terms of reparations to Africa for "wrongs hitherto inflicted upon her," as Trew had expressed.[14] In the minds of Rawle and Parry then, it appeared that a key motive for the proposal of a mission to Africa was, among other things, a consideration of mission as a divine and social justice cause. This was seen as a possible and effective means of repaying Africa for the brutal exploitation and violation of the dignity black Africans through the system of slavery in the centuries-long wretched transatlantic traffic in black Africans as slaves. Righting "the wrongs hitherto inflicted upon her" could only have suggested the need for restitution as an act of social justice, and this was to be provided through the realized benefits of Christianity and civilization. Therefore, they thought that the West Indian church, given its history and achievements, was an appropriate and "peculiarly suited" channel through which this could be achieved.

A third feature of the proposal was the stated intention that this mission would be directed to parts of Western Africa unoccupied by other mission societies of the English or American church.[15] It was clear that the Barbadian churchmen were keen on making the proposed mission a truly West Indian contribution, and hence the concern for their own separate space for mission engagement in Africa. On 16 June 1851, a local missionary society – the West Indian Church Association for the Furtherance of the Gospel in Western Africa (WICAFGWA) – was established in Barbados to promote the West Indian Anglican Mission to Africa. The WICAFGWA expressed the hope that the other dioceses in the West Indies would join them to make this a cooperative venture in order that the missionary work "may become one from the whole Anglo-West Indian church."[16]

Deploying the Mission

On 24 October 1855, Hamble James Leacock and John Duport were selected and within a few days deployed from Barbados to Africa to commence the Anglican Mission from the West Indies to the Rio Pongas in Western Africa.

---

14. Mather and Blagg.
15. Mather and Blagg.
16. Mather and Blagg.

They arrived in Sierra Leone on 14 November, 1855. As pioneers from the Barbados church, Leacock and Duport make interesting case studies. Leacock was an older white Creole Barbadian, born in Barbados in 1795. At the time of deployment to Africa he was sixty years old. He had accepted the Christian faith at a young age, while on a neighbouring island, and had returned to Barbados to study for the Christian ministry at Codrington College. In December 1826, at the age of thirty-one, he was licensed by Bishop William Hart Coleridge (1825–1842), the first bishop of Barbados, and ordained a deacon in the church. The following year, he was made a priest. He later spent twenty-two years away from Barbados, eight of which were in neighbouring Nevis and fourteen in the United States. During this time, Leacock had a varied career as parish priest and magistrate, evangelist and farmer, and thus he was a man with varied life experiences. He returned to Barbados in 1849 and was recalled to the charge at St. Peter's, Speightstown. and later served at St. Leonard's near Bridgetown. In August 1854, he suffered the loss of his wife in the cholera epidemic that ravaged the island. Following that traumatic experience, he volunteered for the Africa mission in 1855.

Leacock's passion for mission work in Africa was expressed in his speech before the Barbados Board of the WICAFGWA in which he announced:

> If the example of an old soldier of the Cross can fire with true missionary spirit and Christian zeal the bosoms of some noble, brave, disinterested, accomplished youth, of our little island, and cause them to rise up, and quit the soft, smooth, downy, attractive elegances of polished life, and prepare and arm them for that rugged, perilous warfare, and follow me in it, I shall then know that I have not lived in vain. . . . I will thankfully go to bed in Afric's dust.[17]

Leacock expressed similar sentiments in his farewell correspondence with John Trew, who, by then, had been appointed Archdeacon of the Bahamas:

> I have nothing to declare but Jesus Christ and "Him crucified," pardon through his blood, justification through his righteousness, sanctification by his Spirit. I know nothing else and I am

---

17. Caswall, *The Martyr of the Pongas*, 68.

determined to know nothing else. This will I teach, and trust in God to give his blessing.[18]

Whatever he might have thought of the prospects of his intended mission in Africa, it is clear that Leacock had, at least, a predetermined theological view of the missionary task. Embedded in this view is a notion that implies a belief in the efficacy of the missionary gospel message and hope for the possibilities of human redemption. That was the view he intended to take with him to Africa. Leacock's passion for mission work in Africa was also expressed in the urgency and deliberateness with which he pursued the project. Sadly, he only survived for seven months in Africa. He was hailed as a "martyr," and Henry Caswall – Chair of the West Indies Committee for the Mission to the Rio Pongas in England, and one of Leacock's main supporters – produced a memoir of him in 1857.[19]

Duport, on the other hand, was a younger black West Indian Creole, born in St. Kitts in 1829. Aged twenty-six, he was half Leacock's age, and had been selected by the Bishop to accompany Leacock as his assistant. Duport was not a "Codringtonian" in the sense that he was not one of those who had achieved scholastic attainment and pastoral training at Codrington College. Instead, he had been trained as a catechist at the Mission House that Rawle had established at Codrington and was, by all official accounts, a diligent and successful student with a disposition towards practical education. Duport's eagerness to learn and his aptitude for mathematics and mechanics identified him as a student with the right skills for the enterprise in Africa. It was only much later, after Leacock's death and at a time when he was the only missionary on the field in the Pongas Mission, that Duport was ordained by the Bishop of Sierra Leone. Duport rendered outstanding service to the Mission during his seventeen years in the Pongas (1855–1872). Due to the mortality of colleagues who came to join him in the work, as well as because he was so far removed from the centre of episcopal influence in Sierra Leone, Duport often found himself alone in the field, and he suffered from isolation and discouragement. But he fought on, and the continuity and leadership he gave to the fledgling mission enabled it, later on, to achieve sustainability as a viable mission.

---

18. Caswall, 70–71.
19. Caswall, *The Martyr of the Pongas*.

John Duport's major contribution to the Mission was in two areas: first, translation of Scripture and the Anglican liturgies into the Susu vernacular, and second, the establishment of a native Anglican church in the coastal area of the Rio Pongas. Sadly, there is no written or photographic legacy of Duport's labours in the Pongas Mission. In 1871, a fire destroyed all his work at his new station in Gene St. Jean in the Rio Nunez. The mission house, church, school, personal items, and all Duport's Susu sermons, manuscripts, and proof sheets – which were described as "a great collection" – were lost. Duport was married twice while in Africa. His first marriage was to a local African woman, the sister of the black chaplain to the Bishop of Sierra Leone. After her death, Duport married one of the Morgan girls who had come from Barbados to serve in the Pongas Mission as a teacher. John Duport went to Liverpool for medical attention and died in 1872, penniless, and leaving his widow and four children in Africa. When the Albert Insurance Company collapsed, Duport lost whatever pension he might have expected upon retirement after having paid out insurance premium for eight years. No memoir was ever written of him.[20]

En route to Africa, Leacock and Duport travelled first to London, where they spent two and a half weeks promoting the cause of the West Indian Africa mission in British churches. The Bishop of Barbados was also in London at the same time and he too used the opportunity to promote the desire of the Anglican Church in the West Indies to make its contribution to the cause in Africa. Despite the boldness of this mission initiative, the means of sustaining it was always an issue, given the declining economic circumstances of post-emancipation West Indian society. Partnership with the mother church in the metropole, even though a last resort, was always considered an option.

Henry Caswall, who by then had been appointed Vicar of Figheldean in Wiltshire, assisted them by arranging speaking opportunities in several churches and missionary meetings of the SPG in England. The presence in England of the two missionaries, Leacock and Duport, and the Bishop of Barbados was seized upon as an opportune moment to form an English Committee through which support for this project of the West Indian church could be channelled. This Committee was to have a significant and lasting

---

20. "Obituary for J. H. A. Duport," *MF* (1 November 1873): 341–343, USPG Archives, Bodleian Library.

effect not only upon the support, continuity, and survival of the West Indies mission in Africa but also in maintaining links with the mother church and other missionary interests in England.

Leacock and Duport left Plymouth Harbour on 24 October 1855 on the *Ethiope* and arrived in Freetown on 14 November. Also on board was J. W. Weeks, the newly appointed Bishop of Sierra Leone, under whose jurisdiction the proposed West Indies mission would operate. Although the Bishop of Barbados had been in contact with Weeks while he was still bishop-elect, Leacock's attempts to call on him while they were in London and present his papers had not been successful. However, during the twenty-one-day voyage to Sierra Leone, there was plenty of time for the West Indian missionaries to exchange ideas with Bishop Weeks about Africa and its prospects, as well as about the proposed mission over which the new bishop would have episcopal jurisdiction.

On 21 November 1855, Leacock and Duport arrived in the Rio Pongas, escorted by naval officers of the West India regiment stationed in Sierra Leone.[21] In accordance with the mandate and object of the Barbados Mission Board – to occupy an area of Africa "not worked by other Missions" – the pioneer missionary party selected the area of Western Africa that was surrounded by the large Rio Pongas. This area, north of Sierra Leone along the Atlantic coast, was straddled by three rivers – the big Pongas, the little Pongas, and the Nunez – which all flowed into the Atlantic Ocean.[22] For over a century, until the late 1860s when the French arrived and took political control, Portuguese, British, and American traders had frequented this area, which was known as the Pongas country.

The Rio Pongas country was populated by native Fullah and Susu peoples. A segment of the population were mulattos, who were descendants and offspring of American, European, and African miscegenation. Local political control in the Pongas area was exercised by the king of the Pongas through a monarchical system in which he wielded absolute power from a military base. His hegemonic control over the Pongas depended upon this military base, as

---

21. *MF* (1856): 50–54, USPG Archives, Bodleian Library.

22. According to Barrow, the name "Rio Pongas," which meant "mud river," was probably given to it by Portuguese traders in the fifteenth century. The mouth of the rivers formed an estuary about three miles long, and there were several islands in the estuary. Barrow, *Fifty Years*, 15.

well as on the economic control that he wielded over clusters of communities formed into small towns. These towns were run by black landowning chiefs or landless mulatto chiefs, who exercised strong economic control over trade in the towns and surrounding villages. In the 1850s, the whole area had some fifteen villages whose combined population was 7,580.[23]

The religious influence which generally prevailed in the area was Islamic, with large mosques and a native African following which penetrated into the interior. The earliest known Christian influence had been a Roman Catholic mission in the sixteenth century. In 1789, the Scottish Presbyterian Mission had sent two medical missionaries, Henry Brunton and Peter Greig, to the area; but when Greig was murdered, the mission was abandoned. In 1808, the Church Missionary Society had also attempted work in the Pongas and, in 1815, had established a station at Kappara, some seventy miles north of Freetown. But after suffering a high mortality of missionary personnel, losing eleven missionaries in fifteen years, the fledgling station was abandoned and the CMS aborted its mission.[24]

After landing in the Rio Pongas country, the first encounter for the West Indian missionaries with the local chiefs was not encouraging. Suspicious of British anti-slavery agents, eight local chiefs rallied to force Kennybeck Ali – the Mohammedan chief of Tintima, where the missionaries had first landed – to reject their empty-handed arrival. Leacock had refused to bear gifts as a gesture of goodwill, as was expected of foreign visitors, and so the missionaries were rebuffed by Kennybeck Ali, who declined to extend a welcome or offer any kind of protection to them. Others, such as the mulatto chief Mrs. Lightburn, displayed even more intransigence and hostility and refused to welcome them. The West Indian missionaries later discovered that the local African chiefs were intent on preserving their economic interests and wanted British education and trade, not religion.

However, Richard Wilkinson, chief of Fallangia, came to the rescue of the mission party, and throughout its existence in the region, Wilkinson and his family became one of the Mission's main local sponsors and protectors. The Wilkinsons provided everything a fledgling, defenceless, and uncertain mission could have wanted in order to secure a foothold in a pioneering

---

23. *MF* (March 1856): 57, USPG Archives, Bodleian Library.
24. Barrow, *Fifty Years*, 17–18.

environment. They provided shelter and space in their piazzas for the missionaries to hold religious services. They summoned people to hear the missionaries, acted as interpreters, and facilitated introductions to other neighbouring, and less hostile, chiefs. Eventually, they even provided land to build a school and a church. The Wilkinsons' actions were interpreted by the missionaries as an act of providential design. Indeed, so involved were the Wilkinsons in the work of the Mission that, within five years, Lewis Wilkinson – son of Chief Richard Wilkinson – had been earmarked to be trained as a missionary in England. It was only the death of the old man, leading to Lewis's immediate appointment as acting chief of Fallangia, that prevented implementation of this proposal. If Lewis had become a missionary, this would undoubtedly have been viewed as a cherished success of the West Indian Mission under Hamble James Leacock.

In a remarkable way, therefore, their first seven months in Africa set the pattern of mission engagement for the pioneering Barbadians. These early months underscored the issues that the West Indian Anglican Mission would, to a lesser or greater degree, encounter over the next four decades. Unfortunately, on 20 August 1856, the pioneer Leacock succumbed to the conditions in Africa and died in Freetown, Sierra Leone. His death marked the end of the first phase of the West Indian Anglican initiative in Africa. Over the next forty years, three other phases may be discerned in the development of this mission in Africa.

Maintaining the Mission

To create and deploy an enterprising mission initiative from the West Indies in the mid-nineteenth century was one thing. To maintain such an initiative was quite another. After the initial deployment of the pioneering team, the task of maintaining the venture became an uphill challenge for the Anglican church in the West Indies. On the field, the issues of negotiating mission engagement in Africa in a slave society, which involved placating local chiefs, dogged the mission from its earliest days. Providing effective episcopal supervision of the Mission also proved problematic. Although episcopal supervision from Sierra Leone was often proposed as a solution to this problem, practically, this was problematic owing to the long distance between the Rio Pongas and Freetown. In thirty years, there were only three episcopal visitations to the

Pongas Mission – the first visit was in February 1858, while the others took place in 1866 and 1878.[25] The problems of transportation, communication, food, physical security, and the upkeep and maintenance of mission property – schools, mission house, and church – also weighed heavily on both the West Indian missionaries in the field and the Mission Board in Barbados.

The West Indian missionaries were also challenged by their encounters with African society, and we will examine these encounters later. In responding both to internal needs and external challenges, the predominant issue confronting the missionaries was the constant shortage and inadequacy of available manpower to effectively carry out their various tasks in the Pongas Mission. This particular issue challenged the will and determination of the Anglican West Indian missionaries in Africa and, inevitably, called into question the capacity of the Mission to fulfil its vision.

The second phase of the Mission to the Rio Pongas, subsequent to Leacock's death, began with this struggle for maintenance. That phase began immediately following the death of Leacock. One of the factors that emerged from the initial deployment of the pioneers, was the question of the leadership qualities of John Duport. After Leacock's burial, Duport offered himself for ordination and spent ten weeks in Sierra Leone preparing to be ordained by the Bishop. Upon returning to the Pongas as a deacon, Duport immersed himself in the work of the mission. With the help of Charles Wilkinson, William Faber, and William Gomez – sons of the local chiefs – Duport erected the first mission church in the Pongas at Fallangia. This was a bold initiative. They built a church 34 x 34 x 12 – with a capacity of about 250 at a time when the population of Fallangia was about 530 – and named it the church of St. James the Apostle.[26] Duport set up classes for baptism and, by Christmas 1856, had baptized twenty-seven adults, youth, and children, including King Jelloram Fernandez's daughter Susanna. Duport also recruited and employed David Cyprian, a black schoolmaster from Sierra Leone, to take charge of

---

25. In addition, the distance and isolation of the Mission from the Mission Board in Barbados, on one hand, and the Committee in England, on the other, were constant issues that affected the Mission. Strong negative racial attitudes in the Pongas, in England, and in Barbados influenced the way in which the prospect of black West Indian superintendence of the Mission was viewed. This further added to the complexity of providing effective management of the Pongas Mission.

26. "Reports of the Rev. J. H. A. Duport," *MF* (1857): 125; see also *MF* (1857): 281, USPG Archives, Bodleian Library.

the school at Fallangia. The Pongas Mission was further strengthened, for a brief period, by a contribution – the only contribution – they received from the diocese of the Bahamas in the person of Mr. Samuel Higgs, who arrived in Fallangia on 9 April 1857. But sadly, Higgs contracted the African fever and died on 21 June 1857, after just two months in Africa. He was buried in Fallangia by Duport.

Despite John Duport's leadership qualities, the Barbados Board, the English Committee, and the local chiefs in the Pongas all – for different reasons – refused to recommend his appointment as Superintendent of the Mission. Instead, they opted to have the mission led by a white superintendent. It appeared that the character and competence of black missionaries to lead was constantly doubted. Addressing the SPG, Henry Caswall, secretary of the English Committee, made his own preference for white superintendence clear: "I fear that black missionaries without a white superintendent would get on badly."[27] The assumption was not merely that a mission to bring Christian civilization to black Africa should be led by a white man as the logical progenitor of "civilization," but that the black man was not yet quite capable of self-management and leadership of a great moral cause. On behalf of the Barbados Board, the English Committee advertised in Britain for a superintendent to take Leacock's place. William Latimer Neville, a graduate of Queen's College, Oxford, was appointed Superintendent of the Pongas Mission, with a stipend of £300 per annum. Duport, now qualified as a deacon, was offered £100 per annum. Duport, who had very little say in the matter, supported the appointment, saying that Neville was "like Leacock's own self" and that he was "the right man in the right place."[28] To show his full support and alignment with the West Indian project, Neville's first sermon in Africa was based on Psalm 68:31 (NIV) – "Envoys will come from Egypt; Cush will submit herself to God" – the most frequently used text by mission leaders in the West Indies in their promotional campaign to drum up support for the West Indian church's missionary adventures in Africa. As it turned out, apart from Leacock, Neville, who served three years (1858–1861) in the Pongas Mission before his death on the field in Africa, became the only other white superintendent of the Pongas Mission. By default, all the other

---

27. Caswall to Hawkins, Correspondence, USPG Archives, Bodleian Library.
28. *MF* (1858): 261, USPG Archives, Bodleian Library.

superintendents of the Pongas Mission were black and West Indian, with the exception of D. G. Williams of Sierra Leone.

With Neville in place as superintendent, the Mission at Fallangia began a period of consolidation, developing in both size and significance. In three years, they had eighty-nine scholars enrolled in the school led by Cyprian, the young Sierra Leonian catechist whom Duport had hired; half of these scholars were children of local chiefs. There were 250 names on the baptism register, 70 were attending weekly classes, 400 were attending Sunday services, 108 were in day school, and 10 girls were doing needlework, which was taught by Mrs. Cyprian. In addition, recognizing the strategic importance of communicating in local vernacular dialects, Duport pursued the task of translating portions of the Book of Common Prayer. These were: The Confession, The Lord's Prayer, The Creed, The Te Deum, The Gloria Patri, some short prayers, and The Ten Commandments into the Soosoo language.[29] For this task of translation work, while Duport relied on the assistance of Chief Wilkinson, he himself did extensive study of the Soosoo dialect. In his report to the SPG in May 1859, he wrote:

> "I have been engaged, at the Bishop's request, in compiling a Soosoo primer. I have completed two specimens, which I have submitted to him for his perusal; but as he is very particular and cautious as to the perfection of translations submitted to the press, he thinks of delaying a little before we print what I have completed, although I believe them quite correct. I am now preparing an alphabet to be adopted by the learners of the Soosoo language, and a few spelling sheets to be printed here. I am striving to acquire more and more of the language, by studying, translating, and revising it. Seldom, however, do I meet with any in Freetown who are sufficiently acquainted with English to add to my stock of knowledge. I am revising my Soosoo vocabulary . . . and also correcting the Soosoo in "Koelle's Polyglotta Africana" . . . we have been searching in the libraries of the Church Missionary Society for translations in the Soosoo language, but without success."[30]

---

29. *MF* (1858): 156–157, USPG Archives, Bodleian Library.
30. *MF* (1 July 1859): 161, USPG Archives, Bodleian Library.

His translations were published by the SPCK and used by Neville in his mission work. In 1859, as things began to settle in the Mission, Duport, who was then thirty years old, married the sister of the Bishop's chaplain in Sierra Leone.

Reinforcements from Barbados

In 1860, when the Barbados Board sent out two more Barbadians – Abel Phillips and Joseph Dean, who were trained at the Mission House at Codrington – to join the mission in Africa, the mission staff increased to its fullest complement to date. However, in the emerging pattern of hope and despair as soon as the stage was set for building and expanding the mission, the mission fell into crisis. In January, Joseph Dean died. This was followed in May by the death of Chief Richard Wilkinson, the main supporter and protector of the West Indian missionaries. In September, the superintendent, William Neville, died, leaving Duport and Phillips as the lone missionaries and Cyprian as schoolmaster. Duport, who had been ordained as a priest earlier in the year, was again left alone in the mission when Phillips fell ill and was forced to return to Barbados in an attempt to regain his health. If all that was not troubling enough, following Neville's death in Fallangia, an accidental fire destroyed the church and mission house. This was one of the lowest points in the Mission's history.

Yet, once again, the Mission bounced back, bolstered by the arrival of additional manpower from the Mission Training House at Codrington. In 1862, J. A. Maurice arrived, along with the first and only black West Indian family to participate in the Pongas Mission. The family consisted of Richard Morgan and his wife, their two adult daughters, a nephew, and five young children,[31] as well as a son – John Edward Morgan, a bright young scholar at Codrington, who arrived two years later and served as a catechist and schoolmaster. The Morgans' contribution was expected to bring some diversity to the programme of the Mission and serve as a model of the skilled black lay Christian family which the missionary agenda was intended to produce as one of its primary goals. The plans for the Mission included a proposal for an industrial school at Fallangia, in which children were to be taught "the arts

---

31. *MF* (1 May 1862): 109, USPG Archives, Bodleian Library.

of blacksmithing, carpentering, tailoring, etc." This proposal also included an agricultural component that specified the planting of groundnuts for the manufacture of groundnut oil for trading. Some of the local towns already had native furnaces for smelting iron.[32] As an agriculturalist, Richard Morgan was expected to establish the experimental farm, not only to teach agricultural skills to students but also to contribute to the development of local domestic agriculture. The Morgan girls were to be schoolteachers, while the nephew was to serve as a catechist.

However, for a variety of reasons, this anticipated new dimension of the West Indian mission work did not materialize as expected. Vassady regards the presence of the Morgan family as perhaps the most destructive element in the Pongas Mission.[33] Their attitude and conduct reinforced the sense of an ethnocentric, Barbadian-controlled mission. Nevertheless, deployment of the Morgan family represented an attempt to broaden the strategy of mission engagement by adding an industrial and commercial aspect to its work. However, their arrival coincided with a period of severe crop failure, food shortage, and famine in the Pongas region. For those and other reasons, it was not possible to start an agriculture-based industrial project at that time. Therefore, the Morgan family turned to teaching and catechizing work.

In 1863, after seven years of service in the field, Duport was given a six-month sabbatical to visit the West Indies. In May, while in Barbados, he and Phillips attended a meeting of the Barbados Board and gave a first-hand report of the Mission. Thereafter, Duport was commissioned by the Board to travel to other West Indian islands to promote the Africa mission, in the hope of raising manpower and support. In his travels to Antigua, St. Vincent, and St. Kitts, Duport received very favourable responses that, according to Bishop Parry, went much beyond his expectation.[34] Local branches of the Anglican Mission Society (The West Indian Association) in these islands used the occasion of Duport's visit to raise funds for the Mission. During Duport's absence from the Pongas, Maurice was put in charge of the Mission. Together with Cyprian, Maurice continued the exploration for new opportunities to establish mission stations. They made a visit to the interior town of Yengisa,

---

32. *MF* (1 June 1862): 133–134, USPG Archives, Bodleian Library.
33. Vassady, *Role of Black West Indian Missionaries*.
34. Parry to Hawkins, Correspondence, USPG Archives, Bodleian Library.

deep in the territory that was under the strong influence of Islam, but were rebuffed and driven away. Xabelle, a brother to the local chief, told the missionaries to go away because they had too many strangers visiting them and, in any case, "it is the business of Missionaries to live near the sea, and not inland."[35]

The issue Maurice and Cyprian encountered in that interior town was suspicion that British-linked missionaries were spies for the anti-slavery movement and fear that their presence would disrupt and undermine the local economy, which was dominated by slave trading. While local chiefs were content to send their children to mission schools for an English education, some resisted the spread of Christianity because of the threat it posed to their overt and covert involvement in the lucrative business of slave trading.[36]

The promise and anticipation of British trade, which was part of the British anti-slavery campaign, complicated matters for the work of the West Indian missionaries in the Rio Pongas. The non-appearance of such trade, even after the passage of the 1833 Emancipation Act in the British Parliament, was reason enough for some chiefs to continue the economic activity of slave trading in the Pongas estuary. As one chief put it, "The English spoil the river by not allowing the Spaniards to make their annual visit for the slave trade."[37] This matter of the lack of trade became a sore point for the West Indies-led mission. In his report in 1863, Maurice revealed that some local people were beginning to question the value of the Mission, arguing that prior to the arrival of the missionaries their material well-being had been better provided for through benefits derived from the slave trade. But with the advent of the missionaries and their attempts to suppress the slave trade with no substitute trade in place, the local people were worse off, with their economic circumstances declining daily. These people viewed the Mission as a stumbling block. Maurice expressed his frustration in his report:

> I am trying to help Mr. Lewis Wilkinson in bringing about the Cotton trade in this part of the country. This I do by putting him in the way how to prepare the soil, as well as in obtaining other assistance from merchant friends of mine in Sierra Leone. . . .

---

35. "Report of Mr. J. A. Maurice," *MF* (1 May 1863): 114–116, USPG Archives.
36. *MF* (1 May 1863): 115–116, USPG Archives.
37. *MF* (1 March 1863): 62, USPG Archives.

> It is not enough to for us to attend only to the spiritual wants of the people, but we must also use our endeavours to better their temporal condition. Then will they believe that the Mission is no delusion.[38]

Feeling exposed and vulnerable with regard to this matter, Chief Lewis Wilkinson, as local patron of the Mission, wrote to the Committee in England expressing his disappointment and pleading for the help needed for his people:

> I pray that something may be done about trade between England and the Pongas country; for my brother and myself have been trying to put down the slave-trade in many ways . . . the Susu nation are willing to do away with the foreign slave-dealing; but they must have an English trade in its place . . . a nation cannot rise without commerce.[39]

Wilkinson went on to point out that they had "in abundance" commodities such as groundnuts, beniseed, coffee, palm oil, palm kernel, beeswax, hides, gold, and various kinds of nuts which would produce oil. He believed that if some philanthropic society in England could provide a groundnut press to produce oil for trade with England, such technological help would be desired by his brother chiefs and they, too, would become involved in legitimate trade. Such trade, he argued, would be the means of advancing civilization and "promoting the kingdom of Christ in this part of Africa."[40]

However, the reality was that the Barbados Board was in no position to influence a course of events towards the realization of this promise. Neither was the English Committee. This effectively weakened the position of the Mission and undermined its practical influence and the social legitimacy it sought. The West Indian missionaries were left bereft of resources and had to find ways of engaging the local African population.

While the problem of the lack of trade was acutely felt in the Pongas area, especially after the American Civil War, when American traders no longer came to that area, the difficulty of conducting mission in a slave society was, perhaps, an even greater challenge. It was expected that being black and

---

38. *MF* (1 July 1863): 162, USPG Archives.
39. *MF* (1 March 1863): 63, USPG Archives.
40. *MF* (1 March 1863): 63, USPG Archives.

West Indian, having knowledge of both slave and emancipation society, and being in some respects "Codringtonians" – where Christianity and slavery co-existed on the Codrington estate prior to emancipation – the Barbadian missionaries would have known how to maneuver around this issue. And, as we shall see, the issue presented itself squarely before them and demanded their response as agents of the Christian missionary enterprise.

In February 1864, John Duport returned to the Pongas Mission and continued in the role of Acting Superintendent. He opened a new mission station at Domingia, and the congregations at both stations, Fallangia and Domingia, comprised domestic slaves as well as freedmen. As they struggled to find effective strategies of Anglican mission engagement in such circumstances, the West Indian missionaries were increasingly frustrated by the absence of episcopal visitation to meaningfully validate their work. They openly pleaded to have a bishop of their own for the Pongas region. In his report at the end of 1864, Duport lamented, "The people are tired of coming. Many have attended for six years without being confirmed. I despair of ever seeing a Bishop of Sierra Leone here . . . When shall we have a Bishop of our own?"[41]

By 1865, the Pongas Mission had been in operation for a decade. In April of that year, the second episcopal visitation of the Mission took place. During his visit, the Bishop confirmed eighty-seven people at Fallangia, while twenty-two candidates who had been prepared for confirmation at Domingia were not so fortunate as the Bishop had no time to visit that station. While at Fallangia, the Bishop consecrated the burial ground in which the remains of Neville, Dean, Higgs, and others were buried.[42] It would be another thirteen years before the Pongas Mission received another episcopal visitation by a bishop. During this period, the West Indians continued to plead for the Pongas Mission to have its own bishop.

Navigating under New Local Political Leadership

The end of that first decade (1855–1865) also saw the emergence of new political leadership throughout the Pongas country. By 1865, except for Mrs. Lightburn – Farrangia's chief – all the chiefs whom the missionaries had

---
41. *MF* (1864): 218, 231, USPG Archives.
42. *MF* (1865): 133, USPG Archives.

known and who had been involved with the Mission in one way or another had died. King Jelloram, the king of the Pongas, had also died, and a new king, William George, had been duly installed. This meant that old assurances, trusts, and collaborations had to be renegotiated, sometimes even despite documentation of old agreements. At a particularly low point, Duport wrote, "The present state of things cannot last . . . at present I am thoroughly done up. One thing I am convinced of, that whatever befalls me, I have spent my strength in the work of the Mission, and I trust it will not prove in vain."[43]

Duport had more than enough reason to wonder if his missionary labours would prove to be in vain. J. A. Maurice, who had experienced difficulties in the Mission since he arrived in 1861, resigned in 1866 and returned to Barbados. Richard Morgan also resigned. The station at Domingia remained unmanned for a while since the young West Indian catechist Paulus also resigned. But, yet again, at a low point in the life of the Mission, new hope was injected when two new Codringtonians, J. F. Turpin and P. H. Doughlin, arrived in 1867. Turpin (1867–1878) and Doughlin (1867–1886) – who remained in the mission for eleven and nineteen years respectively – illustrate two more instances of West Indian adaptation to Africa, longevity in the field, and black leadership in the missionary project. These two missionaries rendered outstanding service to the Mission before retiring to the West Indies. The contributions of Turpin and Doughlin allowed the Pongas Mission, perhaps for the first time, to achieve some real stability and make significant progress towards advancing its goals. This was achieved against the background of the constant pressure of the internal need for resources and the ever-present external challenges of the physical and climatic environment, which included the outbreak of diseases such as smallpox that ravaged the Pongas area from time to time, resulting in many fatalities, including that of influential supporters of the Mission, such as Chief Gomez of Backia village.[44]

By the end of 1867, however, the Mission's prospects brightened once again, with a number of additions to its staff. The West Indian catechist Turpin and the Sierra Leonian Bickersteth were stationed at Domingia; Doughlin was at Fallangia; another Sierra Leonian, William Macaulay, was stationed at Isles de Los; and two West Indian school mistresses were engaged, one at

---

43. *MF* (1865): 219, USPG Archives.
44. *MF* (1867): 362, USPG Archives.

Domingia and one at Fallangia. That year, John Duport, as superintendent, moved the Mission headquarters from Fallangia to Domingia, which he considered more central.[45] In May that year, Duport had suffered the painful loss of his wife, who died after a period of illness, leaving three children, the eldest being eleven years old.[46] Yet, Duport battled on with the work of the Pongas Mission, pursuing his translation work and completing Matthew's Gospel in Susu, which was subsequently published by the SPCK in London.

The Third Phase

The third phase in the development of the Pongas Mission began in 1867. This phase was marked by four major issues. First, the issue of leadership. In 1869, Duport had been temporarily relieved of his responsibilities as superintendent of the Mission when his licence was suspended by the Bishop of Sierra Leone pending an investigation of charges of impropriety and contributing to his wife's death. Rev. D. G. Williams was commissioned to investigate these charges on behalf of the Bishop. Duport was exonerated and his licence reinstated. Duport's work in the Mission came to an end in 1872, when he succumbed to his illness in the Royal Infirmary in Liverpool, where he had been sent for medical treatment. He died on 20 September at the age of forty-three. About a dozen persons, including Turpin, were at his bedside when he died.[47]

After Duport's death, the leadership of the mission effectively passed to Turpin, and then to Doughlin. Both Turpin and Doughlin worked hard to extend the mission, travelling extensively as itinerant preachers. They explored the interior, once travelling 166 miles over a period of eighteen days, visiting thirty-two towns and preaching forty-three times. In 1879, Doughlin, along with McEwen, spent one month visiting fifty-eight towns on foot, distributing tracts and copies of the Book of Common Prayer and the New Testament, and conducting Sunday services.[48] They focused on education and on building schools for boys and girls, and pleaded for funds for the building of a boarding school to provide proper education. Under their leadership, the Mission

---

45. *MF* (1 September 1868): 24, USPG Archives.
46. Duport to Bullock, C/WIN Bar 13, File 13, Correspondence, USPG Archives, Bodleian Library. This was also published in *MF* (2 September 1867): 362, USPG Archives.
47. *MF* (1 November 1873): 341–343, USPG Archives.
48. *MF* (1 July 1875): 195; *MF* (1 December 1879): 554, USPG Archives.

withstood a number of challenges presented by the increasing number of slave-wars. They also had to deal with the growing competitive influence of Islam and the resistance to Christianity that this generated. In addition, the renewal of Roman Catholic missions in the Pongas emerged in the form of the Sisters of Mercy mission. These challenges were described in their reports to the Barbados Board and the English Committee, and published in the *Mission Field*.[49]

With respect to the frequent outbreaks of war, Doughlin gave a chilling account of the impact of war conditions on the local people and on the Mission in his mid-1884 report. He reported:

> This unfortunate war was a great drawback to everything, and greatly demoralised the people. It sprang up over some land matter, and was kept up by the hot blood of the two Princes, who were both heir apparent, and Prime Ministers of the Kingdoms to which they belonged ... each party would fall on an unsuspecting town at night and set all the houses on fire simultaneously, and kill all the men, and sometimes women and children too. Women have been chopped with their children on their backs. Children's feet have been chopped off by sword cuts directed at their mothers. The state of things was awful. Several of our people were caught and sold into slavery, or, which is still more hopeless, the warriors took them away to be their wives. Wherever one goes he finds numbers of free children who are now slaves. Many who would otherwise have not been able to buy slaves have several whom they bought cheaply or caught.[50]

An important feature of this third phase of the Pongas Mission was the fact that, for the first time, the Mission was led and manned exclusively by the black West Indian missionaries. From this time onwards, there was no white West Indian or European missionary participation in the Mission, despite the ongoing preference and requests for white superintendents. For example, as late as 1886, a member of the Barbados Board – Archdeacon Holme of Antigua – inspected the mission on behalf of the Board and recommended in

---

49. *MF* (1873): 197; *MF* (1878): 196, and *MF* (2 June 1884): 178, USPG Archives.
50. *MF* (2 June 1884): 175–179, USPG Archives.

his report that "the great want of the Mission is a European head." Although Holme reported the general good condition in which he found the Mission and the missionaries – despite their unhealthy surroundings – he nevertheless indicated that some of the mission schools were "a failure" and that a European head was urgently needed to "put new life and effectualness into what is already a great work, but one which lacks energy and a directing arm, as well as a wise and encouraging brain."[51] However, no white superintendent was ever sent to the Mission after the death of the British superintendent Neville in 1861. The Pongas Mission was the only mission initiative in Africa from the West Indian churches, in the nineteenth century, to achieve complete black participation, including black superintendence.

Despite the opportunities presented by such an achievement, this did not always work in the interest of the West Indians. Since the manpower for the Pongas Mission was supplied mainly from Barbados, the general feeling that prevailed was that too much control was exercised by a Barbadian-Codrington clique that tended to exclude others, particularly native Africans and those from Sierra Leone. These suspicions and criticisms had been reinforced by the marriages of Duport, Turpin, and Doughlin to three of the Morgan girls from Barbados. Certainly, from the time of the Cyprian's death[52] – when Duport announced that he would no longer employ Sierra Leonians – there was the suggestion that the West Indians, in an effort to fully exercise and demonstrate their emancipation, had taken full control of the Mission and tended to exclude others. Such feelings, it is claimed, were part of the reason for the allegations made against Duport, which led to the investigation of his work by the Bishop of Sierra Leone. Nevertheless, despite these claims, and in spite of Duport's assertion, other Sierra Leonians like T. G. McCarthy[53] and Jeremiah Buckle[54] were employed as catechists and schoolmasters by the West Indians in their management of the mission work in the Pongas.

---

51. *MF* (1 April 1887): 108, USPG Archives. This was indicative of the continued doubt that existed over the capacity of blacks to lead, despite all their efforts and evidence to the contrary.

52. *MF* (August 1864): 218–219, USPG Archives.

53. *MF* (2 June 1879): 277, USPG Archives.

54. *MF* (1 September 1880): 321, USPG Archives.

A Major Breakthrough

In 1888, the Mission experienced a major breakthrough in its evangelizing work in the Pongas when one of the most important chiefs, Mrs. Lightburn, relented and was converted and baptized into the Mission. A rich and powerful female chief, Mrs. Lightburn controlled large amounts of property in the Pongas. According to Doughlin, she was "by far the greatest slaver dealer on this part of the coast." Although she had allowed her grandchildren to attend the mission school in Fallangia, she had been personally opposed to British missionary activity in Farrangia – in the interior, where she presided – and had prohibited all attempts to do mission work there. Several missionaries, including Neville and three bishops, had tried to persuade her otherwise, but it was Doughlin who succeeded in gaining her confidence and counselling her to respond to the missionary message. In an extensive report, Doughlin described the event and impact of her conversion:

> Early Sunday morning Mrs. Lightburn sent the town-crier to walk about the town and proclaim that no one was to leave town that day as an important meeting was to be held there. . . . A very large number of people gathered in the three spacious piazzas of Mrs. Lightburn's house, and soon we began to praise God and to pray to him.[55]

Doughlin preached to the gathering in Susu as Mrs. Lightburn – accompanied by Mr. Marsden, an English merchant who had married one of her granddaughters – requested baptism. Doughlin instructed McEwen to baptize her as "she knelt surrounded by her grandchildren and Mr. Marsden who acted as witnesses, and by her people and was baptised." Two years later, Lightburn died and, amid much fanfare, was given a Christian burial.[56] The effect of her conversion and her endorsement of the Mission gave the missionaries a much-needed foothold and opportunities for new openings in Farrangia, which was a major gateway into the interior.[57]

The second major issue of significance for the Mission during its third phase occurred in 1867, when the imperial government of France took formal

---

55. *MF* (2 December 1878): 583–585, UGSP Archives.
56. *MF* (1 September 1880): 322, USPG Archives.
57. *MF* (2 June 1879): 273–274, USPG Archives.

possession of the Pongas. The French had been trading in the Rio Pongas for several years, and this had created some anxieties among the Susu people, as well as among the West Indians. But once France had taken formal possession of the Pongas, the West Indians knew that their protection and security in the area could not be guaranteed. Furthermore, the British government, through the governor of Sierra Leone, took the view that since the French were now in charge, they should also take responsibility for the education of the natives and, therefore, should support the schools established by the West Indian Pongas Mission.[58] This optimistic view seemed to have been an attempt to find new sources of funding for the Mission, thereby reducing the almost exclusive dependence upon the English Committee to find resources to support its rapidly growing educational work. The West Indian missionaries had introduced a system of school fees as a means of developing local income for the mission schools. However, as Doughlin observed early on after his arrival, "the system of school fees has yet been a complete failure."[59]

Despite their good rapport with some French officials and merchants in the Pongas, the Anglican missionaries' expectation that the French government would fund Protestant mission work in Africa was unrealistic. Besides, French Catholic missionaries were themselves at work in the Pongas region, and they would more naturally commend themselves for French support.[60] No support was ever received from France for the West Indian Mission. Instead, the worst fears of the West Indians were realized when the French government requested that the French language be taught in the mission schools and, later, refused to allow the development of further schools where there was exclusive Protestant control. This marked the beginning of a long period where the West Indian mission work in the Pongas region was eclipsed by the French authorities.

The third issue of significance during the Mission's third phase arose from the opportunity to establish a new field headquarters for the Mission with the opening of a new station in Fotobah on the Isles de Los in 1867. Fotobah represented not merely a third station in the Pongas Mission but also a new phalanx in its strategy for the region. In time, it became the headquarters and

---

58. *MF* (2 September 1868): 244, USPG Archives.
59. *MF* (1868): 245, USPG Archives.
60. *MF* (1 September 1868): 243, USPG Archives.

main station of the Mission. Some twelve miles from the mainland, it was the largest of about five islands in the Rio Pongas and was, at the time, under British rule. The Isles de Los was about half a mile wide, with a range of hills running through the length of the island. In 1865, its population was just over three hundred.[61] For five years, the West Indians had been contemplating, and scouting for, an alternate mission site. Duport had visited the site in 1865 to assess the needs and prospects of a mission station there. He had submitted a report outlining the advantages and disadvantages of the location and drawing attention to the infestation of the place by destructive termites called bugbugs, the difficulty of obtaining labour, the lack of temporary shelter, lack of building supplies, and the need for skilled supervision of the work. On the other hand, he noted that "the island is healthy, provisions abundant, and the soil very good. Meat is very scare, but fowls are plentiful, and so is fish for six months in the year."[62]

The ostensible reason for relocating was to overcome the ravages of the heavy monsoon climate, but also to allow more freedom and control from being beholden to the sponsorship and patronage of local chiefs. The West Indians desired an area that would provide better external security such as that which the British Navy could provide since that would be an effective deterrent to the constant threat of local militia attacks, as well as provide some protection from the French forces. Additionally, the site would afford easier communication with Freetown in Sierra Leone.

While in Barbados on furlough, Duport and Phillips had discussed this possibility with the Barbados Board, and the Board had agreed to pursue the matter with the SPG and the colonial government in Sierra Leone.[63] Maurice, as acting head of the Mission at the time, was requested to discuss the matter with the colonial governor in Sierra Leone, which he did. By 1865, the Mission had obtained a licence for twenty acres of land at Fotobah.[64] Having made three visits in the first quarter of 1867 and "being fully convinced," in October that year, Duport deployed the Sierra Leonian catechist and

---

61. *MF* (1 September 1868): 247, USPG Archives.

62. *MF* (1865): 115, USPG Archives.

63. Parry to Hawkins, D 28A/West Indies, 1860–1867, Correspondence, USPG Archives, Bodleian Library.

64. *MF* (1865): 189, USPG Archives.

schoolmaster William Samuel Macaulay to develop a station on the island.[65] He himself also moved there to carry out the building of this new station. This new initiative was entirely the conception and implementation of the West Indian missionaries, and it demonstrated their imagination, determination, and strategic leadership capabilities in the missionary enterprise in Africa.

The fourth issue that characterized the third phase of the Mission after 1867 was the determined attempts of the missionaries to implement the Venn philosophy of missionary engagement in the Pongas Mission from the new foothold established in Fotobah. Although the SPG, the sponsoring body of the Anglican West Indian Mission, did not overtly embrace the missionary philosophy of Henry Venn (1841–1873) of the Church Missionary Society (CMS),[66] one of the underlying goals of the West Indian Board was that, in time, the church they had planted in Africa would become "self-governing, self-propagating, and self-supporting," as the Venn philosophy of church planting through missionary engagement proposed. This was not entirely a new idea. As already pointed out, various means of generating local income – such as charging school fees – had already been implemented. In addition, the West Indian missionaries used occasions such as harvest, patronal festivals, Christmas, and Easter to encourage the mission churches to be self-supporting. From 1867 this became a determined policy action in the Mission.

Thus, in 1867 the Venn philosophy of mission was put squarely on the agenda of the Pongas Mission for at least three reasons. The first was that, by 1867, the Pongas Mission had grown beyond the capacity of the Barbados Board or the English Committee to sustain. The second was that, as already pointed out in chapter three, the social and economic conditions in the West Indies had declined to such an extent that the West Indian church – having been forced to look inward at its own domestic mission needs, especially in the aftermath of the Morant Bay uprising in Jamaica in 1865 and the increasing poverty in the society – was strapped for resources. The third reason was that the mission in Africa was being forced to develop self-supporting ventures to ensure its survival.

---

65. *MF* (1 September 1868): 246, USPG Archives.

66. As indicated in chapter 1, the Western missionary establishment did not necessarily embrace Venn's three-self philosophy of missionary work, although, as a missionary strategy, it appeared sound and well intentioned.

In May 1867, the English Committee wrote to Stiles Lightburn, who was supreme among the mulatto chiefs, pointing out the need for the local people to show greater ownership and support of the church. They also pointed out that it had never been the intention of the mission to "maintain in perpetuity" the church founded among the Susus to be dependent on help from the West Indies or from England.[67] The letter asserted that the aim of the Mission was to set up a Susu National Church, as exemplified by the CMS Mission in Sierra Leone, and that the local people were expected to demonstrate zeal and readiness to take ownership of the church and the Mission as their own native project. Chief Lightburn forwarded the letter to Duport, indicating that he, as Chief, would have to consult with the people and with the other chiefs before a definitive response could be given. In August, a convention of local chiefs was held, at which Lightburn put the matter before them. Although the Council agreed, in principle, to take steps to help the Mission to become self-supporting, nothing of any real significance materialized even though some chiefs continued to extend pragmatic support of the Mission as they had been doing. As Duport later explained, it was not going to be possible for the Susu church to become self-supporting in the near future for the obvious reasons that (1) there was no money around, (2) the people were slaves and very poor, and (3) the slave masters and the "big people" in society would never encourage it because they saw the presence of the missionaries as an impediment to their slaveholding practices.[68] In the end, the Pongas Mission remained dependent for support on the English Committee and the SPG.

Black Leadership and the Challenge of Maintaining the Mission

Despite the difficulties and challenges it faced, the Pongas Mission in Western Africa was developing steadily under the able leadership of the black West Indian missionaries. However, raising funds to maintain the Mission continued to be challenging. The original hope that the project would be owned and supported by the entire Anglican Church in the West Indies never really materialized despite the church's growth, as evidenced by the creation of

---

67. *MF* (2 September 1867): 364, USPG Archives.
68. *MF* (1 February 1869): 48, USPG Archives.

seven dioceses by 1883: Antigua and Guiana (1842), Nassau (1861), Trinidad (1872), Windward Islands (1879), and British Honduras (1883), in addition to the diocese of Jamaica and the Bahamas, and the diocese of Barbados and the Leeward Islands, which had both been established in 1825.

Despite the growth in episcopal dioceses in the West Indies and the bishops' charges to their clergy to encourage support for the Pongas Mission, as time went on, interest in the mission in Africa declined. Several factors contributed to this trend. At the end of 1869, the West Indian church was dealt a sudden and severe blow when the Secretary of State for the Colonies summarily announced the disestablishment and disendowment of the colonial church. With very little time for preparation, the West Indian church was confronted with a major crisis of self-funding and self-government, to which there were strong reactions, with some church leaders seeing disendowment as "a hostile measure." Jamaican churchmen sent a delegation to London to appeal for support in the face of what they regarded as "a great and unexpected blow . . . utterly unstatesmanlike."[69] In these circumstances, the focus of the church naturally shifted to questions of local survival.

Strapped for resources in a rapidly declining economy, and with little external support, the crisis was further deepened by acts of God in the form of a series of devastating hurricanes in the West Indies, which destroyed schools, churches, chapels, and other mission properties.[70] From time to time, there were outbreaks of communicable diseases such as yellow fever and smallpox that devastated whole populations and affected the work of the church.[71] And the new waves of immigrants presented the West Indian church with a missionary challenge on its doorstep, shifting its focus away from the Africa mission and towards local matters. For example, Rawle – the first Bishop of Trinidad – pleaded for help to serve the "30,000 heathens floated to our shores," adding that "Trinidad cannot be reckoned a feeder to the funds of the West Indian Associated Mission . . . the amount thus given

---

69. *MF* (1 October 1884): 214, USPG Archives. See also the report from Antigua, "Disendowment – Poverty," *MF* (1 February 1878): 93 and *MF* (1 July 1872): 194–195, USPG Archives. Bodleian Library.

70. One such hurricane destroyed over 1,000 houses, in addition to schools, chapels, and churches in the Windward Islands. *MF* (1 April 1887): 98, USPG Archives.

71. *MF* (1 February 1878): 92, USPG Archives.

is very small, and to be valued chiefly as an expression of goodwill."[72] These challenges severely constrained the church's ability to mobilize resources for its domestic needs, let alone its foreign missionary activities.

The diocese of Jamaica serves as a major case in point. From as early as 1858, three years after the Pongas Mission was in operation, Reginald Courtenay, the diocesan bishop, made clear in his charge to a convocation of his clergy their "duty" of supporting missions. In impressing this obligation upon them, he pointed out that the church in Jamaica was, in this respect, "manifestly wanting"[73] and drew a comparison with the church in the Bahamas, which had been able to send personnel and other forms of support to the Pongas Mission. Bishop Courtenay charged the clergy and their congregations to take an active interest in the Mission despite local needs, recommending the establishment of a Missionary Fund to be divided "one portion to Jamaica itself, the other to Africa."[74]

In 1861, in response to their Bishop's charge, as well as other circumstances, the Jamaican clergy set up an indigenous missionary society called the Jamaica Home and Foreign Missionary Society (JHFMS). It is instructive that, in its first year, almost the entirety of the £200 collected by the JHFMS was designated to the Pongas Mission, while only £2 was allocated for Home Mission. The following year, however, over £300 were collected for Home Mission and less than £100 for the Pongas Mission. Thereafter, very little was collected for the mission in Africa.[75] Local needs – including responding to the effects of the religious revival of 1860, the aftermath of the events of 1865, and the immediate consequences of disestablishment in 1869 – captured the focus of the JHFMS and demanded its attention and resources. In 1862, the first report of the JHFMS gave a rationale for the shift to a focus on Home Mission:

---

72. *MF* (1 February 1878): 95–96, USPG Archives.

73. Primary Charge delivered at the Congregation of the Clergy of Jamaica held in Spanish Town, on 15 April 1858 by Reginald Courtenay, D. D. Bishop of Kingston. National Archives of Jamaica, Spanish Town.

74. Primary Charge delivered at the Congregation of the Clergy of Jamaica held in Spanish Town, on 15 April 1858 by Reginald Courtenay, D.D. Bishop of Kingston, National Archives of Jamaica, Spanish Town.

75. Coles, "Jubilee of the Jamaica Church," West India Reference Library, National Library of Jamaica, 8.

> If there be people in this island so debased by vice, ignorance and superstition as to be little better than the heathen, then to take such measures as shall make them partake of that grace of God that bringeth salvation and teacheth them to "deny ungodliness and worldly lusts" will be truly missionary work as sending preachers of the gospel across the ocean into distant and foreign regions.[76]

Between 1850 and 1896, the biggest contribution of the Jamaican diocese to the Pongas Mission was to send W. A. Burris and A. F. O. Marsh, Jamaican agents trained at Codrington in Barbados, both of whom arrived in the late nineteenth century when the Mission was on the verge of closure.[77] In forty years, the Jamaica church never contributed more than a few hundred pounds to the Africa mission.

The diocese of Barbados, where the idea for an African mission originated, also struggled to maintain its support, especially after Parry and Rawle, the pioneers of the mission to Africa, were no longer there to keep the interest alive. Parry had died in retirement in London in 1870 at the age of seventy-six,[78] and Rawle had resigned as principal of Codrington in 1864 after a row with the Board. Between November 1863 and January 1864 sharp exchanges occurred between Parry and Rawle over the Council's acceptance of Rawle's sudden decision for a year's leave of absence from the College, ostensibly for health reasons.[79] This disagreement became public when a local newspaper – *The West Indian* – raised the matter in its editorial of 24 December 1863, drawing attention to the rumours of the "whys and wherefores" of Rawle's resignation. Later, in 1872, Rawle was appointed Bishop of Trinidad and served that diocese for seventeen years before returning to Codrington, where he died in 1889.[80] Following Rawle's resignation, Abel Phillips, tutor and chaplain at the Mission House at Codrington – who had previously

---

76. Coles, "Jubilee," 8.
77. Ellis, *Diocese of Jamaica*, 148; Evans, *History of the Diocese of Jamaica*, 111.
78. *MF* (1 April 1870), USPG Archives.
79. Rawle to Hawkins; Parry to Rawle; Rawle to Hawkins; Rawle to Parry; Parry to Hawkins; Correspondence, USPG Archives.
80. *MF* (1 December 1890): 458–463, USPG Archives.

served in the Pongas Mission – also resigned to take up an appointment in St. Vincent.[81]

The Mission House at Codrington, which Rawle had set up for training missionaries for Africa, had been disused and abandoned for some time. In 1878, seeing that there were no candidates available for training for mission in Africa, the incumbent Bishop Mitchinson began to seriously consider alternative uses for the building. In his article "The Church and Education in a part of the West Indies," Bishop Mitchinson suggested that the Mission House be used as a training school for teachers, an objective that he thought would fulfil the "pious, munificent and philanthropic intentions of the grand old General who founded and endowed Codrington College."[82] In April 1885, within a few months of the arrival of a new principal for Codrington, the facility was completely destroyed in a major fire.[83] In addition to these difficulties, the political climate within the colony was still somewhat unsettled, and both the Barbados church and Barbados society were still trying to come to terms with the peasant uprising of 1876, which was already referred to in chapter 3.[84] The political climate within the colony was still somewhat unsettled. In 1878, Bishop Mitchinson, as Bishop of Barbados, commented that the standard of religious obligation in the island was "lamentably low" and thought that this was borne out by the part "our deluded Church members and even communicants took in that shameful Easter-week of 1876."[85] He also felt that the "week's reign of terror," in what was called the "Confederation Revolt," marred or retarded church work in the colony for "years afterwards."[86] Although disendowment for the Barbados church was introduced gradually through the local legislature, the fear and negative psychology it generated further impacted the church's ability to support and focus on its obligation to the Pongas Mission.[87]

Meanwhile, apart from the changed circumstances in the West Indies, which impacted support for the Pongas Mission, the English Committee

---

81. Phillips to Hawkins, D 28A/West Indies, 1860–1867, USPG Archives.
82. *MF* (August–September 1878): 423–431, USPG Archives.
83. *MF* (1 June 1885), USPG Archives.
84. Belle, "Abortive Revolution."
85. *MF* (August–September 1878): 430, USPG Archives.
86. *MF* (August–September 1878): 430, USPG Archives.
87. Barrow, *Fifty Years*, 129–130.

was itself undergoing its own changes and transitions in leadership. In 1866, Caswall resigned as secretary due to ill health, and successive secretaries – including A. Reece, G. H. Barrow, and A. H. Barrow – gave whatever organizational help they could to the English Committee. A series of honorary chairs, including the Bishop of Antigua, were called upon from time to time to help by giving ongoing leadership to the work of the Committee. Although the Committee endeavoured to continue its support for the West Indian church's mission in Africa, it found this task increasingly difficult and support all round continued to diminish.[88]

Impact on the Mission to Africa

The decline in support from the West Indies for the mission in Africa had several impacts. First, it was an embarrassment to the West Indian church which, despite the inadequacies and one-sidedness of the beginnings of the mission, had come to view this project as a badge of pride and as the West Indian contribution to addressing the "problem of Africa." By the mid-1860s, local branches of the West Indian Anglican Missionary Society were eventually established in almost every West Indian diocese. These branches promoted the mission, raised whatever funds they could, and prided themselves on the fact that their denomination was also engaged in the missionary cause in Africa. The unexpected occurrences of disestablishment and disendowment were singled out as among the major contributory factors to the West Indian church's inability to mobilize support for the Africa mission. But, as Caldecott points out, the difficult challenge of self-funding after disestablishment was not totally without beneficial effects upon the West Indian church since, ultimately, these enforced circumstances helped the West Indian church to develop bases of self-support, self-government, and the active involvement of its lay members. New organizational structures within local dioceses emerged, including the establishment of local synods, constitutions for church government, and a provincial synod in the West Indies as a whole.[89] Nevertheless, despite these positive effects, there was significant fallout in the West Indies, which imperilled the mission to Africa and led even Rawle to later,

---

88. Barrow, 131–132.
89. Caldecott, *Church in the West Indies*, 256–261.

embarrassingly, modify the reasons he had originally put forward for instigating and promoting the Africa mission. In the difficult circumstances of his bishopric in Trinidad in 1878, Rawle maintained that "the cultivation of an interest in Missions is of great value for the improvement of Church feeling and the enlargement of charity. This, more than the effect in Africa, was my object in helping at the foundation of the Mission. I had a strong sense of its home-value, and the results answered my expectations."[90]

The decline in support for the mission from the West Indies also resulted in the loss of management control over the mission by the West Indian church. As Barrow points out, when the reality of its inability to maintain the mission initiative in Africa began to set in, it was decided to first send someone to inspect the Mission and provide both the Barbados Board and the English Committee with an assessment of the situation in which the Mission found itself.[91] Archdeacon H. R. Holme of St. Kitts, to whom this assignment was given, inspected the Mission in 1886 and stated in his report:

> No words of mine could convey to your minds what an actual inspection of the Mission has brought to mine. Its value and importance exceed all that have been hoped for. I cannot believe that a purer and healthier Mission – one more fitted for its work, and more necessary to its surroundings, exists anywhere in the world. . . . That such a mission should be impeded, dwarfed, or abolished, would be a fearful calamity to the district and to the far-off countries with which it is in constant communication. God forbid that this should be![92]

Holme pointed out both what was good and what was bad about the Mission and pleaded for its continuation. But while the missionaries on the field – especially Doughlin in his capacity as Superintendent – kept appealing for a bishop for the Pongas Mission, on the basis that the diocese of Sierra Leone was itself too far-flung for effectiveness,[93] they were repeatedly bypassed and attempts were made to hand over the management of the Mission to the jurisdiction of the Bishop of Sierra Leone. Doughlin, in his report in

---

90. *MF* (1 February 1878): 96, USPG Archives. Bodleian Library.
91. Barrow, *Fifty Years*, 129–132.
92. *MF* (1 April 1887): 104, USPG Archives.
93. *MF* (2 June 1884): 178, USPG Archives.

mid-1884, lamented with deep concern that "our Mission will never do the work which it should do till it has a Bishop of its own. The Bishop of Sierra Leone already has too large a diocese."[94] In 1886, Doughlin retired from the Mission after nineteen years in Africa and returned to the West Indies, where he was made an honorary canon in Trinidad and posted to the parish of St. Clements in South Trinidad. In his retirement, he completed his work of translating the Psalms into Susu.[95]

The Holme report was circulated in time for the second Lambeth Conference in 1888, at which all the West Indian bishops were present. This report formed the basis for discussion among the West Indian bishops concerning the future of the West Indies Africa mission. As difficulties continued to mount, both in Africa and the West Indies, the management and control of the Pongas Mission was eventually transferred from the West Indies Board to the English Committee.

A third result of the gradual decline in the West Indian Anglican Church's ability to support the mission in Africa was a loss of memory within the Church regarding this noble project initiated in the mid-nineteenth century. In 1908, having served as secretary of the English Committee for twenty-six years, the Englishman Barrow was invited to do a tour of the West Indies. In 1913, he published his report of the tour, outlining the history of the Pongas Mission and lamenting that, despite the noble efforts of the West Indian church for half a century and the yearly reports of the SPG about the work of the Pongas Mission, the Mission "still remains comparatively unknown."[96] Barrow eventually served as secretary of the English Committee for more than thirty years. In 1913, J. B. Ellis expressed similar sentiments as he observed that "the Mission is almost lost in the overwhelming records published in the SPG's Annual Reports, and few people could find the Pongas country in an Atlas without the aid of the index of names and places."[97] The historical facts of this mission venture in the post-emancipation life of the Anglican Church in the West Indies are virtually unknown today to its contemporary Church membership.

---

94. Barrow, *Fifty Years*, 130.
95. *MF* (1 July 1890): INSERT PAGE NO, USPG Archives; Barrow, *Fifty Years*, 129.
96. See Barrow, *Fifty Years*; *MF* (September 1913): 275, USPG Archives.
97. Ellis, *The Diocese of Jamaica*, 150.

Eclipse of the Mission

By the beginning of the final decade of the nineteenth century, the Pongas Mission in Western Africa – which had embarked on a pursuit of a very enterprising and noble initiative – had been struggling to survive for four decades. Although its demise never really materialized, one event at the beginning of the 1890s marked the beginning of its eclipse. On 8 March 1894, the French government issued a direct order to close the mission schools in the key places where the Mission was doing its greatest work: Domingia, Fallangia, and Farrangia.[98] This was a major blow for the Mission. When the news reached the West Indies, the bishops discussed what response should be given. They decided to convene a special meeting at the SPG headquarters in London to determine an appropriate response. This meeting, in October 1894, was attended by the Bishop of Sierra Leone, members of the English Committee, and Enos Nuttall, the newly appointed Primate of the West Indies, who had become the fourth Bishop of Jamaica in 1880 and would, in 1897, become the first Archbishop of the West Indies.

At that meeting, it was decided not to withdraw from French-occupied territory in the Pongas nor to expand the Mission but to focus on a new field in the Kambia on the Great Scarcies River. Barrow, as Secretary to the Committee, noted that the decision not to withdraw from the old stations but move to "fresh ground" was met with "hearty approval."[99] This was a calculated decision, which recognized that while there could no longer be much progress in the old stations owing to "the many difficulties put it the way of the missionaries by the French Authorities," it would be unwise to abandon or extend the old stations. If they had decided to abandon the old stations, the question of what to do with mission properties and congregations would have had to be determined. If they had decided to continue the work and expand the mission, they would have had to face and answer questions of security, protection, control, and guarantees. On the other hand, the new prospect of work further south was worth pursuing as it was more in the British sphere of influence. Since the political boundaries in the wake of the European Scramble for African lands were still quite unclear, it was agreed

---

98. Order No. 34 received from the French Colonial Administrator, A. Baillat, 8th March 1894, C/AFR/W2, USPG Archives.
99. Barrow, *Fifty Years*, 140.

that this approach was the best option. The decision to open a new site was implemented by Samuel Cole, a product of the West Indies mission to the Rio Pongas, after inspection of the new location by the Bishop of Sierra Leone.

During the meeting in London, guidelines for the recruitment and engagement of West Indian missionaries for service in Africa were also reviewed. Nuttall, as Bishop of Jamaica, put forward recommendations for better management and recruitment, including new qualifications for clergy and lay persons desirous of serving in Africa. He combined spiritual and theological qualifications with practical skills – for example, medical knowledge about how to treat tropical diseases and construction skills required for building houses, churches, and schools. These new qualifications were expanded and adopted by the English Committee and put forward as new Policy Regulations in 1896. The matter of training, terms of employment, and communication of information about the work of the Mission was also addressed at the meeting.[100]

In February 1895, in reporting to the Synod of the Jamaica diocese, Nuttall outlined the decisions of the London meeting and explained their implications for the West Indian church.[101] He emphasized not only the pressing need to make the management and maintenance of the Mission more efficient and satisfactory, but also the evident need for some "heroic demands" of self-sacrifice and self-surrender on the part of the West Indian church. Nuttall felt that since the West Indian church was not sufficiently engaged in missionary work, a missionary call urging its members to participate in missions might stir enthusiasm and devotion among them and that this would prove beneficial for the whole church. From 1894 onwards, however, the constraints in Africa, as well as the declining support from the West Indies, made the survival of the Pongas Mission even more doubtful.

By 1898, the English Committee – which by now had been given full control of the management of the Mission – in consultation with the West Indies and Sierra Leone, concluded that the support base of the Mission was so much in peril that its future was in real jeopardy. Secretary Barrow wrote to Nuttall stating that "the state of affairs is now great and critical in

---

100. Barrow, *Fifty Years*, Appendix II, 155–157.

101. Nuttall, *West Indian Church*. Extracts from a short address delivered by the Bishop of Jamaica in the Synod of the Church of England in Jamaica, February 1895. The following month, Nuttall presented the same prepared statement at the opening of the Provincial Synod meeting in Georgetown, British Guiana, 2 March 1895.

the extreme, so much so as to threaten the existence of the Mission, after the current year's expenses have been settled."[102] Although accepting the factors which had contributed to this grave state of affairs, Barrow blamed the situation on the failure of the West Indian church to do everything it could to improve the circumstances of the Mission. In an explicit and straightforward letter, he outlined the options, which included the prospect of closure of the Mission, and proposed that any new developments be restricted. While seeking a response and advice from Nuttall, as Archbishop of the West Indies, Barrow, on behalf of the English Committee, appealed for more resources and support from the West Indian church.

Twelve months had hardly passed before Lord Stamford, now Chair of the Committee, wrote to Nuttall proposing the drastic step of retrenching existing agents in the Mission and speculating about an honourable way to relieve the Mission of the expense of J. B. McEwen, an experienced but worn-out missionary who had, by then, served twenty-eight years in the Pongas Mission.[103] Nuttall replied, thanking Stamford for his letter but making no commitment to offer McEwen alternative employment in Jamaica. Nuttall hoped that other West Indian dioceses, which were better endowed, would provide an opening for McEwen.[104] McEwen remained in the Pongas, and his son, S. De Jean McEwen, after graduating from Oxford, served the Pongas Mission for forty years before retiring as Archdeacon in 1946.[105]

The crisis in the Africa mission posed a problem for the West Indian church. It had become clear that a decision had to be made about whether to discontinue the Mission altogether or place it on some other footing. In his report to the Standing Committee of the JHFMS held in Kingston 1899, Nuttall outlined all the developments in the Pongas Mission and suggested that a total reorganization of the Mission was needed. He recommended that local control of and responsibility for the Mission be handed over to the diocese of Sierra Leone and to the missionaries and laymen on the ground,

---

102. Minute Book, Barrow to Nuttall, 22 February 1898, National Archives of Jamaica, Spanish Town, Jamaica.

103. Minute Book, Stamford to Nuttall, 22 March 1899, National Archives of Jamaica, Spanish Town, Jamaica.

104. Minute Book, Nuttall to Stamford, 8 April 1899, National Archives of Jamaica, Spanish Town, Jamaica.

105. *G-PM* (April 1947): 7, USPG Archives. Bodleian Library.

while the West Indian church would continue to contribute manpower and money.[106] This position, which reflected the consensus of a further meeting of the English Committee, the West Indian bishops, and the Bishop of Sierra Leone – which took place during the Lambeth Conference of 1898 in the Library of Lambeth Palace – effectively transferred management responsibility for the Mission from the West Indies to England and Western Africa. The Pongas Mission continued into the twentieth century within the episcopal jurisdiction of the diocese of Sierra Leone until 1935, when it achieved its own status as a diocese with its own bishop. With the installation of a bishop for the Pongas, the West Indian Anglican Church's vision of planting a church in African soil was at last fulfilled, though not without great pain, struggles, and failures.

The value of this West Indian church's contribution to the missionary project in Western Africa as catechists, schoolmasters, and missionary priests was not lost on the European missionary societies or the emergent African church and society. Their role in education, in particular, attracted the attention of both the CMS and bishops of the African church. It was in pursuit of a renewed interest in Africa and the West Indies by the CMS in the late nineteenth century that the CMS sponsored the visit of two African bishops to the West Indies in a recruitment drive for West Indian schoolmasters to serve in Africa. In 1895, the Bishop of Sierra Leone, Dr. Ingham, visited Barbados, the Leeward Islands, and Jamaica. In 1897, the Bishop of Western Equatorial Africa, Bishop Tugwell, visited Jamaica, hosted by the Church of Province of the West Indies.[107] Encouraged by these visits, Bishop Nuttall sent Burris and March – two agents from Jamaica, both trained at Codrington – to the Pongas. Burris worked for nine years in the Pongas Mission, returning to Jamaica in 1926. As a retired priest, he did parish work in Pratville, Manchester. Burris died in 1940 at the age of seventy-nine and is buried in the church cemetery at St. Andrew Parish Church, Kingston, Jamaica. March, however, was relocated from the Pongas to serve in Liberia.[108]

---

106. Minute Book, 295–296. National Archives of Jamaica, Spanish Town, Jamaica.

107. See Ellis, *Diocese of Jamaica*, 150, and Caldecott, *Church in the West Indies*, 266. Ingham published a report of his tour entitled, *The African in the West Indies*.

108. Evans, *History of the Diocese of Jamaica*, 112; *G-PM* (October 1938): 28, UPGS Archives.

Conclusion

Historically, the bold and audacious participation of West Indians in the missionary enterprise in Western Africa in the nineteenth century has been presented as a failed attempt by "nostalgic exiles" to make a useful contribution to the project. Eminent historians such as Ajayi, Neill, Bauer, and others suggest that this perceived failure was because, as New World Africans, they had difficulty adapting to the African environment and this inhibited their contribution to the missionary enterprise, making it less than useful.[109] Wariboko, although focusing primarily on those who were involved in the efforts to evangelize Southern Nigeria in the late nineteenth century, also argues that the West Indians did not have much regard for Africa and were much more interested in the advancement of their personal careers.[110]

However, this study of the participation of the West Indian Anglicans in the Pongas Mission demonstrates their high degree of adaptation and a strong determination to succeed in the enterprise despite the formidable internal and external challenges they faced. Indeed, the longevity of the careers of more than half the number of West Indians who participated in the Pongas Mission suggests a significant level of physical and cultural adaptation, especially at the level of promoting vernacular Christianity and advancing the educational enterprise of the Mission.

The assumption that black West Indians would fare better than white Europeans against the hostile tropical environment in Western Africa was, once again, exposed and proved to be quite unfounded. The West Indians in the Pongas Mission suffered the effects of the African climate just as much as the white European and suffered many casualties and bereavements. Despite this, however, they demonstrated passion and persistence against the odds. In fact, the West Indians had to work harder for acceptance as agents of Christian mission precisely because they were black, as well as because they were from a part of the British Empire where the practice of slavery had been courageously and successfully fought against and abolished after a long and multifaceted struggle. The West Indians' cause in Africa was not helped by the failure of the British to back up the anti-slavery movement's agenda of providing legitimate trade and commerce with West African

---

109. Neill, *History of Christian Missions*; Bauer, *2000 Years of Christianity*.
110. Wariboko, *Ruined by "Race."* 207.

regions like the Pongas, which had been mooted as part of the campaign in British proposals for the abolition of slavery in Africa and as a remedy for Africa's wrongs. The Pongas Mission, despite its vision and its best efforts, failed to open the door for legitimate trade and, in fact, was constantly constrained in its ability to effectively change and transform the socio-economic realities on the mission field. On the other hand, the Mission did break new ground, as was their aim and intent. They went to a part of Western Africa that had been neglected or abandoned by the Western missionary enterprise after its failure to establish a mission in that region in the mid-nineteenth century. The Pongas Mission demonstrated the capacity of West Indian agents to participate in every aspect of the missionary enterprise. They understood the importance of introducing Christianity in the vernacular idioms and were very keen to do so even as a bicultural exercise, where the English language was used in services and in religious rites. Without doubt, Duport's translations into the Susu language of the Book of Common Prayer, the Liturgy for Marriage and the Burial of the Dead, the Psalms, the Gospels, and the Epistles – which were published by the SPCK – were an outstanding contribution of the Mission. These laid the groundwork not only for training other missionaries but also for the emergence of an indigenous leadership of the Susu church.

The schools established by the Pongas Mission, with the help of Sierra Leonian schoolmasters, produced a class of locally educated scholars who were able to find good employment among the French traders and contribute to the development of their community. Some, like the young native Thomas Curtis, stood out among them. In an environment in which the spread of Islam in Western Africa was on the increase, they interacted as much with African Mohammedans as they did with European or American merchants. While the West Indian missionaries' strongly Christian-Protestant-Anglican background may or may not have been sufficient preparation for dealing with the challenge of Islam that they encountered in the Pongas country, they confronted that challenge and wrestled with all the issues arising from it. Some of those issues included Islamic sanction for the practice of slaveholding, greegree-merchandising, polygamy, and the pastoral problem of interfaith marriages. Samuel Hughes provided a good description of the pastoral challenge of such a marriage in his report in 1882, where he described how, in addition to his counselling, he had to send "a bigman of Fotoba" to talk the "palaver" with the bride's Mohammedan parents to resolve an interfaith problem.[111]

As agents of Christian mission, the West Indian missionaries influenced and affected the material culture of the Pongas with the introduction of new technologies in building construction, agriculture, family sociology, and religion. While challenging aspects of African indigenous culture that nineteenth century Protestant missionaries on the whole regarded as "superstition," they demonstrated a determination to use Christian agency as a means of African liberation from its slave-based culture and economy. They regarded this cultural problem of slavery, which impacted the local economy, as the principal source of the ubiquity of African violence and death and the root cause of Africa's underdevelopment and perceived moral degradation. To all the challenges that confronted them, they responded using Anglican rites, including observance of saints' days and religious festivals to absolve, heal, comfort, and educate.

In the end, despite all its noble attempts, due to declining economic circumstances in the West Indies and external political pressures in Western Africa, the West Indian church was unable to sustain the mission that they had initiated to the Rio Pongas. The fledgling church that it had created in Western Africa had to become part of the larger network of the church in Africa in order to survive and be sustainable.

---

111. *MF* (1 September 1882): 293, USPG Archives.

Part 3: Interpretation

Nostalgic Exiles or Missionary Enterprisers?

CHAPTER 7

Encountering Africa

Critical examinations of the encounter between the Christian missionary enterprise and Africa in the nineteenth century have formed a complex and highly contested field of inquiry. Interpreters of the encounter have vilified and repudiated both the messengers and the message of Christian mission. Equally, they have been exonerated and appropriated by others. Nineteenth-century agents of Christian mission have been portrayed either as covert imperialists, who laid the ground for "a state of colonialism in anticipation of the colonial state," or as overt collaborators with the colonial state, who sought to transform the African heart and mind into colonial conformity with European values and norms.[1] Indeed, the problem, as stated by the Comaroffs, is that

> the impact of Protestant evangelists as harbingers of industrial capitalism lay in the fact that their civilizing mission was simultaneously symbolic and practical, theological and temporal. The goods and techniques they brought with them to Africa presupposed the messages and meanings they proclaimed in the pulpit, and vice versa. Both were vehicles of a moral economy that celebrated the global spirit of commerce, the commodity, and the imperial marketplace.[2]

The problem, however, was not that simple. Indeed, some agents of the Western missionary enterprise did in fact act in collaboration with the

---
1. Comaroff and Comaroff, *Of Revelation and Revolution*, 11.
2. Comaroff and Comaroff, 9.

colonial enterprise and were harbingers of a moral economy which "celebrated the global spirit of commerce, the commodity, and the imperial marketplace," as the Comaroffs assert. But, as John Peel has shown, "though the links between Christian mission and 'civilization' were extremely powerful and consequential, they were historically contingent and subject to strains."[3] There were other significant nineteenth-century Western mission actors – like mission strategist and thinker Henry Venn (Secretary of the CMS from 1840–1872) and those agents who understood and pursued his philosophy of mission – whose influence over missionary engagement in Africa might best be described as facilitators or midwives of African self-liberation and self-development and progenitors of modern African nationalism. Indeed, some missionary agents in nineteenth-century Africa appeared, at times, to act in ways that seemed intended to subvert the colonial project. In their engagement with Africa, their genuine pro-African orientation and self-giving commitment to the enablement of African self-development often placed them at odds with the colonial state.

Christian missionaries who were inclined this way showed a strong inclination and motivation to redress what was regarded, in globalized perspectives, as "the problem of Africa." As Peel cryptically puts it, "the double irony of Christian missions since the early nineteenth century is that they have become progressively estranged from the dominant culture of the societies that sent them, while they have often succeeded in their target areas less for their own reasons than for the reasons of those they have evangelised."[4] And, as he has shown in the case of the Yoruba in Western Africa, Western missionary encounter with Africa in the nineteenth century was not just a matter of the "transmission of a message," but the "appropriation" of the message in ways which created religious change and the making of a new African religion. Such missionary pursuits, often by nonconformist missionaries, were executed intentionally, without the aid or support of the colonial state or any forms of reliance on the imperial projects of Europeans.

Perceiving this reality and ambiguity in the complexity of Christian missionary engagement, the Comaroffs acknowledge:

---

3. Peel, *Religious Encounter*, 5.
4. Peel, *Religious Encounter*, 5.

Indeed, it is in the signifying role of evangelical practice (often very mundane, material practice) that we begin to find an answer to the most basic, most puzzling question about the historical agency of Christian missionaries: how it is that they, like other colonial functionaries, wrought far-reaching political, social, and economic transformations in the absence of concrete resources of much consequence.[5]

Within this range of perspectives, the question, therefore, is this: How did the West Indians encounter Africa, and how should their encounters be interpreted? The black West Indians participating in the civilizing missions in Africa encountered Africa in a variety of ways, not least as ostensibly civilized subjects of an Empire that was seeking to redeem Africa. No doubt conditioned by the massive negative propaganda on Africa, especially by the mission leaders in the West Indies, they participated in the enterprise with stereotypical nineteenth-century images and perceptions of Africa and, at times, acted as if they were white European masters of the project. While acknowledging these realities, it must also be noted that the response of the West Indians to encounters with Africa varied according to individual personalities, circumstances, and modalities of engagement. Even the dictates of the philosophies, conceptions, and regulations of the missionary societies which had recruited and deployed them helped to determine their response to whatever they encountered in Africa. If, however, there was a common factor which influenced and shaped their response to issues encountered in Africa, it was the social context of the West Indian slave societies from which they came, and the freedom and life in a free society which they innately understood and valued.

As pointed out in the previous chapter, the Anglican Mission to the Pongas is the one West Indian mission initiative to Africa in which the West Indians were most in command and possibly had the widest-ranging contact with African life and society. Surprisingly, in the aftermath of the collapse and failure of the British CMS-led Niger Mission of 1841, the concept of "native agency" gained remarkable ground in Europe as being the most realistic method for the effective transmission of Christianity in African soil. There

---

5. Comaroff and Comaroff, *Of Revelation and Revolution*, 9.

were strong sentiments in both Britain and in the West Indies that the West Indian Mission to the Rio Pongas was an exercise in "native agency." Mission leaders in Britain and in the West Indies strongly asserted this view.[6] Given the scope of their contact with African life and society, the Pongas Mission might, therefore, provide a good basis on which to investigate the realities of the encounter between the West Indian missionaries and Africa in the nineteenth century. Since each of the three missionary projects in this study were affected, influenced, and shaped by encounters with Africa, reference will be made to each of them; but the main focus will be the Pongas Mission. Attempts will be made, where possible, to discern and draw any relevant connections and conclusions concerning the ways in which the West Indian agents of Christian mission in the nineteenth century encountered and responded to Africa.

The Basel Mission to the Gold Coast

The Basel Mission, which was situated in the Akwapim mountains on the Gold Coast of Africa, had a structure and philosophy of missionary engagement that was based on the concept of mission work centred around a Christian settler-colony. The missionaries lived in circumscribed mission compounds and, at least in the initial years, contact with real African society – especially for the West Indians – was very limited and closely monitored. In addition to the physical environment of the mission, Jon Miller points out that the practice of "mutual watching" was also a means of reporting breaches of the missionary code by colleague missionaries. Such breaches were then reported to the Committee in Basel. "Mutual watching" was also used as a tool to maintain the moral character and public reputation of the Mission.[7] In this type of environment, the physical and psychological conditions of the Mission were very restrictive and carefully guarded against "African influences."

On the eve of their historic departure to Africa, the Moravian elders in Jamaica solemnly warned the Jamaicans recruited for the mission to "keep

---

6. See "Report on The Pongas Mission," *MF* (1 May 1863): 113. USPG Archives. This report was editorialized as follows: "The Missionaries and all others in the employ of the mission are now, without exception, Africans by origin." See also "The Present Position and Prospects of Christian Mission in Africa", *MF* (1 May 1873): 129–133, USPG Archives. Bodleian Library.

7. Miller, *Social Control*, 103–107.

yourselves from idols" (1 John 5:21 KJV). One of the implications of this charge was that they, as a band of Christianized West Indians recruited to engage in the missionary task in Africa, should endeavour to not compromise the missionary project by undue association with African culture and society. Implied in the charge was the notion that "idols" meant associating with anything "African," particularly in religion and culture, which Europeans considered idolatry or "superstition." It is difficult to judge to what extent this advice was taken to heart and followed in Africa by the West Indians. The fact is that, given their African ancestry, there would naturally have been some degree of curiosity, and even anticipation, on the part of the West Indians for real contact with African life. From all indications, they approached the missionary task with that kind of curiosity and intent.

The Jamaicans' experience in Africa, especially in the first five years, was shaped as much by the internal conditions in the Akropong Mission as by the external conditions of West African society. To their surprise, one of the most significant and troubling issues they encountered was the continuing practice of African slavery, an issue that was also problematic for the Basel Mission. While the Moravians, as a Christian missionary movement, tacitly accepted the institution of slavery and were by no means anti-slavery advocates,[8] the Baslers had no clear pronouncement on the subject either. But the West Indians, for whom slave emancipation meant a great deal, could not have been expected to countenance the coexistence of slavery and Christian mission in Akropong, especially in light of the example of the Moravian missionaries on the Mount Carmel estate in Jamaica.

One of the most troubling concerns for the West Indians in Akropong, therefore, was the fact that Andreas Riis, the Mission leader, employed Africans as slaves in his household and appeared to have been engaged in trading in slaves in Akropong. This concern came to a head in 1845 in the incident involving the public flogging of West Indian Jonas Hosford on allegations of theft by one of Riis's African slaves. The band of West Indian settlers reacted swiftly and strongly to Riis's involvement in this flogging. The humiliation caused by his actions was not only a disappointment to the West Indians, who had cherished high hopes for the Mission, it also brought

---

8. Hutton, *History of the Moravian Church*; Sensbach, *Separate Canaan*; Haenger et al., *Slaves and Slaveholders*.

them into sharp conflict with Riis and strengthened their resolve to protest against his leadership and his racial attitudes towards the Africans, as well as his treatment of them. It not only brought the issue of African slavery into sharp focus for them but may also have served to bolster their determination to stand up for their welfare and their human dignity, as implied in their protest letter to the Basel Committee.[9] This humiliating incident also appeared to have been instrumental in Hosford eventually leaving the Mission and returning to the West Indies.

As the West Indians engaged in evangelizing work among the Akwapims in Akropong, their encounters with African culture only served to further heighten their curiosity, which sometimes placed them in awkward situations. For example, being West Indians of African ancestry, they would naturally have been curious about elements of African religion which had to do with rituals of death, burial, and the meaning of sacred places. Faced with the task of establishing western-style education through the mission schools, while at the same time experiencing personal insecurity from the social exclusion practised in the Akropong Mission, appeared to have disturbed and confused these mission workers.

Undoubtedly, as time went on, they desired to encounter and experience much more of African life than the Basel leadership allowed. The experience of Ed Walker, who bravely walked away from the Mission to find an alternative life outside it, demonstrated how hard and disorienting this was for the West Indians. Nevertheless, the West Indians persevered and reached out to encounter Africa and Africans, as evidenced from the examples of John and Mary Hall – who were among the pioneers of the first Basel congregation in Akropong – and Alexander Worthy Clerk – who became an outstanding evangelist in the mission and itinerated into the hinterlands of the Akwapim mountains in pursuit of converts and new mission stations in the mid-1850s.

Unfortunately, records pertaining to these encounters are fragmentary, due to lack of adequate recording and issues related to preservation of the West Indian experience in Africa. Nevertheless, available sources such as the autobiography of Peter Hall – son of John and Mary Hall – who grew up in the mission and became the First Moderator of the Presbyterian Church

---

9. Letter from West Indians, 13 January 1845, Letter-books Correspondence ‚Afrika III (1842–1848): vol. D-1, 2, BMS Archives.

of Ghana, tell part of this story and provide some insight into how the West Indians viewed their encounters with Africa. In addition, Correspondence and reports to the Basel Committee in Switzerland provide evidence of their frustrations, anxieties, and concerns in Africa. The story of Catherine Mulgrave – detailing her contribution to the development of the mission schools, while simultaneously undergoing a deep personal crisis in her marriage to George Thompson – highlights the kind of personal struggles the West Indians experienced in Akropong while supporting the work of the Mission. In Catherine's case, her piety and devotion to the Mission were well communicated in her correspondence with the Basel Committee.

Limited and circumscribed though contact with Africa was for West Indians in the Basel Mission in Akropong, especially in the early formative years, the evidence suggests that they were unafraid to respond to whatever challenges they encountered and, in fact, demonstrated their willingness to make courageous adjustments in their new environment.

The Baptist Mission to the Cameroon

In contrast to the Basel Mission at Akropong on the Gold Coast, the Baptist Mission to the Cameroon allowed its missionaries much more freedom to operate and make decisions. Given the relatively flexible and entrepreneurial nature of the Baptist organization, its missionary agents enjoyed much greater freedom of contact with Africa and African life. The many problems and challenges they encountered, both in Clarence Bay and on the mainland, brought them into direct contact with African realities in all their varied forms. Although the Baptist missionaries from Jamaica encountered Africa in multiple ways, they too were given strict guidelines – in line with standard European missionary field policy – concerning contact with the natives. The issue of white superintendence was a constant and overriding presence, ensuring that European perceptions both of Africa and of the enterprise of Christian mission were reinforced and upheld. As described in chapter five, the case of the Jamaican Baptists in the Cameroon Mission showed the extent to which those who remained after 1846 creatively utilized the freedom and flexibility they enjoyed to persevere and respond to African encounters in the communities in Clarence Bay and around Mt. Cameroon.

Like other West Indian agents in Western Africa in the nineteenth century, the Jamaican Baptists also exhibited curiosity about Africa and were often ambivalent, or had strong reactions to encounters with African cultural realities. J. J. Fuller, for example, upon landing in Cameroon Bay on his first day in Africa, exhibited a mixture of curiosity, ignorance, and westernized perceptions of African life as he encountered what he described as a "a real savage." Describing his anxious curiosity to see the phenomenon, he immediately wandered off and was surprised at what he encountered. "I had not gone far in the bush when I heard a noise and looking before me I saw a man, so hideously dressed that I took to my heels and ran as fast as I could go." Fuller then described the phenomenon:

> He was naked but rubbed all over with red clay. His hair all thickly matted in clay, around his neck he had a necklace of small shells broken and strung like beads broad, the same on both arms, thigh and waist, a piece of monkey skin formed his only covering, to the end of which was fastened a wooden bell. In his left arm was a knife, on his head was a broad hat made of palm leaves, covered with wild animal skin. On one side a rosette of parrot's feathers and in the front, a monkey's skull. His face daubed with red ochre on one side, on the other with chalk. He carried three spears in his hands.[10]

Fuller's swift response in taking to his heels and running as fast as he could probably indicates the extent of his shock, fright, and ignorance of African customs. He later learned that this was the formal African dress code that was adopted when meeting and welcoming strangers and new arrivals. Later, Fuller was able to laugh at the fact that he had run away from the very "heathen we had come to Africa to convert." John Clarke, the Mission leader, ever a keen observer, writing from Fernando Po in 1841 during his reconnaissance mission, describes a similar experience in relation to native dress during a visit to the interior town of Hiccory:

> The dress of this people is a covering of clay and palm oil, the head loaded with clay in a thousand locks of hair, resting at night on a piece of wood, and by day on the shoulders, ornamented

---

10. Fuller, MS *Autobiography*, 23, BMS Archives.

with the skulls of dogs and monkeys, pieces of broken plate, shells broken into small round pieces and vertebrae of snakes, a hat of a flat, and bowl shape fastened to the clay with a long iron nail and ornamented with feathers, snake skins, shells, skulls, and such like finery. The neck is ornamented with goat's fat, pieces of skinney fat, white beads, straw or grass plaited, ornaments and strings, snake skins, and vertebrae, calabashes, stuffed skins of small animals, shells, etc. arms, wrists, knees, and ankles, and the top of a walking staff similarly ornamented, a knife in the left arm; and a few lances of barbed wood in hand.[11]

As a white man in Africa, Clarke's impression was that "if they do not know you, they and their children turn around, and run into the woods to hide themselves." Just as Fuller and his West Indian colleagues had to assess and interpret their African encounters, so too did Clarke and his European colleague missionaries. As we shall see later, what was evident in the Baptist Mission to the Cameroon was the extent to which the West Indians persevered with their missionary task in the face of enormous challenges and the ways in which they responded to various African encounters.

The Anglican Mission to Rio Pongas

One of the first encounters for the West Indian missionaries in Africa was, of course, with the African landscape. Upon arriving in Africa, the West Indian missionaries were eager to explore the African landscape and see how the reality compared with the Africa they had imagined. Invariably, comparisons were made between what they encountered in their day-to-day experiences in Africa and the West Indian landscape they had left behind. For example, when the Barbadians Leacock and Duport arrived in Freetown in 1855, their first physical impression of Africa disabused Leacock of any ideas or images he might have had about the "wilds of Africa." As Leacock noted:

> The scenery, the trees, the shrubbery, the fruits, the flowers, the climate, the people; everything and every person, reminds me of home. Even devil-grass (called here Bahama–grass), the pest

---

11. Clarke, *BHFA* (1841), BMS Archives.

and plague of our Barbadian planters, is here. It was among the first things that attracted my notice, and for the first time in my life I delighted to behold it.[12]

Leacock, as an elderly white Barbadian, perhaps had romanticized imaginations of Africa, as he expressed in his anticipated missionary encounter of Africa of desiring to "go to bed in Afric's dust."[13] The reminders of "home," such as those offered by these early impressions of the Western African physical landscape, evidently affected the manner in which he, and no doubt others from Barbados, encountered and engaged with Africa. This might also have had a bearing on their determination to succeed in the enterprise. Nevertheless, despite such apparent or readily imagined affinities with the African landscape, the missionaries attempted to recreate a sense of "home" in Africa, as revealed by Chief Lewis Wilkinson, one of the early local patrons of the Mission. In his description of the Christmas service at the Fallangia church in 1865. Wilkinson described how "two days before Christmas the church was adorned with palm branches and beautiful scented tropical flowers, and amongst these 'The Barbadian pride' and other West Indian flowers."[14] While the missionaries might have thought that these adornments would embellish the religious aesthetics of the Anglican ritual that marked the high season of the church's liturgy, such adornments might also have aided their adjustment by attempting to recreate a sense of "home" within the African landscape. For the Barbadians, the "Barbadian pride" distinctly marked "home" in the way landscapes shape memory.

As they traversed the landscape of the Pongas region of Western Africa in their itinerant evangelization work, the West Indians, like other Western missionaries in Africa, often noted and described various aspects of the physical environment, the plants, animals, insects, rivers, dwelling houses, and the social and economic interactions of the communities they encountered. At times, they tried to interpret these elements from an African perspective and assess their impact on African life. For example, occurrences of natural disasters – such as tornadoes, hurricanes, famine – and outbreaks of communicable diseases – such as smallpox, yellow fever, and other plagues – were

---

12. Caswall, *The Martyr of the Pongas*, 111.
13. Caswall, 111.
14. *MF* (1866): 60, USPG Archives.

seized upon as opportunities for teaching and interpreting natural phenomena in spiritual terms. In their Christianizing mission work, they used any experience and opportunity to propose new models and interpretations of Western Christian spirituality in the context of African realities.

In the countryside in which the Pongas Mission was located, one of the impacts of frequent disasters, natural or otherwise, was a state of deprivation experienced by the people and their communities. In describing the privations of the people – and indeed, their own privations – the West Indian missionaries often spoke in ways that suggested an insider, codependent relationship with the community that was now their adopted home. At the same time, the privileged position they occupied, as outsiders who had access to external help, was never too far from the surface. For example, in describing the abatement of a devastating famine in Fallangia in 1862, John Duport told of the daily prayers he offered on behalf of the community and his thankfulness that the distress had been greatly relieved. At the same time, he noted, "We have suffered much, in common with others, as we were obliged to send to Sierra Leone to purchase rice at a very high rate of 15s. per bushel –the same rice which we usually bought at 6s. per bushel. But we are only too thankful that we have obtained some, while the poor people here fed on leaves and palm-cabbage."[15]

This suffering "in common with others," was certainly the element of privation and want of staple food in a situation of famine. But the comparison as insiders stopped there. As outsiders, the missionaries had access to external resources, in contrast to those who had no access to outside help and had to continue suffering from want of their staple diet in a situation of famine. Presumably, while the nature of Duport's thanksgiving at the relief of the social crisis might have been the same as that of the native people, in terms of gratitude for provision of food, the reality of his privileged position would have set him apart.

Nevertheless, suffering "in common with others" meant sharing a common life with the people in the Pongas, even if as an "insider-outsider," and this also meant sharing common social problems. One of those problems was vulnerability to the loss of prized property due to simple larceny or persistent attacks from predatory animals. For example, one month, the main

---

15. *MF* (1 January 1863): 18–19, USPG Archives.

Mission House at Fallangia lost "ten sheep, three bullocks, and a good cow in calf" through attacks from what was described as a "bush cat."[16] Leopards and snakes (red, black, and green) often visited the compound and relieved the Mission of valuable stocks such as turkey or other poultry being raised by the mission staff for its food supply. In describing this situation, Duport noted that "these creatures are numerous and they come into the yard at night."[17] Losses incurred from such acts were not only a menace, they represented forms of deprivations to which the missionaries were subjected and which they then mentioned in their reports. In his report of 1884, Doughlin described a plague of insects that the West Indians experienced. Noting the impact of *chigoes* on the land and the people, he observed that "the chigoe has only been here for eighteen months, and it has spread over the whole country. . . . It is the *Pulex penetrans*, which is in the West Indies, but is in a savage state. There is a venom in the sting which is not in that in the West Indies. The people suffer much from them. It is sad to think that they will never be driven from the country again."[18]

Challenges Faced in Encountering Africa
A Plague of Locusts

From Samuel Cole, we get another example of the kind of environmental challenge the West Indians encountered in the Pongas. As if symbolic of the way in which the Mission was being eclipsed at that stage of its development, Cole provided a vivid description of a plague of locusts which afflicted the Pongas country between January and June of 1893:

> These destructive creatures made their appearance on January 28th and took over two hours and twenty minutes in passing over. It looked very much as if there was an eclipse during their transit. Their second visit was made in April, when they continued until June, devouring almost the entire rice-crop that was just springing up. There was much unrest and consternation among the people. Immediately after the heavy rains their third visit

---

16. *MF* (1865): 39, USPG Archives.
17. *MF* (1 February 1860): 42, USPG Archives.
18. *MF* (2 June 1884): 177, USPG Archives.

was made, when large quantities of guinea-corn, rice and other plants were devoured. The anxiety for the future is very great, and food is beginning to be scarce.[19]

It was not long after these occurrences that the French government moved to eclipse the West Indian Mission in the Pongas. They ordered the closure of its mission schools in all three centres, Domingia, Fallangia, and Farrangia. This unpleasant and unwelcome political encounter with the French authorities was a severe blow to the West Indians. Already troubled by the threatening plagues in the natural environment, to which they and the whole community had to respond, they now had to contend with this major blow to the continuation of their mission in Western Africa caused by external imperial forces.

The manner in which the West Indian missionaries responded to these issues – in both spiritual and practical terms – demonstrates their commitment to Africa and African society, and to the project in which they were engaged. In times of social distress, they called their congregations to prayer and fasting, seeking spiritual help and divine intervention. For example, after the failure of the groundnut crop in the Pongas region in 1866, and the negative effect this had on the local economy, Duport and his team used the Lenten period that followed as a time of fasting and prayer for economic recovery. The crop failure had resulted in depression among the merchants and people and left the poor without means of purchasing food and clothing. Therefore, the church proclaimed that the first day of Lent be observed as a day of Solemn Fast. Duport reported that this first day of Lent was "strictly observed by our people"[20] and noted that there was "a large congregation in the morning and a much larger in the evening at 7:15." There were night services twice a week, on Wednesdays and Fridays, during the season of Lent.

Since the practice of fasting was part of the religious rite of Islam, it was not a new phenomenon in the Pongas. Duport, as the advocate of Christianity, used the opportunity to differentiate between the Christian practice of intercessory fasting and the Muslim ritual of obligatory fasting. In his report, Duport did not elaborate on the difference but noted that "the Mohammedans having their fast of thirty days I availed myself of the opportunity of explaining to our people the difference between the Christian and the Mohammedan

---

19. Barrow, *Fifty Years*, 138–139.
20. *MF* (1866): 96–97, USPG Archives.

fast." Fasting was also strictly observed in the Mission church on Good Friday.[21] The difference, presumably, lay not only in the length and seasonality but also in the liturgical experience and meaning of the Christian rite of fasting.

In their task of establishing Christianity in Africa, the West Indians had to find ways of institutionalizing Christian traditions. Alert to every opportunity to present Christianity as a religion relevant to Africa, they were always on the lookout for parallels between the natural environment or local conditions and the prescribed cycle of Anglican ritual observances. This became an important tool of their missionary engagement in the Pongas Mission.

As periods of fasting were introduced, so too were periods of thanksgiving. St. Andrew's Day, on 30 November, was appointed as a day of General Thanksgiving in the Pongas Mission and appropriate liturgical exercises were instituted.[22] These spiritual exercises, to a large extent, not only enabled the West Indians to manage, appreciate, and adapt themselves to the physical and social environment of the parts of Western Africa they had made their missionary "home" but also helped to undergird the missionary goal they pursued and counteract the challenges of mission work, including constant personal threats – illness, suffering, and death from the "African fever" – and dislocations and privations caused by other factors. As they served in Africa, making spiritual adjustments was as important as physical or cultural adaptation.

In terms of practical responses to social and economic adversities, the West Indian missionaries provided assistance in different forms to people in various communities. For example, in responding to the frequent outbreaks of disastrous fires, they introduced preventive measures such as limiting the growth of bush grass that caused many fires in the dry season.[23] They emphasized land cultivation and introduced measures of soil conservation and crop diversification. Reporting on the people's response following the great famine of 1862 in Fallangia, J. A. Maurice noted that "famine has taught the people a lesson. . . . They have planted corn, yams, and a large quantity of rice – besides a good deal of cotton." This kind of response evidently gave the missionaries a feeling of optimism, and Maurice expressed the hope that

---

21. *MF* (1 April 1867): 315, USPG Archives.
22. *MF* (1866): 35, USPG Archives.
23. *MF* (1 January 1863): 19, USPG Archives.

Fallangia would someday become an important place – "the Antioch of the Rio Pongas."[24]

Contesting African Culture

One of the challenges of the nineteenth-century Western missionary enterprise was the way in which it encountered and sought to contest local culture and traditional religious beliefs. In Africa, the West Indians should hardly have been surprised, let alone horrified, at manifestations of the African religious beliefs they encountered. Given their background in the repressive slave societies of the West Indies, where the retention of African religious beliefs had been instrumental in sustaining and preserving ethnic identity and survival, it would be natural to expect that they would at least have appreciated the cultural significance of similar manifestations in Africa. But it is important to understand that it was as agents of Christian mission – and, as such, as advocates of Western mission Christianity – that these missionaries responded to phenomena such as spirit possession, blood sacrifice, acts of ritualized atonements, and attempts at controlling or submitting to the powers of nature that they encountered in Africa. Stories of the missionaries' encounters with witchcraft, obeah, and forms of myal religion in Africa suggest that they had some knowledge and familiarity with such manifestations.[25] For example, before he went to Africa – while serving as parish priest in the West Indian island of Nevis – Hamble Leacock had the experience of confronting an obeah man who "possessed a certain charm, and was an accomplished poisoner."[26]

In encountering similar manifestations in Africa, perhaps expressed in varied cultural idioms, the West Indian missionaries generally responded rationally, expressed scepticism, and questioned the belief systems which they thought undergirded such phenomena. They proposed counter-religious claims and generally asserted what they believed was the superiority and authority of the Christian religion over all other belief systems. A case in point was their general response to the phenomenon called *gree-grees*. A *gree-gree* was a fetish or ornament that was widely used throughout the Pongas country

---

24. MF (1 December 1863): 279, USPG Archives.
25. Handler and Bilby, *"On the Early Use,"* 87–100.
26. Caswall, *Martyr of the Pongas*, 52.

for protection against evil spirits. Leacock described a *gree-gree* as consisting of "a few words of the Koran, written in Arabic, and enclosed in a leather case."[27] Not long after his arrival in Africa, John Duport found himself alone at the mission station in Fallangia. He gave vivid accounts of his encounters with several people and reported the widespread use of *gree-grees*, and he was quick to add people's alleged confessions of their experience of the inadequacy of the *gree-grees* to solve their problems. Not only did Duport declare the impotence and inadequacy of such devices to achieve their purported intentions, he also decried as false the basis on which claims for their advantageous and beneficial use were made. Duport noted in his journal:

> Sunday, June 8, 1856. There were present at morning and evening service sixty-three persons, and many more. I again compared the power of Jesus to the power of gree-grees (if they have any power at all), taking for my subject the resurrection of Lazarus at the command of Jesus.[28]

Duport did not merely assert the superiority of Christianity over local African custom but compared the power of Jesus and the power of the fetish. He contested the efficacy of the power of the fetish. He noted:

> After evening service old Bantra told me that everything I said concerning gree-grees was very true, for he had proved it himself, and that those that made them were only robbing the people, and deceiving them. Thomas's mother told me that she once had plenty of them, but since we began to speak about them, she has cast them all away, and besides, she herself has proved them to be all lies; for she had a severe pain in her head, and a gree-gree was sent her to place on it; she did so, but it appeared to her that the pain increased; she took it from her head and cast it away. Very similar confessions were made by Eliza, Maria, and Mammy Sue. . . . At night I continued on the subject. On Monday morning a woman brought a bottle of greeters and

---

27. *MF* (1856): 230, USPG Archives.
28. Caswall, *Martyr of the Pongas*, 241–242.

asked me to destroy it, as she was afraid to do so. I took it from her and have it in my possession.[29]

From the commencement of the Pongas Mission, the West Indians campaigned against the practice of using *gree-grees* as a fetish and a means of self-protection, and they made every effort to eradicate its use. Yet, despite their relentless campaign, the practice persisted, as missionary R. J. Clarke discovered as late as 1879 on his tour of Isles de Los. In the Mohammedan town of Kapora, Clarke found a man preparing for war with both *gree-grees* and the crucifix on his person.[30] As if to show the extent of the influence of both Christianity and Islam, this man employed both the Mohammedan and Christian fetish to make doubly sure of his protection as he prepared to engage in local hostilities and war.

The practice of "blood sacrifice" as a ritual for social cleansing was another custom which the West Indians encountered and challenged. This practice, which ran deep within the local culture, was based on the *Kolungi* –the native sacrifice for the dead – and involved an organized ritual that included a ceremony around an altar decorated with rice, goat blood, kola nuts, liqueur, and perhaps bottles of some local wine. The ceremony consisted of an individual costumed in the images of a male devil or a female devil officiating around an altar. The officiating priest would perform exorcisms or inducement of spirits as requested. The West Indians condemned this practice, calling it "devil-worship," since it seemed to them to have diabolical consequences on whole communities. Their response to this type of phenomenon might have been the normative missionary response to what was generally regarded by the Western missionary establishment as "superstition." But this phenomenon was also perceived as something that threatened to block or retard the progress of the Mission, hence their strong condemnation.

The Bahamian Abel Phillips drew attention to two such ceremonies in the foothill towns of Mawunde and Yengisa, some eight to twelve miles from Fallangia. In 1860, while itinerating from his station at Domingia, he entered Mawunde and met large groups of people leaving the town for a ceremony that was to be held just outside its borders. Phillips observed rice with palm oil, together with the clothes in which a deceased person had died, placed at

---

29. Caswall, 241–242.
30. *MF* (1 June 1880): 192, USPG Archives.

the entrance to the town. In his report, he commented, "It is customary in this country, when one dies, to put rice, etc, outside the town, together with palm oil, rum, pipes, tobacco, and whatever the deceased loved in his life, in order (as they fancy) to draw the spirits away from the place, and to prevent his relatives and friends from being haunted by his ghost."[31]

Although, as a West Indian, Phillips might have understood this practice as a form of myalism, he gave no indication in this report of his own feelings or response to it. In contrast, he reacted strongly to the activities of local Islamists in the town and, in the same report, noted that:

> the Mohammedans are trying their utmost to convert the young people of Yengisa, and, I am sorry to say, not without some success. It seems to me that unless we can follow-up the first attack on heathenism, we had almost better not attempt to convert then at all. As soon as the heathen begin to have any misgivings, if we are not at hand to cherish those misgivings, and to direct them to their blessed Saviour, a Mohammedan teacher is always at hand to take advantage of their feeling after God, and to induce them to adopt his own perversion of the truth.[32]

Nevertheless, the fact that Phillips mentioned this ritual practice in his report suggests that it had caught his attention and he had tried to attach meaning to it. He witnessed a similar ceremony at the town of Yengisa, with the added feature of large bundles of hair – instead of rice and palm oil – placed by the widow as an expression of sorrow over the loss of her dearly departed.[33]

Witchcraft

On the whole, the West Indian missionaries showed less tolerance towards the practice of witchcraft than towards any other cultural practice they encountered in Western Africa. The reason seems to have been the excessive use of violence that was associated with witchcraft. Whenever they encountered situations where individuals or villages had been destroyed, allegedly

---

31. *MF* (1 August 1862): 178–179, USPG Archives.
32. *MF* (1 August 1862): 179. USPG Archives.
33. MF (1 August 1862): 179, USPG Archives.

using witchcraft, the missionaries invariably expressed horror and took some form of action. For example, within three months of his arrival in the Rio Pongas, the Barbadian Hamble Leacock reported the existence of witchcraft in most villages and noted that "in some villages it is enough that suspicion only rests on an individual to cause him severe punishment; but when the circumstances is proved, the poor wretch, having a weight tied to him, is thrown into the river, to be devoured by alligators, or he is tied to a stake and burnt."[34] While Leacock was quick to point out that not all cases were as dramatic or as aggressively violent, he noted that other, less violent, courses of action were often taken. In the same account, he cited the case of a slave who was accused and convicted of practising witchcraft; such a slave would have either been banished into the interior or sold to foreign slave merchants.

The missionaries Neville and Doughlin later found out that rivers and alligators were often linked with local responses to the practice of witchcraft. William Latimer Neville was the only Englishman and sometime Superintendent of the Pongas Mission. He gave good service to the Mission and, sadly, succumbed to missionary mortality on the field of engagement. In his work, he compared the strength of belief in witchcraft in Africa with witchcraft in England before the arrival of Christianity and told the story of a purchase order for wood by the Bishop of Sierra Leone from a village on the shore of the river some fifteen miles from Freetown. When the material was not forthcoming, inquiries were made and it was discovered that the village had been destroyed by neighbouring villagers on the grounds of it being a "witch village." Their story was that a crocodile had come out of the river and carried off a woman in their village. These villagers believed that the animal had been possessed by witches – or that the witches themselves had assumed the form of a crocodile – and so they had destroyed the whole village by setting fire to it.[35] Neville mentioned this story not only to show the existence of local beliefs in witchcraft and local reactions to it but also to underscore the fact that these were pre-Christian practices which the Christian missionary enterprise in Africa had to address.

---

34. *MF* (1856): 205, USPG Archives.
35. *MF* (1 February 1859): 35, USPG Archives.

Witchcraft Eradication

Due to the prevalence of witchcraft, one of the key targets of the West Indian missionaries in the Pongas Mission was the eradication of this phenomenon in the region. Doughlin, for example, reported two cases at Tofia and Backia, where women were caught by alligators and local people attributed their demise to witchcraft. Another woman at Backia was burned to death on similar suspicion. The association of the alligator with witchcraft was apparently a long-standing local custom in the Pongas, which had developed from a ritualized placation of the alligator. As the alligator became linked to the menacing problem of witchcraft, either the individual who stood accused of being the embodiment of the witch had to be put away and removed from society or the alligator itself had to be executed. This was how Chief Lewis Wilkinson of Fallangia understood this practice. In telling Caswall the story of the shooting of an alligator on a Christmas morning, Wilkinson said:

> This animal, before the Christian religion came among us, used to be worshipped at a certain time of the year. Bread or flour was put in a white plate, or calabash, and thrown into the entrance of his cave at low water, and a blessing was asked of him by a heathen priest in behalf of all the people, that plants and souls might be spared from sickness and death. His length was a fathom and a half. The heathens in our neighbourhood hearing of this alligator being shot, now affirms the truth of the Christian religion.[36]

On learning of less violent, but nonetheless fatal, measures being introduced in Backia to deal with individuals accused of witchcraft, Doughlin resolved to intervene and prohibit such forms of capital punishment. He noted that there was "some talk of giving sassy water to some people at Backia who are suspected of witchcraft. I hope to succeed in putting a stop to it."[37] The West Indian Richard Morgan, who was based at the station at Farrangia, described sassy water as "deadly poison," noting that when it was administered, "death generally ensues a few hours after, and then it is said . . . he or

---

36. *MF* (1866): 60, USPG Archives.
37. *MF* (1 April 1882): 110, USPG Archives.

she is a witch."³⁸ Morgan pointed out that underlying the infliction of such punishment was the belief that God would not allow ferocious wild animals to "molest human beings, unless under very strange circumstances." Since the anti-human behaviour of creatures like the alligator would thus be contrary to nature, any manifestation of such behaviour was viewed as a mark of the presence of evil and wrongdoing. Typifying the world view of the Western missionary enterprise, Morgan thought that "the belief in these absurdities warps the mind and makes their votaries resort to charms, *gree-grees,* and such like delusions."³⁹

Islam

As interesting as the encounters with African religion and witchcraft were, two larger issues defined the West Indians' encounters with Africa in the Rio Pongas Mission. One was the challenge of being agents of Christian mission in a predominantly Muslim environment. The other was the continuing practice of internal African slavery. When Leacock and Duport were first deployed to Africa in the mid-nineteenth century, they did not envisage that their mission would be carried out in a predominantly Muslim environment. There was, therefore, no predetermined strategy for dealing with such issues. The West Indians seemed to have responded to the situation as best they could. While they welcomed Muslim onlookers, particularly at celebrations such as the dedication or opening of a new station, church, house, or school, they exercised great caution and care in their dealings with the local Muslim community. Inevitably, however, an adversarial relationship developed between the Christian missionaries and the Muslims. Although the antagonism between Christianity and Islam predated the arrival of the West Indian missionaries, now that these two religious groups had to coexist in a religiously competitive environment, and since both were engaged in the enterprise of religious claim-making in Africa, each group had to justify and demonstrate their efficacy and capacity to deal with African problems.

In the trading economy of the Rio Pongas, where much of the trading was carried on by Muslims, missionary engagement was bound to be a challenge to the Muslims since, as Leacock observed, "their chief means of support

---

38. *MF* (1 October 1883): 334–5, USPG Archives.
39. *MF* (1 October 1883): 335, USPG Archives.

is making and selling to the heathens, charms or amulets, which they call '*greegrees*.'" Sounding a note of cynicism about the belief system and religious claims behind the Mohammedan merchandising of this practice, Leacock commented that

> the warrior rushes into battle covered with these charms, for each of which he has, perhaps, given four or five dollars; and when, notwithstanding, he receives the deadly wound from the adversary's sabre or unerring bullet, the Mohammedan's cry is "His time is come." The preservation of life and health, down to the hour of death, they ascribe to the power of the *"greegrees"*; but death, let it come when or how it may, *comes at the appointed time*.[40]

The civilizing mission, of which the West Indians were participants and agents, would have disposed them to reject the religion of Islam based upon Western Christianity's Eurocentric "enlightened" rationalistic world view. However, it was the economic motives and practices of the Mohammedans that the West Indian missionaries perceived as the real danger. In their response, the West Indian missionaries sought to align themselves with those whom they thought were being exploited, in both religious as well as in economic terms. The West Indians were conditioned to react against any perceived acts of social injustice. This would also have disposed them to develop an antipathy towards Islam that led them to condemn and attempt to counteract the perceived economic exploitation of the people. They viewed the religious and economic practices of the Mohammedans as clear indicators of the need to protect vulnerable populations in the community.

The West Indian Anglican missionaries' attitude towards Islam inevitably invited a backlash from the Mohammedans. As Maurice discovered, when he tried to expand his mission to the town of Yengisa in 1863, the Islamists sometimes used their influence with chiefs and kings to prevent expansion of the Christian mission in the Pongas Nevertheless, it is worth noting that the level of suspicion, rivalry, jealousy, and competitiveness between the Christian missionaries and the Muslims in the Pongas region did not prevent them from engaging in mutually beneficial business transactions. The West Indians were

---

40. *MF* (1856): 230, USPG Archives.

certainly not afraid to do business with their Muslim neighbours when it was deemed necessary, as in the case of transportation, which was a constant need in the Mission.

The missionaries required transport to traverse the territory of the Pongas country, and the Mission required a boat, from time to time to transport goods and people along the rivers. Over a period of time, through funds raised in England, the Mission had acquired two boats, one of which had been wrecked but later repaired. Maurice described the repaired boat as being "thirty feet long, and seven broad, schooner-rigged and coppered, with a small cabin. It was built in America, and was a rapid sailer, having made the passage between Sierra Leone and the Pongas in twenty-four hours."[41] Twenty years later, the missionaries were still complaining that their chief cause of anxiety in the Mission was "the want of a good boat."[42] On land, they either walked for miles to do their itinerant work or, as Duport did, found some other form of transport.

In the mid-1860s, a new mode of transportation – in the form of horses – was introduced in the Pongas, probably by Mohammedan traders. In 1868, Duport hired a horse from a Mohammedan to travel from Fallangia to Domingia. In describing his missionary activities for the first quarter of 1868, he commented, "This is the second horse I have seen during my thirteen years in the country."[43] Within a few days, Doughlin also hired a horse, which created quite a sensation among the people, perhaps on account of the novelty of the creature and its use as a means of transportation. Doughlin wrote:

> My presence on horseback caused the greatest consternation amongst the people, as very few had ever seen a horse before. They gave me as wide a berth as possible, taking refuge behind houses, walls, and trees, whence they patiently observed the beast I rode, which was not a good one.[44]

In the religiously competitive atmosphere that prevailed in the Rio Pongas, the relationship between Christians and Muslims was not restricted to trading activities alone. As we have seen, some Mohammedans were not afraid to

---

41. *MF* (1 December 1863): 278–279, USPG Archives.
42. *MF* (1 September 1882): 294, USPG Archives.
43. *MF* (1 September 1868): 244, USPG Archives.
44. *MF* (1 September 1868): 245, USPG Archives.

make use of the West Indian missionary contribution to education through its mission schools. Many Muslim students were sent to the Christian mission schools established by the West Indian missionaries, partly because of the high standard of the education curriculum and partly because these schools offered an English-based education – which was seen as contributing towards building an educated African class that would be able to communicate with the outside world.

African Slavery

The second major issue that the West Indian missionaries encountered and confronted in Africa was the continuing practice of African slavery. For several reasons, this was the biggest underlying challenge that confronted the West Indians in their encounters in Africa. For one thing, being black West Indians from the former slave societies of the British West Indies, their presence and engagement in Western Africa as agents of Christian mission invited suspicion that they were agents of the anti-slavery movement. Not long after his arrival in the Pongas, Leacock rejoiced and gave thanks that God had directed them to "the greatest slave-market in all Africa."[45] Little would he have realized, then, that his early alliance with the mulatto chiefs would invite suspicion and opposition to the British-connected Mission he founded. In time, the issue was complicated by the entourage of black West Indians who had come from the former slave society of the British West Indies to serve as agents of British Christian mission in the Pongas region.

This suspicion often led to rejection of the Mission by slaveholding chiefs like Mrs. Lightburn, who had acquired up to one thousand slaves. Perhaps another reason for Lightburn's initial opposition – before her conversion in 1867 – to the British-connected Mission was her bad previous experience of British anti-slavery agents who had visited her area and, while enjoying her hospitality, destroyed her village on suspicion of it being a slaveholding area.[46] Likewise, the presence of the West Indian missionaries attracted opposition and hostility from Mohammedan slave traders, who saw them as obstacles

---

45. *MF* (March 1856): 61, USPG Archives.
46. *MF* (1866): 83, USPG Archives.

to their economic well-being.[47] Some Mohammedan slaveholders even prohibited slaves from attending the mission church or school.[48] This climate of suspicion during the early phase of the mission meant that the security of the West Indians was at risk, making them vulnerable to various forms of attack. This, in turn, made the West Indians reliant on British protection or the protection of local chiefs who were sympathetic towards them. The issue of the continued practice of slavery in Africa was also problematic for the West Indians because some of those chiefs – such as the Wilkinsons, who offered protection and became local sponsors of the Mission – were also slaveholders. In 1878, Doughlin reported from Fallangia: "The chief of the town, Mr. Charles Wilkinson, lately manumitted his head-man, making the nineteenth whom he has set free in nine years."[49]

The West Indians often drew attention to the actions of chiefs who offered protection to the Mission. For instance, in 1867, Stiles Lightburn, head of the mulatto chiefs, having heard of the threat to the Mission, "came with his long boat, fully manned and armed, and bringing some cannon. His first care was to place a strong guard over the Mission station."[50] In 1861, on the death of Richard Wilkinson, the first chief to sponsor the Mission, Duport noted that "without him, humanly speaking, the Mission could never have gained a foothold in this country. When open hostilities and private stratagems were at work to overthrow the Mission, he stood firm by us, unmoved."[51]

By the 1850s, a decade after slavery was abolished in the British Empire, slave trading was still very much a part of the economic structure of West African society. In an attempt to restrain the continuing trade, the British government not only made contractual agreements with local kings and chiefs to prohibit the trading of slaves, they also deployed men-of-war ships in the Rio Pongas and the Rio Nunez to carry out patrols and intercept slave trading ships. Some local kings and chiefs, while pledging to carry out their contractual agreements, were deceitful in their dealings, as Duport discovered. In 1860, five years after the commencement of mission work in the Pongas,

---

47. *MF* (March 1856): 227, USPG Archives.
48. *MF* (1869): 67, USPG Archives.
49. 519 MF (April 1 1870):196, USPG Archives.
50. *MF* (1 June 1867): 236, USPG Archives.
51. MF (1 August 1861): 185, USPG Archives.

Duport assessed the accomplishments of the Mission and drew attention to the positives and negatives. One significant drawback of the Mission he noted was the continuing slave trade, and Duport also observed that "King Calom, who is in treaty with the British Government, and receives a yearly stipend of British money for the suppression of the slave-trade, is deeply engaged in it. It was to him that the vessel came and he himself has shipped many slaves in her."[52] The vessel to which Duport referred was a slave ship anchored in the river "laden with human beings ready to be carried to Spanish or French Islands, but most of the crew are ill with fever which has caused delay." Describing a situation of general commotion in Domingia in 1866, Duport noted that the commotion had developed because, acting on intelligence that a French merchant in Domingia was dealing in the slave trade and that a slave ship was expected, a British man-of-war had arrived. The king of the Nunez had apparently alerted some local chiefs to prepare a cargo of slaves so that the expected ship might not be delayed. When challenged regarding his connection with these activities, the King had replied, "As long as white men come to buy, we must supply them."[53] On occasion, Duport reportedly challenged the actions of the local chiefs, to which they responded that as the English were not providing an alternative trade, they must take the trade offered by the French or Spanish.[54] It was simply a case of demand and supply. To his embarrassment, Duport sometimes found that his own position, as a black West Indian and an agent of Emancipation through the Christian missionary enterprise, and that of the Mission was compromised by the fact that some of the chiefs from whom he "expected better things" had joined others in the "nefarious traffic" of slave trading.[55] Duport was obviously uncomfortable with this situation; although he did not name these chiefs, they were those who had acted as sponsors of the Pongas Mission, on whose patronage and protection he depended.

Yet another reason the issue of slavery was inescapable for the West Indian missionaries in Africa was because the overwhelming majority of their congregations were slaves. These were mainly domestic slaves, who were sent

---

52. *MF* (1 March 1861): 68, USPG Archives.
53. *MF* (1867): 17, USPG Archives.
54. *MF* (1864): 231, USPG Archives.
55. *MF* (1864): 231, USPG Archives.

to the Mission by their owners, sometimes as part of their patronage of the Mission. Since these slaves formed the majority of the baptism and Sunday school classes, the times of the services were adjusted to suit their availability and convenience. For example, at Fallangia –which was the first church of the Pongas Mission – Duport reported that the baptism class "consists wholly of slaves."[56] In his report of 1864, he observed that "the missionary work has continued as usual, but the people being chiefly slaves, their attendance at church and at the classes is far from regular."[57] After the first episcopal visit to the Mission in 1865, the times of services were adjusted from 6:00 a.m. to 5:00 a.m. and from 5:30 p.m. to 6:15 p.m. to suit the convenience of the people, "most of whom are slaves."[58]

Pursuing Christian missionary endeavours in the context of a slave society was never easy and, among other things, it made the black West Indians acutely aware of the plight of the black African slaves, albeit domestic slaves. But they were also conscious of their own vulnerable position. Duport, for example, refused to baptize any slave without the consent of that slave's master or owner,[59] presumably so that he did not jeopardize his relationship with the powerful slaveholder chiefs. While, on the one hand, this action might suggest that Duport was supportive of the slave system and the beneficiaries of slave trading, yet, on the other hand, he worked ardently for the release of slaves from their bonds. Duport and other West Indians acted as agents for British anti-slavery funds, in pursuit of the manumission of Christian slaves in the Pongas region.[60] How did they reconcile these two things? This would only be possible if the ultimate driving vision of the West Indian missionaries in Africa is understood. That vision was the effective planting of Christianity in Africa through the institutional church, and through the apparatus of Christian mission, and the expansion of the emancipation dream they experienced as a lived reality in the West Indies.

---

56. *MF* (1 January 1863): 20, USPG Archives.
57. *MF* (1865): 59, USPG Archives.
58. *MF* (1865): 133, USPG Archives.
59. *MF* (January 1867): 15, USPG Archives.
60. *MF* (January 1867): 15, USPG Archives.

Fighting the Anti-slavery Cause in Africa

It was only in the 1870s, after the arrival of Turpin and Doughlin, that a more open and activist anti-slavery position became evident in the Pongas Mission. By then, so-called slave-wars – initiated for the purpose of kidnapping and capturing to enslave – had become a regular feature of the Pongas region. Reporting in 1881, Doughlin took note of the fact that slave-wars had become quite common and were having a demoralizing effect on the local populations. He highlighted the fact that "the appetite for enslaving their fellows rages very much" and "war-men are seen prowling about the country committing acts of wanton lawlessness and oppression." He pointed out that "if they are disturbed by one who has never been to war, they seize the person and sell him."[61] Morgan, in Farrangia, also reported that there were "constant wars between native tribes in which the chief motive is the acquisition of slaves."[62] And, in 1886, when Archdeacon Holme of Antigua inspected the Mission, he encountered in Debreeka "large caravans from the interior, composed of Mohammedan masters and gangs of slaves bearing merchandise."[63] In an attempt to reduce the climate of war, the French government had intervened, prohibiting the sale of gunpowder for a time. But this was a short-term measure and was unlikely to have had much effect.

At his station in Domingia, Turpin encountered the problem of some slaveholders passively resisting the West Indian Mission and prohibiting their slaves to attend the mission church. These slaveholders claimed that the slaves, through association with the Mission, "learn to speak English and as soon as they can speak a little English they are in a position to run away."[64] And given the fact that "other domestics" who had been in attendance had been withdrawn for the season, class attendance at his station had become quite irregular.

In the late 1870s, faced with a general decline in their missionary endeavours and frustrated by their inability to grow the Mission, Turpin and Doughlin decided to tackle the problems of the Mission in three ways. The first way was that, they extended the practice, begun by Duport, of acting as

---

61. *MF* (1 April 1882): 109, USPG Archives.
62. *MF* (1 October 1883): 335, USPG Archives.
63. *MF* (1 April 1887): 102, USPG Archives.
64. *MF* (1 September 1867): 246, USPG Archives.

agents for British Anti-Slavery funds, and worked aggressively for the manumission of Christian slaves in the Pongas region. In 1878, Doughlin received £20 through the SPG from four ladies in England for the manumission of John Brown, a Christian slave of whose plight they had heard him speak.[65] With that sum, he was able to obtain the release of two men – John Brown and William DaSilva – and also one boy. John Brown was set free without payment of the manumission costs as his Christian owner refused to accept the money as a price for "a fellow communicant." The other man, William DaSilva, became a lay helper in the Fallangia church under J. B. McEwen, supplementing the very overstretched missionary manpower.[66] Doughlin referred to this activity as the work of "redeeming with money." Turpin also added a scheme of lending money to Christian slaves so that they could purchase their own freedom by manumission. This money came from a revolving fund which he had established, to which the manumitted slave would be obliged to make returns. Two men who benefitted from Turpin's scheme found employment as a sailor and a boatman on the rivers and attached themselves to the Mission.[67]

The second way was that, Turpin and Doughlin identified the primary reasons for the Mission's decline and determined to change their strategy of mission engagement. Since the West Indian Mission to the Pongas region had its origins among the mulattos and their slaves, it was sometimes perceived as not being a mission to the native peoples of the region but, rather, to the expatriates and the middle class. This perception sometimes led to incursions against the Mission or physical threats to its expansion among native Soosoos, who alleged or suspected an alliance between the missionaries and mulattos to acquire more and more of the land which they considered belonged to the native peoples. Duport, well aware of these feelings, frequently made interventions and clarifications to quell such suspicions.[68] The work of the West Indian mission at every station was being frustrated by irregular and uncertain participation by the slave congregations. Passive acceptance had crept in, as Doughlin discovered in Fallangia where, as he noted, "the

---

65. *MF* (1 April 1878): 196, USPG Archives.
66. *MF* (1878): 196; *MF* (1879): 277, USPG Archives.
67. *MF* (1 April 1882): 110, USPG Archives.
68. *MF* (1 June 1867): 236, USPG Archives.

people are saying they are coming and never come."[69] Samuel Macaulay, the schoolmaster and catechist from Sierra Leone, reported from his station at Domingia that there was reluctance to participate in the rites of the church because "the natives, I regret to say, still consider themselves as having no part in it."[70] No good progress could be made without regular and consistent attendance and participation. Therefore, as the vulnerability of the Mission became increasingly exposed, Turpin and Doughlin changed the strategy of engagement by shifting the focus from black slaves and their coloured masters to freemen and native Soosoos.

As it developed, the West Indian mission was greatly challenged by the prevalence of African slavery in the Rio Pongas region. Its strategic long-term development was also inhibited, if not impaired, by preoccupations with whether the Mission was perceived as pro-slavery or anti-slavery. It was in this context of concern for the real orientation of the Mission that several extensive scouting expeditions were pursued from 1868 onwards, ten years after the initial arrival of the West Indians. In the first quarter of 1868, Duport went on a scouting expedition well into the interior, visiting towns and villages like Kissin and Kossinsi. The chief object of that expedition, he said, was "to have establishments in the pure Susu towns, as there is a general impression that we are sent to the Mulattos only."[71] Evidently, Duport's intention was to seek ways of moving away from the cosmopolitan atmosphere of the Pongas Mission and into truly native Susu communities. To that end, he negotiated and secured promises of land for new stations in the interior.

During the period 1874–1875, Doughlin and Turpin made their own joint scouting excursions deep into the Soosoo interior, spending eighteen days on this single mission, covering 104 miles and visiting 32 towns.[72] They visited the important towns of Brahmaia and Korera and ventured through the Baggo kingdom of Debrika. Following this expedition, they became convinced that the Pongas Mission was not just a mission to "heathens" but also very much a mission to "Mohammedans" as well. They also insisted that their key strategy for evangelization should be through education of native children in the

---

69. *MF* (1 September 1868): 246, USPG Archives.

70. *MF* (1 June 1870): 172, USPG Archives.

71. *MF* (1 September 1868): 244–245, USPG Archives.

72. *MF* (1 July 1875): 195, USPG Archives.

setting of a boarding school, as the Roman Catholic missionaries had done in Sierra Leone.[73] In other words, the Mission needed a new plan and a new strategy. Later, Doughlin and the new missionary, McEwen, spent one month on a missionary reconnaissance tour further into the interior, visiting fifty-eight towns.[74] McEwen returned convinced of the need for a new strategy of mission engagement and added his voice to the call for a boarding school, without which, he said, "we will never make progress."[75]

By 1882, ten years after Duport had died, and four years after Turpin had returned to Barbados, Doughlin, as superintendent of the Mission, thought it was time to implement the change in strategy which had long been contemplated. His policy proposal was, no doubt, influenced not just by the factors to which he attributed the decline of the Mission but also by the increase in frequency and destructiveness of the slave-wars from the 1870s into the early 1880s. In a statement to the Barbados Board, Doughlin expressed discouragement at the state of the operational strategy of the Mission and proposed a new course of action in 1882:

> I cannot say that I derive much encouragement from the work among the slaves. Our lines are not cast in pleasant places. The slaves are moved about very much and sent out of our reach, and their spiritual welfare is never thought of by their master and mistresses. Sometimes their days are taken away altogether, and they are forced to work on Sundays to get food to eat.[76]

In his critique of the status quo in the Pongas Mission, Doughlin appeared to have expressed some amount of impatience and offered decisive leadership, as he requested the Board's approval to change course. "We have been working hitherto among slaves and their masters. It is time that we should penetrate among the free people."[77] In addition to pleading for a boarding school as part of this new strategy, he proposed to strategically deploy the next missionary to either Lokkatah or Baga Shore. During his next four years at the Mission, Doughlin pursued this goal of a change in mission strategy,

---

73. *MF* (1 July 1875): 193–198, USPG Archives.
74. *MF* (2 June 1879): 554–555, USPG Archives.
75. *MF* (2 June 1879): 278, USPG Archives.
76. *MF* (1 April 1882): 110, USPG Archives.
77. *MF* (1 April 1882): 110, USPG Archives.

deploying new missionaries such as Samuel Cole and Samuel Hughes, who arrived in 1881, to establish new outstations.[78] However, the outcome of their work was eclipsed by other events beyond the missionaries' control.

The third way that Doughlin and Turpin responded to the problems of the Mission was to continue their advocacy for active and beneficial commercial trade with the Pongas region, to supplant and substitute for the slave-trading economy that had persisted in Africa despite British anti-slavery measures. While exploring the interior regions, they observed factories for commercial development in largely Mohammedan areas. Doughlin, for example, was so impressed with the "many rising factories" he saw at Kworrira and the new openings for merchant activity at Zokhata after the quelling of the slave-wars that he felt that "we the Missionaries, should go and open Gospel operations. We should put out our own factories too."[79] He commenced regular services among the traders at Kworrira and was determined to capitalize on the opportunities being opened with the development of a significant internal market economy.

While they advocated trade and commerce, however, Turpin and Doughlin – and later McEwen, Cole, Hughes, Morgan, and others – believed that their best contribution was to be made in the area of education and training. Having been trained in the environment of Codrington College, they agitated passionately for a boarding school as the best way to effect change and transformation in the populations of the Pongas country. During the period in which the Pongas Mission was being established, three types of education had been attempted, each with its own attendant problems. From the beginning, the missionaries had established a mission school which was more or less part of the process of building a church. This was a *Christian education programme* based on the Sunday school and its curriculum. Even in its most rudimentary form, Duport, the schoolmaster, delighted in it. In one of his earliest reports, he described the way in which the school was conducted:

> First, as I enter the School, the children repeat the Morning Hymn; then prayer. After prayer, we repeat the Psalms in the Prayer-book which they have learned, then the Ten Commandments, and the Creed, with its questions and answers

---
78. *MF* (1 April 1882): 290–291, USPG Archives.
79. *MF* (2 June 1884): 178, USPG Archives.

given in the Church Catechism. Then I examined each child from my vocabulary of words, in Soosoo and English. Secondly, reading and spelling, counting, weights and measures, numeration and multiplication table up to five times; then arithmetic. I use mangoes and the fingers, to give them some idea of addition ... Third, play-hour. Fourth, reading and spelling, writing and dictation, the map of the Holy Land, & Fifth, Evening Hymn and other Psalms; then evening prayer.[80]

Duport established a system whereby school education was offered Sunday morning and Sunday night, so that boys who were not able to attend during the day could attend at night. Using the Anglican Prayer Book as his basic text, Duport employed a variety of techniques to provide basic education and the development of literary and numeracy skills. Some of his techniques included the introduction of liturgical music with the aid of an instrument called the harmonium. From such practices came the development of the church choir and the introduction of hymnodical music in the mission church.[81] While demanding a great deal of physical energy, this also enabled Duport to gain more knowledge and fluency in vernacular Soosoo.

From these rudimentary beginnings, the curriculum of the mission schools was expanded to a second level of education, which included more classical and scholastic requirements. Duport produced a primer which included an English-Soosoo vocabulary. The SPG also donated books to the Mission for the development of reading skills. At this level, boys and girls were separated, and the education of girls took on more elements of domesticity and gender development, according to current notions of female socialization. Duport even produced an edition of the *Churching of Women* for use in the mission schools[82] and, by his organizing skills and translations of texts, laid a solid foundation for the development of the Soosoo church. Interest in the education of females continued throughout the life of the Mission. In 1897, Samuel Cole, the missionary stationed at Kambia, in describing the development of the school at his station drew attention to the performance of the girls in the schools: "The girls are also progressing in the art of sewing.

---

80. *MF* (1856): 229, USPG Archives.
81. *MF* (1866): 59–60, USPG Archives.
82. *MF* (1866): 9, USPG Archives.

It was a hard job at the beginning with them even to thread a needle or to use a thimble, but they have so mastered all now that one can scarcely remember what they were."[83]

A third level of education was the plan to develop what was called *Industrial Education*, which was aimed at diversifying the educational programme of the Mission to help meet local needs for economic development. The recruitment of Richard Morgan and the Morgan family from Barbados was intended to fulfil this objective. This plan, which was proposed in 1862, envisaged a school for training native boys in the practical industrial skills of blacksmithing, carpentering, tailoring, and agriculture.[84] The proposal was encouraged and supported by local chiefs, who saw the growing need for employment and industrial development in their towns. Chief Faber of the Kubia region, for example, who saw the benefits to be derived for his people who were increasingly becoming traders, encouraged Duport and Phillips to develop such a plan. There was also potential for the development of trade in oil extracted from groundnut, instead of the traditional rice cultivation.[85] However, as noted in chapter six, the plan for the industrial school failed due to a multiplicity of internal and external factors, including a severe period of drought, crop failure, food shortage, and famine in the Pongas region. It was a difficult period of social, economic, and environmental struggle, in which it was not possible to start an agricultural-based industrial development project. So, the Morgans turned, instead, to catechizing and other educational work.

In the end, what remained was the second level of education, which the West Indians missionaries continued to pursue and, with the employment of Sierra Leonian and local schoolmasters – such as T G McCarthy, Jeremiah Buckle, William Da Silva and others – the educational work of the Pongas Mission struggled on. The problem of maintenance, which generally affected the Mission's expansion and development work, naturally affected the educational programme too. Despite local demand for education, factors such as attendance – which fluctuated according to social and economic conditions such as famine, smallpox, economic depression, and the introduction of fees – cost of maintenance of increased mission staff and mission infrastructure such

---

83. *MF* (1 January 1897): 17, USPG Archives.
84. *MF* (1 June 1862): 133, USPG Archives.
85. *MF* (1 June 1862): 134, USPG Archives.

as churches, schools, and mission houses, and the problem of the declining prospects of financial support from the West Indies tested the sustainable limits of the Mission's primary programme of education. Despite opportunities for expansion and development, the Mission was constrained in its ability to do more than it was already doing.

With the arrival of deacon C. W. Farquhar of Antigua in 1890, the long-hoped-for boarding school was finally introduced. Farquhar – with fifteen years of experience in Antigua as a Master of the Mico model of education – established the school in the new station at Isles de Los and had it inspected by the principal of the Fourah Bay College in Sierra Leone. Farquhar served the Mission for thirty-nine years and died as Archdeacon in 1929. Joseph McEwen, OBE – one of his former pupils – wrote brief reflections on Farquhar's life in an article titled "Conakry and Isles De Los Re-Visited."[86] Joseph McEwen himself, son of missionary J. B. McEwen from Barbados, was raised in the Mission's boarding school and served in the colonial service in Nigeria for nearly thirty years. Later, other boarding schools were instituted and played an important role in the development of the Pongas Mission, becoming one of the most enduring features of the Mission and the basis of its educational legacy. The boarding schools laid the foundation for the emergence of a truly native African Christian church in this part of Western Africa. The boarding school at Domingia, for example, produced church workers as well as native priests known as "Burris boys." Luther Benjamin, the first native priest in the Pongas, was one of these Burris boys. He was ordained in 1939 by the bishop of the Gambia-Pongas diocese and retired as Archdeacon of Guinea in 1968.[87]

Polygamy

In the West Indian missionaries' encounters with the Muslim populations in Western Africa, perhaps no other issue was more contested than the issue of polygamy. The Muslim practice of polygamy represented a direct challenge to Christian teachings concerning marriage and family.

---

86. *G-PM* (April 1939): 9–10; *G-PM* (April 1940): 6; *G-PM* (April 1947): 4; *G-PM* (December 1968): 22–23, USPG Archives.

87. *G-PM* (April 1940): 6; *G-PM* (April 1947): *G-PM* (December 1968): 22–23, USPG Archives.

In their reports, the West Indian missionaries invariably cited cases of careful premarital pastoral counselling as well as cases of refusal to sanction requests for the marriage rite to be performed for people not concerned with or belonging to the Mission. The witness of Christian family life was a key missionary goal. The Barbadian Turpin, for example, referred to polygamy as "a great immorality" which was a stumbling block to Christian missionary progress in Africa.[88]

If the West Indian missionaries were zealous for converts – and they were – at the same time, they were also obliged to be uncompromising in their teaching with regard to the issue of monogamy. Since, in Christian teaching, monogamy is the standard for marriage and family, in mission, it was considered an important means of public witness to the moral virtue of Christianity. The marriage rite, with all its biblical, social, and cultural elements, was a spectacle which missionaries were keen to use pedagogically as a witness to the redemptive work of the gospel. As a result, one of the issues that became a political matter in Fallangia was the question of interfaith marriage. It became such a problem that, in the mid-1860s, Chief Lewis Wilkinson prohibited interfaith marriages because Mohammedan fathers were prohibiting children of such unions from attending the mission schools. Reports said that "the chief has lately put a stop to the practice of Christian women intermarrying with Mohammedan husbands. The children of such marriages, who ought to swell the numbers of the training and infant schools, are prevented from attending by fathers, who object to their being taught the Christian religion."[89]

The question the West Indian mission to the Rio Pongas had to address was to what extent Christian missionaries could bless marriages between Christians and Muslims and how they could help to resolve differences over religious beliefs and religious practices. Missionary Samuel Hughes gave an account of a bride and groom whom he had counselled and later married. The bride, Seeray, was Mohammedan in family background but had been baptized by West Indian missionary, R. J. Clarke and given the name Sarah. She had also been confirmed by the Bishop of Sierra Leone. According to Hughes, Lambert, the groom, was "a prominent member of the church to

---

88. *MF* (1 July 1875): 196, USPG Archives.
89. *MF* (1866): 59, USPG Archives.

whom the Lord blessed my words and he yielded to me to have his marriage solemnized in the presence of God and His people." Both Seeray (Sarah) and Lambert consented to be married and requested the West Indian missionary to bless their marriage. Yet, difficulties still "stared at the face," according to Hughes. Seeray's Mohammedan parents had to give consent. To get the parents' consent, Hughes had to send "a bigman of Fotoba" to talk the "palaver" with the parents in the town of Boom. That intervention succeeded, and the marriage was solemnized in the mission church, with the mother and other relatives of the bride attending.[90]

While noting the absence of the father of the bride due to illness, Hughes drew attention to the fact that during the marriage ceremony – in keeping with the Christian practice of the woman being symbolically released to be married – when the question, "Who giveth this woman to be married to this man?" was asked, "a Mohammedan stepped forward, took the hand of Seeray, and delivered her to me." Hughes evidently saw the public performance of this Christian rite as a mark of witness to the community and an accomplishment for the Mission. He commented that "the above marriages are among the special favours of God on us in this Mission. They are among the first in this island." He further claimed that such an event had some immediate effect on the local community as "many of the natives have been led to exclaim 'What hath God wrought.'"[91] This did not, however, appear to have resulted in an increase in attendance at the Mission nor serve as an encouragement of interfaith marriages between Christians and Mohammedans.

From the time of their arrival in the Pongas region in the mid-1850s, the West Indians encountered the challenge of working in an area predominantly influenced by Islam. However, it was not until the mid-1870s, after Doughlin and Turpin ventured into the upper regions of the Pongas country, that the Pongas Mission was recognized as a mission to the Mohammedans that required a particular strategy of engagement if it were to succeed.[92] It was left

---

90. *MF* (1 September 1882): 292–293, USPG Archives.
91. *MF* (1 September 1882): 292–293, USPG Archives.
92. "Pongas Mission: Progress of Christianity and Mohammedanism", *MF* (1 July 1875): 193–198, USPG Archives. This article begins by asserting that "it is not, perhaps, generally known that the S.P.G. carries on, in many parts of the world, Missions to the Moslem population.... On the Pongas Mission the ministers of Christ are confronted by agents of the false prophet.... unless the Mission clergy are enabled to fight Islam with its own weapons, though they may bring salvation to individual souls, they cannot win a country for Christ."

to Doughlin, as the superintendent of the Mission, to develop and articulate that strategy. As we have seen, soon after his arrival in the Pongas, Doughlin assessed the work of the Mission and concluded that the mission schools were not functioning as effectively as they should. In fact, by 1868, the school system had broken down, and Doughlin had reported that "classes may be said to be wholly deserted at Fallangia. This has been a cause of grief to all the missionaries. The system of school fees has yet been a complete failure."[93] With the new energy and vision which he and Turpin brought, they set about correcting this situation by employing new catechists and schoolmasters and reorganizing the schools. In the course of this reorganization, the vision of a boarding school as an important and necessary means of control was also developed. Responding to the problems of pursuing consistent education in the mission schools due to the irregular and inconsistent attendance by students, all the West Indian missionaries in the Pongas Mission were united in their advocacy and campaign for a boarding school approach to education. Missionary McEwen expressed the frustration of the West Indian missionaries in a very blunt report in 1879, in which he noted:

> It is impossible to have much influence over them unless they are within the Mission yard. One cannot help throwing the greater portion of the blame of the failures of our schools to the want of a boarding-school in our Mission. Give us a boarding-school – give us a boarding-school – has been our cry for years, and it is our cry now, and it will be our cry till one is established amongst us. Such is the condition of the country in which we live that our friends may be assured that we will never make progress in the training and education of the children and younger natives until such an institution is established.[94]

As we have seen, it took twenty years before this vision and dream was finally realized in 1890, when C. W. Farquhar of Antigua was sent to implement a boarding school at the Isles de Los station.[95] Farquhar focused on the formalization of the Mission's primary task and objectives in the area

---

93. *MF* (1 September 1868): 245, USPG Archives.
94. *MF* (2 June 1879): 278, USPG Archives.
95. Barrow, *Fifty Years*, 133.

of education and training, and the key component of his strategy was the establishment of residential boarding schools over which the Mission would exercise full control.

By the 1870s, the Pongas Mission had a track record of over two decades in the area of education. Driven by local demand, as well as by a need to find a competitive edge to rival the spread of Mohammedan religious activities, Doughlin, Turpin, McEwen, and the band of West Indian missionaries badgered their Mission Board and English supporters for means to pursue a broader educational agenda, which they saw as a critical tool in the struggle for African converts and also, equally, an instrument for social transformation and, ultimately, the redemption of Africa.

Conclusion

In their Christianizing efforts in Africa in the mid-nineteenth century, as part of the Western missionary enterprise, the West Indian missionaries encountered Africa in multidimensional and uneven ways. Given the variety of factors they had to contend with – their social background, the policy constraints of their sponsoring missions, tribal and cultural resistance across the broad span of West African life in the nineteenth century, encountering a resurgent Islam in Western Africa, and a variety of other issues they encountered on the field – some failed in this encounter and returned to the West Indies, but several persevered, had long careers in Africa, and succeeded in establishing a foothold for Christianity in Africa. Overall, the West Indians made outstanding contributions to the effective planting and transmission of Christianity to Western African societies. A critical examination of three of these missions from the West Indies – the Moravian Mission to the Gold Coast, the Baptist Mission to the Cameroon, and the Anglican Mission to the Rio Pongas – reveals that, despite some formidable challenges which Africa posed, the West Indian agents responded with a strong desire and determination to make a contribution not only to the enterprise of Christian missions but, specifically, to the development of Africa itself, their ancestral homeland. Among the many challenges they encountered were the entrenched cultural practices of witchcraft, domestic slavery, and polygamy, and the competing influence of Islam. To overcome these challenges, they adopted different strategies. Some of these strategies –such as education, agriculture, and

Christian marriage rites – conformed to the Western missionary agenda of missionary engagement, while others – such as the determined attempts at effecting the manumission and release of slaves – appeared as a distinctly West Indian interest.

In all the encounters, however, the underlying interest of the West Indian missionary agents appeared to have been a passionate concern for African freedom and development. No doubt shaped by the slave context of their origins, the agents of each of these three enterprises vigorously pursued their mission as a mission of freedom and social justice.

While the Anglican Mission to the Rio Pongas probably provides the most significant illustrations of the variety of phenomena and local issues that West Indian missionaries encountered and responded to in Western Africa, the other missions encountered similar phenomena and evidenced responses in generally similar patterns. Some of these phenomena followed patterns familiar to them from the African world of their West Indian cultural origins, and others were completely new experiences. Some issues were highly complex and involved matters beyond their control, such as finding substantial and legitimate alternatives to trade in African slaves. In most instances, they were stretched in their capacity to handle these situations but rose admirably to the challenge.

In Africa, the West Indian missionaries were often placed in a binary position. On the one hand, they had arrived with a strategic mission to engage in evangelizing work with a view to establishing Christianity in an area of Africa where no such work was being done by other missionary agencies or where such work had been tried and abandoned. On the other hand, to achieve this mission, there was the pragmatic need for a viable space to establish a foothold for an operational base in the section of Africa selected for such work. This required local support, protection, and provisions. Such was the case for all three missions, even though the Moravians in the Gold Coast Mission went to an already existing mission base in Akropong-Aquapim, which Andreas Riis, leader of the Basel Mission, had previously secured.

In the case of the Pongas Mission, the fact that such local needs were provided for by mulatto chiefs – whose power and authority were derived largely from control of the local economy, which was dominated by slave trading activities – only added to the complexity of the missionary task, as the West Indians eventually discovered. Leacock and Duport – the Barbadian pioneers – were truly grateful for the physical protection and generous assistance of Chief Richard Wilkinson of Fallangia as they sought to establish a base for their pioneering operation and lay the foundation for the Pongas Mission. The Mission, however, became reliant on the patronage offered by Wilkinson, his sons – Charles and Lewis – and other chiefs with similar social backgrounds such as Lightburn, Gomez, and Faber.

In the circumstances in which the West Indians placed themselves, the issues that they encountered in Africa – the landscape and climate, famines and plagues, witchcraft and domestic violence, Islam and polygamy, tribal wars and slavery – all required specific responses. There is every indication that the missionaries attempted to respond to each of these issues in bold, mission-affirming ways. The responses of those who achieved long careers in Africa –such as Catherine Mulgrave, J. J. Fuller, John Duport, and Philip Doughlin –indicate their high level of commitment towards Africa and their readiness, as New World Africans, to make the necessary adjustments and accommodation.

From this examination then, the preponderant evidence points both to a clear, determined response to encounters with Africa on the part of most West Indian missionaries in Africa in the nineteenth century and to a high level of passionate commitment to the missionary enterprise and a strong desire to succeed in it. For example, over the eighty years (1856–1936) of the West Indian Mission to the Rio Pongas, the determination to achieve their intended goal was backed up by a persistent and relentless agitation for two things: (1) a bishop for the Mission and (2) a boarding school as a critical instrument for their mission engagement; and the missionaries did not let up until both demands were met. The realization of this missionary dream attests not only to their perseverance despite the daunting challenges but also to the strength of motivation that sighted their missionary vision in Africa in the first place.

It was only the external interventions of German and French imperial forces in the "Scramble for Africa" and, in some measure, the loss of real support from the West Indies due to the declining fortunes of the West Indian economy, that caused the eclipse of the fulfilment of the West Indian missionary vision for Africa. That vision was the establishment of a truly native African church through which Christianity could help to produce moral change and Africa's advancement. This was the originally stated aims and objects of the West Indian missions to Africa, to be delivered by the aggressive pursuits of representative agents, as best they could. That motivation and commitment could be seen also in the discernment and determination to change strategy when a shift in strategic engagement was required to achieve the aims and objects of the Mission. The example of the Pongas Mission is a studied case in point.

In the end, the clearest indication of the strategic goal and achievement of the missions lay in the work of linguistic translation and educational development. As David Brown – the schoolmaster-catechist from Sierra Leone – recognized in 1879, this was "the striking feature of the work of the Mission." Brown pointed out the value of having both minister and convert reading from the same text in the same language without the medium of an interpreter.[96] From his point of view, to achieve this was to achieve mission.

Although the project of translation of English texts into vernacular languages through the work of Western missionary agents had been problematic and subjected to a variety of interpretations – whether considered pre-imperialist, imperialist, or anti-imperialist – this translation work did open up new possibilities by providing alternative universes of thought and discourse.[97] Through this activity, the West Indians saw the opportunity not only to effectively communicate the message and build a native African church but also a means to indigenize themselves in Africa. The cases of the Moravian (Basel) Mission to the Gold Coast, the Baptist Mission to the Cameroon, and Anglican Mission to the Rio Pongas show the extent to which the West Indian missionaries recognized the importance of vernacular translation and engaged assiduously in this task in their respective missions. Scripture translations and translations of important texts such as the Anglican prayer book, the Catechism, Service Orders, and school primers – which John Duport achieved in the Pongas Mission, and which was also pursued by others such as Maurice, Doughlin, and Morgan – were significant achievements of these West Indian missionaries in Africa. They knew that this work would not only serve the spiritual goals of the Mission but also enhance the development of education in Africa.

---

96. *MF* (June 1879): 279, USPG Archives.
97. Sanneh, *Translating the Message*.

CHAPTER 8

Conceptions of Christian Mission

The participation of West Indians in the missionary enterprise in Africa in the mid-nineteenth century was, in part, the outworking of the missionary dream of the Western missionary enterprise that sought to "remedy" Africa through the means of Christian mission. Enlisting the participation of the West Indians was an attempt to ensure the successful planting and transmission of Christianity into sub-Saharan African soil at a time when European missionary mortality in Africa was haemorrhaging European efforts and demonstrating what a formidable task this project was. Africa was indeed the "white man's grave." West Indian participation was also, in part, the outworking of an opportunity for the newly emancipated Christianized Africans in the British West Indies to contribute to a project to which they were thought to be "especially suited." Either way, their participation raises important questions regarding not only their suitability and the nature of their contribution but also their conception and particular understanding of the project as a whole. It would be instructive to discern and extrapolate more fully, if possible, their unique understanding of the project in which they so passionately engaged and the perspectives from which they might have conceived of and envisioned their participation in this enterprise. To what extent was there alignment or variance between their conception and vision and that of their sponsors? Did they demonstrate any distinctive elements in their missionary engagement in Africa that might be identified as uniquely West Indian?

In the attempt to discern any such distinctive elements in the West Indian participation in the missionary enterprise in Africa, it was necessary to investigate more deeply the activities in which they were engaged and the opinions they expressed in their missionary engagement. This study revealed how the West Indians conceived of the enterprise and what priorities, activities, choices, and strategies of engagement they pursued in Africa, and why.

Mission and Civilization

Christian mission, as pursued by the Western missionary enterprise in the nineteenth century, was conducted in an "Age of Empire," when European powers were in active competitive pursuit of their separate imperial ambitions across the globe, in Africa, Asia, and Latin America. Their singular aim was resource extraction and transfer to the metropole to strengthen and build up economic and political power. One of the consequences of this was the link drawn between the project of Christian mission and empire-building, and the imperialistic expansion of European civilization. David Bosch, the noted South African missiologist, points out the often-stated view that Western missionaries in the nineteenth century "became promoters of Western imperial expansion."[1] This view posits that "whether they liked it or not, the missionaries became pioneers of Western imperialistic expansion." It is a perspective widely shared by those who consider the Western missionary project as merely a vehicle for civilizing "heathens" and "savages" in order to bring them into the mainstream of modern nation-states.[2] Bosch argued that "it was only natural for missionaries to be regarded as both vanguard and rear-guard for the colonial powers."[3]

Basing his work on Hans Kung's six paradigms of the history of Christianity, Bosch notes, that the nineteenth-century notion of mission as a harbinger of civilization was a paradigm shift. This was an idea that originated during the Victorian era, in which Christian mission was viewed as a civilizing force. Influenced by the European Age of Enlightenment, this Enlightenment conception of Christian mission interpreted the effects of the Christian gospel in terms of modernity, which sought to revolutionize every aspect of modern life. Beginning in the late eighteenth century, this idea flourished in the nineteenth century with the self-proclaimed triumph

---

1. Bosch, *Transforming Mission*, 282.
2. See Sindima, *Drums of Redemption*; Hall, *Civilising Subjects*.
3. Bosch, *Transforming Mission*, 304.

of mission Christianity in the urban industrial centres of Europe. Such notions of the virtues of Christian mission were also transported to the British colonies in the West Indies.

However, there is another perspective, which views the role of Christian mission in the nineteenth century quite differently. As the noted West African scholar Jacob Ajayi points out, "Missionaries who set out to change a people's religion and beliefs are, by definition, reformers and they must be regarded as Developers."[4] Viewed from this perspective, Ajayi suggests that "there were many missionaries who denied that they had any business promoting civilization." Chief among them, in Ajayi's view, was Henry Venn. As missionary theorist, strategist, and long-time secretary of the Church Missionary Society, Venn's far-sighted pro-African policy and anti-colonial strategy for missionary engagement aimed to develop Africa and African society through African participation as native agents. As Venn articulated his philosophy of native agency and native pastorates, what emerged was a conception of mission whose aim was to establish indigeneity and localization as a means of subversion and planting Christianity in local soil. This philosophy of mission deliberately set out to create a middle class that was seen as the best way to subvert and supplant an old subsistence culture. There was precedence for this strategy in European history in the way in which the Industrial Revolution in Europe produced a middle class that upset the mercantilist system on which the European slave trade itself was based.[5] This was a radical concept that fostered local initiative, local governance, and local ownership.

In light of these twin conceptions of Christian mission in the nineteenth century, how did the West Indian missionaries conceive of the role of Christian mission in Africa? Were they part of the vanguard or rearguard of European imperialism or were they pro-African developers, seeking to build native African institutions for Africa's sake?

To start with, the West Indians in the three missions in Western Africa embraced the missionary project fully and left the West Indies with high expectations of making a distinctive contribution to the enterprise in Africa. Their understanding of the project was, as Ed Walker, the Jamaican Moravian who took part in the Basel Mission to the Gold Coast, stated, one in which

---

4. Ajayi, "Henry Venn," 59.
5. Ajayi, 61.

they were going to make a contribution and "have brethren and sisters to pray for Africa and for us ... when we go there."[6] As expressed by Walker, the West Indians saw themselves as being recruited to carry out a mission, while enjoying the support of "brethren and sisters" at home. But on the field in Africa their enthusiasm and expectation of active engagement were dampened by their experience of disappointment in the leadership of Basel missionaries and the control they exercised over the settler colony in Akropong-Aquapim. This certainly mitigated against any meaningful contribution they might have envisaged making, especially in the early years of the Mission. The problems they encountered undoubtedly contributed to the early struggles the Mission experienced in Africa in its second attempt in 1844 to establish a mission. That undoubtedly circumscribed and retarded their full and active participation in the project. The goal of creating a Christian settler colony in Africa with West Indians but proscribing their contact with African life and society was a misplaced decision that certainly affected the West Indians' perception of the project and their participation in it.

Even though the first five years of their involvement were admittedly difficult and generally unproductive as far as missionary work was concerned, the West Indians laboured alongside the Basel missionaries and helped to organize work projects in the Mission. They formed the nucleus of the first Christian church among the Akan and Ga peoples in the Aquapim mountains. They participated in its construction and also assisted as lay helpers in its leadership. As auxiliaries, they contributed to building the infrastructure for schools, mission houses, and support systems for outreach to and engagement with the Ga peoples. The outstanding work of Catherine Mulgrave in education – both on her own and, later, alongside her second husband Johannes Zimmermann – and Alexander Worthy Clerk in evangelism and catechism, are examples of areas of ministry in which the West Indians participated and excelled. They also made attempts to initiate new outreach stations, such as the one at Ussu in 1846, merely three years after their arrival in Africa. As new stations were opened, they participated in their development through the evangelization of the new areas, thus expanding the boundaries of the Basel Mission in the Akropong-Aquapim region of the Gold Coast.

---

6. In Zorn to La Trobe, 4 January 1843, Afrika III (1842–1848): vol. D-1,2, BEMS Archives.

Despite their internal disaffection over conditions in the Basel mission, and disagreements among the missionaries about resources, strategy, and appropriateness of each proposed new site which were major obstacles to any real advance, the West Indians continued in their labours in the mission.[7] The eight stations which were opened after 1850 – which included Akropong, Christiansborg, Abokoi, and Aburi – involved West Indian participation. From these stations, significant foundational evangelizing and missionary outreach was carried out. From 1850, they contributed to the growth of the Basel Mission and saw the rise of a truly African church in the hinterlands above the Aquapim mountains. New stations that were later opened at Kibi, Odumase-Krobo, Anum, and Aida also had West Indian inputs.

Schools were established at each of these stations, which enabled the Mission to concentrate on education as an important vehicle of missionary transmission. Native workers were trained in industrial crafts and skills for trade and commerce. Food networks for the Gold Coast, pioneered by the West Indians, were developed, and experiments with cash crops – notably cotton, coffee, and cocoa – proved quite successful in these networks. Domestic agriculture also developed under the Basel Mission with the participation of the West Indians. The Basel missionaries established a school for theological training, aimed at producing native leadership for the emerging African church. The first to graduate from this theological training institute was the Jamaican Alexander Worthy Clerk. As the West Indians participated in each of these activities, they did so with the attitude that this was a noble enterprise in which they had been given the privilege of participating. Both out of practical necessity and as an expression of their commitment to the task and the goals of the enterprise, they exerted themselves as converts and agents to a project they believed in and fully embraced.

Therefore, when considered against the background of the needs of Western Africa in the mid-nineteenth century and the vision of the Western missionary enterprise, it is understandable that the West Indians exerted their energies in the project as if engaged in development work. Mission as development and development as a means of freedom seemed to have formed the framework of their missionary motive for engagement. Their labours and

---

7. Mader makes this point in his Correspondence. See Mader to Josenhans, Missionary personal files, Afrika III, vol. D-1, 2, Correspondence, BEMS Archives.

commitment to the project could be taken as indicators that they accepted a conception of Christian mission as an agency of development. From the record of their conduct and activities in the Basel Mission, the issues for which they fought, especially during the early years in Akropong, demonstrate their belief that if Christian mission was a means of civilization, it must produce a civility that respects and enhances human dignity, freedom, and human aspirations. They perceived Christian mission as being as much about social justice that elevated human dignity as it was about spiritual salvation and human moral redemption.

Likewise in the Baptist Mission to the Cameroon, the West Indians experienced similar issues and struggles to those of the other two groups, even though they might have enjoyed slightly more freedom of operation. They laid a solid foundation for the Christian Mission enterprise in the Cameroon. In their labours and legacy, they provided and demonstrated sufficient evidence of their grasp of the nature and task of the enterprise they were engaged in. For them, the task was clearly one concerned with the effective planting and transmission of the Christian missionary message, without which the object of forming a truly native African church as the vehicle by which African redemption would be achieved could not be realized.

The goal of establishing Christianity in parts of Western Africa – including what is now Cameroon – was certainly part of the long-held hopes and dreams of the Western missionary enterprise for sub-Saharan Africa. The efforts of the Jamaican and British Baptists in the Cameroon between 1844 and 1888, the Jamaican Moravians in the Basel Mission in Akropong between 1846 and 1870, and the Anglican Mission from Barbados to the Rio Pongas between 1856 and 1897 enabled those hopes and dreams to become reality. The contribution of the West Indians to the enterprise may be seen in the various missionary activities around which the enterprise centred, which will be discussed below. This contribution attests to their understanding, commitment, and conception of the project in which they laboured with great effect and endurance.

Church Planting

The goal of the nineteenth-century missionary was to plant a church – that is, to gather a nucleus of people around which Christian rites and witness would be organized, practised, and demonstrated. The first step to realizing this goal was to establish a regular preaching station as a platform from which evangelizing work could be carried out. After a while, a place was set aside where Christian initiation, catechizing, and various forms of Christian education were conducted. There, the public witness of the Christian rites of marriage, baptism, and burial could be regularly and publicly demonstrated. Engaging in this institution-building dimension of the missionary project as a long-term strategy of planting Christianity in sub-Saharan Africa became a priority for the West Indian missionaries and their active engagement in this dimension of the project demonstrated their understanding and conception of the project.

Although the black West Indian missionaries were not the founders of the first church at Clarence Bay in the Cameroon Mission, Richard Merrick and his family, Alexander Fuller and others formed part of the nucleus and leadership of that church, which included carrying out regular preaching duties. When the Baptist Mission was relocated to the mainland in 1846, they helped to initiate and establish the church at Bimbia and surrounding areas and formed part of the leadership of these newly planted churches. In contrast to the experience of the Jamaican Moravians in the Basel Mission at Akropong, the Jamaican Baptists in the Cameroon Mission and the Barbadian Anglicans in the Pongas Mission were active participants in all the activities of the Mission, including leadership and preaching roles.[8] In the Baptist Mission in the Cameroon, the preacher-evangelists – Gallimore, Trusty, Duckett, and Ennis – as well as Merrick and Fuller, were pioneer church planters, who engaged vigorously in efforts to establish new stations in the interior of the mainland. Pinnock actually established a base at the foothills of Mt. Cameroon but, sadly, was driven out by resistant tribesmen. He settled, instead, in Victoria and spent over twenty years in the Mission. His son, John Pinnock, who was born in Africa, joined the Congo Mission in 1887 and served at Underhill, Kibokolo, and Matadi.[9]

---

8. As we have seen, this may have been due, in part, to the enterprising nature of Baptist ecclesiology and missiology, which much more readily emphasized lay leadership, as well as to the fact that the Anglicans from Barbados did not have much support in the form of European personnel. The structure of the Mission in Akropong, on the other hand, was quite restrictive for the West Indian participants.

9. Payne, *Free Church tradition in the Life of England*, 84.

Perhaps no West Indian was more successful in the work of church planting than J. J. Fuller who enjoyed longevity in the field.[10] Fuller not only contributed to the building of several stations, including Jubilee at Bimbia, Bethel, and Aqua Town, but he also extended the work of the Mission by building his own stations at Hickory Town – also called Mortonville – Jaburi, and Dibombari. After nearly 28 years in the Cameroon Fuller requested extended leave which was granted by the BMS. He spent 18 months on furlough during which he visited Jamaica in 1872 where he raised money to build a chapel in Mortonville and named it after Sir Morton Peto, the BMS treasurer. Around the mission stations, Fuller built schools, trained teachers, and appointed native deacons for his various churches. His example illustrates the freedom and wide-ranging activities of a Baptist missionary in Western Africa and highlights the fact that many of the BMS's church planting tasks in the Cameroon were either driven or strongly supported by the Jamaicans. Those who doubted the capacity and ability of the black missionaries to exercise leadership need only have considered the case of Richard Merrick, Joseph Fuller, and others in the Cameroon Mission, or John Duport, Phillip Doughlin, and others in the Pongas Mission. These people are shining examples of black leadership which enabled the missionary project not only to survive but to succeed in its long-held hopes of effectively planting Christianity in sub-Saharan Africa.

African Philology and Vernacular Scripture Translation

One of the consequential outcomes of the Western missionary enterprise is the study of the use of language as an instrument of cultural transmission, which has given rise to the development of modern philology.[11] In the enterprise in Africa, it led to the disciplined study of African languages by Western

---

10. Newman, "West Indian Contribution," 220–231.

11. Philology, according to The New Oxford Dictionary (2003), is "the branch of knowledge that deals with the structure, historical development and relations of a language or languages." The Penguin English Dictionary, 2nd Edition (2003) offers four definitions of the term "philology," including this one: "The study of the historical development of a language or the comparison of different languages especially based on the analysis of texts, historical linguistics, and/or comparative linguistics."

missionaries as a strategy for penetration of African culture and society.[12] In this aspect of the missionary task, the West Indian missionaries also ventured bravely to contribute since they did not wish to be excluded from any aspect of the enterprise. The development of vernacular Scriptures, liturgical texts, and school primers were considered by them to be well within their capability. Those who succeeded as missionary pioneers in Africa – such as Fuller, Mulgrave, Duport, and Doughlin – seemed propelled by a sense of calling to this missionary task, which meant total engagement in the project.

The fact that the West Indian missionaries were from the margin of the British Empire, rather than from the metropole, may have provided added impetus. As West Indian Creoles, their Christian formation occurred in an environment in which vernacularization was very much a part of the creolization process. Therefore, they understood the significance of language as an instrument of self-identity, as well as a means of symbolic communication. As emancipated African West Indians, they endeavoured to use this natural facility in Africa.[13] Burton, Brathwaite, and others note the effect of their long encounter with the colonial state that created within them a flair for the manipulative use of words, often in the guise of play.[14] In the Creole society of the West Indies, the creative and skilful use of language was an imperative in the learned behaviour of the middle and underclasses. In slave society, the African slaves had become skilled in the art, vocabulary, and use of symbolic language. Indeed, it was in their struggle to deal with the effects of slavery

---

12. The argument put forward by Sanneh, *Translating the Message*, Bediako, *Theology and Identity*, 109–125, and Walls, *Missionary Movement*, 26–42, not only draws attention to the role of Scripture translation into vernacular languages by the missionary enterprise as an important means of faith transmission but, equally, to the nature of cultural penetration and the development of local languages through the translation principle.

13. The special interest in African languages and linguistics that John Clarke – as leader of the Baptist Mission from Jamaica – had developed was bound to influence the Jamaican missionary team in the Cameroon Mission. As already noted, in preparation for their mission to Africa, Clarke and others had begun to build a lexicon of African vocabulary while in Jamaica, and they avidly expanded this while in Africa. After returning to the West Indies from the Cameroon Mission, Clarke published his collection, and it has been suggested that Koelle's *Polyglotta Africana* might well have been influenced by Clarke's work. Groves notes that Clarke was the first to publish records of the speech of the indigenous Bubis. Groves, *Planting of Christianity in Africa*, 31, citing H. H. Johnson, *A Comparative study of the Bantu and Semi-Bantu Languages 1*, 813, and F. W. H. Migeod, *Languages of Africa*, I, 189.

14. Burton, *Afro-Creole*, 1–12; Brathwaite, *Folk Culture*, 364–383.

as "social death," as Patterson termed it, that they created, manipulated, and used language as an instrument of survival, resistance, and defiance.[15]

The two West Indians whose contribution to African philology and vernacular translations were the most useful in the Baptist Mission in the Cameroon were Joseph Merrick and J. J. Fuller. In their separate roles and capacities, each of them demonstrated their understanding of the significance of vernacular communication as an important tool of missionary transmission. Merrick, for instance, in 1848, the year before his untimely death, expressed his views on the matter in correspondence with an English supporter:

> I have often felt as if my heart would break in a thousand pieces, when the heathen have assembled before me without being able to hear in their own tongue the wonderful words and works of God. . . . It is my opinion that where the missionary does not acquire the people's language, so as to present truth, in all its various shades and colours, and as powerful a manner as he can present it in his own tongue, neither the Gospel of Christ nor the people have had a fair trial. . . . For this reason every missionary should regard it as his primary and imperative duty to acquire the native tongue, and as a general thing, I should say that if, after a fair trial, a missionary finds that he cannot do this, he should seriously consider, whether it is his duty to remain in a heathen land.[16]

In his letter, not only was Merrick communicating his frustration in dealing with and overcoming communication barriers of being unable to communicate in "the people's language," he also communicated his passion for presenting "the wonderful words and works of God." This passion was evident throughout his short five years in Africa. As John Clarke's Jamaican protégé, Joseph Merrick certainly broke new ground in Africa by publishing

---

15. The published tales of Jamaican planter, Monk Lewis, in which he recounted colourful stories of communicating with his household slaves and others on the plantation illustrate precisely how skilled the African slaves in the New World environment had become in the manipulation of language. Citing Monk Lewis, Brathwaite says, "it was in language that the slave was perhaps most successfully imprisoned by his master, and it was in his (mis) use of it that he perhaps most effectively rebelled." Brathwaite, "The 'Folk' Culture of the Slaves," 381.

16. Merrick to Coby, General Missionary Correspondence, BMS Archives.

vernacular translations of the Old Testament.[17] He preached often from the Old Testament and made many allusions to Old Testament stories, especially the story of Joseph. The inevitable comparison with African slavery and the slave experiences of the ancient Jews no doubt reflected his experience of the slave society of Jamaica, and Spanish Town in particular which, during the time Merrick lived and worked there, had a Jewish population and a synagogue. From his station at Bimbia, Merrick also prepared and published a grammar and comparative dictionary of the Isubu, Baquiri, Monggo, Balung, Duala, and Balimba dialects, as well as schoolbooks, lessons, and a hymn book in Isubu.[18]

For his part, J. J. Fuller made several attempts to produce some works in translation but was always overshadowed by Alfred Saker, who took control of the translation project of the BMS in the Cameroon after Merrick's death. There is no doubt that Saker depended heavily on Fuller as printer and collaborator in his translation work. Fuller did make his own contribution to the philological output of the BMS by translating Bunyan's classic work, *The Pilgrim's Progress* into the Duala language.[19] But Fuller's real legacy lay in the practical and vital work – of building several missionary stations – and in the enormous skill and flexibility with which he kept the enterprise in the Cameroon alive. Based on his considerable exertions and unquestionable commitment to the missionary project over forty years, the nature of Fuller's missionary engagement in the Cameron mission suggests that he understood Christian mission as a vital instrument for human freedom from all kinds of bondages, and an invaluable tool for experiencing divine justice and human development.

---

17. van Slageren, *Origins of the Evangelical Church*, has drawn attention to the fact that translating Old Testament books was new to the missionary enterprise in the 1840s. He suggests that Merrick's background in Jamaica may have been an influence in his choice of the Old Testament for translating into African dialects.

18. Extracts of his Scripture translations are available for inspection in the BMS Archives, Angus Library, Regent's College, Oxford.

19. A beautifully bound copy of Fuller's translation of *Bunyan's Pilgrim's Progress in the Duala Language* is in the BMS Archives, Ref. 1.f.34. In the preface to his book, Fuller stated that he thought that "no book, apart from the Holy Scriptures" would help the Dualas to expand their knowledge of the Christian religion as much as "the present volume can." The significance of *Pilgrim's Progress* to African literature and imagination has been highlighted by Isabel Hofmeyr, "Dreams, Documents and 'Fetishes'," 84–119, and Comaroff and Comaroff, *Of Revelation and Revolution*, 172–178, 332.

Education

As already pointed out, the nineteenth-century Western missionary enterprise placed great emphasis on education. Along with agriculture, it was the single most important instrument to be employed in the "civilization" of "uncivilized" and "barbarous" peoples.[20] In the "Age of Enlightenment," education as a civilizing tool meant the development of human rational capacity, the introduction and broadening of knowledge, and the embrace of the scientific method with its modern technology. The modality for delivering this "education" was to be through the institutionalization of "school." Therefore, in Christian mission, great emphasis was placed on the establishment of schools as a key component of the strategy of engagement. Through mission schools, the fundamentals of knowledge were to be acquired through books, corporate socializing, and the culture-forming regimen of the scholastic habit. It was important, therefore, to establish classes for the young to be taught and trained in the rudiments of general and moral knowledge. For the Christian missionary, this was seen not merely as the introduction of superior knowledge and techniques but, equally, as the means whereby Christian formation and shaping of the next generation could be ensured. Through scholastic education the expectation was that the next generation would emerge and be able to exert and provide Christian leadership in the local community. In many instances, this became the basis and beginning of a colonial education system that – as Ajayi has shown in the case of Nigeria – produced a new black African elite that, in time, became the progenitors of African nationalism.[21]

In Western Africa, the demand for mission school education in the mid-nineteenth century was at times quite high. Local chiefs, members of the merchant class, and all who aspired to benefit from trading and other contacts with Europeans desired a Western education. Over time, however, a conflict developed over the delivery of "education" by Western missionaries. This conflict manifested itself as a choice between local demand for Western education on the one hand, and the missionary delivery of vernacularized education on the other. For Western missionaries, the priority was the penetration of local culture through vernacular translations of European texts; but for reasons of politics and commerce, the African elders desired their young to learn and

---

20. Ingleby, *Education as a Missionary Tool*.
21. Ajayi, *Christian Missions in Nigeria*.

master the European texts in European languages. At times, the West Indian missionaries in Africa found themselves caught in this tension. Some, like the Baptists in the Cameroon, gave full support to the translation project, while others, like the Anglicans in the Pongas Mission, served both interests.

Knowing the value of missionary education from their own formation in the West Indies, education was therefore a natural avenue of activity for engagement for West Indian missionaries in Africa. The "successful" experiments in mission-led education in the West Indies was the foundation that helped the West Indian missionaries in Africa to prioritize education as a strategy of engagement in Africa. From the Baptist Mission in Jamaica, for example, schools and Sabbath classes were proud achievements of missionary endeavour. In 1843, when John Clarke arrived in Spanish Town during his recruitment tour of Jamaica, he took particular note of teachers and even those who had a teacher as a relative, as he interviewed and recruited candidates for the mission to Africa. He recorded in his journal:

> Examined Messers Norman & Ennis and accepted them with their wives and children for Africa ... Mr. & Mrs. Ennis and Miss Davis are coloured people Mr. Norman is Teacher at Kitson's Ville, in St. Johns ... Emily Davis, a Sambo Creole aged 24 years, has been a member at Spanish Town for 6 years. Her sister keeps the day school at Lucky Valley in St. Thomas-in-the vale. [22]

In Africa, Clarke laid out a careful plan for the mission schools, a plan in which teachers seemed to have been given pride of place.[23] Every BMS missionary to the Cameroon, Jamaican as well as British, followed this plan and established classes for ongoing and graded instructions in the mission schools. The Jamaicans went a step further by introducing the technology of printing, which facilitated the educational process.[24] From funds raised in

---

22. Clarke, *African Journal*, vol. 3, Box 2: *Journals of West Africa*, BMS Archives.

23. Stanley, *Bible and the Flag*, 109. Stanley suggests that part of the internal problems of the early settlement in Fernando Po might have stemmed from a perception of a hierarchy of status and privileges afforded to the teachers.

24. Richard Merrick taught the technology of printing to young J. J. Fuller. As Fuller later acknowledged, "I had no knowledge of printing but Mr. Merrick being a Printer by trade promised to teach me and gave me a Printers Dictionary with certain instructions. . . . I helped put up the first Mission Press and in the evenings began a course of study under Mr.

England and Scotland in 1842, Merrick bought a printing press and used it to produce primers for schools. With this press, they were able to produce educational primers in Duala for young scholars in Bimbia, Victoria, and other stations. They also began the process of codifying the local Bantu dialects in the Cameroon and laid the foundation for the development of the educational system.

Interestingly, the method of education used in the West Indies by the British Baptists missionaries was known as the Lancaster method. This method of education involved the use of formal and informal systems of education. The formal system was the classroom-based instructional curricula that centred on the fundamentals of literary education and the "three Rs" – reading, writing, and arithmetic – while the informal method was personal self-development through extracurricular programmes. An important component of this method was a leadership development system of "monitors," whereby older students would be given responsibilities to instruct and guide younger students. The idea was to inculcate self-discipline, peer leadership, and peer learning among the young scholars. As an example, in the recruitment of Jamaican Baptists for the mission in Africa, twelve-year-old Samuel Fuller – son of Alexander Fuller and younger brother to J. J. Fuller – and eleven-year-old Ebenezer Norman – son of William and Martha Norman, who were both teachers – were selected to go to Africa with the expectation that they would act as monitors in the mission schools in Africa. Young Fuller and Norman began well but failed to live up to the expectations and demands placed upon them by the Mission and its leaders. Succumbing to the pressures exerted upon them, they opted out and were dismissed by the BMS. Nonetheless, the BMS-founded schools in the Cameroon developed an educational system that left a recognizable educational legacy in that country.[25]

Merrick . . . at the same time tried to get a knowledge of the native language, and being young I soon mastered that and was able to speak to the people in their own tongue." Fuller, MS *Autobiography*, 29, BMS Archives.

25. Aka, "Joseph Merrick."

Villages and Social Formation

In addition to the moral formation of individual persons, the civilizing missions of the nineteenth century included plans for community formation. From the nineteenth-century European standpoint, the notion of civilization included, among other things, the modernization of a way of life that took into account everything from the formation of individual personhood to community formation, including proper housing, social interaction, civil social discourse and, of course, religion (church attendance) and family life. The idea behind this was the perceived need to tame the "noble savage" and create a way of life in which social discourse was civil instead of savage, constructive instead of destructive. If Christian mission was to be the harbinger of "civilization," this meant that its agents would necessarily have to concern themselves with the social dimension of the missionary task. In the Victorian age, this social dimension of life was highly affirmed and valued and contributed to the building of a class-structured society.

Therefore, one of the activities undertaken by the West Indians in Africa was the establishment of villages as model communities. As one of the major social projects in which missionaries were actively involved in the post-emancipation West Indies, the Jamaican Baptists transported the model of the free village to Africa. The design of these villages resembled late medieval villages in Europe. At the centre of the village was the Mission church. On one side of the church were the dwelling homes of the missionaries and Christian families. On the other side, there was the school and commercial enterprises that provided legitimate commerce and trade for the community. Surrounding these structures in the centre were roads leading from the centre to other areas that offered more possibilities for housing, gardening, and other agricultural pursuits such as horticulture and the growing of cash crops for local markets.

In the Cameroon, Joseph Merrick was intent on establishing this model of the Jamaican free village in the township of Bimbia and went as far as to purchase land from King William for this purpose.[26] Merrick and J. J. Fuller acquired the land, designed plans for the construction of the village, hired workers, and began the process of building houses to establish a community. In addition to the technology of printing, the Jamaican Baptists had

---

26. van Slageren and van Slageren, " Jamaican Missionaries in Cameroon," 149.

also brought to Africa a technology of building, which included the skills of brickmaking and bricklaying, carpentry, and innovative roofing systems. Fuller, like his father before him, had learned the skills of brickmaking and bricklaying as a young apprentice in Spanish Town. His technical expertise and pragmatic approach to the project proved extremely useful in the Cameroon Mission. He utilized his skills in almost all the building projects in the Mission and also trained many local young Isubus in these skills and techniques. These construction projects added to the skills bank of the Isubu and Duala communities, as well as to the housing stock of the local communities.

Although the villages were never developed as fully as envisaged, nonetheless the Jamaican Baptists' spirit of freedom, enterprise, and resistance to external threats seemed to have been transmitted to the community. This was manifested on several occasions. For example, when, after Merrick's untimely death at sea and Clarke's departure back to the West Indies, Alfred Saker attempted to close down the Bimbia mission station, he met strong resistance and opposition from the local village community established by the black Jamaican missionaries.

Recognizing that stable and secure housing was important for the health of the missionaries, Merrick and Fuller were anxious to improve the quality of the housing for the missionaries on the field but were often constrained by the lack of resources and the need for approval from the BMS in London. They voiced their frustrations in correspondence with the BMS. For example, after the departure of John Clarke from the Cameroon back to Jamaica, Merrick felt impelled to write to the Society and express his personal views on the situation in the Mission:

> A few days before brother Clarke left for Jamaica, while he was dangerously ill, the rain beat most furiously into his bedroom, and wetted the bed on which he was lying. When I think of this, and remember that the same circumstances may happen soon after brother Clarke's return, you will not be surprised to hear that I feel painfully embarrassed between the probability of incurring the censure of the Committee for building without obtaining their concurrence, and neglecting that which, if

performed, might perhaps prevent the serious illness of one of our most valuable missionaries."[27]

Merrick's embarrassment was coupled with a feeling of impotence. He was impatient and frustrated at his inability to take action to improve the physical infrastructure of the Mission due to the constraints of BMS policy in the metropole.

Feeling similarly constrained by the lack of resources and wishing that he had a subsidiary network of support outside the BMS, Fuller, later reminisced, "Many had been the time when I have sat low-spirited, especially when I received a letter from England to say I must on no account extend my work without the Brethren's consent, or that the friends of the Society will not allow it."[28] Perhaps this policy of control by means of obtaining approval was right and necessary in the circumstances. But the enterprising, and yet compliant, West Indians knew its adverse effects on the field. Given their drive and enthusiasm for the missionary project, a lot more might have been achieved if the necessary resources had been made available, particularly in respect of the construction and development of the physical infrastructure of the Mission. The intentionality with which the West Indians laboured for the development of the missions in Africa, is an indication that they believed they were also labouring for the development of new, modern African communities. By the construction of villages for new community life and the spiritual mission in which they were engaged, they appeared convinced that their participation in the project was laying the foundation for the upliftment of African dignity and freedom.

Domestic Agriculture and Health Care

As previously noted, the development of local agriculture was an essential component of each of the three West Indian missions in Africa in the nineteenth century. While this was mostly to satisfy domestic needs, producing agricultural crops for export was also contemplated as a source of income generation for sustaining the missions. Agricultural work was also a part of the creative and educational work of the mission. In the Baptist Mission

---

27. Merrick, *MH* (January 1848), BMS Archives.
28. Fuller, *MH* (January 1884): 188, BMS Archives.

in the Cameroon, the British Baptist missionary Alfred Saker was credited with revolutionizing domestic agriculture in the country by his introduction of new species such as breadfruit, pomegranates, mangoes, avocados, and mamee apples. He was also credited with introducing medicine, arts and crafts, new architecture and local housing construction technology such as carpentry and ironmongery. He was seen as being ahead of his time in his considerable contribution to vernacular translations of the Bible into Dualla.[29] As a rugged pioneer who blazed a trail in the missionary enterprise in Western Africa, Saker's achievements in the Cameroon were undoubtedly outstanding. However, much of what are claimed to be Saker's introductions or innovations in Cameroon life were in fact brought over from the West Indies on the *Chilimark* by the Jamaican Baptist missionary group.

Before leaving the West Indies in their transatlantic voyage to Africa, the Jamaican Baptists, regardless of what they might have imagined Africa to be, were evidently determined to ensure that they made a valuable contribution not only to the spiritual needs of "bleeding Africa" – as the popular reputation of Africa suggested – but also to its material needs. They wanted to bless "Mother Africa" with whatever resources they had in the West Indies. The matter of food supply for sustaining the Mission was, therefore, given practical consideration by Baptist congregations across Jamaica as their contribution to the enterprise in Africa. When the missionary group disembarked at Clarence Bay on 16 February 1844, Clarke noted in his journal the fact that Alfred Saker had refused to help with offloading the food crops taken by the Jamaicans. Subsequently, it was the Jamaican missionary settlers – who were assigned agricultural tasks – who planted these food crops.

One of the essential elements for agricultural development was a reliable water supply, but the water systems available were inadequate to compensate for periods of drought on the Gold Coast and in the Cameroon. This was one of the problems that the Baptist Mission encountered when they relocated to the mainland. Whenever such periods of drought occurred, the West Indians dug artesian wells to try to find a source of water supply. In describing one such well he dug, J. J. Fuller noted the unexpected reaction

---

29. Livingstone is alleged to have said that the work of Alfred Saker is "the most remarkable on the African continent." Sir Harry Johnson, the British Consul in the Bight of Africa also commended Saker for converting the Duallas to "real and permanent civilization." Stanley, *Bible and the Flag*.

of the local community to his discovery of water. His ability to find water in an otherwise barren environment resulted in a drop in attendance at the Mission church. Upon investigation, Fuller discovered that the local people were staying away from the Mission because they thought he was a witch, possessing magical powers, because he had been able to produce water from the earth.[30] This water source, however, not only irrigated the domestic gardens of the Mission but also nurtured their poultry and other livestock. The local community also benefitted as the Mission was able to assist them by supplying water to the villagers during times of drought.

In addition to water, the health needs of the Mission were vital and constant. As already noted, the notorious health impact of the West African environment on Westerners was a major deterrent and impediment to the Western missionary enterprise in Africa. Malaria, and the prevalence of other diseases such as smallpox, and tropical parasites such as chiggers were an incessant danger to life in Western Africa. Even the two doctors in the Baptist Mission, Sturgeon and Prince, succumbed on the field and became part of the high missionary casualty rate in the early efforts to establish the Mission. Recognizing and identifying the problem, the West Indian missionaries searched for solutions to the health challenges they faced. For example, Merrick took steps to establish a sanatorium in the highlands of Mt. Cameroon and Fuller and others worked hard to procure vaccines and medicines for the people in their villages to fight against outbreaks of smallpox as well as other environmentally transmissible diseases. When the prescribed Western medicines failed or were not available, the West Indians had no hesitation in resorting to what they knew. As Creole West Indians, they drew upon their ethnic background and experience in the West Indies of employing "bush" remedies when faced with the challenge of finding remedies and medical solutions in Africa.

For example, when J. J. Fuller was faced with a personal health crisis in his family, after normal prescribed medicines had been tried but yielded no positive results, he unhesitatingly employed the healing options of local "bush" medicines. When his second wife, Charlotte Diboll – daughter of John Diboll, the British BMS missionary in the Cameroon – had a severe case of lockjaw, no remedy could be found to help her, and she almost died; but Fuller sent to neighbouring Sierra Leone for a coloured man who, he said, "understood

---

30. Fuller, MS *Autobiography*, BMS Archives.

this complaint." The man came to the Cameroon and prescribed what Fuller described as "herbs from the bush." Charlotte recovered and contributed many years of useful service to the missionary cause until their retirement in England in 1888.[31]

The West Indian missionaries were generally successful in confronting the various health challenges they encountered in Africa. Despite their losses, failures, and misapprehensions, they sought solutions and found ways of persevering in the missionary cause to keep the enterprise alive.

Marriage and Family, Death and Dying and the Struggle for Human Dignity

If the objective of the civilizing missions of the nineteenth century was in fact to create a new moral order among missionized peoples, then a vital instrument in achieving this task, in addition to education and agriculture, was the Christian institution of marriage and family. The Western missionary establishment believed that through the formative influences of Christian institutions such as "the Christian home" and "the school," uncivilized human beings could be reared and nurtured in Christian moral knowledge and moral awareness. In Africa, one of the obstacles to the achievement of the objective in the view of the European missionaries was the practice of polygamy. Western Christian notions of marriage and family stood in direct contrast and conflict with this practice. Inevitably, polygamy was perceived to be one of the major stumbling blocks to the progress of Christian mission in Africa. While observing African society during the reconnaissance mission in 1841, John Clarke, leader of the Jamaican Baptist missionary group, noted that "polygamy and belief in Jujus seem to be the greatest barriers in the way" and remarked that "the last will fall soon, but the first, with the kings and head men, has a firm hold; not too firm, however, for the gospel to destroy."[32] Therefore, a way had to be found to deal with this problem. That way was through the direct promotion of the Christian rite of marriage – which was considered a Christian sacrament – and monogamous family life.

---

31. Fuller, MS *Autobiography*, 185, BMS Archives.
32. Clarke, *BHFA* (29 April 1841): 312, BMS Archives.

Christian marriages were, therefore, strongly encouraged.[33] Many marriages were performed in the missions in Africa by the West Indian missionaries in their pursuit of the goals of the Western missionary project. For example, after eleven months in Africa, on their first visit to Clarence, Clarke and Prince baptized five persons and married sixty-six couples before they left the island to report to the BMS in London.[34] This practice of performing baptisms and marriages was carried on by the Jamaicans under Clarke's leadership of the Cameroon Mission. As vanguards of this new moral mission, the West Indians were expected to model this new order as settlers, auxiliaries, or missionaries. They were to be model families, displaying Christian virtues of monogamy, filial love, and domestic aesthetics. This expectation forced many to conform and pattern their family life on the basis of European rather than African norms. Not all succeeded. Many conflicts emerged, and there were some casualties – such as the breakdown of the marriage of George Thompson and Catherine Mulgrave and their subsequent divorce in the Basel Mission in Akropong.

By attempting to engage Africa in this Victorian way of marriage and family, the nineteenth-century missionary enterprise has been seen as a colonial project seeking to domesticate and colonize Africa in Western cultural forms.[35] As a strategy in the proposed remedy for Africa, this kind of intervention in African family systems has been taken as an example of the unrealistic and mythic expectation concerning Africa's redemption through the agency of Western paradigms of Christianity.

When it came to the prevailing culture of violence, perhaps in no other sphere of activity in Africa was the West Indian view of the missionary task more clearly expressed than in their unrelenting struggle against African violence, bloodshedding, and death. In their ministry activities, the West Indian missionaries were constantly preoccupied with issues of death and dying. With extraordinary sensitivity to encounters of African internecine violence, they recognized that tribal wars were often used as a cobelligerent means of supplying the slave trade. In response the West Indian agents took counteractive measures to reduce the levels of violence, including slave wars,

---

33. Parrinder, "Christian Marriage in French West Africa," 260–268.
34. Clarke, *BHFA* (6 September 1842): 191, BMS Archives.
35. Comaroff and Comaroff, *Of Revelation and Revolution*, 138.

and passionately demonstrated a conception of the missionary enterprise as a struggle for human freedom and the upliftment of human dignity. Their vigorous reactions and struggles with the endemic problem of African violence and the slave trade in its various forms impelled them to act as if they were, in truth, as Lamin Sanneh characterized African Americans in the nineteenth-century missionary enterprise, "Abolitionists Abroad."[36]

One of the violence-cultivating issues against which the Jamaican Baptists fought vigorously in the Cameroon was the practice known as "killing for the dead."[37] This practice was a local custom among the coastal Bantus which centred around the death of an important local personage such as a local chief or member of a chief's family. Immediately following the death of such a person, a raid would be made upon the nearest village and one or two persons captured and taken to the burial ceremony of the deceased. That person would then be killed or buried alive with the deceased, ostensibly to accompany the deceased to the other world. In reality, the practice was a political device to spread fear and terror in neighbouring villages in order to establish and demonstrate the power base of a new chief or to maintain the balance of power among rival chiefs contending for political hegemony.

John Clarke gave a chilling account of his encounter with this practice:

> A captain of a ship near the coast where these practices were performed requested that they might not be put to death so near the coast where he must of necessity witnessed it. They attended to his wish and planted from 40 to 50 posts at the back of the town, the victims that were brought had a bandage tied round their eyes. They were then secured to a post, after this the executioner went round, cutting the throats of each one as he passed along. This lasted for 14 days after the death of a King.[38]

J. J. Fuller also gave a vivid description of a similar event that took place following the death of Chief Preso Bell's eldest son, in which he highlighted his own indignant intervention:

---

36. Sanneh, *Abolitionists Abroad*.
37. Clarke, *BHFA* (6 September 1842): 191–194, BMS Archives.
38. Clarke.

The cloud gathered again when Preso Bell's eldest son died. In the silence of the night he sent off his war canoe, and next morning a poor fellow was beheaded to accompany this young man to the other world. I remonstrated with the old chief in such a way that although I did not to all appearance in any way shake his belief in the desirability of such an act, yet he seemed ashamed that he should have given me the trouble to speak to him. But it was his last, for the poor man after a time took ill, and as if haunted, he went from one witch doctor to the other, and from one place to another. At last he got out from the Town and settled on an island opposite. There he lived for a time, during which I visited him, and pointing him to a Saviour in Christ Jesus. But poor man, he was so steeped in his superstition that he seemed as if he could not let go. Several were accused of bewitching him, but thank God none were put to death, and I am grateful to God for the influence I had upon other chiefs. At last he died and with him the custom of burying with the dead.[39]

Whatever the social or political justification for this practice, the West Indian missionaries regarded it as a terrifying ordeal for the captured and a travesty of human life. In their missionary excursions into the interior, the Baptist missionaries often encountered populations of fearful villagers hidden in the hinterland in and around Mt. Cameroon. Such villagers had taken flight into the interior out of fear of raids from nearby villages for the purpose of capturing humans to make sacrifices for the dead. The West Indians responded to such situations with great humanitarian and abolitionist fervour. Through preaching, teaching, pastoral watch, and direct intervention, they engaged with and contested the practice as advocates of the humanitarian concern for dignity, freedom, and justice for every human being. They viewed the prevailing burial rites in African customs as corrupt and unenlightened "superstition" because they included practices such as the use of libations, drumming, animal sacrifices, and celebratory activities. In contrast to this local custom, the West Indians used the opportunity to introduce a new custom of Christian burial of the dead with compassionate, positive,

---

39. Fuller, MS *Autobiography*, 208–211, BMS Archives.

family-affirming liturgical rites. It is arguable whether this new Christian rite of burial of the dead was more akin to older African burial rites which were community-affirming rather than community alienating. Some historians have drawn parallels with the burial customs practiced by African slaves in the West Indies and the ancestral practices in Africa. In citing ways in which the death, funeral, and burial customs practised by African slaves in Jamaica had similarities with such customs among the Ga in the Gold Coast, Edward Kamau Brathwaite quotes Monk Lewis's description of such practices in a slave village in Jamaica and his description of a Ga funeral. Both included sacrifices, libations, drumming, and revelries, but the sacrifices were non-human, usually a bird or pig. Brathwaite contends that the meaning of these elements and ceremonies were not only understood by Africans as preparation for and helpful passage to the next life but were often misunderstood by Europeans as trivial and debasing.[40]

In June 1888, J. J. Fuller was invited to address the Centenary Conference of Protestant Missions of the World in Exeter Hall, London. In his address, Fuller claimed that, as a result of the missionary intervention in the Cameroon in Western Africa, the practices of "human sacrifice has been abolished, and many of the evils and customs of the country have been put a stop to." In concluding his platform speech, Fuller stated that in comparison with the conditions prevailing when he had arrived in Western Africa, the present situation of the people on the west coast of Africa was "a cause for the greatest thanksgiving." He declared, "God has done great things for us, and God intends that Africa, which has long had to bear the burdens and oppressions of all nations, shall take her place among the children of men." [41] This may have been a case of the usual optimistic and hyperbolic claim-making in missionary-speak, so characteristic of Western missionaries in the nineteenth century. If in fact it was not the case that "many of the evils and customs of the country" had been abolished as a result of the Western missionary intervention, it was nevertheless an attempt to recognize the fact that, over the forty years of the Jamaican Baptist Mission in Cameroon, some reduction at least had taken place in such practices involving the ritualistic violent sacrifice of

---

40. Brathwaite, "The 'Folk' Culture of the Slaves," 367.

41. Fuller's address is in Johnston, *Report of the Centenary Conference*, 267. This historic conference was attended by 1,600 participants representing 138 missionary societies.

human life. Perhaps Fuller, as a missionary from the West Indies, saw this issue more acutely than his missionary colleagues from the metropole. For the West Indian missionaries, Christian mission as a civilizing force was not just a means of intellectual or spiritual enlightenment but a struggle for social justice for the oppressed. It was a clear means towards the affirmation of human dignity, and the upliftment of Africa in the eyes of the world. This became very evident in the examples of their struggles for the release of Africans in bondage to so many forms of enslavement.

Temperance and Anti-slavery Societies

In their drive to create in Africa a moral society according to Baptist principles and tradition, one of the instruments used by the Baptist mission in the Cameroon was the establishment of temperance and anti-slavery societies. As soon as the Clarke-led Baptist Mission to Western Africa arrived in Fernando Po in 1844, one of the first community actions they undertook was to institute a temperance society and an anti-slavery society. A temperance society was a voluntary group in which individual participants pledged to abstain from substances that inhibited, impaired, or undermined their human capacity to function in normal ways. Members of these groups shared fellowship together and received mutual support. One of the motives for establishing a temperance society in Fernando Po might have been a desire to contain and influence the morally dissolute cosmopolitan port community in Clarence Bay. But it was also a way of creating social difference between the missionary group and the local people while inculcating discipline and moral virtue among the missionary group themselves. This was considered important in order to spotlight the missionary group and ensure the integrity of Baptist witness among the peoples encountered in Africa. However, in Fernando Po the Baptist Mission faced internal obstacles to the formation of a temperance society. The Englishman Alfred Saker, for example, refused to comply with the order for temperance among the missionary group. His indulgences became known in the Mission, and he was ultimately reported to the BMS in London by fellow English missionary Alexander Inness. This resulted in a Commission of Enquiry in 1863 into Saker's conduct in Africa. Nonetheless, a temperance society was established in Fernando Po and it had a positive value in drawing attention to publicly stated Christian moral standards and Mission policy, as well as, at times, restraining or moderating individual conduct.

The temperance and anti-slavery societies formed by the Baptists in the Cameroon were part of the organizational life of every mission station and congregation set up by that mission in Africa. Through these voluntary social organizations, the missionaries kept watch over the moral state of the villages, first at Clarence Bay and later at every other station on the African mainland. In their role as advocacy groups, the local temperance and anti-slavery societies served as constant reminders of the Mission's struggle for human freedom, dignity, and upliftment in Africa and elsewhere, in all aspects of life.

The Mission to the Rio Pongas

Like the Jamaican Baptists in the Cameroon Mission, the Barbadian Anglicans in the Mission to the Rio Pongas spent over forty years on the West African coast. In fact, as Gibba has shown, the Pongas Mission continued well into the twentieth century, lasting for more than eighty years.[42] This is a reasonable period of time within which to examine their achievements and failures and assess what conceptions of mission may possibly be discerned from their engagement in Africa. Given the variety of issues they encountered over this period of time, and the ways in which they responded, the Anglican West Indian missionaries demonstrated the capacity of marginal, non-metropolitan people, flawed though they were, to participate in every aspect of the enterprise of Christian mission in the nineteenth century. They engaged fully in the missionary task of evangelism, catechizing, planting and building a native African church. In their effort to create a new moral Christian consciousness in African society, they engaged fully in the social dimensions of the project in the areas of education, health care, agriculture, village formation, building construction, and domestic family formation. They engaged fully in issues of vernacular translation for meaningful Christian textual transmission and also engaged passionately in anti-slavery activities. Their attempts to undermine and eradicate African slavery seemed predicated on the grounds of its fundamental human indignity and injustice and was part of the "wrongs done to Africa." In this, they showed the emancipatory spirit of the Creole

---

42. Gibba, "West Indian Mission to West Africa."

West Indian character in slavery and emancipation after the collapse of the slave regime in the West Indies. And in this, it may be possible to discern their understanding and conception of Christian mission as an agency for social justice, human freedom and redemption, and upliftment. Although this conception was directed towards Africa and Africans, it also applied to themselves and their own well-being in the missionary project. No difference was seen between pursuing freedom and justice for slaves in Africa, on the one hand, and agitating relentlessly for improvement in their own security and social conditions in their missions, on the other. Their passion for social justice was exhibited both ways.

It might have been that the abolitionist spirit which imbued the missionary work in the West Indies contributed to the collapse of slavery and the commencement of the emancipation project in the British West Indies. This same spirit was eagerly transported across the Atlantic to the missionary enterprise in Africa in which West Indian participation had been intentionally sought and recruited.

Summary

From this study, several things have been established or may be inferred. First, it is evident that in all three West Indian missions in Africa in the nineteenth century, the level of participation of West Indian agents in the enterprise was extensive and encompassed all aspects of the enterprise. No part of the missionary project was considered by them to be beyond their horizon of engagement or capabilities. Their involvement encompassed the multidimensional nature of the enterprise and, in the main, they measured up to the tasks assigned. Their approach to the task demonstrated that even those from the margins of the Empire, if given the chance, could make contributions as valuable and as worthwhile as those from the metropole. The disappointments and failures of some West Indians may, in part, be accounted for by an examination of the terms and conditions of their contractual engagement, the inability of their European sponsors to fulfil their end of the contracts, and the manner in which they were treated and regarded as sub-alterns by the European managers of the missions. In many cases, the terms and conditions of engagement and the relational environment of the missions seemed to have made the critical difference between happiness and unhappiness, conflict and peace, failure and success in the missionary endeavour in Africa.

The three West Indian missions considered in this study were invariably embroiled in one internal conflict or another. Most of these conflicts were manifestations of class conflicts inherent in the structured class, colour and social status-based system of apportioning work. Invariably, the leadership of the missions failed to grasp the potential conflicts inherent in the nature of the work systems they devised. For example, ascriptions of a higher class status, particularly that of "missionary," seemed to have been a source of much conflict. The term held important meanings for the Europeans that might have been challenged by the West Indians. To be a "missionary" and engage in missionary work required ordination or recognition of a special status. Settlers and others, although thought to be very important to the project, were auxiliaries, who were perceived and treated as sub-alterns of a lower status or class and remunerated accordingly. "Missionaries" received marginally higher remuneration than others. The strategy of deployment according to the gifts and natural talents of individuals also appeared to have had the effect of honouring and empowering some, while disempowering or even dishonouring others. Despite this, however, to be given the opportunity to be involved in this project had the effect of honouring and empowering previously "socially dishonoured persons" as a whole.[43] What also seemed to have made a difference in the enterprise in Africa was the extent to which those selected from the West Indies were reasonably prepared in terms of their social background, mental attitude, and skills training prior to deployment for the mission work in Africa.

Second, the extensive nature of the missionary participation of the West Indians in the Africa missions appeared to have provided a dynamic existential context that shaped or reshaped their perceptions of the project for which they were recruited. Based on the manner in which they generally responded to African encounters – as described in this study – they might have entered Africa as subjects of the Empire and behaved in colonialist and Victorian terms. They pursued mission as a civilizing force, along the lines of European norms and values. However, an examination of the agendas, priorities, and record of their engagement in Africa also reveals the nature

---

43. Patterson, *Slavery and Social Death*, 10–14, 99–101.

and extent of personal transformation which some underwent on the field, especially those who had long and impactful missionary careers in Africa. Encountering Africa in its various forms presented the challenge of pursuing mission not as colonizers but as instruments of freedom and justice, or even – in the minds of the proposers of the Pongas Mission in Barbados – as "reparations for wrongs" done to Africa. Their motivations appeared to have been driven more by their West Indian background than by the interests and values of their European sponsors.

Third, from their motivation, agendas, and extensive engagement in the Africa enterprise, it may be possible, therefore, to discern some distinctive lines of conceptions of the missionary project on the part of the West Indian agents. Based on the ways in which they engaged Africa, Christian mission appears to have been perceived, understood, and pursued by the West Indians both as a civilizing force – encompassing all human beings and not just Africans – and as a force for social justice and the upliftment of human dignity and freedom. As Vassady concludes, "failure was not a necessary outcome" of the West Indian expeditions in Africa.[44] For example, as pioneers and trailblazers in the Cameroon, despite all the problems, failures, and disappointments they faced, the Jamaican Baptists managed to lay a foundation for the arrival and transmission of Christianity in that part of Western Africa where other mission attempts had failed.[45] That foundation, along with the social legacy it produced, functioned as a midwife that helped the Baptist Missionary Society of Great Britain to regain its vision for Africa.[46] From the foundations laid in the Cameroon, the BMS undertook a mission to the Congo, which was the biggest African project in its history. In the Cameroon, the Jamaican Baptists had lit a flame for Christianity that would continue to burn, leaving behind a legacy that is at least beginning to be recognized. As DeLancey acknowledges:

> These first steps of Christians in Cameroon owe much to the efforts of ... the Jamaicans ... and produced a Christian, literate, skilled group of clerks, teachers, craftsmen, pastors, and

---

44. Vassady, "Role of the Black West Indian Missionary," 101.
45. van Slageren, *The Origins*, 145–156.
46. Russell, *Missionary Outreach*; Stanley, *History of the Baptist Missionary Society*, 106–139.

other appendages of the colonial era, an elite that would in time become a significant factor in the growth of Cameroon nationalism.[47]

---

47. DeLancey, *Cameroon Federal Republic*, 8. The link between Cameroon Baptists and the Jamaican Baptist Union continues today, with reciprocal exchanges and mutual support. Le Vine, *Cameroon Federal Republic*; DeLancey, *Cameroon Federal Republic*, 8; Gifford, *African Christianity*, 284–287.

CHAPTER 9

Assessments and Implications

'I confess I do not see what are we to do next for Africa. I hope in due time the right way may open.'[1] E. N. Buxton. February 8, 1842

In an attempt to understand more fully the historical participation of West Indians in the missionary enterprise in Western Africa in the nineteenth century, this study has examined the question of how it was that, in the global nature of the nineteenth-century Western missionary enterprise, the West Indies came to be seen and considered as a possible source of supply for Christian mission in Africa. Furthermore, it examined what contribution, if any, did West Indians make to that project, and did their contribution suggest any special meaning or unique conception of the enterprise? The central issues of the transatlantic slavery industry between Africa and the New World from the seventeeth century, and the resistance and struggle for freedom on the part of the enslaved throughout the long period of enslavement, which shaped the broad context in which the impact of the imperial colonial project on the West Indies, the dialectics of the margins of the British Empire in the early nineteenth century, and the emergence of new contours in modern Christianity and Christian mission in the nineteenth century were considered as part of a complex set of motivations for the initiatives from the West Indies to Africa in the aftermath of emancipation in the mid-nineteenth century. This project may be considered as a reverse transatlantic episodic enterprise.

As early as the 1830s the West Indies was seen as a potential source of supply for the missionary enterprise in Africa, especially given that the

---

1. Edward North Buxton to Priscilla Johnston, Buxton Papers, Reel #9, USPG Archives;

prospects of the collapse of the slave regime that governed the British West Indies loomed before them. Baptist, Methodist, Moravian, and Anglican communities dreamed of such prospects and possibilities as new ventures that could further demonstrate the efficacy and success of Christian missionary endeavours. As missionary endeavours grew in the West Indies, and as slave societies showed signs of collapsing, these Christian communities began to contemplate ways in which this dream could be realized in other fields. Through transatlantic channels and networks, especially the British and American anti-slavery movements, European missionaries promoted the idea as a project particularly suited to the West Indian church as an appropriate response for the blessings of the success of the missionary impact on the African slaves in the West Indies. Given the abnormal and peculiar context in which West Indian slave societies emerged and developed from the seventeenth to the nineteenth centuries – including the complex, highly defended, and vigorously contested nature of these societies, as described in chapter three – these initiatives represented a bold and ambitious vision. It was an idea that would have automatically attracted sceptics and opponents, especially those who had doubts about the so-called "Negro character".[2]

The fact that there were five separate mission initiatives from the West Indies to Africa in the nineteenth century not only suggests some degree of enthusiasm and desire for adventure but also some degree of competitive ambition and possible opportunism. Given the formidable challenges they faced, these initiatives would not have been easily mounted and, furthermore, were not easily sustained. This would have been difficult for several reasons. Assuming that the dream originated among the white European missionaries in the West Indies, the African population in the West Indies would have had to overcome their existential doubts and be convinced and persuaded about the necessity, safety, viability, and legitimacy of this idea if they were to accept it and participate in it. Emerging from years of collective memory of the infamous Middle Passage journey from Africa to the West Indies, the torturous and death-inducing life of plantation slavery, and the relentless struggle for freedom by the slave population, this would have been a difficult challenge to purue. However, it was not only the Africans in the West Indies who had to be convinced, champions of Christian mission in Britain had to

---

2. Cawley Bolt, *Some Evangelical Missionaries' Understanding*.

be persuaded too. Edward Underhill, as secretary of the Baptist Missionary Society, noted that some British Baptists had objections to the idea on the grounds that (1) the obstacles to such an enterprise in Africa had hitherto been insuperable, so why bother, (2) attempting to preach the gospel to the children of Ham was a profane interference with a divine decree because the African natives were suffering from the judicial sentence of God against them, and (3) the mental inferiority of the Negro race rendered them incapable of accepting the gospel.[3]

To overcome these obstacles required not only a rational and plausible justification but also a promotional campaign to persuade various publics. Africa had to be reimagined and a new racial theory of the African had to be invented. The relationship between race and slavery, and the ways in which this had affected the African persona in slavery in the New Transatlantic World became a long intellectual debate.[4] A biblical text from the Book of Psalms, "Princes shall come out of Egypt; Ethiopia shall soon stretch out her hands unto God" (Ps 68:31 KJV) was identified and used to reintroduce Africa in popular religious discourse and reshape missionary imagination to focus solicitously on a needy Africa begging for help. It was the text most widely used throughout the West Indies by all mission societies to promote and propagandize the idea of a missionary project from the West Indies to Africa. It was employed in whipping up missionary interest and enthusiasm for Africa and also in reinterpreting and recasting the racialized view of the African. Once the "cursed and despised sons of Ham," the Africans were now to be viewed as the blessed sons of Abraham whose redemption was at hand. This new imaging, based on biblical imagery, depicted Africa as one with arms stretched out to God, pleading and awaiting redemption. Africa in the mid-nineteenth century was perceived as being ready to produce a nobler race of princes and rulers and, quite possibly, a new civilization, through the agency of Christian mission.

During the 1840s, every European missionary in the West Indies preached on this text and applied this new theological interpretation in these terms. In 1844, D. J. East, a Baptist missionary to Jamaica, published a pamphlet on the subject in which he sharply reflected the shift in missionary thinking towards

---

3. Underhill, *Alfred Saker*, 11.
4. See Jordon, *White Over Black*; Campbell and Oakes, "The Invention of Race."

Africa in the 1830s, as the prospect of the collapse of the slave system loomed before them. East saw in Psalm 68:31 not only the fulfilment of prophecy but also the removal of a curse on the sons of Ham (Gen 9:22–27). From his point of view, and perhaps from the Baptist point of view:

> The believer in revelation sees in the condition of Africa the fulfilment of Divine prediction – the execution of a curse pronounced by the Almighty nearly four thousand years ago, and still standing on record in holy oracles (Gen 9:22–27; Ps 68:31), but the curse which for so many generations has rested upon the unhappy descendants of Ham, is not to be perpetual. . . . The same inspired authority which records the curse, predicts the blessing.[5]

William Knibb, Baptist missionary to Jamaica, who was one of the most passionate promoters in the West Indies of the idea of a missionary contribution from the West Indies to Africa, championed this new theological thinking regarding Africa on his visits to Britain, using the text of Psalm 68:31 as the basis of his exhortations. In the spring of 1833, when Knibb was despatched to London to explain the alleged involvement of Jamaican Baptists in the so-called Baptist War of Christmas 1831–1832, he boldly announced that the Baptist community in Jamaica were ready to undertake a bold missionary venture to Africa using African West Indians. He made this speech in a public address at St. Mary's Church in Islington, London, the month before the British Parliament passed the Slavery Abolition Act, which brought to an end slavery throughout the British Empire. In his speech, Knibb suggested that for this project to be achieved, even as a newly realized retributive act of British justice, the support of British Baptists would be needed. He further implied that they themselves might need some prodding to get on board. Basing his vision on Psalm 68:31, he appealed directly for British Baptist attention to be focused specifically on Africa. And, as if to address both those who were entirely sceptical of the idea and those who might need just a little extra prodding, he asserted that

> thither, we trust, shortly some of the most pious Christian converts will return with a full recompense for all the wrongs we

---

5. East, *West Africa*, 2.

have inflicted on that race, by proclaiming that freedom which Christ alone can bestow. Then shall Africa stretch out her hand and say, "While our enemies thought to do us evil, God meant it for good."[6]

When he spoke again in London the following year, Knibb returned to this subject more fully. Speaking on "the Spiritual Prospects of Africa," he again used as his text Psalm 68:31, to expound his views on the prospective opportunity, along the lines of the new thinking on Africa. Knibb linked the idea of the sufferings experienced by the enslaved Africans in the West Indies with their acceptance of the Christian gospel and the way in which that had prepared them to contribute in a particular way to the spiritual prospects of Africa. In his discourse, he argued that

> a race of Christians was rising up in the house of bondage, trained by God in the school of affliction, and on whom the sword of persecution has rested. They bore on their backs the marks of the Lord Jesus Christ, and thousands of them would bear those marks to the grave, and probably wear them in heaven. Trained in the school of adversity, they knew well the consolations which flow from the cross which Jesus bore. That Christianity which found them in sorrow, has now lifted them in the scale of society, and make them fit to return to their native country to preach salvation through the blood of the Son of God.[7]

Knibb's extensive discourse on this popular text was to form the basis of the rest of his mission in Jamaica until his death in 1845.

This kind of vigorous advocacy of the idea of a West Indian missionary project to Africa occurred not only in Jamaica but also in several other parts of the British West Indies – for example, St. Kitts, Antigua, Barbados, and Guyana – in the mid-nineteenth century.[8] As the new thinking developed, the campaign to recruit African West Indians for Christian missionary work

---

6. Knibb, "Sermon preached on behalf of the BMS," *The Pulpit* (Thursday, 27 June 1833), BMS Pamphlet Collection, BMS Archives.

7. Knibb, "Spiritual Prospects," BMS Collection, BMS Archives.

8. It should be noted that Africa was not the only place to which West Indian missionaries contemplated sending Creole West Indians. Missionaries working in Trinidad and Guyana in

in Africa was theologically justified on the basis of a new doctrine of providential design.⁹ This doctrine had its origins in the biblical story of Joseph in Egypt (Gen 37; 50:15–26). In another speech in London in 1842, Knibb alluded to this story while commenting on the Old Testament text "Ye thought evil against me, but God meant it unto good" (Gen 37; 50:15–26 KJV). In the biblical story, Joseph was sold by his brothers into slavery in Egypt, survived the ordeal in Egypt, and was, later, providentially used to redeem his brothers and their families. The link between the theological notion of providential design and the missionary vision for Africa was based on the view that, in the history of African slavery in the New World, the time had now come for Africa and African redemption through the efficacious agency of Christian mission. In the historical workings of God, "Ethiopia" (meaning Africa) was now "stretch[ing] out her hands unto God" (as a plea for redemption), and it was now time for responding and reaching out to Africa on behalf of God.

The Moravian Community in Jamaica

Although the campaign for the recruitment of West Indians for missionary work focused on Africa, in the Jamaican Moravian community, for example, there had always been missionary interest in other lands as well. The Moravians in Jamaica eventually sent missionaries to Central America to work among the native Indians, just like other Moravian missions among native North American Indians.¹⁰ Therefore, the way in which the call for participation in missionary work in Africa was promoted, heard, and responded to in the West Indies was important. From the slow beginnings of their missionary work on slave plantations in Jamaica in the mid-eighteenth century, the Moravians developed and practised their own notions of Christian missionary engagement in the communities they established in the western and central parishes of the island. Their involvement with African slaves in these communities produced a sensitivity towards African culture and religious manifestations that their strict beliefs disregarded as "superstition." As we have seen, the deployment of black Moravians from Jamaica to the Gold

---

the mid-nineteenth century also contemplated the possibility of training and sending Indo-West Indians to the Indian subcontinent.

9. Sindima, *Drums of Redemption*, and Killingray, "Black Atlantic Missionary Movement."
10. Westmeier, "Becoming All Things."

Coast of Africa presented many challenges that these missionary agents had to overcome. Although some failed, many succeeded in this missionary venture, despite the cross cultural difficulties.

Expressions of African religious culture – whether retained from the motherland or invented in Creole West Indian society – were part of plantation life in Jamaica. Beliefs in ancestral spirits, the healing and protection rituals of Mayal religion, and the malevolent judicial spirit possession of obeah were part of the Afro-West Indian world. These practices were often conducted in a clandestine manner at nightfall and sometimes formed part of an alternative justice system to that which existed in the formal state.[11] Therefore, when the invitation came for a mission to Africa, it is not surprising that Moravian mission leaders in Jamaica were keen to select those who did not subscribe to such beliefs and could be trusted to practice Christianity as they did, adhering to the ideals of European values, norms, and doctrines. These African West Indians, they thought, would be ideal agents to promote Christianity in Africa as a means of attacking and supplanting the roots of "African superstitions." They hoped that these missionary agents would lead the way in civilizing Africa and bring about real transformation, thus fulfilling the prophecy of Psalm 68:31.

Therefore, Jacob Zorn and others considered Psalm 68:31 a good, prophetic biblical text that signalled both the advent and fulfilment of this dream for Africa. Zorn was eager to make a case for the "strength and usefulness" of his Jamaican Negroes, even while he expressed some concerns about their engagement in Africa. In spite of his concerns, he was praised for his farsightedness in erecting a school in 1835 to train African West Indians for future missionary service in Africa.[12]

The extent to which Zorn's vision and concerns were demonstrated in the individuals he selected and sent to Africa might be debatable. But the vision of Africa to which he imagined that his Jamaican Moravians would make a distinctive contribution is clear. At the heart of that vision was the new thinking about Africa, embodied in the reimagined interpretive use of the biblical text about the outstretched arms of Ethiopia reaching out to God. For Zorn, this represented an open invitation and opportunity for Africans

---

11. Paton, *No Bond but the Law*, 13–19.
12. Buchner, *Moravians in Jamaica*, 136. Also cited in Antwi, "The African Factor," 6.

outside Africa to help fulfil the biblical prophecy of Psalm 68:31 and, on the eve of their departure from Jamaica to Africa, this was what Zorn impressed upon his recruits. No doubt his reimagined vision of Africa played a role in their motivation to go. However, in Africa they were surprised, disappointed, frustrated, and somewhat disoriented by the manner in which the project was administered by the Basel Missionary Society. As a result, some of them returned to Jamaica; but most remained in Africa and struggled on to ensure that the missionary project succeeded.

The Anglican Community

The Anglican Mission responded even more slowly than the Moravians to the "call" to Africa. As already pointed out, it was John McCammon Trew (1792–1869), the Irish CMS missionary to Jamaica and the Bahamas, who first proposed the idea of West Indian Anglican participation in Africa. Trew, who had a varied career in the West Indies from 1817 to 1861 – first as rector in the central parish of Manchester, then in the eastern parish of St. Thomas in the East – was recalled to London in 1834 to serve as secretary and principal agent for the Mico Educational Trust which had launched several educational projects throughout the West Indies. One of them was the Mico Educational Trust named after, and was the legacy of, Lady Jane Mico, widow of Sir Samuel Mico who died around 1666. By the 1830s, the Trust had accumulated sums of over £100,000. Given the British Parliament's focus at the time on improving the welfare of slaves and the poor, large sums were channelled towards the education of the negroes project in the British West Indies. Thomas Fowell Buxton, a great-grandson of Charles Buxton, was involved with the companies of the Mico families, and he steered the Trust towards setting up elementary schools throughout the British West Indies and teachers' training colleges in Jamaica and Antigua. The schools were later handed over to various religious societies, but Mico College in Kingston remained the responsibility of the Mico Trustees in London.[13]

In 1838, when full emancipation took place in the British West Indies, Trew was in London, serving as secretary of Thomas Fowell Buxton's organization, the Africa Colonisation Society (ACS). It was the ACS that organized

---

13. Wesley, "Rise of Negro Education," 68–82.

the failed Niger Mission of 1841, a project in which Trew had been heavily involved. As Secretary to the ACS, he was fully acquainted with the vision and strategy that surrounded the conception, deployment, and collapse of the Niger Mission. And when that Mission failed, attention was then turned to the possibility of employing Africans on the Continent and in the West Indies to help achieve the elusive goal of planting Christianity in sub-Saharan Africa.

Given his background and missionary experience in the West Indies, Trew seized upon the opportunity to put into operation his dream of the full involvement of the West Indian church in the enterprise in Africa. He became increasingly impatient when such involvement was not forthcoming from the Anglican dioceses throughout the West Indies. In 1844, Trew was appointed Archdeacon of the Bahamas by Aubrey George Spencer, the second bishop of Jamaica. During his term as Archdeacon (1844–1857), Trew made sure to enlist at least one Bahamian, Samuel Higgs, for the Pongas Mission to Western Africa, which was launched from Barbados in 1855. In all Trew's varied career posts associated with the West Indies what stood out was his concern to see the transformational and redemptive benefits of missionary work in Africa, just as he had witnessed in Jamaica and throughout the West Indies.[14]

Of course, while Trew was agitating for Anglican West Indian participation in missionary work in Africa, the Jamaican Baptists were already at work in the Cameroon and the Moravians, recruited by the Basel Mission, were setting up their mission on the Gold Coast. As the last of the West Indian mission initiatives in the mid-nineteenth century, the Anglican Church eventually took on board the Africa cause and mounted its own mission to the Rio Pongas as its contribution to the missionary enterprise in Africa.

Reshaping Africa in European Imagination

By the mid-nineteenth century, coincidental with the new-found need to recast the image of Africa and the Africans in the European mind, events in Africa and in Europe were at work influencing and shaping these new understandings and perceptions. As public response to the publicity surrounding David Livingstone's arrival in Southern Africa in 1841 developed, his activities began to spotlight Africa in public imagination. In 1857, the

---

14. Hughes, "Impact on Jamaica," 22.

publication of Livingstone's *Missionary Travels and Researches in South Africa* dealt with matters that had intrigued Europeans for a long time and helped to dispel the notion that "dark Africa" was the source of the slave trade.[15] Public discussions about the morality of the slave trade and the continued existence of slavery despite the 1807 Act of Abolition of the slave trade ultimately impacted and influenced a shift in public attitude towards African slavery.

In Britain, many were now beginning to feel that it was time to focus on solving the problem of Africa in Africa by specific actions to remedy the bleeding of Africa. After nearly two centuries of the brutal transatlantic African slave trade and the backlash it produced in the rise of the transatlantic anti-slavery movement, public attention in Britain by the 1830s was now also shifting towards the moral and humanitarian outcry concerning the institution of British slavery in the colonies. Inevitably, attention was drawn to the continent of Africa itself as the ostensible source of a nefarious industry of slave trading on which British and European metropolitan societies depended and were the primary beneficiaries.[16]

Mobilizing for Missionary Participation

When making a the case for West Indian participation in the missionary enterprise in Africa, not only had African West Indians to be persuaded, they also had to be recruited for this mission. This posed a challenge of a different sort. Despite the extravagant claims by some European missionaries in the West Indies – such as the Baptist leaders William Knibb and John Clarke – that thousands of Christianized Africans in the West Indies were ready for this missionary call to Africa, the reality was that these Christianized Africans were preoccupied with other pressing issues closer to home, which demanded their energy and attention.[17] In the transitional state of the immediate post-emancipation West Indian society, what was naturally uppermost in their minds were critical issues of personal security, economic survival, orientation to a new social order and to the new social status of post-slavery freedom.

---

15. Livingstone, *Missionary Travels*, preface and chapters 6-8.

16. Deveneaux, "Public Opinion and Colonial Policy," 45–6.

17. Knibb and Clarke spoke repeatedly of thousands of Africans in the West Indies who had been converted to Christianity and who were ready for this missionary call to Africa.

Chapter 2 cited an ex-slave's speech on the occasion of the commemoration of the fourth anniversary of emancipation in Jamaica. This former slave's words indicate that these critical issues included the practical matters of land access, wage labour, adequate housing, food security, and the real prospect of enjoying the hard-won freedom from bonded slavery. The pursuit of "lived freedom," as Sheller calls it, was their chief concern and priority.[18] The prospect of settling into a new post-slave society and pursuing personal welfare involved critical life-choices, and this was a key reason why the recruitment campaign for Africa by the Baptists, Moravians, and Anglicans proved a difficult exercise. Additionally, the less-than-attractive contractual terms of the recruitment campaign were also problematic. The European mission leaders in the West Indies promoted the idea of mission to Africa as a "back to Africa" opportunity for would-be settlers and colonists. Those who accepted the opportunity would do so understanding that they were serving a European project. The West Indians, as emigrants, were expected to serve the white missionaries and model black Christian presence in Africa as exhibits of the success of Christian missionary endeavours. How would this have benefitted them? What was in it for them?

In this environment, the term "missionary" was almost always reserved for the white European who was licensed to preach, teach, and conduct the primary missionary tasks of education, Bible translation, and church planting. That is why the West Indians, when deployed in Africa, instinctively reacted and resisted the circumscribed interpretation of their role and sought freedom to engage in all aspects of the missionary enterprise. Such acts of resistance frequently resulted in their being regarded as troublemakers, who were ungrateful, merely trying to imitate white Europeans, and obstacles to the real progress of the missionary project in Africa. Their persistent agitation, however, not only expanded the capacity of the white European leaders in the mission field, it also opened and broadened the space for the West Indians to make their own distinctive contribution to the enterprise.

The composition of the three West Indian missionary expeditions to Western Africa in the mid nineteenth-century, examined in this study, had among them those who were recruited on the basis of this mixed agenda of settlers, colonists, and missionaries. In their deployment, one of the problems

---

18. Sheller, *Democracy after Slavery*, 65–68.

of understanding and interpreting their encounters with Africa was interpreting the conflicts that arose from the management of this combination of roles and mixed agendas. While other factors also affected their performance and full participation in the project, the common factor across these three West Indian missions in Africa in the nineteenth century was the similarity of the basis on which those who went as agents of Christian mission were recruited and deployed.

Another difficulty in the ambitious and problematic proposal of mounting and sustaining the missionary enterprises from the West Indies to Western Africa was that those who were recruited had to be transported across the Atlantic and then deployed, maintained, and supervised in Africa. This was a management issue. Despite the optimism and enthusiasm for the prospects of West Indian participation in Africa, what was the real probability of making the vision of black Christianized West Indians doing Christian missionary work in Africa happen? In addition to working out the modalities of logistics, the Africa mission proposers also faced the challenge of ensuring a selection of individuals and families who were most likely to make a useful contribution to the project. Although their ethnic origins and ancestry may have been derived from Africa, it may have been questionable the extent to which these African West Indians could realistically be expected to function as "native agents" in Africa. And yet, as we have seen, this was the primary assumption on which the project was proposed, recruitment made, and West Indians deployed in Africa. It was assumed that, as New World Africans, they would have the necessary immunity to withstand and overcome the climate and conditions in Africa, especially in the area of health. As it turned out, the West Indians' immediate vulnerability to the torrid equatorial conditions in Africa and the early deaths of some soon disabused mission leaders of this notion.

The European-sponsored recruitment of West Indians for Mission in Africa also presumed that the West Indians possessed the capacity to survive and work cheerfully as "native agents" alongside Europeans in an auxiliary capacity. In reality, the West Indians were neither authentically "native agents" – able to fully understand and function in the African context as though they were truly native to Africa – nor Europeans in ancestry, social background, knowledge, attitude, and training. They were Creole West Indians and could only act authentically on the basis of who and what they were in their New World formation. The evidence considered in this study suggests that, despite these challenges, their participation, perseverance, and contribution in Africa were important to the success of the overall missionary goal of establishing Christianity in sub-Saharan Africa. In Western Africa, the West Indian agents not only exerted themselves on behalf of the Western missionary enterprise in every aspect of the enterprise, but some – like the Baptists Merrick and Fuller, the Moravians Mulgrave and Hall, and the Anglicans Duport and Doughlin – had long careers in Africa missions, made invaluable groundwork contributions that laid a solid foundation for the planting and transmission of Christianity in the parts of Western Africa in which they laboured. Without their contribution, Christianity might not have gained the foothold it achieved nor survived in parts of Southern Nigeria, Ghana, the Cameroon, and, what is today The Gambia.

Fulfilment of the Emancipation Dream

After the collapse of the Niger Expedition of 1841, the frank confession of a member of the Buxton family summed up the European feeling towards Africa. In confessing, "I do not see what are we to do next for Africa. I hope in due time the right way may open,"[19] this Buxton family member spoke right to the heart of European despair and questions about the prospects for Africa in the mid-nineteenth century. The Buxton family had invested so much in British philanthropic concern for Africa and generated so much public expectation. What were they to do in response to the perceived problem that Africa represented to the world? The answer came in the realization that Europeans were limited in what they could do to transform Africa. Salvation for Africa lay in the hands of Africans. In this new realization, it was acknowledged, perhaps for the first time, that there was a role in the Christian missionary enterprise in Africa for native agents in Africa and others in the African diaspora. This realization began to shape the geopolitical thinking of the Western missionary establishment and coincided with the missionary vision of the European missionaries then working in the West Indies. The

---

19. This remark was made by Edward North Buxton (1812–1858), a younger brother of Thomas Fowell Buxton (1786–1845). Edward North Buxton to Priscilla Johnston, Buxton Papers, Reel #9, February 8, 1842. USPG Archives.

coincidence of these mutual interests gave rise to the expeditions to Africa from the West Indies in the mid-nineteenth century.

Did the West Indian expeditions help to fulfill the trans-Atlantic dream of rescuing "dark Africa"? There are several ways in which the widespread engagement and contribution of the West Indian agents to the planting and sustainable rise of Christianity in Western Africa contributed to bridging and highlighting the Euro-American and native African presence in the enterprise in sub-Saharan Africa in the nineteenth century. As we have seen, they helped the project to succeed along the lines of its desired goal of producing an indigenous native African church. The role of the Jamaican Baptists among the Dualas in the Cameroon, the Jamaican Moravians among the Akans in the Basel Mission in Akropong, and the Barbadian Anglicans among the Susus in the Rio Pongas region (now The Gambia) deserve better consideration and recognition in the history of West African Christianity.

In the end, what most significantly impacted the West Indian agents in Africa was the challenge of mobilizing resources to maintain these ambitious missionary projects. The inability to do so was one of the primary reasons for the failure to achieve far more and to prevent the collapse of their mission initiatives in Africa. Support was simply not available or forthcoming from an increasingly impoverished and economically declining West Indian society in the late nineteenth century. Each of the missions struggled with this issue, and none succeeded in responding adequately to it. In addition, leadership, supervision, and management issues on the field tended to restrain positive and enthusiastic engagement in the project on the part of the West Indian agents. As they struggled with welfare needs and management issues on the field in Africa, the call to engage in missions in Africa seemed to have required unusual levels of commitment in order to stay the course and to confront and overcome the obstacles and challenges encountered in the pursuit of bringing the light of Christian civilization to Africa. From what we have seen, a number of West Indian agents rose to the challenge and demonstrated the level of determination and commitment required. Given better support and more favourable conditions, perhaps a lot more might have been achieved and West Indian participation and contribution much more substantially demonstrated.

Conceptions of Christian Mission

One of the questions investigated in this study was the possibility of determining the conceptions of Christian mission evidenced by the West Indians in their participation in the enterprise in Africa. This study argues that in order to answer that question – as well as the important questions of motives, meaning, and contribution to Africa – the careers of those who achieved some longevity in the Africa missions should be examined. That is why this study has highlighted the careers of John and Mary Hall, Alexander Worthy Clerk, and Catherine Mulgrave-Zimmermann in the Basel Mission in Akropong, and Joseph Merrick and Joseph Jackson Fuller in the Cameroon Mission and John Duport and Phillip Doughlin in the Rio Pongas Mission. It is from those who achieved long careers in Africa that it may be possible to discern and understand why and how they, and other West Indians who laboured alongside them, conceived of, understood, and pursued the enterprise of Christian mission in which they so assiduously engaged in Africa.

In examining further some internal and external factors that could have influenced how the West Indian agents understood Christian mission in Africa, two things stood out. One was the sociopolitical context and environment in which their formation occurred. This was a context dominated by the grand narratives of slavery and emancipation, in which the persona and self-identity of the African in the West Indies had to undergo forms of radical social transformation in order to enable authentic public self-identity and social validation to occur. This was the milieu in which the West Indian church had its origins and which, in turn, nurtured the construction of a black Christianized Creole West Indian persona and identity. If slavery in the British West Indies was in fact "social death," as Patterson deemed it, and the manifestation of this was in forms of "natal self-alienation,"[20] then emancipation not only required the resurrection, restoration, and reassertion of the conscious self, it also required psychosocial space for this new self to be actualized. Despite the lack of state provisions for the emancipated African population in the West Indies to establish themselves after the abolition of slavery, and despite the problems of adjustments and disappointment in expectations of the new social status of emancipation, the psychosocial

---

20. Patterson, *Slavery and Social Death*, 7–8.

space that the newly formed West Indian churches afforded provided the existential freedom needed as an important dimension of post-emancipation British West Indian society. This was highlighted in the ex-slave's speech at the fourth anniversary celebration of emancipation (as noted in chapter 2).

The second thing that stood out was the way and degree to which mission Christianity was appropriated by the African slaves on the plantations in the British West Indies. This was a remarkable feature of the growth and spread of mission Christianity in the West Indies in the first three decades of the nineteenth century. Viewing the formation of mission communities in this context, the message of salvation proclaimed by the missionaries in the West Indies provided the slaves with the opportunity for an empathetic ontological explanation for their suffering and bondage, as well as an existential experience of liberation in the midst of their suffering and bondage. Slave conversion through the message brought by the missionaries in the British West Indies did not supplant or replace their desire for freedom. Rather, it enhanced it, as the radical insurrectionist leadership of Samuel Sharpe, the Jamaican Baptist slave-deacon, demonstrated. For Sam Sharpe, the words of the biblical text "no man can serve two masters" (Matt 6:24 KJV), received in slavery, justified his involvement in the mission church and leadership of the pivotal slave protest and revolt in Jamaica in 1831, known as "the Sam Sharpe Rebellion" or "the Baptist War."

The appropriation of Christianity by the enslaved Africans in the West Indies, even as it was perceived as the religion of the masters, was used in the construction of a Creole West Indian Christian identity. This identity included a persona that was conditioned, at best, to resist – passively or actively – and, at worst, when pushed, to revolt against forms of oppression in the pursuit of freedom. This was part of what Beckles called the "self-liberating ethos" of the slaves.[21] Perhaps on account of the fact that mission Christianity was mediated through the evangelical missions in the environment of plantation slave societies, it was communicated and received as a religion that championed social justice. Since freedom as "lived freedom" was a negotiated existence in which basic rights and freedoms had to be vigilantly pursued, secured, and safeguarded, sensitivity towards injustice in any form was always at the forefront of the consciousness of the West Indian slave population. Any

---

21. Beckles, "Caribbean Anti-Slavery," 869 – 878.

perceived denial of basic rights and freedoms, or any attempt at exploiting or manipulating such freedoms, was to be resisted and fought against. In its social role, religion was important to life and freedom, and could not to be separated from it. As religion played a part in the recovery and shaping of identity for African slaves in the New World environment, it was therefore natural to imagine a role for it in the vision of creating a new African persona and a new African society in Africa.

In responding to the public need and outcry for the creation of a new social order in the aftermath of the collapse of British West Indian slave society, the part played by the mission churches provided the much-needed space for nurturing this identity. Their role in helping the ex-slaves to transition from a slave-based society into a free and more open society – with all the economic, social, and political implications and opportunities involved in adjusting to a new status of social freedom – was not only an instructive episode in missionary work but also appeared to have shaped and underscored a conception of Christian mission as an agency of liberation and justice.

It is highly probable, therefore, that this pursuit of the emancipation dream – including the restoration of self-dignity, self-esteem, and self-affirmation of the African in the modern world – could help explain the motivation and conduct of the West Indian agents in Africa in the nineteenth century. As we have seen, the European missionaries serving alongside them consistently failed to grasp this reality, despite the fact that they themselves were pursuing a similar dream. Nevertheless, this dimension of their formation is not the sole explanation for their missionary conduct in Africa. Their encounters in Africa – which we have already examined – must also be considered since these encounters had a significant impact on their perception and conception of the enterprise in which they were engaged.

For example, one feature common to all three West Indian missions was the fact that, as black agents from the African diaspora, they were in the main treated as no more than subalterns in a European project. Even in the Pongas Mission, where they were the primary agents on the field, there was reluctance on the part of their European sponsors to recognize and appoint a black missionary as superintendent. As Vassady and Wariboko have shown, pay scales were differentiated according to type of work and whether one was married of not but also according to colour as well.[22] The West Indians' reactions to these matters of personal well-being and to the management styles of the mission leaders created internal conflicts that gave rise to considerations of repatriation on their part. As Christianized West Indians – and therefore "civilized subjects" of the Empire – they were expected to be eager to carry out the work of the civilizing missions as an act of gratitude and, thereby, contribute to fulfilling the mission goals.[23] When they failed to live up to these expectations, demanded amelioration of their conditions, or asked that they be repatriated to the West Indies, they were considered to have failed in the project.

Mission as Justice and Freedom

Based upon a comparative analysis of the three missionary projects from the West Indies to Western Africa in the mid-nineteenth century that were examined in this study, the African West Indians seemed to have approached the task of actively engaging in Christian mission as if it were an agency for divine justice and freedom. In all three missions, if there was any discernible conception of Christian mission throughout their engagement in Africa, it was in this relationship between an evangelizing mission and justice and freedom. For the West Indians, it was evident that justice and freedom were integrally related to the gospel message and was good news – both in its existential and its ontological sense – to those in the margins of the British Empire. It may also be possible to infer, from the circumstances of their formation in the West Indies, that they may have derived that understanding of justice and freedom from the Hebraic principle proclaimed in the Old Testament Scriptures – for example, where the Psalmist pleads for the endowment of Israel's ruler with the twin virtues of justice and righteousness that he may "deliver the needy when he crieth; the poor also, and him that hath no helper . . . and shall save the souls of the needy . . . redeem their soul from deceit and violence and precious shall their blood be in his sight."[24] For the enslaved and oppressed ancient Hebrew people, understanding this relationship between freedom

---

22. Vassady, "Role of the Black West Indian Missionary," and Wariboko, *Ruined by "Race."*
23. Hall, *Civilising Subjects*, 380–406.
24. Psalm 72:12–14 KJV.

and justice was crucial to their self-understanding and sense of mission in the world. Oppressed peoples know, through hard existential experience, that where there is no justice there is no freedom.

This understanding of the integral link between justice and freedom has been a part of a biblical understanding of the redemptive potential of human society as the Exodus narratives of the Old Testament indicate.[25] It is instructive that in the case of both the ancient Hebrews' enslavement in Egypt and the African enslavement in the West Indies, the understanding of this notion of the integral link between justice and freedom was mediated through the prism of a slave culture in which human injustice, violent resistance, and the persistent struggle for liberation were salient features. Likewise, the message of divine intervention and ultimate redemption that emerged from these two cases of ancient and modern slavery pointed to an outcome that resulted in missiological engagement by those who had been redeemed from bondage by justice that is received as divine.

Christian Mission as *Missio Dei*

If the conception of Christian mission as an agency of divine justice and freedom was in fact the way in which the West Indian missionaries perceived and understood their engagement in Africa in the nineteenth century, it would seem to be an important missiological understanding that emerged and flourished among subject peoples in the margins of an a global empire based on an oppressive slavery-based economic system in the nineteenth century. Its importance and significance lay in the fact that not only was it reflective of a Hebraic conception of mission as *missio Dei*,[26] it was also reflective of St. Paul's insights into the nature of freedom, which he demonstrated in a passionate fight and advocacy for the justice and legitimacy of gentile Christian identity in the Graeco-Roman Empire in the 1st century AD.

In his apostolic missions to the nascent gentile communities scattered and persecuted throughout the Roman Empire, St. Paul made an integral

---

25. See Exodus 3:7; 15:1–18.

26. In the Jewish understanding of mission as *missio Dei*, Yahweh's mission was understood as a mission in which there was an integral link between righteousness and justice, on the one hand, and justice and freedom on the other (Ps 103:6–8; Isa 56:1–2).

link between justice and freedom, and between justice and righteousness. He articulated and championed this principle in his letters, discourses and apologia for gentile Christian identity in the early church of the first century AD. For example, in his letter to the church in Galatia, he used his astute Hebraic understanding of freedom to argue for gentile freedom in a remarkable and revolutionary way. As a Jewish scholar, he argued that in the Jewish Christ "there is neither Jew nor Gentile, neither slave nor free, nor is there male and female, for you are all one in Christ Jesus. If you belong to Christ, then you are Abraham's seed, and heirs according to the promise."[27] In other words, in Yahweh's divine justice in the historic phenomenon of the incarnate person and earthly mission of his Son, Jesus Christ, both ontological and existential freedom from all social barriers of race, religion, social status, and gender exist. Therefore, gentile Christian identity is a legitimate claim and was achieved in the judicial mission of Jesus the Christ. His act of executing divine justice and atonement for a transgressive humanity is a bridge to reconciliation and freedom, first with Yahweh and then with fellow humans, across all social barriers. Freedom, in turn, is guaranteed by seal and is determined by righteousness – or right relationships and conduct – that was the supreme characteristic of Jesus as Messiah.

The parallel between St. Paul's missiological experience in establishing Christian communities in the Roman Empire outside of Palestine in the first century AD and the European missionary experience of establishing Christian communities in the British West Indies in the Age of Empire and Slavery in the 19th Century provides two contextual frameworks within which this understanding of the link between righteousness and justice and the justice-freedom link finds historical grounding. This concept also appears as an essential component of the message of redemption in Judeo-Christian theology. As a logical consequence, the link is not only further established between that message of divine redemption and its missiological outworking, it is also explicitly cited by St. Paul as a divine obligation on the part the redeemed and liberated. For example, in his second letter to the church at Corinth, in validating and legitimizing gentile Christian identity, Paul passionately pleads for justice for gentile Christians and, in turn, lays a missiological obligation on the gentile church:

---

27. See Galatians 3:28–29 (NIV).

> Since, then, we know what it is to fear the Lord, we try to persuade others. What we are is plain to God, and I hope it is also plain to your conscience. We are not trying to commend ourselves to you again, but are giving you an opportunity to take pride in us, so that you can answer those who take pride in what is seen rather than in what is in the heart. If we are "out of our mind," as some say, it is for God; if we are in our right mind, it is for you. For Christ's love compels us, because we are convinced that one died for all, and therefore all died. And he died for all, that those who live should no longer live for themselves but for him who died for them and was raised again. So from now on we regard no one from a worldly point of view. Though we once regarded Christ in this way, we do so no longer. Therefore, if anyone is in Christ, the new creation has come: The old has gone, the new is here! All this is from God, who reconciled us to himself through Christ and gave us the ministry of reconciliation: that God was reconciling the world to himself in Christ, not counting people's sins against them. And he has committed to us the message of reconciliation. We are therefore Christ's ambassadors, as though God were making his appeal through us. We implore you on Christ's behalf: Be reconciled to God. God made him who had no sin to be sin for us, so that in him we might become the righteousness of God.[28]

The West Indian missionaries in Africa in the nineteenth century were placed in a missiological dynamic and understood the missiological obligation that was communicated to them by the European missionaries in the West Indies. The redemptive love of Jesus the redeeming messiah "compels us" to be ambassadors for Christ. The records of the West Indians eager desire for engagement in the Africa missions suggest that they had understood and grasped this implication of their missionary obligation. This included the understanding that the missionary goal of conversion and salvation could not be fully understood, pursued, and realized outside of a commitment to the socio-religious value of the justice-freedom, freedom-righteousness

---

28. 2 Corinthians 5:11–21 NIV.

message that lay at the heart of Judeo-Christian teaching. At the core of this teaching was the affirmation of the inherent dignity of the human being as a reflection of the image and likeness of God, which creation narratives affirm.[29]

Implications

What then are possible implications arising from this study? The primary objective of this study was a critical analysis of the participation of West Indians as agents of Christian mission in the Western missionary enterprise in Africa in the mid-nineteenth century. In the pursuit of this objective, several factors emerged. First, there was a clear indication that, despite the enthusiasm and desire on the part of European mission leaders in the West Indies to showcase their mission success, the recruitment of African West Indians for the missionary project in Africa was difficult and proved to be less than what was hoped for. The three missionary expeditions examined in this study experienced similar problems of recruitment, management, and capacity to sustain the ventures in Africa. The West Indians who were successful in being recruited to go to Africa, were deployed amid perceptions of Africa and suffered adverse treatment as marginal groups of people from the margins of the Empire, who were endeavouring to be involved in a project larger than their horizons. The fact that they struggled for acceptance and recognition of their value and contribution to the enterprise has led to the charge of their presence in Africa as "misguided exiles" in a mythic quest for an imagined homeland. Their struggles on the field must be taken into account for the way they affected their participation and gave rise to negative assessments of their role and contribution.

A second factor observed in this study was that in the historiography of West African Christianity, the role and contributions of the West Indian agents in the planting and rise of Christianity in Western Africa have received relatively scant attention and, even where mentioned, have not been given the treatment they merit. If mentioned at all, the West Indian agents have been portrayed as having had no real voice, no face, no zeal, and as being marginal to the project. Research into what they represented and their role in Africa has been neglected not only in West African Christian history but

---

29. Genesis 1:26–27 NIV.

also in post-emancipation studies in the West Indies. One reason for this has been the difficulties of access to research material on the subject. This phenomenom in post-emancipation West Indian history has also been affected by the predilections of post-colonial African and West Indian historians, and a lack of intellectual tools of historical analyses of Church History and its modern offshoot, Mission History.

A third factor that emerged was the possibility of discerning and attributing meaning to the historical phenomenon being examined. In examining in closer detail, this particular case of the unique and unusual participation of ex-slaves from the other side of the Atlantic in the Western missionary enterprise in Africa in the nineteenth century, a number of issues emerged that suggested possibilities in discerning some significance and attributing some meaning to their engagement and encounters in Africa, especially in light of the lengthy careers and perseverance of some in the enterprise in all three cases examined. As already indicated, by evaluating the careers of those who achieved some longevity in Africa – such as Richard Merrick and Joseph Jackson Fuller in the Cameroon Mission, Catherine Mulgrave and Peter Hall in the Basel Mission, John Duport and Phillip Doughlin in the Pongas Mission– not only can a better understanding of their contribution be achieved but the significance of their participation can be better understood. That significance seems to be in understanding the pursuit and enlargement of the emancipation dream derived from their experience of slavery and emancipation in the West Indies. In the mission field, that dream was translated into a valiant fight for African freedom and African development. Without grasping this significance and meaning of the phenomenon of their participation in the missionary ventures in Africa, the record and legacy of their involvement cannot be logically and meaningfully understood and will, perhaps, be forever lost to the history of both Western Africa and the West Indies.

There are further implications arising from these three factors. One of these implications relates to the possibility of a historiography of mission Christianity that, as Lamin Sanneh points out, transcends the old imperialist-nationalist historiography.[30] He, and John Peel, among others, suggest other ways other ways in which this kind of historical phenomenon can be read

---

30. Sanneh, "Horizontal and the Vertical."

and understood. This, however, will only emerge when marginal groups like the West Indian missionaries in Western Africa in the nineteenth century are recognized and their role and contribution properly researched and taken into account. As John Peel has emphatically shown, it is possible to employ a different kind of research and analysis to help understand the role and contribution of marginal groups of people to engaged in the mega project of Christian transmission in sub-Saharan Africa.[31] His research effectively demonstrates the impact of the dynamic and interactive roles of native and non-native agents of mission Christianity upon local Yoruba culture in the nineteenth century. This kind of research and analysis seeks proper and deeper understanding of the self-perception, motivation, and engagement on the part of the enterprisers in Christian mission, especially those who engage from the margins of social and political power dynamics. The availability and utilization of this kind of research methodology has the potential to uncover new sources and new understandings about the making of Christianity as a global religion.

The methodology used by John Peel could lead to very fruitful results and move Mission Studies in new directions. Among African historians, the works of Kalu, Sanneh, Bediako, Antwi, and others point in this direction. They recognize and highlight not only the role of native agents in the planting of Christianity in Africa but also the possibility for a leveraging role of a third culture such as the West Indian agents represented. It was this possibility that the Western missionary establishment – represented by such influential organizations as the Basel Evangelical Missionary Society, the British Baptist Missionary Society, the Church Missionary Society, and the United Society for the Propagation of the Gospel – perceived after the trial and failure of their own efforts in Western Africa. Their failure made them face up to the realization that African agents were capable of delivering the goals of the project if properly engaged and enabled to do so. It led them to accede to petitions for their sponsorship support.

A further implication of this study concerns approaches to conceptual understandings of Christian mission. One of the findings of this study is the way in which the European missionaries in the West Indies in the nineteenth century were forced to adjust their understandings and strategy of mission

---

31. Peel, *Religious Encounter*, 1–26.

engagement in the strongly controlled and contested context of the slave societies of the nineteenth-century West Indian society. As we have seen, the conceptions and understandings of mission that they brought with them to the West Indies were reshaped by the realities of the socio-political situation in the local context in which strong cross-currents of social and political debate were inescapable. Similarly, conceptions of Christian mission that the West Indians might have taken with them in the reverse transatlantic journey to Africa had to be readjusted and realigned when confronted with the inescapable realties of the issues involved in mission engagement and encounters in Africa in the nineteenth century. On the basis of these findings, it may be possible to infer that conceptions of mission can be derived not merely from officialdom but also from mission praxis in the field of engagement. Grasping such understanding can be of value and importance in realizing how conceptions and approaches to Christian mission are formed and shaped. Certainly, what appears to be an understanding of Christian mission as a mission of justice and freedom has important meanings and implications that need to be pursued. This is what the West Indian agents appeared to have demonstrated by their vigorous engagement in the mission enterprise in Western Africa.

West Indian Missionaries and The Modern Global Missionary Movement

The modern western missionary enterprise itself – which had its genesis in the late eighteenth century, in what was called the Great Religious Awakening, and which gave rise to new churches in the Far East and the Global South[32] – had to undergo its own adjustments and metamorphosis in conceptualizations of mission throughout the nineteenth century. As a transatlantic religious revival, the Great Awakening spurred great Christian missionary activities aimed particularly at the urban poor on both sides of the Atlantic. It led to the formation of a large number of parachurch mission societies in Europe and the United States of America. Those mission societies flourished in the nineteenth century and, with their advent, a new missiological dimension was added to the life of the Western church. This expansion in modern Christian missionary endeavours took place at the same time as the expansion

---

32. Buhlmann, *Coming of the Third Church*.

of European and American geopolitical and commercial interests were occurring. All this at a time when anti-imperial revolutions and revolutionary sentiments were widespread in what is called an Age of Revolution.[33]

As a consequence of Christian missionary expansion in an Age of Empire and amid anti-imperial revolutions, it was inevitable that questions arose about the relationship between colonial empires and Christian mission, and the nature of Christian missionary engagement under conditions of colonialism and Empire-building. Even as David Livingstone was highlighting and championing the missionary task in Africa in the mid-nineteenth century, as bearers of "Christianity, Commerce, and Civilization," mission theorists such as Henry Venn (1841–1873) of the Church Missionary Society and Rufus Anderson (1832–1880) of the American Board of Foreign Missions were proposing the concept of the "euthanasia of mission." Their theoretical construct of the "three-self" model of missions – that is, that a church, once planted, should grow towards becoming self-governing, self-supporting, and self-propagating – focused less on the long-term agency of the missionary and more on the development of an indigenous native church. Throughout this study, it was evident that the West Indian agents in Africa understood and accepted the Venn-Anderson conception of the enterprise. Nevertheless, in their field encounters in Africa, they demonstrated their own unique conception of the enterprise in terms of mission as an agency of justice and freedom in which the goal of building a native church was an integral part of their strategy. That strategy involved the employment of every facet of the missionary apparatus. Contributions from the margins should not, therefore, be treated as insignificant for they may offer insights not only into the complexities of cross-cultural and transnational transmission of Christianity but also into the nature and translatability of the Christian message itself.

While these implications relate to the emerging discipline of Mission Studies, there are also implications for the field of Emancipation Studies. The case of these marginal groups of newly emancipated West Indians pursuing the struggle to realize the full potential of human freedom may, as Orlando Patterson has argued, illustrate further the dialectical contribution

---

33. Heimert, *Religion and the American Mind*; Vidler, *Church in an Age of Revolution*; and Hobsbawm, *Age of Extremes*.

by formerly oppressed peoples to the enlargement of freedom.[34] In the three missions examined, the West Indians pushed the boundaries of the enterprise by insisting on their ability and capacity to engage in every aspect of the project. They refused to submit to the marginal or subaltern role in which they were placed. They resisted imposed interpretations of their status and capabilities based on race, gender, or powerlessness. In seeking to enlarge freedom for themselves and for their fellow Africans, they pursued freedom as the foundation for personal and communal development. They engaged in the enterprise on behalf of the Western missionary establishment as non-state actors seeking to open up opportunities for Africa's development of its human, moral, and spiritual capital. This was part of the remedy sought for Africa for the misery that resulted from its exploitation by European imperial powers.

The pursuit of the emancipation dream in Africa by the West Indian agents of Christian mission was very much in keeping with the kind of discovery and discourse of some development economists in recent times. While the social virtue of freedom is highly valued by marginal groups – such as the West Indians in the Africa missions in the mid-nineteenth century – the economic value of freedom is underscored by development economists like Nobel Laureate Amartya Sen. In his highly respected work, Sen argues that "development consists of the removal of various types of unfreedom that leave people with little choice and little opportunity of exercising their reasoned agency."[35] As an economist, his conclusion that "the expansion of freedom is the primary end and the primary means of development" is well worth noting. On this basis, the type of engagement that the West Indian agents pursued in Africa, as described in this study, should be seen in this light as an opportunity for pursuing the expansion of existential as well as ontological freedom.

The West Indian missions to Western Africa in the nineteenth century might have emerged from the margin of the Empire; as such, these endeavours, though ambitious, were small projects in relation to other missionary endeavours in Africa in the nineteenth century. But – like the visionary pioneers of African Methodism,[36] the CMS agents among the Yorubas,[37] and

---

34. Patterson, "Slavery: The Underside of Freedom" and *Freedom in the Making*.
35. Sen, *Freedom as Development*, xii.
36. J. Campbell, *Songs of Zion*.
37. Peel, *Religious Encounter*.

the Universities' Mission to Central Africa (UMCA)[38] in the mid-nineteenth century – their legacy in Africa recalls the wisdom of the rhetorical biblical question, "Who dares despise the day of small things?" (Zech 4:10 NIV).

---

38. Anderson-Morshead, *History of the Universities' Mission.*

APPENDIX I

From the Archives of the Basel Evangelical Missionary Society, Basel, Switzerland

Photo of Catherine Mulgrave, Johannes Zimmermann, and family. (Pictured from left is an unidentified person, Johannes, Catherine, Gottfried, Johannes, Johanna, Rosine, Gottleib Christophe). ca 1872.

Basel Missionary Archives, QS-30.002.0237.02, "The Zimmermann-Mulgrave Family", 01.01.1872-31.12.1873. https://www.bmarchives.org/items/show/100208370.

APPENDIX II

From the Archives of the Baptist Missionary Society, Regents Park College, Oxford

Photo of Joseph Jackson Fuller, Baptist Missionary to the Cameroon (1845-1888)

Used by kind permission of BMS World Mission Angus Library and Archive, Regent's Park College, Oxford

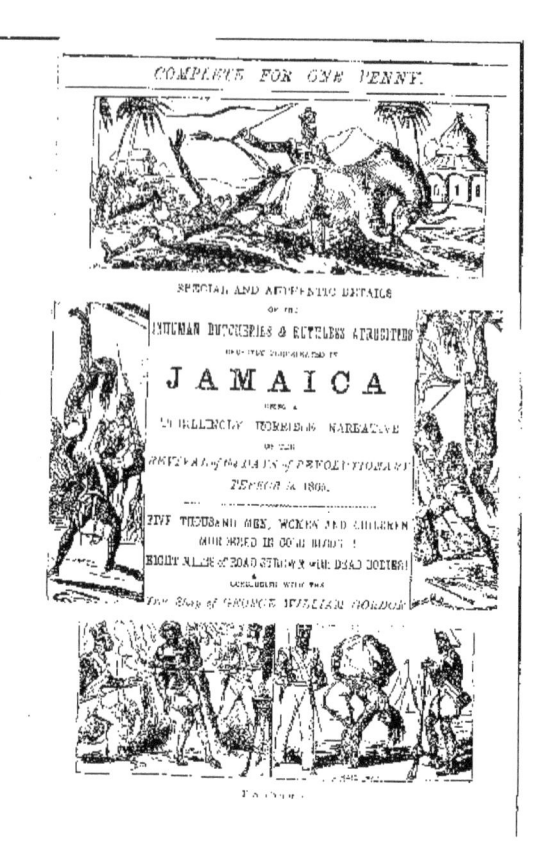

Illustrated Story of the Morant Bay uprising in Jamaica 1865 in The Times of London

Hamble James Leacock
Pioneer Missionary from Barbados to the Rio Pongas
Died in Sierra Leone, 1856
(Source: Henry Caswall. 1857. The Martyr of The Pongas)

APPENDIX III
From the USPG Archives, Rhodes House, Oxford

THE LORD'S PRAYER IN SOOSOO, TRANSLATED BY
MR. DUPORT.

A = AH.

Woung   Fáfa,   Makángua arréyannà,   Ekelo Senèyankoo.
Our   Father, that is there in heaven, Thy name hallowed be.
Ekha   yámanà fa.   Bsagwhánningáma donn, anákhènà arreyannà.
Thy kingdom come. Thy will be done on earth, as it is in heaven.
Mookookeetò mŭkŭkee locŏ locŏ tarmorn Aunoo emookoo younoobee
Give us to-day our daily bread and our trespasses

caffáreo, mookoofang caffáreo mookoolòràbà. Noo enáma mookoora-
forgive,   as we   forgive our neighbours,   and lead us not
soo   fàkùbeo   Emookoorámùnù lákùboo: Etanangbà yámanàra
into temptation, deliver us from evil; For thine the kingdom,
saimhàra annoo daraja Abada annoo abada.   Amoun.
the power, and the glory, for ever and ever.   Amen.

Sample of John Duport's translation of the Lord's Prayer in Susu. Taken from Henry Caswall (1857), A Martyr of the Pongas: Memoir of Hamble James Leacock, page 252

Bibliography

Books/Articles/Theses

Ajayi, J. F. Ade. *Christian Missions in Nigeria, 1841–1891: The Making of a New Elite*. London: Longman, 1965.

———. "Henry Venn and the Policy of Development." In *Tradition and Change in Africa: The Essays of J. F. Ade Ajayi*, edited by Toyin Falola, 57–68. Trenton; Asmara, Eritrea: Africa World Press, 2000.

———. "Native Agency in Nineteenth-Century West Africa." In *Tradition and Change in Africa: The Essays of J. F. Ade Ajayi*, edited by Toyin Falola, 101–127. Trenton; Asmara, Eritrea: Africa World Press, 2000.

Aka, Emmanuel Aloangamo. "How the Basel Mission was Established in Cameroon." *Cameroon Tribune*, 28 November 1986. BMS Archives, Angus Library, Regent's College, Oxford.

———. "Joseph Merrick, Alfred Saker and the Foundations of Christianity in the Cameroons, 1844–1876." *Cameroon Tribune*, 8 October 1986. BMS Archives, Angus Library, Regent's College, Oxford.

Alagoa, E. J., and L. Z. Elango. "The Niger Delta and the Cameroon Region." In *Africa in the Nineteenth Century until the 1880s*, edited by J. F. Ade Ajayi, 725–791. UNESCO. Berkeley: University of California Press, 1989.

Alho, Olli. *The Religion of the Slaves: A Study of the Religious Tradition and Behaviour of Plantation Slaves in the United States, 1830–1865*. Helsinki: Suomalainen Tiedeakatemia, 1976.

Altink, Henrice. "An Outrage on all Decency: Abolitionist Reactions to Flogging Jamaican Slave Women, 1780–1834." *Slavery and Abolition* 23, no. 2 (2002): 107–122. doi:10.1080/714005229.

Anderson, Gerald H., ed. *Biographical Dictionary of Christian Missions*. New York: Macmillan, 1998.

Anderson-Morshead, A. E. M. *The History of the Universities' Mission to Central Africa, 1859–1908*, rev. ed. London: UMCA, 1955.

Anstey, Roger. *The Atlantic Slave Trade and British Abolition, 1760–1810*. London: Macmillan, 1975. doi:10.1007/978-1-349-01886-4.

Antwi, Daniel. "The African Factor in Christian Mission to Africa: A Study of Moravian and Basel Mission Initiatives in Ghana." *International Review of Mission* 87, no. 344 (January1998): 55–66. https://doi.org/10.1111/j.1758-6631.1998.tb00066.x.

Antwi, Daniel, and Paul Jenkins. "The Moravians, the Basel Mission and the Akuapem State in the Early Nineteenth Century." In *Christian Missionaries and the State in the Third World*, edited by Holger Bernt Hansen and Michael Twaddle, 39–51. Oxford: James Currey, 2002.

Ardener, Edwin. *Kingdom on Mount Cameroon: Studies in the History of the Cameroon Coast, 1500–1970*. Edited and with an introduction by Shirley Ardener. Cameroon Studies 1. Oxford: Berghahn, 1996.

Austin-Broos, Diane J. *Jamaica Genesis: Religion and the Politics of Moral Orders*. Kingston: Ian Randle, 1997. doi:10.7208/Chicago/9780226924816.001.0001.

———. "Redefining the Moral Order: Interpretations of Christianity in Post-Emancipation Jamaica." In *The Meaning of Freedom: Economics, Politics, and Culture after Slavery*, edited by Frank McGlynn and Seymour Drescher, 221–243. Pittsburgh: University of Pittsburgh Press, 1992.

Ayandele, E.A. "The Missionary Factor in Northern Nigeria, 1870–1918." In *The History of Christianity in West Africa*, edited by O. U. Kalu, 133–158. London: Longman, 1980.

———. *The Missionary Impact on Modern Nigeria, 1842–1914: A Political and Social Analysis*. London: Longman, 1966.

Bakan, Abigail B. *Ideology and Class Conflict in Jamaica: The Politics of Rebellion*. Montreal: McGill-Queen's University Press, 1990.

Barrow, A. H. *Fifty Years in Western Africa: Being a Record of the Work of the West Indian Church on the Banks of the Rio Pongo*. London: SPCK, 1900.

———. *West Indian Church Africa Mission: Report of a Tour in the West Indies to the English Committee of the Pongas Mission*. London: SPCK, 1908.

Bauer, John. *2000 Years of Christianity in Africa: An African History 62–1992*. Nairobi: Paulines Publications, 1994.

Beckles, Hilary McD. "Caribbean Anti-Slavery: The Self-Liberation Ethos of Enslaved Blacks." *Journal of Caribbean History* 22, nos. 1–2 (1988): 1–19.

———. *A History of Barbados: From Amerindian Settlement to Nation-State*. Cambridge: Cambridge University Press, 1990.

Beckles, Hilary, and Verene Shepherd, eds. *Caribbean Freedom: Economy and Society from Emancipation to the Present*. Kingston: Ian Randle, 1993.

Bediako, Kwame. *Christianity in Africa: The Renewal of a Non-Western Religion*. Edinburgh: Edinburgh University Press; Maryknoll: Orbis Books, 1995.

———. *Theology and Identity: The Impact of Culture upon Christian Thought in the Second Century and in Modern Africa.* Oxford: Regnum Books, 1992.

Bell, Kenneth N., and W. P. Morrell, eds. *Select Documents on British Colonial Policy, 1830–1860.* Oxford: Clarendon Press, 1928.

Belle, George. "The Abortive Revolution of 1876 in Barbados." In *Caribbean Freedom: Economy and Society from Emancipation to the Present*, edited by Hilary Beckles and Verene Shepherd, 181–191. Kingston: Ian Randle, 1993.

Bernau, J. H. *Missionary Labours in British Guyana, with Remarks on the Manners, Customs, and Superstitious Rites of the Aborigines.* London: John Farquhar Shaw, 1847.

Besson, Jean. "Religion as Resistance: The Baptist Church, Revival Worldviews, and the Rastafari Movement." In *Rastafari and Other African-Caribbean Worldviews*, edited by Barry Chevannes, 43–76. London: Macmillan, 1998. doi:10.1007/978-1-349-13745-9_3.

Bisnauth, Dale A. *A History of Religions in the Caribbean.* Kingston: Kingston Publishers, 1989.

Black, Clinton V. *The History of Jamaica.* London: Collins, 1958.

Blyden, E. W. *Christianity, Islam and the Negro Race.* London: W. B. Whittingham, 1887; repr. Edinburgh: Edinburgh University Press, 1967.

Blyth, George. *Reminiscences of a Missionary Life.* Edinburgh: William Oliphant, 1851.

Bolt, Cawley St. Clair. "Some Evangelical Missionaries' Understanding of Negro Character in Jamaica, 1834–1870: With Particular Reference to Selected Baptist Missionaries." PhD thesis, Oxford Centre for Mission Studies/University of Wales, 2006.

Bolt, Christine. *Victorian Attitudes to Race.* Toronto: University of Toronto Press; London: Routledge & Kegan Paul, 1971.

Bosch, David J. *Transforming Mission: Paradigm Shifts in Theology of Mission.* Maryknoll: Orbis Books, 1991.

Brathwaite, Edward Kamau. *The Development of Creole Society in Jamaica, 1770–1820.* Oxford: Oxford University Press, 1971.

———. *The Folk Culture of the Slaves in Jamaica*, rev ed. London: New Beacon Books, 1981.

———. "The 'Folk' Culture of the Slaves". *The Slavery Reader.* Eds Gad Heuwman and James Walvin. London, New York: Rutledge. 2003.

———. "The Spirit of African Survival in Jamaica." *Jamaica Journal* 42 (1978): 44–63.

Brodber, Erna. *Myal.* London; Port of Spain: New Beacon Books, 1988.

Brown, Terry. "Memoir of Bishop William Hart Coleridge." *Colonial Church Chronicle, and Missionary Journal* 4 (July 1850): 3–11. http://anglicanhistory.org/wi/coleridge_memoir1850.html

Buchner, J. H. *The Moravians in Jamaica: History of the Mission of the United Brethren's Church to the Negroes in the Island of Jamaica from the Year 1754 to 1854.* London: Longman, Brown and Co, 1854.

Buhlmann, Walbert. *The Coming of the Third Church: An Analysis of the Present and Future of the Church.* Maryknoll: Orbis Books, 1974.

Burton, Richard D. E. *Afro-Creole: Power, Opposition, and Play in the Caribbean.* Ithaca: Cornell University Press, 1997. doi:10.7591/9781501722431.

Buxton, T. F. *The African Slave Trade and Its Remedy.* London: Frank Cass, 1840.

———. *Debate on the Motion of T. Fowell Buxton, M.P.* The House of Commons. London, 1834, July1. USPG Archives, Rhodes House, Oxford.

Caldecott, Alfred. *The Church in the West Indies.* London: SPCK, 1898.

Campbell, Archibald Montgomery. *A Sermon, Preached in Lambeth Chapel, on Sunday, July XXV, M. DCCC. XXIV at the Consecration of Christopher Lipscombe Lord Bishop of Jamaica and of William Hart Coleridge Lord Bishop of Barbados and the Leeward Islands.* London: Rivington, 1824. http://anglicanhistory.org/wi/jm/

Campbell, Horace. *Rasta and Resistance: From Marcus Garvey to Walter Rodney.* Trenton: Africa World Press, 1987.

Campbell, James, and James Oakes. "The Invention of Race: Rereading White Over Black." *Reviews in American History* 21 (March 1993): 172–183. doi:10.2307/2702971.

Campbell, James T. *Songs of Zion: The African Methodist Episcopal Church in the United States and South Africa.* New York: Oxford University Press, 1995.

Caswall, Henry. *The Martyr of the Pongas: Being a Memoir of the Rev. Hamble James Leacock.* London: Rivington, 1857.

Catherall, G. A. "Baptist War and Peace: A Study of British Baptist Involvement in Jamaica, 1783–1865." PhD thesis, University of Keele, 1970. BMS Archives, Angus Library, Regent's Park College, Oxford.

Chevannes, Barry ed. *Rastafari and Other African-Caribbean Worldviews.* London: Macmillan, 1998. doi:10.1007/978-1-349-13745-9.

Clarke, John, W. Dendy, and J. M. Phillippo. *The Voice of Jubilee: A Narrative of The Baptist Mission, Jamaica, from Its Commencement.* London: John Snow, 1865.

Comaroff, Jean, and John Comaroff. *Of Revelation and Revolution: Christianity, Colonialism, and Consciousness in South Africa,* vol. 1. Chicago: University of Chicago Press, 1991.

Craton, Michael. "Continuity Not Change: The Incidence of Unrest among Ex-slaves in the British West Indies, 1838–1876." In *Caribbean Freedom: Economy and Society from Emancipation to the Present,* edited by Hilary Beckles and Verene Shepherd, 192–206. Kingston: Ian Randle, 1993.

———. *Empire, Enslavement, and Freedom in the Caribbean.* Kingston: Ian Randle, 1997.

Bibliography

———. *Testing the Chains: Resistance to Slavery in the British West Indies.* Ithaca: Cornell University Press, 1982.
Curtin, Philip D. "The British Sugar Duties and West Indian Prosperity." *Journal of Economic History* 14, no. 2 (Spring 1954): 157–169. doi:10.1017/S002205070006544X.
———. *The Image of Africa: British Ideas and Action, 1780–1850.* Madison, University of Wisconsin Press, 1964.
———. *Two Jamaicas: The Role of Ideas in a Tropical Colony, 1830–1865.* Cambridge: Harvard University Press, 1955.
———. "'The White Man's Grave:' Image and Reality, 1780–1850." *Journal of British Studies* 1 (November 1961): 94–110.
da Costa, Emilia Viotti. *Crowns of Glory, Tears of Blood: The Demerara Slave Rebellion of 1823.* New York: Oxford University Press, 1994.
Davis, David Brion. *The Problem of Slavery in Western Culture.* Oxford: Oxford University Press, 1988.
Dayfoot, Arthur Charles. *The Shaping of The West Indian Church, 1492–1962.* Kingston: University of the West Indies Press, 1999.
Debrunner, H. W. *A History of Christianity in Ghana 1470–1957.* Accra: Waterville Publishing House, 1967.
DeLancey, Mark W. *Cameroon Federal Republic.* London: Westview Press, 1989.
DeLancey, Mark W., and H. Mbella Mokeba, eds. *Historical Dictionary of the Republic of Cameroon.* 2nd ed. Metuchen; London: Scarecrow Press, 1990.
Deveneaux, Gustav Kashope. "Public Opinion and Colonial Policy in Nineteenth-Century Sierra Leone." *International Journal of African Historical Studies* 9, no. 1 (1976): 45–67. doi:10.2307/217390.
Dickson, Kwamina B. *A Historical Geography of Ghana.* Cambridge: Cambridge University Press, 1969.
Duncan, Peter. *A Narrative of the Wesleyan Mission to Jamaica.* London: Paternoster, 1849.
Eliot, Edward. *Christianity and Slavery: In a Course of Lectures Preached at the Cathedral and Parish Church of St. Michael, Barbados.* London: J. Hatchard, 1833.
Elkins, Stanley M. *Slavery: A Problem in American Institutional and Intellectual Life.* Chicago: University of Chicago Press, 1959.
Ellis, J. B. *The Diocese of Jamaica: A Short Account of Its History, Growth, and Organization.* London: SPCK, 1913.
Evans, E. L. *A History of the Diocese of Jamaica.* Kingston: Diocese of Jamaica, 1975.
Falola, Toyin ed. *Tradition and Change in Africa: The Essays of J. F. Ade. Ajayi.* Trenton; Asmara, Eritrea: Africa World Press, 2000.

Furley, O. W. "Moravian Missionaries and Slaves in the West Indies." *Caribbean Studies* 5 (1965): 3–16.

Gallagher, J. "Fowell Buxton and the New African Policy, 1838–1842." *Cambridge Historical Journal* 10, no. 1 (1950): 36–58. doi:10.1017/S1474691300002675.

Genovese, Eugene D. *Roll Jordan Roll: The World the Slaves Made*. New York: Random House 1974.

Gibba, Bakary. "The West Indian Mission to West Africa: The Rio Pongas Mission, 1850–1963." PhD thesis, University of Toronto, 2011. https://tspace.library.utoronto.ca/bitstream/1807/31759/1/Gibba_Bakary_201111_PhD_thesis.pdf

Gifford, Lord Anthony. "Don't Doubt Justice of Reparations Claim." Guest Column, *The Gleaner*, Wednesday, 30 April 2014. https://jamaica-gleaner.com/gleaner/20140430/cleisure/cleisure4.html.

———. "The Legal Basis of the Claim for Reparations." Paper presented at the First Pan-African Congress on Reparations, Abuja, Federal Republic of Nigeria, 27–29 April 1993.

Gifford, Paul. *African Christianity: Its Public Role*. London: C. Hurst, 1998.

Gilroy, Paul. *The Black Atlantic: Modernity and Double Consciousness*. London; New York: Verso Books, 1993.

Goodridge, Sehon S. *Facing the Challenge of Emancipation: A Study of the Ministry of William Hart Coleridge, First Bishop of Barbados, 1824–1842*. Bridgetown, Barbados: Cedar Press, 1981.

Grey, Earl Henry George. *The Colonial Policy of Lord John Russell's Administration*, vol. 1. London: Bentley, 1853.

Grey, Richard. "The Origins and Organization of the Nineteenth-Century Missionary Movement." In *The History of Christianity in West Africa*, edited by O. U. Kalu, 14–21. London: Longman, 1980.

Groves, C. P. *The Planting of Christianity in Africa*, vol. 2: 1840–78. London: Lutterworth Press, 1954.

Gwei, Solomon Nfor. "History of the British Baptist Mission in Cameroon, with Beginnings in Fernando Po, 1841–1886." BDiv thesis, Rüschlikon-Zürich: Baptist Theological Seminary, 1966.

Haas, Waltraud. "The Nineteenth-Century Basel Mission and Its Women Missionaries." In *Texts and Documents: Mission History from the Woman's Point of View*, 12–29. Basel Mission: Nr. 13, 1989.

———. "On Being a Woman in the Nineteenth-Century Basel Mission" in *Texts and Documents: Mission History from the Woman's Point of View*, 30–44. Basel Mission: Nr. 13, 1989.

Haenger, Peter, Christina Handford, J. J. Schaffer, and Paul E. Lovejoy. *Slaves and Slaveholders on the Gold Coast: Towards an Understanding of Social Bondage in West Africa*. Basel: Schlettwein, 2000.

Hall, Catherine. *Civilising Subjects: Metropole and Colony in the English Imagination, 1830–1867*. Cambridge: Polity Press, 2002.

Hall, Douglas. *In Miserable Slavery: Thomas Thistlewood in Jamaica, 1750–86*. London: Macmillan, 1989.

Hall, Neville A. T. *Slave Society in the Danish West Indies*. Kingston: University of the West Indies Press, 1992.

Hall, Peter. *Autobiography of Rev. Peter Hall*. Accra: Waterville Publishing House, 1965.

Handler, Jerome S., and Kenneth M. Bilby. "On the Early Use and Origin of the Term 'Obeah' in Barbados and the Anglophone Caribbean." *Slavery and Abolition* 22, no. 2. (August 2001): 87–100. doi:10.1080/714005192. PMID:18782932.

Hark, Walter and Adolph Westphal. *The Breaking of the Dawn: Moravian Work in Jamaica, 1754–1904*. London: William Strain & Sons, 1904.

Hastings, Adrian. *The Church in Africa, 1450–1950*. Oxford: Clarendon Press, 1994.

Heimert, Alan. *Religion and the American Mind: From the Great Awakening to the Revolution*. Cambridge: Harvard University Press, 1966.

Heuman, Gad. *The Killing Time: The Morant Bay Rebellion in Jamaica*. Knoxville: University of Tennessee Press, 1994.

———. "Riots and Resistance in the Caribbean at the Moment of Freedom." *Slavery and Abolition* 21, no. 2 (August 2000): 135–149. doi:10.1080/0144390008575309.

———. "A Tale of Two Jamaican Rebellions." *Jamaica Historical Review* 19 (1996): 1–8.

Heuman, Gad, and David V. Trotman, eds. *Contesting Freedom: Control and Resistance in the Post-emancipation Caribbean*. Oxford: Macmillan Caribbean, 2005.

Hewitt, Gordon. *The Problems of Success: A History of the Church Missionary Society, 1910–1942*. London: SCM Press, 1971.

Higman, B. W. "Slavery Remembered: The Celebration of Emancipation in Jamaica." *Journal of Caribbean History* 12 (1979): 55–74.

Hinchliff, Peter. "Voluntary Absolutism: British Missionary Societies in the Nineteenth Century." *Studies in Church History* 23 (1986): 363–379. doi:10.1017/S0424208400010706.

Hinton, John Howard. *Memoir of William Knibb, Missionary in Jamaica*. London: Houlston & Stoneman, 1847.

Hobsbawm, Eric. *Age of Extremes: The Short History of the Twentieth Century, 1914–1991*. London: Abacus, 1994.

Hoekendijk, J. C. "The Church in Missionary Thinking." *International Review of Mission* 41, no. 3 (July 1952): 324–336. doi.org/10.1111/j.1758-6631.1952.tb03688.x.

Hofmeyr, Isabel. "Dreams, Documents and 'Fetishes': African Christian Interpretations of the Pilgrim's Progress." *Journal of Religion in Africa* 32, no. 4 (2002): 440–456. doi:10.1163/157006602321107649.

———. "How Bunyan Became English: Missionaries, Translation, and the Discipline of English Literature." *Journal of British Studies* 41 (2002): 84–119. doi:10.1086/386255.

Holt, Thomas C. *The Problem of Freedom: Race, Labor, and Politics in Jamaica and Britain, 1832–1938*. Baltimore; London: Johns Hopkins University Press, 1992.

Howe, Stephen. *Afrocentrism: Mythical Pasts and Imagined Homes*. London: Verso Books, 1999.

Hughes, H. B. L. "The Impact on Jamaica of the Evangelical Revival." *Jamaica Historical Review* 1, no. 1 (June 1945): 7–23.

Hutton, J. E. *History of the Moravian Church*. London: Moravian Publication Office, 1909.

Ifemesia, C. C. "The 'Civilizing' Mission of 1841: Aspects of an Episode in Anglo-Nigerian Relations." In *The History of Christianity in West Africa*, edited by O. U. Kalu, 81–102. London: Longman, 1980.

Ingham, Ernest Graham. *The African in the West Indies*. London: H. H. Hodgson, 1895.

Ingleby, Jonathan. "Education as a Missionary Tool: A Study in Christian Missionary Education by English Protestant Missionaries in India with Special Reference to Cultural Change." PhD thesis, London: Oxford Centre for Mission Studies/Open University, 1998.

Isichei, Elizabeth. *A History of Christianity in Africa: From Antiquity to the Present*. London: SPCK, 1995.

Jacobs, Sylvia M., ed. *Black Americans and the Missionary Movement in Africa*. Westport: Greenwood, 1982.

Jakobsson, Stiv. *Am I Not a Man and a Brother? British Missions and the Abolition of the Slave Trade and Slavery in West Africa and the West Indies, 1786–1838*. Uppsala: Gleerup, 1972.

Jenkins, David. *Black Zion: The Return of Afro-Americans and West Indians to Africa*. London: Wildwood House, 1975.

Jenkins, Paul. "Andreas Riis (1804–1854)." In *Biographical Dictionary of Christian Missions*, edited by Gerald H. Anderson, 571. New York: Macmillan, 1998.

———. "Johannes Zimmermann (1825–1875)." In *Biographical Dictionary of Christian Missions*, edited by Gerald H. Anderson, 762. New York: Macmillan, 1998.

———. "The Scandal of Continuing Intercultural Blindness in Mission Historiography: The Case of Andreas Riis in Akwapim." *International Missionary Review* 87, no. 344 (January 1998): 67–76. doi.org/10.1111/j.1758-6631.1998.tb00067.x.

Johnston, Franklyn A. J. "Education in Jamaica and Trinidad in the Generation after Emancipation." DPhil thesis, Oxford University, 1970.

Fuller, J. J. Conference Address. In Johnston, Rev. James, ed. *Report of the Centenary Conference on the Protestant Missions of the World, Exeter Hall, London: 9–19 June 1888*, 1:265–267. London: James Nisbet & Co, 1889.

Jordon, Winthrop D. *White Over Black: American Attitudes toward the Negro, 1550–1812*. Chapel Hill: University of North Carolina Press, 1968.

Kalu, O. U. "Introduction." In *The History of Christianity in West Africa*, edited by O. U. Kalu, 10–13. London: Longman, 1980.

Kiernan, Victor G. *The Lords of Human Kind: European Attitudes to Other Cultures in the Imperial Age*. London: Weidenfeld and Nicolson, 1969.

Killingray, David. "The Black Atlantic Missionary Movement and Africa, 1780s–1920s." *Journal of Religion in Africa*. 33, no. 1 (January 2003): 3–31. doi: 10.1163/157006603765626695.

Knight, Franklin W., and Margaret E. Crahan, eds. *Africa and the Caribbean: The Legacies of a Link*. Baltimore: Johns Hopkins University Press, 1979.

Koua, Solomon. "The Planting of Christianity in Cameroon Town, 1841–1886." PhD thesis, University of Paris, 1984.

Kwast, Lloyd E. *The Discipling of West Cameroon: A Study of Baptist Growth*. Grand Rapids: Eerdmans, 1971.

Lampe, Armando. *Mission or Submission? Moravian and Catholic Missionaries in the Dutch Caribbean during the Nineteenth Century*. Gottingen: Vandenhoeck & Ruprecht, 2001.

Lanternari, Vittorio. *The Religions of the Oppressed: A Study of Modern Messianic Cults*. New York: Alfred A. Knopf, 1963.

Le Vine, Victor T. *The Cameroon Federal Republic*. Ithaca: Cornell University Press, 1963. Repr. Ithaca; London: Cornell University Press, 1971.

Lewis, Gordon K. *Main Currents in Caribbean Thought: The Historical Evolution of Caribbean Society in Its Ideological Aspects, 1492–1900*. Baltimore: Johns Hopkins University Press, 1983.

Lewis, Kingsley. *The Moravian Mission in Barbados, 1816–1886: A Study of the Historical Context and Theological Significance of a Minority Church among an Oppressed People*. Frankfurt: Peter Lang, 1985.

Lipscomb, Christopher. *Church Societies a Blessing to the Colonies: A Sermon preached at the Parish Church of St. Michael-Le-Belfry, York*. London: Rivington, 1840. http://anglicanhistory.org/wi/jm/

Livingstone, David. *Missionary Travels and Researches in South Africa*. London: John Murray, 1857.

Lynch, Hollis R. "The Native Pastorate Controversy and Cultural Ethnocentrism in Sierra Leone, 1871–1874," In *The History of Christianity in West Africa*, edited by O. U. Kalu, 270–292. London: Longman, 1980.

Lynn, Martin. "Britain's West African Policy and the Island of Fernando Po, 1821–1843." *Journal of Imperial and Commonwealth History* 18, no. 2 (1990): 191–207. doi:10.1080/03086539008582815.

Mather, George, and Charles John Blagg. *Bishop Rawle: A Memoir*. London: Kegan Paul, 1890.

Miller, Jon. *The Social Control of Religious Zeal: A Study of Organizational Contradictions*. New Brunswick: Rutgers University Press, 1994.

Mintz, Sidney W. "From Plantations to Peasantries in the Caribbean." In *Caribbean Contours*, edited by Sidney W. Mintz and Sally Price, 127–153. Baltimore: Johns Hopkins University Press, 1985.

———. "The Historical Sociology of Jamaican Villages." In *Afro-Caribbean Villages in Historical Perspective*, edited by Charles V. Carnegie, 1–19. Kingston: African Caribbean Institute of Jamaica, 1987.

Morrell, W. P. *British Colonial Policy in the Age of Peel and Russell*. Oxford: Clarendon Press, 1930.

———. *British Colonial Policy in the Mid-Victorian Age*. Oxford: Clarendon Press, 1969.

Murphy, Patricia Shaubah. *The Moravian Mission to the African Slaves of the Danish West Indies, 1732–1828*. St. Thomas: Caribbean Research Institute of the College of the Virgin Islands, 1969.

Neill, Stephen. *Colonialism and Christian Missions*. London: Lutterworth, 1966.

———. *A History of Christian Missions*. London: Penguin Books, 1964.

Newbury, C. W., ed. *British Policy towards West Africa: Select Documents, 1786–1874*. 147–148. Oxford: Clarendon Press, 1965.

Newman, Las. "A West Indian Contribution to Christian Mission in Africa: The Career of Joseph Jackson Fuller, 1845–1888." *Transformation* 18, no. 4 (October 2001): 220–231. doi:10.1177/026537880101800403.

Odamtten, S. K. *The Missionary Factor in Ghana's Development, 1820–1880*. Accra: Waterville Publishing House, 1978.

Offer, Avner. "The British Empire, 1870–1914: A Waste of Money?" *Economic History Review* 46, no. 2 (May1993): 215–238. doi:10.2307/2598015.

Paget, Hugh. "The Free Village System in Jamaica." *Caribbean Quarterly* 1, no. 4 (1950): 7–19. doi:10.1080/00086495.1950.11829205.

Parrinder, E. G. S. "Christian Marriage in French West Africa." *Africa* 17, no. 4 (October 1947): 260–268. doi:10.2307/1156657.

Pascoe, C. F. *Two Hundred Years of the S.P.G.: An Historical Account of the Society for the Propagation of the Gospel in Foreign Parts, 1701–1900*. London: SPG, 1901.

Paton, Diana. *No Bond but the Law: Punishment, Race, and Gender in Jamaican State Formation, 1780–1870*. Durham: Duke University Press, 2004. doi:10.1215/9780822386148.

———. "Popular and Official Justice in Post-Emancipation Jamaica." In *Contesting Freedom: Control and Resistance in the Post-Emancipation Caribbean*, edited by Gad Heuman and David Trotman, 1–19. Oxford: Macmillan, 2005.

Patterson, Orlando. *Freedom in the Making of Western Culture*, vol. 1. Cambridge: Harvard University Press, 1991.

———. *Slavery and Social Death: A Comparative Study*. Cambridge: Harvard University Press, 1982.

———. "Slavery: The Underside of Freedom." *Slavery & Abolition* 5, no. 2 (September 1984): 87–104.

———. *The Sociology of Slavery: An Analysis of the Origins, Development, and Structure of Negro Slave Society in Jamaica*. Rutherford, NJ: Fairleigh Dickinson University Press, 1967.

Payne, Ernest A. *The Free Church Tradition in the Life of England*. London: SCM. Press, 1933.

———. *Freedom in Jamaica: Some Chapters in the Story of the Baptist Missionary Society*. London: Carey Press, 1946.

Peel, J. D. Y. *Religious Encounter and the Making of the Yoruba*. Bloomington: Indiana University Press, 2003.

Phillippo, J. C. *Cholera in Jamaica in 1850, 51 and 54 and the Lessons to be Learnt therefrom*. Kingston: Geo Henderson., 1887.

Phillippo, J. M. *Jamaica: Its Past and Present State*. London: John Snow, 1843.

Piggin, Stuart. "Assessing Nineteenth-Century Missionary Motivation: Some Considerations of Theory and Method." In *Religious Motivation: Biographical and Sociological Problems for the Church Historian*, edited by Derek Baker, 327–337. Studies in Church History. 15. Oxford: Basil Blackwell, 1978.

Pinnington, John. "Church Principles in the Early Years of the Church Missionary Society: The Problem of the 'German' Missionaries." *Journal of Theological Studies* 20, no. 2 (1969): 523–532.

Porter, Andrew. "Cambridge, Keswick, and Late-Nineteenth-Century Attitudes to Africa." *Journal of Imperial and Commonwealth History* 5, no. 1 (1976): 5–34. doi:10.1080/03086537608582471.

———. "'Commerce and Christianity': The Rise and Fall of a Nineteenth-Century Missionary Slogan." *Historical Journal* 28, no. 3 (1985): 597–621. doi:10.1017/S0018246X00003320.

———. *The Imperial Horizons of British Protestant Missions, 1880–1914*. Grand Rapids: Eerdmans, 2003.

———. *Religion versus Empire?: British Protestant Missionaries and Overseas Expansion, 1700–1914*. Manchester: Manchester University Press, 2004.

Price, Richard. *Alabi's World*. Baltimore: Johns Hopkins University Press, 1990.

Raboteau, Albert J. *A Fire in the Bones: Reflections on African-American Religious History*. Boston: Beacon Press, 1995.

———. *Slave Religion: The 'Invisible Institution' in the Antebellum South*. Oxford: Oxford University Press, 1980.

Russell, Horace O. "The Emergence of the Christian Black: The Making of a Stereotype." *Jamaica Journal* 16 (1983): 51–58.

———. *The Missionary Outreach of the West Indian Church: Jamaican Baptist Missions to West Africa in the Nineteenth Century*. New York: Peter Lang, 2000.

———. "A Question of Indigenous Mission: The Jamaica Baptist Missionary Society." *Baptist Quarterly* 25, no. 2 (April 1973): 86–93. doi:10.1080/0005576X.1973.11751390.

Sanneh, Lamin. *Abolitionists Abroad: American Blacks and the Making of Modern West Africa*. Cambridge: Harvard University Press, 2001.

———. "The Horizontal and the Vertical in Mission: An African Perspective." *International Bulletin of Missionary Research* 7, no. 4 (1983): 165–171.

———. "Mission and the Modern Imperative –Retrospect and Prospect: Charting a Course." In *Earthen Vessels: American Evangelicals and Foreign Missions, 1880–1980*, edited by Joel A. Carpenter and Wilbert R. Shenk, 301–316. Grand Rapids: Eerdmans, 1990.

———. *Translating the Message: The Missionary Impact on Culture*. Maryknoll: Orbis Books, 1989.

———. *West African Christianity: The Religious Impact*. London/Maryknoll: C. Hurst/Orbis, 1983.

Sawyerr, Harry. "Christian Evangelistic Strategy in West Africa: Reflections on the Centenary of the Consecration of Bishop Samuel Adjayi Crowther on St. Peter's Day, 1864." *International Review of Missions* 54, no. 215 (1965): 343–352. doi:10.1111/j.1758-6631.1965.tb01883.x.

Schweizer, Peter A. *Survivors on the Gold Coast: The Basel Missionaries in Colonial Ghana*. Accra: Smartline, 2001.

Sen, Amartya. *Freedom as Development*. Oxford: Oxford University Press, 1999.

Sensbach, Jon F. *A Separate Canaan: The Making of an Afro-Moravian World in North Carolina, 1763–1840*. Chapel Hill: University of North Carolina Press, 1998.

Sharpe, Eric J. "Reflections on Missionary Historiography." *International Bulletin of Missionary Research* 13, no.2 (April 1989): 76–81. doi:10.1177/239693938901300207.

Sheller, Mimi. *Democracy after Slavery: Black Publics and Peasant Radicalism in Haiti and Jamaica*. London: Macmillan, 2000.
Shenk, Wilbert R. "Henry Venn." In *Biographical Dictionary of Christian Missions*, edited by Gerald H. Anderson. New York: Macmillan, 1998.
———. *Henry Venn: Missionary Statesman*. Maryknoll: Orbis Books, 1983.
Shepherd, Verene, and Hilary McD. Beckles, eds. *Caribbean Slavery in the Atlantic World*. Kingston: Ian Randle; Oxford: James Currey; Princeton: Markus Weiner, 2000.
Short, K. R. M. "Study in Political Nonconformity: The Baptists 1827–1845, with Particular Reference to Slavery." DPhil thesis, University of Oxford, 1972. Regent's Park College, Oxford.
Sindima, Harvey J. *Drums of Redemption: An Introduction to African Christianity*. Westport: Praeger, 1992.
Smith, Noel. *The Presbyterian Church in Ghana: A Young Church in a Changing Society*, Accra: Ghana University Press, 1966.
Stanley, Brian. "Alfred Saker (1814–1880). In *The Biographical Dictionary of Christian Missions*, edited by Gerald H. Anderson, 587. New York: Macmillan, 1998.
———. *The Bible and the Flag: Protestant Mission and British Imperialism in the Nineteenth and Twentieth Centuries*. Leicester: Inter-Varsity Press, 1990.
———. *The History of the Baptist Missionary Society (1792–1992)*. Edinburgh: T& T Clark, 1992.
———. "Baptists, Race and Empire, 1792–1914," Baptist Quarterly, 54:1, 4–17, DOI: 10.1080/0005576X.2022.2114246. 2023
Stock, Eugene. *History of the Church Missionary Society. Its Environment, Its Men and Its Work*. Vol. 4. London: Church Missionary Society, 1916.
Sundkler, Bengt, and Christopher Steed. *A History of the Church in Africa*. Cambridge: Cambridge University Press, 2000.
Thompson, H. P. *Into All Lands: The History of the Society for the Propagation of the Gospel in Foreign Parts, 1701–1950*. London: SPCK, 1951.
Thompson, Livingston. "The Church and Politics." *The Jamaica Moravian* 12, no. 17 (July-December 1998). Kingston.
Thornton, John. *Africa and Africans in the Making of the Atlantic World, 1400–1800*. Cambridge: Cambridge University Press, 1998.
Titus, Noel. "The West Indian Mission to Africa: Its Conception and Birth." *Journal of Negro History* 65, no. 2 (Spring 1980): 93–111. doi:10.2307/2717049.
Trew, J. M. *Africa Wasted by Britain and Restored by Native Agency*. London: J. Hatchard & Son, 1843.
———. *Hints, Briefly Suggestive, of Jamaica's Future*. London: James Nisbet, 1866.
Turner, Mary. *Slaves and Missionaries: The Disintegration of Jamaican Slave Society, 1787–1834*. Urbana: University of Illinois Press, 1982.

Underhill, E. B. *Alfred Saker: Missionary to Africa*. London: Alexander & Shepherd, 1884.

———. *The Tragedy of Morant Bay: A Narrative of the Disturbances in the Island of Jamaica in 1865*. London: Alexander & Shepherd, 1895.

Underhill, E. B., and J. T. Brown. *Emancipation in the West Indies*. London: British and Foreign Anti-slavery Society, 1861.

van Slageren, Jaap. *The Origins of the Evangelical Church of Cameroon, European Missions and Indigenous Christianity*. Leiden: Brill, 1972.

———. "Jamaican Missionaries in Cameroon." *Exchange* 30, no. 2 (2001): 145–156.

Vassady, Bela. "The Role of the Black West Indian Missionary in West Africa, 1840–1890." PhD thesis, Temple University, 1972.

Vidler, Alec R. *The Church in an Age of Revolution: 1789 to the Present Day*. London: Penguin Books, 1974; repr. 1990.

Waddell, Hope Masterton. *Twenty-Nine Years in the West Indies and Central Africa: A Review of Missionary Work and Adventure, 1829–1858*. London: T. Nelson & Sons, 1863.

Walker, James W. St. G. *The Black Loyalists: The Search for a Promised Land in Nova Scotia and Sierra Leone, 1783–1870*. New York: Dalhousie University Press, 1976.

Walls, Andrew F. "The Legacy of David Livingstone." *International Bulletin of Missionary Research* 11, no. 3 (July 1987): 125–129. doi:10.1177/239693938701100306.

———. "The Legacy of Thomas Fowell Buxton." *International Bulletin of Missionary Research* 15, no. 2 (April 1991): 74–77. doi.org/10.1177/239693939101500207.

———. *The Missionary Movement in Christian History: Studies in the Transmission of Faith*. Maryknoll: Orbis Books, 1996.

———. "Missions: Origins." In *Dictionary of Scottish Church History and Theology*, edited by Nigel M. de S. Cameron, 567–594. Downers Grove: InterVarsity Press, 1993.

Walvin, James. *Black Ivory: A History of British Slavery*. London: HarperCollins, 1992.

Wariboko, Waibinte E. "I Really Cannot Make Africa My Home: West Indian Missionaries as 'Outsiders' in the Church Missionary Society Civilizing Mission to Southern Nigeria, 1898–1925." *Journal of African History* 45, no. 2 (2004): 221–236. doi:10.1017/S0021853703008685.

———. "The Pongas Mission and Its Impact on Black Personhood: A Neglected Theme in the Caribbean-African Connection, 1855–1952." Paper presented at Conference of the Transatlantic Research Group, Echeruo Center for Public Policy, Owerri, Nigeria, 28–30 July 2006.

―――. *Ruined By "Race": Afro-Caribbean Missionaries and the Evangelization of Southern Nigeria, 1895-1925.* Trenton: Africa World Press, 2007.

―――. "Why There Is No West Indian Church among the Susus in West Africa Today: A Critique of the Pongas Mission and Its Portrayal of Blackness, 1855-1935." Paper presented at the Conference of the Transatlantic Research Group, Echeruo Center for Public Policy, Owerri, Nigeria, 28-30 July 2006.

Warneck, Gustav. *Outline of a History of Protestant Missions from the Reformation to the Present Time.* London: Oliphant, Anderson & Ferrier, 1906.

Warren, Max A. C. "The Missionary Expansion of Ecclesia Anglicana." In *New Testament Christianity for Africa and the World*, edited by M. E. Glasswell and E. W. Fashole-Luke, 124-140. London: SPCK, 1974.

―――. *The Missionary Movement from Britain in Modern History.* London: SCM, 1965.

―――. *Social History and Christian Mission.* London: SCM, 1967.

Watts, Michael R. *The Dissenters: Volume II: The Expansion of Evangelical Nonconformity (1791-1859).* Oxford: Clarendon Press, 1995.

Wesley, Charles H. "The Rise of Negro Education in the British Empire – II." *Journal of Negro Education* 2, no. 1 (January 1933): 68-82. doi:10.2307/2292220.

Westmeier, Karl-Wilhelm. "Becoming All Things to All People: Early Moravian Missions to Native North Americans." *International Bulletin of Missionary Research* 21, no. 4 (October 1997): 172-176.

Williams, Eric. *Capitalism and Slavery.* Chapel Hill: University of North Carolina Press, 1944.

Wilmore, Gayraud S. "Black Americans in Mission: Setting the Record Straight." *International Bulletin of Missionary Research* 10, no. 3 (July 1986): 98-102. doi:10.1177/239693938601000301.

―――. *Black Religion and Black Radicalism: An Interpretation of the Religious History of Afro-American People.* Maryknoll: Orbis Books, 1983.

Wilmot, Swithin. "Emancipation in Action: Workers and Wage Conflict in Jamaica, 1838-1840." *Jamaica Journal* 19 (1986): 55-62.

―――. "Emancipation in Action: Workers and Wage Conflict in Jamaica, 1838-1840." In *Caribbean Freedom: Economy and Society from Emancipation to the Present*, edited by Hilary Beckles and Verene Shepherd, 48-54. Kingston: Ian Randle, 1993.

Yates, T. E. *Venn and Victorian Bishops Abroad: The Missionary Policies of Henry Venn and Their Repercussions upon the Anglican Episcopate of the Colonial Period, 1841-1872.* London: SPCK; Uppsala: Swedish Institute of Missionary Research, 1978.

Young, Robert J. C. *Colonial Desire: Hybridity in Theory, Culture and Race.* London: Routledge, 1995.

Archival Sources

BEMS: Archives of the Basel Evangelical Missionary Society, Basel, Switzerland (now called Mission-21.org)

Correspondence

Dieterle to Hoffmann. Akropong. 17 February 1848. Missionary personal files. Afrika III 1842–48, vol. D-1, 2.

Dieterle to Hoffmann. Akropong. 19 February 1848. Letter-books Correspondence, missionary personal files. Vols. D-1, 1 to D-1, 4.

Ed Walker to Basel Missionaries at Akropong. 1 April 1849. Afrika III, vol. D-1, 2.

Green to Inspector Hoffmann. Akropong. 12 December 1844. Personal file. Afrika III, vol. D-1, 2.

Letter from West Indians. 13 January 1845. Letter-books Correspondence. Afrika III 1842–48, vol. D-1.

Mader to Josenhans. Akropong. 29 September 1851. Missionary personal files. Afrika III, vol. D-1, 2.

Meischel to Hoffmann. 20 May 1848. Afrika III 1842–48, vol. D-1, 2.

Sebald to Hoffmann. Akropong. 16 May 1845. Missionary personal files. Afrika III 1842–48, vol. D-1, 2.

Walker to Meischel. 10 November 1848. Afrika III 1842–48, vol. D-1, 2.

Walker to Meischel. 21 January 1849. Afrika III 1842–48, vol. D-1, 2.

Widmann to Inspector Hoffmann. Mico Institution. 30 January 1843. Africka - II 1842–1848, vol. D-1, 2.

Widmann to Hoffmann. Akropong. 8 January 1846. Personal file. Afrika III 1842–48, vol. D-1, 2.

Widmann to Hoffmann. 16 January 1846. Letter-books Correspondence, missionary personal files. Vols. D-1, 1 to D-1, 4.

Widmann to Hoffmann. Akropong. 12 July 1847. Afrika III 1842–48, vol. D-1, 2.

Widmann to Hoffmann. 11 November 1847. Letter-books Correspondence, missionary personal files. Vols. D-1, 1 to D-1, 4.

Widmann to Hoffmann. Akropong. 7 March 1848. Correspondence. Afrika III 1842–48, vol. D-1, 2.

Zorn to La Trobe. Fairfield. 26 December 1842. Africka - III 1842–1848, vol. D-1, 2.

Zorn to La Trobe. Fairfield. 4 January 1843. Africka - III 1842–1848, vol. D-1, 2.

Letter-books Correspondence, missionaries' personal files, vols. D-1, 1 to D-1, 4, and abstracts from Correspondence, 1828–1851.

Letter-books *in* Correspondence from Ghana. 1829–1851. Vols. D-1, 1 to D-1, 4.

Letter-books *in* Correspondence from Ghana. 13 January 1845. Afrika III 1842–48, vol. D-1, 2.

Letter books *out* Correspondence from Basel. 1828–1835. Contains replies, instructions from the Basel Committee to missionaries.
"Report on Missionaries' Conference." Akropong. 21 March 1848. Afrika III 1842–48, vol. D-1, 2. No. 7.
Stanger. 2 June 1851. Missionary personal files. Afrika III, vol. D-1, 2.
"Stipulations for the West Indian Brethren." Danish Accra. 4 June 1847. Afrika III 1842–48, vol. D-1, 2. No. 6.
Mission Magazine (1843): 231–242. Afrika III 1842–1848.
Mitchinson. "Church Discipline beyond the Seas." Basel. *Mission Field* (1 February 1888): 41–44.
Reindorf, Carl Christian. *History of the Gold Coast and Asante*. Basel: 1895.
Archives of the Basel Evangelical Missionary Society, Basel, Switzerland.

BMS: Archives of the Baptist Missionary Society, Angus Library, Regent's College, Oxford

Briggs, P. E. T. *The Church in the Cameroons: The Early Days, 1841–1887.*
Clarke, John. *Journals of West Africa* (two boxes).
Clarke to Sir Morton Peto, Br. Trestrail, and E. B. Underhill, Savanna la Maar, Ja. 13 March 1862.
Box 1 contains vol. 1. Transcript of *African Journal*, 1840–1841, and vol. 2. 1841–42. 4/2/2 A3.
Box 2 contains three volumes of *African Journal*. Vol. 3, August 1843–November 1844 (second journey). Vol. 4, November 1844–August 1845 (second journey). Vol. 5, August 1845–November 1846. 4/2/2 A3.
Fuller, J. J. Documents and manuscripts by J. J. Fuller. A/5/16–19 (2 boxes)
———. MS notes on Cameroon and Fernando Po by Mr. Fuller and Mr. Grenfell. A/5/17.
———. MS *Autobiography of J. J. Fuller of Cameroon: From Jamaica to the Cameroon, 1850–1888*. A/5/18.
———. *Bunyan's Pilgrim's Progress in the Duala language*. 1.f.34.
Knibb, William. "Report of the Proceedings at an Extraordinary Meeting of the Baptist Missionary Society." Exeter Hall, London: 22 May 1840. Sermon by William Knibb. 5.d.7 (b.b.)
———. "A Sermon preached on behalf of the Baptist Missionary Society at the Poultry Chapel, June 19, 1833." BMS Pamphlet Collection 1823–1851. 5.c.12 (o).
———. "The Spiritual Prospects of Africa." Sermon delivered at Eagle Street Chapel, London: 17 August 1834. BMS Collection 1823–1851. 21.a.5 (t).
Merrick, Joseph. Merrick to H. H. Dobney, 3 August 1848.
Merrick, Joseph. Memoirs of Richard Merrick and Joseph Merrick. London: 1850. J. Merrick, Missionary from Jamaica to Cameroon 1843–1849. 13.e.11

Pinnock. Africa file A/1
General missionary Correspondence W1/W1/2 W1/3
The Baptist Herald and Friend of Africa (BHFA)
The Baptist Magazine (BM)
The Missionary Herald (MH)

USPG: Archives of the United Societies for the Propagation of the Gospel, Rhodes House, Oxford (now found in the Bodleian Library, Oxford)

Occasional Papers Relating to the West Indian Mission to Western Africa. 1859. Bodleian Library, Oxford. C/AFW-2.

Copy of the French Order to close the Mission Schools at Domingia, Fallangia, and Farrangia, March 8th from the Colonial Administrator, A Baillott. 1894. C/AFR/W2.

USPG Correspondence:

Correspondence from the West Indies to the SPG. D 28A/West Indies.

Alexander Kennedy to Buxton. Port of Spain. Buxton Papers.

Buxton, Sir Thomas Fowell. *The Papers of Sir Thomas Fowell Buxton*, Reels #1–9. Contains Correspondence.

Buxton to Trew. 2 October 1835. Trew to Buxton. 31 December 1835. Buxton Papers, 14, 15, Reel #5.

Buxton to Ward. Rome. 27 December 1839. Buxton Papers.

Buxton to Knibb. 27 October 1840. Buxton Papers.

E. N. Buxton to Mrs. Johnston. 7 February 1842. Buxton Papers, Reel #9.

Edward North Buxton to Priscilla Johnston. 8 February 1842. Buxton Papers, Reel #9.

T. F. Buxton to Dr. Ramsey. 10 March 1843. Buxton Papers, Reel #9.

Caswall to Hawkins. 2 March 1863. D 28A/West Indies, 1860–1867.

Charles Thwaites to Buxton. Willoughby Bay, Antigua. 22 March 1839.

Duport to Bullock. Fallangia. 4 June 1867. C/WIN Bar 13, File 13.

George Peter Thompson to T F Buxton. Kingston. 25 January 1843. Buxton Papers, Reel #9.

Mrs. Johnston to Dr. Philip. 11 February 1842. Buxton Papers, Reel #9.

Parry to Hawkins. 8 May 1863. D 28A/West Indies, 1860–67.

Parry to Hawkins. 25 July 1863. D 28A/West Indies, 1860–67.

Phillippo to Buxton. 21 January 1839. Buxton Papers.

Phillips to Hawkins. 19 February 1864. D 28A/West Indies, 1860–67.

Rawle to Hawkins. 24 November 1863. Parry to Rawle. 26 November 1863. Rawle to Hawkins. 3 December 1863. Rawle to Parry. 16 January 1864. Parry to Hawkins. 25 January 1864.

Reginald Kingston to Bullock. 8 April 1863. Bullock to the Bishop of Kingston. Henry Venn to the Lord Bishop of Jamaica. January 1867:227. *West Indies 1860–1867*. D28A, 179.
Reply of the Society to the Earl of Bathurst. 23 June 23 1823. C/WIN/Bar 15.
Rev. G. D. Hill to Bishop Lipscombe. 20 April 1840. C/Win/Jam 2., File #157.
Rev. John Watson to Bishop of Barbados. 18 December 1846. C/Win/Bar 13, File # 13.
Thomas E. Ward to Buxton. Falmouth, Jamaica. 15 October 1839. Buxton Papers.
Thompson to Buxton. Kingston. 25 January 1843. Buxton Papers, Reel #9.
William Wemyss Anderson to Buxton. Kingston. 1 May 1839.
Papers for the Codrington Estates. C/Win/Bar-12.
Mather, George, and Charles John Blagg. "The Life of Bishop Rawle." *Mission Field* (1 December 1890): 458–463.
Mitchinson, J. "Church Discipline beyond the Seas." *Mission Field* (1 February 1888):41–44.
The Gambia-Pongas Magazine (G-PM). The Diocese of Gambia and the Rio Pongas. 1938–1947.
The Mission Field (MF) Vols. 1–86. This magazine contains printed reports and articles from USPG missionaries on the mission field (1856–1941).
"Pongas Mission: Progress of Christianity and Mohammedanism." *Mission Field* (1 July 1875): 193–198.
"Proposed Mission from the Church in the West Indies to Western Africa." *Barbados Church Society* (1850).
"Report of Mr. J. A. Maurice. Fallangia, Rio Pongas. 15 February 1863." *Mission Field* (1 May 1863): 114–116.
Trinidad Association of the SPG. "Appeal of the Trinidad Association for the Propagation of the Gospel." May 1845. C/Win/Bar 13, file #11.

CMS: Archives of the Church Missionary Society, University of Birmingham

Correspondence from Jamaica to the CMS

James Stephen Wiltshire to Henry Venn (expressing a desire to go to Africa as a missionary). CMS/231-1-57.

LMS: Archives of the London Missionary Society, SOAS, Russell Sq., London

Documents relating to West Indian missionaries

Register of Missionaries, Deputations, 1796–1923, (fourth edition).
Correspondence from the West Indies, Jamaica - Box 11.

Edward Holland to LMS Foreign Secretary. Mount Regale, Chapelton, Jamaica. 29 January 1843. Correspondence West Indies, Jamaica - Box 11.

The National Archives of Jamaica, Spanish Town
Books and pamphlets of missionary work in Jamaica
The Jamaica Standard and Royal Gazette.
Minute Book.
Courtenay, Reginald. "Primary Charge delivered at the Congregation of the Clergy of Jamaica held in Spanish Town," on 15 April 1858 by Reginald Courtenay, D. D. Bishop of Kingston. National Archives of Jamaica, Spanish Town.
Nuttall, Enos. *The West Indian Church and West African Missions.* Extracts from a short address delivered by the Bishop of Jamaica in the Synod of the Church of England in Jamaica. February 1895. National Archives of Jamaica, Spanish Town.

The National Library of Jamaica, Spanish Town
Books and pamphlets of missionary work in Jamaica
Barbados Church Society. Proposed Mission from the Church in the West Indies to Western Africa. 1850.
Coles, C. H. "Jubilee of the Jamaica Church of England Home and Foreign Missionary Society, 1861–1911." West India Reference Library.
The Falmouth Post (FP)

Langham
PARTNERSHIP

Langham Literature, with its publishing work, is a ministry of Langham Partnership.

Langham Partnership is a global fellowship working in pursuit of the vision God entrusted to its founder John Stott –

> *to facilitate the growth of the church in maturity and Christ-likeness through raising the standards of biblical preaching and teaching.*

Our vision is to see churches in the Majority World equipped for mission and growing to maturity in Christ through the ministry of pastors and leaders who believe, teach and live by the word of God.

Our mission is to strengthen the ministry of the word of God through:
- nurturing national movements for biblical preaching
- fostering the creation and distribution of evangelical literature
- enhancing evangelical theological education

especially in countries where churches are under-resourced.

Our ministry

Langham Preaching partners with national leaders to nurture indigenous biblical preaching movements for pastors and lay preachers all around the world. With the support of a team of trainers from many countries, a multi-level programme of seminars provides practical training, and is followed by a programme for training local facilitators. Local preachers' groups and national and regional networks ensure continuity and ongoing development, seeking to build vigorous movements committed to Bible exposition.

Langham Literature provides Majority World preachers, scholars and seminary libraries with evangelical books and electronic resources through publishing and distribution, grants and discounts. The programme also fosters the creation of indigenous evangelical books in many languages, through writer's grants, strengthening local evangelical publishing houses, and investment in major regional literature projects, such as one volume Bible commentaries like the *Africa Bible Commentary* and the *South Asia Bible Commentary*.

Langham Scholars provides financial support for evangelical doctoral students from the Majority World so that, when they return home, they may train pastors and other Christian leaders with sound, biblical and theological teaching. This programme equips those who equip others. Langham Scholars also works in partnership with Majority World seminaries in strengthening evangelical theological education. A growing number of Langham Scholars study in high quality doctoral programmes in the Majority World itself. As well as teaching the next generation of pastors, graduated Langham Scholars exercise significant influence through their writing and leadership.

To learn more about Langham Partnership and the work we do visit **langham.org**